D1153879

SOCIALIZATION
AND THE
LIFE CYCLE

SOCIALIZATION
AND THE
LIFE CYCLE

Peter I. Rose, Editor
SMITH COLLEGE

ST. MARTIN'S PRESS   NEW YORK

HQ783
S57

Library of Congress Catalog Card Number: 78–65243
Copyright © 1979 by St. Martin's Press, Inc.
All Rights Reserved.
Manufactured in the United States of America.
32109
fedcba
For information, write St. Martin's Press, Inc.,
175 Fifth Avenue, New York, N. Y. 10010

cover design: Tom McKeveny
typography: Judith Woracek

ISBN: 0–312–73800–5

ACKNOWLEDGMENTS

ART

Cover: *Andante*, © Estate of Ben Shahn, 1979.

Part I: *Children of the Streets*, © Estate of Ben Shahn, 1979.

Part II: *Unexpected Meetings*, © Estate of Ben Shahn, 1979.

Part III: *Welder*, © Estate of Ben Shahn, 1979.

Part IV: *To Parents One Had to Hurt*, © Estate of Ben Shahn, 1979.

Part V: *Beside the Dead*, © Estate of Ben Shahn, 1979.

SELECTIONS

Margaret E. Adams: "The Single Woman in Today's Society" is reproduced by permission from the *American Journal of Orthopsychiatry*, Vol. 41, No. 5. Copyright © 1971 the American Orthopsychiatric Association, Inc.

Acknowledgments and copyrights continue at the back of the book on pages 411–412, which constitute an extension of the copyright page.

All the world's a stage,
And all the men and women merely players;
They have their exits and their entrances,
And one man in his time plays many parts,
His acts being seven ages. . . . At first the infant,
Mewling and puking in the nurse's arms:
Then the whining school-boy, with his satchel
And shining morning face, creeping like snail
Unwillingly to school: and then the lover,
Sighing like furnace, with a woeful ballad
Made to his mistress' eyebrow: then a soldier,
Full of strange oaths and bearded like the pard,
Jealous in honour, sudden and quick in quarrel,
Seeking the bubble reputation
Even in the cannon's mouth: and then the justice,
In fair round belly with good capon line,
With eyes severe and beard of formal cut,
Full of wise saws and modern instances,
And so he plays his part. . . . The sixth age shifts
Into the lean and slippered pantaloon,
With spectacles on nose and pouch on side,
His youthful hose, well saved, a world too wide
For his shrunk shank, and his big manly voice,
Turning again toward childish treble, pipes,
And whistles in his sound. . . . Last scene of all,
That ends this strange eventful history,
Is second childishness, and mere oblivion,
Sans teeth, sans eyes, sans taste, sans everything.

As You Like It
WILLIAM SHAKESPEARE

Preface

Socialization and the Life Cycle is about love, labor, and loss. It deals with the affection and guidance of family, teachers, and friends, and the intimacy of primary relationships; with the rites of passage from childhood to adulthood; with the problems of dating and mating; with the critical importance of occupation and the significance of occupational roles in the adult years; and with the crises of middle age and the later years. It consists of a variety of articles by prominent sociologists and sociologically sensitive writers whose research reports and commentaries offer the reader a close look at the process of socialization from cradle to grave—and, in a sense, beyond the grave, since the functions of bereavement for survivors are also considered.

The five sections of the book are presented in a sequence paralleling the life cycle and are tied together with brief introductory essays. These essays, along with the headnotes that precede each selection, serve to alert the reader to the major sociological issues embodied in the selections.

The theoretical basis for the book is the symbolic interactionist view, which suggests that self and society are interdependent, that reality is socially constructed, that interaction with others is the main means of learning the rules and roles of society, and that what we generically label "*the* process of socialization" is not one but a series of processes. The selections make use of a wide variety of data. In fact, almost every type of research commonly used in the social sciences is represented in one or another of the selections.

Socialization and the Life Cycle should help students gain a better understanding of society, themselves, and their own life situations. It is not a how-to-be-a-successful-person book, but it is a guide to the sociological analysis of those critical aspects of life that most readers have already experienced, are currently wrestling with, or will some day have to face.

As they peruse the selections presented here, readers will see how the processes of socialization depend, in large measure, upon learning the tolerance limits of social situations and upon mastering appropriate responses to particular circumstances. They will also recognize that social change and growth often involve testing the limits set by society and, sometimes, breaking away and seeking independence from the constraints of the traditional order.

The processes of growing up and growing old are not easy. Nor are they easy to explain. Just as feedback is important to persons learning new roles as children, adolescents, adults, or senior citizens, it is important to authors and editors of books. I hope that users of this book will share with me their comments, criticisms, and suggestions for further editions.

Peter I. Rose

Contents

PART I. THE SIGNIFICANCE OF OTHERS   1

Introduction   2

Becoming a Member of Society, PETER L. BERGER AND
   BRIGITTE BERGER   4

Growing Up Confused, RICHARD FLACKS   21

Kids, Clubs, and Special Places, ROBERT PAUL SMITH   33

Children and Their Caretakers, NORMAN K. DENZIN   36

Sexual Stereotypes Start Early, FLORENCE HOWE   52

Encounter in Color, THOMAS J. COTTLE   64

PART II. ESTABLISHING NEW RELATIONSHIPS   77

Introduction   78

The Peer Group, JOSEPH BENSMAN AND
   BERNARD ROSENBERG   79

The Urge to Merge, GAIL SHEEHY   97

Who Has the Power? The Marital Struggle,
   DAIR L. GILLESPIE   108

Transition to Parenthood, ALICE S. ROSSI   132

The Single Woman in Today's Society,
   MARGARET ADAMS   146

The Six Stations of Divorce, PAUL BOHANNAN   158

PART III. WORKING 175

Introduction   176

A Cog in the Machinery, RAFAEL STEINBERG
   AND THE EDITORS OF TIME-LIFE BOOKS   177

Routine Work, BARBARA GARSON   190

Stress: From 9 to 5, ROBERT L. KAHN   205

Women in the Workplace, LOUISE KAPP HOWE   213

Professionalization, RICHARD N. HARRIS   223

Surgery as an Activity System, ERVING GOFFMAN   257

Rebirth in the Airborne, MELFORD S. WEISS   271

PART IV. COPING WITH CHANGE 277

Introduction   278

Stages of Adulthood, DANIEL J. LEVINSON ET AL.   279

Setting Off on the Midlife Passage, GAIL SHEEHY   294

The Menopause that Refreshes, GERALD NACHMAN   306

Middle-class Professionals Face Unemployment,
   DOUGLAS H. POWELL AND PAUL F. DRISCOLL   309

*In Controlled Environments: Four Cases of Intensive
   Resocialization*, PETER I. ROSE, MYRON GLAZER,
   AND PENINA MIGDAL GLAZER   320

PART V. THE LATER YEARS 339

Introduction   340

Growing Old Happy, Kenneth Woodward   341

It's Like Your Own Home Here, JUDITH WAX   345

Downward Mobility in Old Age, THOMAS TISSUE   355

Last Rites: Three Practitioners, STUDS TERKEL   368

Learning to Die, THOMAS POWERS   378

Bereavement, AUSTIN H. KUTSCHER   393

SOCIALIZATION
AND THE
LIFE CYCLE

PART I
THE SIGNIFICANCE OF OTHERS

THERE IS AN OLD NOTION THAT EACH BABY ENTERS THE WORLD WITH a *tabula rasa*, a clean slate, on which parents and others inscribe the rules of society. Once this has been accomplished, it is argued, the new societal member is ready to take his or her place within the community of adults. Although the imagery is dramatic, it is somewhat inaccurate.

No one is born with a clean slate. Each individual has a double inheritance, one biological, the other social. The first inheritance refers to the genetic makeup, the so-called natural endowments. The second is a combination of things: the norms and values of the societies, communities, and groups into which a person is born and those pertaining to the family's place within them. Often the two inheritances become as one; think, for example, of the difference's between persons who are born male or female or white or black in our society.

In a very real sense, much general socialization—the shaping of a person's social being—is preordained. We enter the human race with socially defined advantages and liabilities and go on from there. This is not to say that anatomy is destiny or that social stigmata can never be overcome. In a rapidly changing society life offers all sorts of possibilities to every individual. Nevertheless, there is more than a kernel of truth in the old expression, "It is easier to climb the ladder of success when daddy owns the ladder."

Fathers and mothers do more than give infants their place in society. They are, in most places, what sociologists call primary agents of socialization. From birth the newborn must start learning what is considered right and wrong, good and bad, pleasurable and painful; and it is up to the parents to give this basic instruction. The early years are crucial for molding the social self.

It was the social psychologist George Herbert Mead who used the phrase "significant others." Mead was referring to the fact that early socialization greatly depends upon the people with whom one has intimate and lasting contact. Parents or close friends are among the most common models. Modeling behavior after certain significant others or following their close instructions and admonitions means that, in many ways, people appear to be what they think others think they should be. In a complex society there are many role models and many sets of expectations within each community and group. Parents may say one thing, peers another. What is learned from either may be appropriate in certain social settings but absolutely inappropriate in others. Moreover, wider cultural norms as mediated and transmitted by others may be applied selectively or categorically. Thus, there frequently are double standards for men and women, whites and nonwhites, rich and poor, parents and children.

Part One of *Socialization and the Life Cycle* looks at the significant role others play in the early years of life. The section begins with a selection on "Becoming a Member of Society," which sets the stage for further discussion.

Part One includes an examination of the conflicting demands of parents and others in times of social turmoil and rapid cultural change, a witty and penetrating glimpse into the secret world of children, essays on "sexist" training and on the meaning of race to boys and girls. Each selection attempts to illustrate the connections between the self and society, especially during the crucial periods of childhood and adolescence.

In this opening essay, sociologists Peter and Brigitte Berger explain that "the process through which an individual learns to be a member of society is called socialization." They describe the process in simple, straightforward language, emphasizing the ways in which new members are indoctrinated with the rules, roles, and cultural norms of their society, community, and social group. Using examples from various cultures, the Bergers show how training through imitation and symbolic communication prepares individuals for life.

Socialization does not stop once the child can give the proper signs, speak the vernacular, or follow simple rules laid down by parents or other teachers. It is a dynamic process, one that involves many "others." Although the early years are obviously very important, the individual continues to change as he or she meets new people, encounters new situations, and learns to play new roles while moving through the life cycle.

As you read "Becoming a Member of Society," think about how most Americans initiate their children to the ways of our society. Keep in mind such notions as the double inheritance mentioned in the Introduction to Part One, as well as the importance of language and gesture, role taking and role playing, and of significant and generalized others in the process of socialization.

Becoming a Member of Society

PETER L. BERGER AND BRIGITTE BERGER

BEING AN INFANT: NON-SOCIAL AND SOCIAL COMPONENTS

For better or for worse, all of us begin by being born. The first condition we experience is the condition of being an infant. When we begin to analyze what this condition entails, we obviously come up against a number of things that have nothing to do with society. First of all, being an infant entails a certain relationship to one's own body. One experiences hunger, pleasure, physical comfort or discomfort and so forth. In the condition of being an infant one is assaulted in numerous ways by the physical environment. One experiences light and darkness, heat and cold; objects of all sorts impinge upon one's attention. One is warmed by the rays of the sun, one is intrigued by the smoothness of a surface or, if one is unlucky, one may be rained upon or bitten by a flea. Being born means to enter into a world with a seemingly infinite richness of experience. A good deal of this experience is not social. Needless to say, an infant at the time does not make such distinctions. It is only in retrospect that it is possible to differentiate the social and the non-social components of his experience. Having made this distinction, however, it is possible to say that the experience of society also begins at birth. The world of the infant is populated by other people. Very soon he is able to distinguish between them, and some of them become of overwhelming significance for him. From the beginning, the infant not only interacts with his own body and with his physical environment, but with other human beings. The biography of the individual, from the moment of birth, is the story of his relations with others.

More than that, the non-social components of the infant's experience are mediated and modified by others, that is, by his social experience. The sensation of hunger in his stomach can only be assuaged by the actions of others. Most of the time, physical comfort or discomfort is brought about by the actions or omissions of oters. The object with the pleasurably smooth surface was probably placed within the infant's grasp by somebody. And very likely, if he is rained upon, it is because somebody left him outside without cover. In this way, social experience, while it can be distinguished from other elements in the infant's experience, is not in an isolated category. Almost every aspect of the infant's world involves other human beings. His experience of others is crucial for *all* experience. It is others who create the patterns through which the world is experienced. It is only through these patterns that the organism is able to establish a stable relationship with the outside world—not only the social world but the world of physical environment as well. But these same patterns also penetrate the organism; that is, they interfere with the way it functions. Thus it is others who set the patterns by which the infant's craving for food is satisfied. But in doing so, these others also interfere with the infant's organism itself. The most obvious illustration of this is the timetable of feedings. If the child is fed at certain times, and at certain times only, the organism is forced to adjust to this pattern. In making this adjustment, its functioning changes. What happens in the end is not only that the infant is fed at certain times but that he is hungry at those times. Graphically, society not only imposes its patterns upon the infant's behavior but reaches inside him to organize the functions of his stomach. The same observation pertains to elimination, to sleeping and to other physiological processes that are endemic to the organism.

TO FEED OR NOT TO FEED: A QUESTION OF SOCIAL LOCATION

Some of these socially imposed patterns may be due to the individual peculiarities of the adults who deal with the infant. For example, a mother may feed her infant whenever he cries, regardless of schedule, because she has very sensitive eardrums or because she loves him so much that she cannot bear to think that he might be in discomfort for any length of time. More commonly, however, the decision of whether to feed the infant whenever he cries, or whether to impose a fixed timetable upon him, is not a peculiar decision of the mother as an individual but is a much broader pattern of the society in which the mother lives and which she has learned as the proper one for the problem at hand.

This has a very important implication: in his relations with others, the child experiences a tightly circumscribed micro-world. Only much later does he become aware of the fact that this micro-world has as its background an infinitely vaster macro-world. Perhaps, in retrospect, one envies the infant for this ignorance. Nevertheless, this invisible macro-world, unknown to him, has shaped and predefined almost everything he experiences in his micro-world. If his mother switches from a rigid feeding schedule to a new regime of feeding him whenever he cries, it will of course not occur to the infant to credit anybody but her for this pleasurable change in his circumstances. What he does not know is that the mother acted upon the advice of some expert who reflects the notions currently in vogue in, say, the American college-educated upper middle class. In the final analysis, then, it is not so much the mother as that invisible collective entity that has (in this case pleasurably) invaded the infant's physiological system. There is a further implication, however. Namely, if the infant's mother had belonged to another class, such as the non-college-educated working class, the infant would still be screaming for his food to no avail. In other words, the micro-worlds of the infant's experience differ from each other according to which macro-worlds they are imbedded in. Infancy is experienced relative to its overall location in society. The same principle of relativity pertains to later childhood, adolescence or any other biographical stage.

Feeding practices may be taken as an important case in point. A large number of variations in this are, of course, possible—feeding the infant on a regular schedule as against so-called demand feeding, breast feeding as against bottle feeding, different timetables for weaning and so on. Not only are there great differences between societies in this but also between classes within the same society. For example, in America bottle feeding was first pioneered by middle-class mothers. It then rather rapidly spread to other classes. Later, it was once more middle-class mothers who led a reaction against it in favor of breast feeding. Quite literally, therefore, the income level of an infant's parents decided whether, when hungry, he would be presented with his mother's breast or with a bottle.[1]

Between societies, the differences in this area are truly remarkable. In the middle-class family in Western society, before the spread of various notions concerning demand feeding by experts in the field, there was a rigid, almost industrial regime of feeding schedules. The infant was fed at certain hours and at those hours only. In between he was allowed to cry. This practice was variously justified either in terms of practicality or its alleged contribution to the infant's health. By contrast, we may look at the feeding practices of the Gusii in Kenya.[2]

Among the Gusii there are no feeding schedules at all. The mother nurses the infant whenever he cries. At night the mother sleeps naked under a blanket with the child in her arms. As far as feasible, the infant has continuous and instant access to his mother's breast.

When the mother is working, she either carries the infant tied to her back, or he is carried alongside her by someone else. On these occasions also, when the infant starts to cry, he is fed as quickly as possible. The general rule is that the infant is not allowed to cry for more than five minutes before he is fed. Compared with most feeding patterns in Western society, this strikes one as very "permissive" indeed.

There are, however, other aspects of Gusii feeding practices that impress one in a rather different way. Thus, beginning a few days after birth, the infant is fed a gruel as a supplement to his mother's milk. It appears from the data that the infant does not take to this gruel with much enthusiasm. This does not help him any; he is fed by force. This forced feeding is done in the rather unpleasant manner of the mother holding the infant's nose. When, in order to breathe, the infant then opens his mouth, the gruel is poured into it. Also, while other individuals may do so, the infant's mother shows very little affection, and actually rarely fondles the infant. Probably this is done so as to avoid jealousy from onlookers, but it means in practice that the infant experiences more affection from other people than from his own mother. Thus, there are other aspects of Gusii child-rearing at this early stage which, when compared with Western patterns, impress us as quite harsh. On the other hand, when it comes to weaning, the Gusiis again show a very high degree of "permissiveness" as compared with Western societies. Thus, while in

[1] John and Elizabeth Newson, *Patterns of Infant Care* (Baltimore, Penguin Books, 1965), pp. 176ff.
[2] Beatrice Whiting (ed.), *Six Cultures—Studies in Child Rearing* (New York, Wiley, 1963), pp. 139ff.

Western societies the very great majority of children is changed from the breast to the bottle before the age of six months, Gusii children are weaned up to the age of twenty-two months.

TOILET TRAINING: THE BUSH OR "INSPIRATION"

Toilet training is another area of the infant's behavior in which, in a very obvious way, social patterns are imposed upon the very physiological functioning of the organism. Generally speaking, there are rather few problems in this area in primitive societies. The general rule is that as soon as children can walk they follow the adults into the bush or into some other area designated by the community as appropriate for elimination. There is especially little problem in warm climates where little or no clothing is worn by small children. Thus, among the Gusii, toilet training consists of the relatively simple matter of getting the child to defecate outside the house. This, on the average, is usually done around twenty-five months of age, and usually takes about one month to accomplish. There seems to be little concern over urination. Since small children wear no lower garments, there is no problem of soiling clothes. Children are taught modesty in eliminating functions, but apparently this is learned in a process of simple imitation without threats or sanctions.[3]

By contrast, toilet training is a very great preoccupation in Western societies. (It seems likely that if Freud had been a Gusii, it would never have occurred to him to give toilet training such an important place in his theory of child development.) If one compares, say, American society with that of the Gusii, it is not difficult to see why toilet training should be more of a problem in the former. There is, after all, the multiplicity of clothing worn by children, the complexity of housing arrangements, not to mention the general unavailability of bush. Thus, the tribulations, successes and failures of toilet training are a frequent topic of conversation among American mothers. In a recent study of a community in New England,[4] the observers found an amazing range of punitive measures inflicted on children who did not respond to toilet training as they were supposed to. These measures ranged from rubbing the infant's nose in his own feces, to the use of suppositories or enemas to get the infant used to regularity. (Actually, from one-fourth to one-third of the mothers interviewed reported use of the latter measures.) It seems that small children cordially dislike enemas, and the threat of their use was usually enough to "inspire" the child to defecate when his mother wanted him to.

If a Gusii sociologist, however, concluded from this material that American toilet-training practices are particularly rigid, he would be mistaken in generalizing from this to the way Americans treat their children in other areas of

---

[3] Whiting, *ibid.*, pp. 154ff.
[4] *Ibid.*, pp. 944ff.

behavior. For example, Americans take for granted that children want to be very much in motion, and by and large this is tolerated even in the lower grades of school. Frenchmen, by contrast, have a very different view of this matter.[5] In a recent study of French child-rearing practices, an American observer was amazed at the way in which French children are taken to play in a park dressed in elegant clothes and somehow manage not to get dirty. American children, of course, manage to get themselves absolutely covered with dirt within no time at all in comparable situations. The explanation of the difference lies in the relative immobility of French children. The American observer noticed this in French children between two and three years of age, and was amazed by their capacity to remain absolutely still for long periods of time. The same study tells of the case of a French child sent by his teacher to see a school psychologist for no other reason than because the child would not sit still in class. The French schoolteacher, completely unused to such behavior, concluded that the child must be ill. In other words, a degree of motor activity taken for granted in an American school was looked upon as evidence for some sort of pathology in France.

SOCIALIZATION: RELATIVE PATTERNS EXPERIENCED AS ABSOLUTE

The process through which an individual learns to be a member of society is called *socialization*. There are a number of aspects to this. All the processes just discussed are aspects of socialization. In this sense, socialization is the imposition of social patterns on behavior. And, as we have tried to show, these patterns even interfere with the physiological processes of the organism. It follows that, in the biography of every individual, socialization, and especially early socialization, is a tremendously powerful and important fact. From the point of view of the outside observer, the patterns that are imposed in socialization are highly relative, as we have seen. They depend not only upon the individual peculiarities of the adults who are in charge of the child but also upon the various social groupings to which these adults belong. Thus, the patterns of a child's behavior depend not only upon whether he is a Gusii or an American but also whether he is a middle-class or working-class American. From the point of view of the child, however, these same patterns are experienced in a very absolute way. Indeed, there are reasons to think that if this were not so, the child would become disturbed and socialization could not proceed.

The absoluteness with which societies' patterns confront the child is based on two very simple facts—the great power of the adults in the situation, and

[5] Margaret Mead and Martha Wolfenstein (eds.), *Childhood in Contemporary Cultures* (Chicago, Phoenix Books, 1955), pp. 106ff.

the ignorance of the child of alternative patterns. Psychologists differ in their view as to whether the child experiences the adults at this stage of life as being very much under his control (because they are generally so responsive to his needs) or whether he feels continually threatened by them (because he is so dependent upon them). However this may be, there can be no question that, objectively speaking, adults have overwhelming power in the situation. The child can, of course, resist them, but the probable outcome of any conflict is a victory on the part of the adults. It is they who control most of the rewards that he craves and most of the sanctions that he fears. Indeed, the simple fact that most children are eventually socialized affords simple proof of this proposition. At the same time, it is obvious that the small child is ignorant of any alternatives to the patterns that are being imposed upon him. The adults confront him with a world—for him, it is *the* world. It is only much later that he discovers that there are alternatives to this particular world, that his parents' world is relative in space and time, and that quite different patterns are possible. Only then does the individual become aware of the relativity of social patterns and of social worlds—in the extreme case, he might even follow up this insight by becoming a sociologist.

INITIATING A CHILD: *THE* WORLD BECOMES *HIS* WORLD

There is, thus, a way of looking at socialization from what one might call the "policeman's point of view"; that is, socialization can be viewed primarily as the imposition of controls from without, supported by some system of rewards and punishments. There is another, if you will, more benign way of looking at the same phenomenon, namely one can look upon socialization as a process of initiation in which the child is permitted to develop and expand into a world available to him. In this aspect, socialization is an essential part of the process of becoming fully human and realizing the full potential of the individual. Socialization is a process of initiation into a social world, its forms of interaction and its many meanings. The social world of his parents first confronts the child as an external, vastly powerful and mysterious reality. In the course of socialization, that world becomes comprehensible. The child enters it, becomes capable of participating in it. It becomes *his* world.

LANGUAGE, THINKING, REFLECTION AND "TALKING BACK"

The primary vehicle of socialization, especially in this second aspect, is language. We will return to language in somewhat greater detail a little later on. At this point we would only stress how essential language is for socialization and, indeed, for any continuing participation in a society. It is in acquiring language that a child learns to convey and retain socially recognized meaning. He begins to be able to think abstractly, which means that his mind becomes able to move beyond the immediate situation. It is also through the acquisition of language that the child becomes capable of reflection. Past experience is reflected upon and integrated into a growing, coherent view of reality. Present experience is ongoingly interpreted in terms of this view, and future experience can not only be imagined but planned for. It is through this growing reflection that the child becomes conscious of himself as a self—in the literal sense of re-flection, that is, of the child's attention *turning back* from the outside world to himself.

It is very easy, and, of course, up to a point correct, to think of socialization as a shaping or molding process. Indeed, the child is shaped by society, molded in such a way that he can be a recognized and participant member of it. But it is also important not to see this as a one-sided process. The child, even the very young infant, is not a passive victim of socialization. He resists it, participates in it, collaborates with it in varying degrees. Socialization is a reciprocal process in the sense that not only the socialized but the socializers are affected by it. This can be observed fairly easily in everyday life. Usually parents succeed to a greater or lesser degree in shaping their children in accordance with the overall patterns established by society and desired by themselves. But the parents also are changed by the experience. The child's capacity for reciprocity, that is, his capacity to act on his own upon the world and the other people inhabiting it increases in direct relation to his capacity to use language. Quite literally, the child then starts to *talk back* to the adults.

In the same vein, it is important to recognize that there are limits to socialization. These limits are given in the child's organism. Given an average intelligence, it is possible to take an infant from any part of the world and socialize him into becoming a member of American society. Any normal child can learn English. Any normal child can learn the values and patterns for living that are attached to the English language in America. Probably every normal child could also learn a system of musical notation. But clearly every normal child could *not* be developed into a musical genius. Unless the potential for this were already given in the organism, any efforts at socialization in this direction would come up against hard and impregnable resistance. The present state of scientific knowledge (especially in the area of human biology) does not permit us to describe the precise limits of socialization. All the same, it is very important to be aware that these limits exist.

TAKING THE ATTITUDE OF AND TAKING THE ROLE OF THE OTHER

What are the mechanisms by which socialization proceeds? The fundamental mechanism is a process of interacting and identifying with others. A crucial step is when the child learns (in Mead's phrase) *to take the attitude of the other.*[6] This means that the child not only learns to recognize a certain attitude in someone else, and to understand its meaning, but that he learns to take it himself. For example, the child observes his mother taking an attitude of anger on certain occasions—say, on occasions where he soils himself. The attitude of anger not only is expressed by various gestures and words but also conveys a particular meaning, namely, that it is wrong to soil oneself. The child will first imitate the external expressions of this attitude, both verbally and nonverbally. It is in this process of interaction and identification that the meaning of this attitude is appropriated by the child.

This particular phase of socialization will be successfully accomplished when the child has learned to take the same attitude toward himself, even in the absence of his mother. Thus, children can be observed "playing mother" to themselves when they are alone—for example, by rebuking themselves for infractions of the rules of toilet training, sometimes by acting out a complete little skit in imitation of similar previous performances on the part of the mother. Eventually, it is no longer necessary to go through the skit. The attitude has become firmly imbedded in the child's consciousness, and he can refer to it silently and without acting it out. Similarly, the child learns *to take the role of the other.* For the present purpose, we can simply understand a role as an attitude that has become fixed in a consistent and reiterated pattern of conduct. Thus, there are not only a variety of attitudes which the mother takes toward the child, but there is an overall pattern of conduct which can be called the "mother role." A child not only learns to take on specific attitudes but to take on these roles. Playing is a very important part of this learning process. Everyone, of course, has watched children playing at being their parents, at being older brothers or sisters, and then later at being policemen, cowboys or Indians. Such playing is not only important for the particular roles that it involves but for teaching the child to play *any* role. It doesn't matter, therefore, that this particular child will never be either cowboy or Indian. But, in playing the role, a reiterated pattern of conduct is learned in the first place. *The point is not to become an Indian, but rather to learn how to play roles.*

SOCIALIZATION: FROM "SIGNIFICANT OTHERS" TO "GENERALIZED OTHER"

Beyond this general teaching function of "playing at" roles, the same process may also communicate social meanings that are "for real." How American children play the role of policeman will greatly depend on what this role

---

[6] These and the following concepts were coined by George Herbert Mead. See our recommendations for readings for this chapter.

means in their immediate social milieu. To a white suburban child the police-man means a figure of authority and reassurance, someone to turn to in the case of trouble. To a black child of the inner city, the same role very likely im-plies hostility and danger, a threat rather than reassurance, someone to run away from rather than to. We may also assume that playing the roles of cow-boy and Indian has very different meanings indeed in white suburbia or on an Indian reservation.

Socialization thus proceeds in a continuous interaction with others. But not all the others encountered by the child are equally important in this process. Some are clearly of central importance. In the case of most children, these are the parents and whatever brothers and sisters might be around. In some cases there are added to this group such figures as grandparents, close friends of the parents and domestic servants. There are other people who stay in the back-ground and whose place in the process of socialization could best be described as one in which background noise is provided. These are all sorts of casual con-tacts, ranging from the mailman to the neighbor whom one only sees occa-sionally. If one thinks of socialization as a kind of drama, one could think of it in terms of ancient Greek theater, in which case some of the participants may be compared to the major protagonists of a play while others function as a chorus.

The major protagonist in the drama of socialization Mead called *significant others*. These are the people with whom the child interacts most frequently, to whom he has an important emotional relationship, and whose attitudes and roles are the crucial ones in his situation. Obviously, it is very important for what happens to the child just who or what these significant others are. By this we mean not only their individual particularities or eccentricities but their location in the larger society. In the earlier phases of socialization, whatever attitudes or roles are taken by the child, it is from the significant others that they are taken. In a very real sense they *are* the child's social world. As sociali-zation proceeds, however, the child begins to understand that these particular attitudes and roles refer to a much more general reality. For example, the child then begins to understand that it is not only his mother who is angry when he soils himself but that that anger is shared by every other significant adult that he knows, and, indeed, by the adult world in general. It is at this point that the child learns to relate not only to specific significant others but to a *generalized other* (another Meadian term) which represents society at large. This step can be easily seen in terms of language. In the earlier phase, it is as if the child says to himself (in many cases he will actually do so), "Mom-my doesn't want me to soil myself." After the discovery of the generalized other, it becomes a statement such as this: "One does not soil oneself." The particular attitudes have now become universal. The specific commands and prohibitions of individual others have become general norms. This step is a very crucial one in the process of socialization.

INTERNALIZATION, CONSCIENCE AND
SELF-DISCOVERY

It will now make sense that one of the terms used to describe socialization, and sometimes used almost interchangeably with it, is that of *internalization*. What is meant by this is that the social world, with its multitude of meanings, becomes internalized in the child's own consciousness. What previously was experienced as something outside himself can now become experienced within himself as well. In a complicated process of reciprocity and reflection, a certain symmetry is established between the inner world of the individual and the outer social world within which he is being socialized. The phenomenon we usually call conscience illustrates this most clearly. Conscience, after all, is essentially the internalization (or, rather, the internalized presence) of moral commands and prohibitions that previously came from the outside. It all began when somewhere in the course of socialization a significant other said, "Do this," or "Don't do that." As socialization proceeded, the child identified with these statements of morality. In identifying with them, he internalized them. Somewhere along the line, he said to himself, "Do this," or "Don't do that,"—probably in much the same manner that his mother or some other significant person first said them to him. Then these statements became silently absorbed into his own mind. The voices have become inner voices. And finally it is the individual's own conscience that is speaking to him.

Once more it is possible to look upon this in different ways. One can look at internalization from what we previously called the "policeman's point of view," and it will be correct to do so. As the example of conscience clearly illustrates, internalization has something to do with controlling the individual's conduct. It makes it possible for such controls to be continuous and economical. It would be terribly expensive for society, and probably impossible, to constantly surround the individual with other people who will say, "Do this," and "Don't do that." When these injunctions have become internalized within the individual's own consciousness, only occasional reinforcements from the outside are necessary. Most of the time, most individuals will control themselves. But this is only one way of looking at the phenomenon. Internalization not only controls the individual but opens up the world for him. Internalization not only allows the individual to participate in the outside social world but also enables him to have a rich inner life of his own. *Only by internalizing the voices of others can we speak to ourselves. If no one had significantly addressed us from the outside, there would be silence within ourselves as well. It is only through others that we can come to discover ourselves.* Even more specifically, it is only through significant others that we can develop a significant relationship to ourselves. This, among other reasons, is why it is so important to choose one's parents with some care.

"HE'S ONLY A CHILD"—BIOLOGICAL GROWTH AND BIOGRAPHICAL STAGES

There is, of course, a certain parallelism between the biological processes of growth and socialization. If nothing else, the growth of the organism sets limits to socialization. Thus, it would be futile if a society wanted to teach language to a child one month old or calculus to a child aged two years. However, it would be a great mistake to think that the biographical stages of life, as defined by society, are directly based on the stages of biological growth. This is so with regard to all stages of biography, from birth to death, but it is also true of childhood. There are many different ways of structuring childhood not only in terms of its duration but in terms of its characteristics. It is no doubt possible for the biologist to provide a definition of childhood in terms of the degree of development of the organism; and the psychologist can give a corresponding definition in terms of the development of the mind. Within these biological and psychological limits, however, the sociologist must insist that childhood itself is a matter of social construction. This means that society has great leeway in deciding what childhood is to be.

Childhood, as we understand and know it today, is a creation of the modern world, especially of the bourgeoisie.[7] It is only very recently in Western history that childhood has come to be conceived of as a special and highly protected age. This modern structure of childhood is not only expressed in innumerable beliefs and values regarding children (for example, the notion that children are somehow "innocent") but also in our legislation. Thus, it is today a just about universal assumption in modern societies that children are not subject to the ordinary provisions of criminal law. It was not so very long ago that children were simply looked upon as little adults. This was very clearly expressed by the manner in which they were dressed. As recently as the eighteenth century, as we can see by looking at paintings from this period, children walked around with their parents dressed in identical fashion—except, of course, in smaller sizes. As childhood came to be understood and organized as a very special phase of life, distinct from adulthood, children began to be dressed in special ways.

A case in point is the modern belief in the "innocence" of children, that is, the belief that children ought to be protected from certain aspects of life. For fascinating comparative reading, we may look at the diary kept by the royal

[7] Philippe Ariés, *Centuries of Childhood* (New York, Knopf, 1962).

physician during the childhood of Louis XIII of France at the beginning of the seventeenth century.[8] His nanny played with his penis when Louis was less than one year old. Everyone thought that this was great fun. Soon afterward, the little prince made a point of always exhibiting his penis amid general merriment. He also asked everyone to kiss it. This ribald attention to the child's genital parts continued for several years and involved not only frivolous maids and the like but also his mother, the Queen. At the age of four the Prince was taken to his mother's bed by a lady of the court and told, "Monsieur, this is where you were made." Only after he reached about seven years of age did the notion arise that he ought to have a certain degree of modesty about this part of his body. One may add that Louis XIII was married at the age of fourteen, by which time, as one commentator remarks wryly, he had nothing left to learn.

DIFFERENT WORLDS OF CHILDHOOD

A classical case of the different worlds of childhood, known to almost everyone, is the contrast between Athens and Sparta in this respect.[9] The Athenians were very much concerned that their young men should grow up into well-rounded individuals, as capable in poetry and philosophy as in the arts of war. Athenian education reflected this ideal. The world of the Athenian child (at least the male child) was a world of ongoing competition, not only physically but mentally and aesthetically. By contrast, Spartan education stressed only the development of discipline, obedience and physical prowess—that is, the virtues of the soldier. Compared with Athenian practices, the way in which the Spartans raised their children was overwhelmingly harsh if not downright brutal. The practice of letting children go hungry, forcing them to steal their own food, was only one of many expressions of this conception of childhood. Needless to say, it was much more agreeable to be a little boy in Athens than in Sparta. But this is not the major sociological point. Rather the point is that Spartan socialization produced very different kinds of individuals from socialization in Athens. Spartan society, which glorified the military aspect of life over any other, wanted such individuals, and in terms of these goals the Spartan system of child-rearing made perfect sense.

The kind of childhood which was developed in the modern West is, today, rapidly spreading throughout the world. There are many reasons for this. One of them is the dramatic decline in infant mortality and children's diseases which has been one of the truly revolutionary consequences of modern medicine. As a result, childhood has become a safer and happier phase of life than

[8] *Ibid.*, pp. 100ff.
[9] Compare, for example, H.I. Marrou, *A History of Education in Antiquity* (New York, Mentor Books, 1956).

it has ever been before, and this has encouraged the spread of the Western conception of childhood as a specially valuable and to-be-protected stage of life. Compared with previous periods of history in the West and elsewhere, socialization today has taken on unique qualities of gentleness and concern for all the needs of the child. It is very likely that the spread of this conception of socialization and the structure of childhood that goes with it are having very important effects on society, even in the political sphere.

MEETING OURSELVES: THE MEADIAN CONCEPTS OF "I" AND "ME"

So far we have emphasized the way in which socialization introduces the child into a particular social world. Equally important is the way in which socialization introduces the child to himself. Just as society has constructed a world into which the child can be initiated, so society also constructs specific types of self. Not only is the child socialized into a particular world but he is socialized into a particular self. What takes place within the child's consciousness in this process has been expressed by the Meadian concepts of the *I* and the *me*.[10] We have already mentioned as an interesting consequence of socialization that a child can speak to himself. The *I* and the *me* are the partners in precisely this kind of conversation. The *I* represents the ongoing spontaneous awareness of self that all of us have. The *me*, by contrast, represents that part of the self that has been shaped or molded by society.

These two aspects of the self can enter into conversation with each other. For example, a little boy growing up in American society is taught certain things that supposedly are appropriate to little boys, such as fortitude in the face of pain. Suppose he bangs his knee and it starts to bleed. The *I* is registering the pain and, we might imagine, wants to scream its head off. The *me*, on the other hand, has learned that good little boys are supposed to be brave. It is the *me* that makes out little boy bite his lip and bear the pain. Or suppose that the little boy has grown a little older and has a very attractive teacher in school. The *I* registers the attraction and wants nothing more than to grab the teacher and make love to her. The *me*, however, has appropriated the social norm that such things are simply not done. It is not difficult to imagine a silent inner conversation between these two aspects of the self, the one saying, "Go ahead and get her," the other warning, "Stop; this is wrong." Socialization, then, in a very important way, shapes a part of the self. It cannot shape the self in its entirety. There is always something spontaneous, something uncontrollable, which sometimes erupts in unforeseen ways. It is that spontaneous part of the self that *confronts* the socialized part of the self.

[10] These concepts are also taken from Mead.

APPROPRIATING AN IDENTITY: BEING ASSIGNED OR SUBSCRIBING

The socialized part of the self is commonly called *identity*.[11] Every society may be viewed as holding a repertoire of identities—little boy, little girl, father, mother, policeman, professor, thief, archbishop, general and so forth. By a kind of invisible lottery, these identities as assigned to different individuals. Some of them are assigned from birth, such as little boy or little girl. Others are assigned later in life, such as clever little boy or pretty little girl (or, conversely, stupid little boy or ugly little girl). Other identities are put up, as it were, for subscription, and individuals may obtain them by deliberate effort, such as policeman or archbishop. But whether an identity is assigned or achieved, in each case it is appropriated by the individual through a process of interaction with others. It is others who identify him in a specific way. Only if an identity is confirmed by others is it possible for that identity to be real to the individual holding it. In other words, identity is the product of an interplay of identification and self-identification. This is even true of identities that are deliberately constructed by an individual.

For example, there are individuals in our society who are identified as male who would prefer to be female. They may do any number of things, all the way to surgery, in order to reconstruct themselves in terms of the desired new identity. The essential goal which they must achieve, however, is to get at least some others to accept that new identity, that is, to identify them in these terms. It is impossible to be anything or anybody for very long all by oneself. Others have to tell us who we are, others have to confirm our identity. There are, indeed, cases where individuals hold on to an identity that no one else in the world recognizes as real. We call such individuals psychotics. They are marginal cases of great interest, but their analysis cannot concern us here.

DIFFERENT SOCIETIES, DIFFERENT IDENTITIES: AMERICAN AND SOVIET SOCIALIZATION

If the relationship between socialization and identity is understood, then it will be clear how it comes about that entire social groups or societies can be characterized in terms of specific identities. Americans, for instance, can be recognized not only in terms of certain patterns of conduct but also in terms of certain characteristics that many of them have in common—that is, in

[11] It is not quite clear who first used the concept of identity in this sense. Its popularity in recent years is largely due to the work of Erik Erikson, who may be described as a sociologically inclined psychoanalyst. See his *Childhood and Society* (New York, Norton, 1950).

terms of a specifically American identity. Numerous studies have shown how certain basic American values, such as autonomy, individual achievement and seriousness about one's career, are introduced into the socialization process from the beginning, especially in the case of boys.[12] Even the games which American children play reflect these values, for example in their emphasis on individual competition. There are severe penalties for failure to live up to these values and to the identity which they intend. These penalties range from being made fun of by other children to being a failure in the occupational world.

By contrast, Soviet society has emphasized discipline, loyalty and cooperation with others for collective achievement. It is these values which have been emphasized in Soviet child-rearing and educational practices. The goal here, of course, has been to produce an identity that is suitable to the Soviet ideal of socialist society. The Soviet child thus grows up in a situation in which he is much more firmly controlled than his American contemporary, but in which he is also more protected against unsettling necessities to make choices of his own. As a result, as has been observed by some American investigators, Soviet children show a much greater serenity than American children of the same age.[13] One may leave aside the question whether the Soviet claim to have produced the "new socialist man" is justified. What is clear, however, is that Soviet society, for better or for worse, has set up such socialization processes as are conducive to a specific type of identity which is in accordance with the ideals and needs of that society.

SECONDARY SOCIALIZATION: ENTERING NEW WORLDS

In talking about education, we have already implied that socialization does not come to an end at the point where an individual child becomes a full participant in society. Indeed, one may say that socialization never comes to an end. In a normal biography, what happens simply is that the intensity and scope of socialization diminish after early childhood. Sociologists distinguish between *primary* and *secondary socialization*. By primary socialization is meant the original process by which a child becomes a participant member of a society. By secondary socialization are meant all later processes by which an individual is inducted into a specific social world. For example, every training in an occupation involves processes of secondary socialization. In some cases, these processes are relatively superficial. For example, no profound changes in the identity of an individual are required to train him to be a certified public

[12] This is an influential (well-merited) study of life in a Canadian suburban community, with special emphasis on family and childhood patterns: J.R. Seeley, R.A. Sim and E.W. Loosley, *Crestwood Heights* (New York, Basic Books, 1956), pp. 118ff.
[13] David and Vera Mace, *The Soviet Family* (Garden City, N.Y., Dolphin Books, 1964), pp. 264ff.

accountant. This is not the case, however, if an individual is to be trained to be a priest or to be a professional revolutionary. There are instances of secondary socialization of this kind that resemble in intensity what goes on in the socialization of early childhood. Secondary socialization is also involved in such widely different experiences as improving one's general social position, changing one's place of residence, adapting to a chronic illness or being accepted by a new circle of friends.

RELATIONS TO INDIVIDUALS AND THE SOCIAL UNIVERSE

All processes of socialization take place in face-to-face interaction with other people. In other words, socialization always involves changes in the micro-world of the individual. At the same time, most processes of socialization, both primary and secondary, relate the individual to complex structures of the macro-world. The attitudes which the individual learns in socialization usually refer to broad systems of meaning and of values that extend far beyond his immediate situation. For example, habits of neatness and cleanliness are not only eccentric notions of a particular set of parents but are values of great importance in a broad middle-class world. Similarly, roles learned in socialization refer to vast institutions that may not be readily visible within the individual's micro-world. Thus, learning the role of being a brave little boy is not only conducive to approval by one's parents and playmates but will have significance to the individual as he makes his career in a much broader world of institutions, ranging from the college football field to the military. Socialization links micro-world and macro-world. First, socialization enables the individual to relate to specific individual others; subsequently, it enables him to relate to an entire social universe. For better or for worse, being human entails having such a relationship on a lifelong basis.

Readings

The conceptual approach of this chapter is based on George Herbert Mead, especially his *Mind, Self and Society* (Chicago, University of Chicago Press, 1934). Mead is not an easy author to read for the beginning student. For the latter, we would recommend Anselm Strauss (ed.), *George Herbert Mead on Social Psychology* (Chicago, Phoenix Books, 1964), which contains selections from Mead's work and a useful introduction by the editor. One of the best books for an understanding of the different worlds of childhood is Philippe Ariès, *Centuries of Childhood* (New York, Knopf, 1962), available in paperback.

In this essay sociologist Richard Flacks indicates the importance of cultural values in determining the general nature of socialization. Flacks begins by examining certain American values, including those related to economic activity, technological advances, and corporate organization. He then explores our child-rearing practices, emphasizing certain contradictions in social responsibilities and the confusion that has resulted from recent challenges to traditional ideas about the roles of parents—and the roles of children.

As you read "Growing Up Confused," pay particular attention to the significance of values and to problems of value-conflict and role-conflict.

Growing Up Confused

RICHARD FLACKS

It is not too great an oversimplification to say that the central, unifying theme of American culture has always been that cluster of values Max Weber called the "Protestant Ethic." In particular, Americans agreed that the meaning of life was given by one's work, that personal fulfillment and social responsibility required that males be fully engaged in a vocation, and that virtue was measured in terms of success in an occupation. The most valued work was entrepreneurial activity; the most valued model was the rational, thrifty, hard-working, self-denying, risk-taking entrepreneur.

Undoubtedly, the vitality of these values was important in the phenomenal growth of the American technological and economic system in the nineteenth century. In a period when accumulation and production were society's central problems, it was fortunate that the average man was highly motivated to produce, to work hard, and to save—in short, to resist temptations that might divert him from doing his part in building the country. It was also fortunate that aspirations for monetary success could be fulfilled by many, while many others could believe that their failure lay in themselves—in their own inability to achieve the cultural ideal—rather than in the ideal itself.

In the American ideal women were not regarded as virtuous if *they* sought independence and success in the world of work. Instead, they were valued if they supported their husbands' capacity to be single-mindedly devoted to

21

work, if they themselves were skilled at producing a self-sufficient household, and if they raised their male children to be independent, self-reliant, self-denying, and achievement-oriented individuals.

Given the entrepreneurial opportunities, the open frontier, and the evident dynamism of American life, it is not surprising that most American young people who were socialized into this cultural framework accepted it with enthusiasm. Boys were eager to become men in the image of their fathers—although encouraged by their fathers and mothers, they were profoundly eager to surpass their fathers' achievements in work and status.

Observers agree that this cultural framework has been severely eroded or at least modified by what has happened in America in the twentieth century. What, in brief outline, happened?

1. An economic system organized around problems of capital accumulation and the need for saving, entrepreneurship, and self-reliance—a system of free market and individual competition—has been replaced by an economic system organized around problems of distribution and the need for spending, interdependence, bureaucratic management, planning, and large-scale organization.

2. As a consequence, work is now coordinated by massive private and public bureaucratic organizations, and work achievement is defined not in entrepreneurial terms, but in terms of successful fulfillment of a career within a bureaucratic or professional hierarchy.

3. These developments have permitted and been required by a tremendous technological leap. Consequently, a vast array of commodities for individual consumption is produced. On the one hand, this situation required that men consume; on the other hand, it obviated the sense of the need to save, postpone gratification, and be self-denying that had been justified by scarcity.

As a result of these massive changes—from individual entrepreneurship to large corporate organization, from free market competition to bureaucratic coordination and planning, from accumulation and scarcity to consumption and affluence—the vitality of the "Protestant Ethic" has declined. Throughout society during the past sixty years, more and more people have felt less committed to the entrepreneurial character and its virtues. Increasingly, self-worth and worth in the eyes of others is organized as much by one's style of life and one's consumption patterns as by one's occupational status as such. Furthermore, although instrumental and rational activity is still highly valued, all observers report that there has been a relaxation on prohibitions against expressiveness and hedonism. Indeed, a society in which the consumption of goods has become a fundamental problem requires that men cease to be ascetic and self-denying and abandon many of the guilts that they experience when they express their impulses.

By the middle of the twentieth century, the American society was qualitatively different from the society that had given birth to the cultural framework of capitalism. The family firm had been superseded by the giant corporation, the free market by the "welfare-warfare" state, and the entrepreneur by the manager and the bureaucrat. Technology had created a superabundant economy in which the traditional virtues of thrift, self-denial and living by the sweat of one's brow seemed not only absurd, but actually dangerous to prosperity. Technology seemed to promise not only an abundance of goods, but a world in which hard physical labor could be eliminated.

Yet, despite the need for new values and a new cultural framework, a cultural transformation was not occurring. Politicians, teachers, and preachers continued to give lip-service to the Protestant Ethic, while the mass media, without announcing the fact, purveyed an increasingly blatant hedonism. Many of the classic symptoms of "anomie" were widespread. Breakdown was widely evident, but new values were not.

I suppose that the best indication of the coherence of a culture is the degree to which parents can transmit a sense of it to their offspring with clarity and effectiveness. Cultural breakdown has reached the point of no return when the process of socialization no longer provides the new generation with coherent reasons to be enthusiastic about becoming adult members of the society. Perhaps the best way I can illustrate what I mean by cultural instability and breakdown is to discuss the American middle class family as it seemed to most observers to be functioning by mid-twentieth century. An examination of family patterns and childrearing not only illuminates the cultural crisis, but also provides some clues to the sources of youthful discontent.

When you read what follows, remember that I am not criticizing American parents for faulty childrearing practices. On the contrary, the main point I am trying to make is that parental confusion is virtually inevitable in a society in which the culture is breaking down. Moreover, the outcomes of that confusion should not be labeled "pathological," in my opinion. On the contrary. When parents raise their children in a manner that causes them to have significant problems of "adjustment," if anything, this is a "healthy" circumstance. I am arguing that the basic source of socially patterned maladjustment is a culture that no longer enables a person to find coherent meaning in his life. The maladjustment of youth offers one of the few hopes that new meanings can be found—that a new culture can be created.

The family, of course, is the primary institution for the inculcation of basic values and molding of culturally appropriate character structures. All observers agree that the American family, particularly the white, "middle class" family, has undergone a substantial transformation over the past several decades—a transformation that both reflects and contributes to the cultural crisis in the society at large.

A major structural change in the middle class family has been its "reduction"—that is, the erosion of close ties to relatives outside the nuclear family unit. Dissolution of extended family bonds is highly functional in a society based on technological development because it permits people to be relatively free of emotional and economic ties to "homes" and "relatives" and enables them to move freely in response to changing occupational requirements, and to take advantage of opportunities for career advancement wherever and whenever they become available. Since the nuclear family is expected to establish a self-contained household, it becomes a highly efficient mechanism for absorbing a vast array of consumer goods—each small family unit seeks to purchase the house, car, furnishings, appliances, and other commodities that will ensure its independence. (On the other hand, an extended family complex living contiguously probably would share many such goods, thereby reducing the need for each household in the network to buy its own.) Thus, in a structural sense the nuclear middle class family meshes nicely with the economy's demand for a mobile labor force and an actively consuming public.

In the typical middle class family, the father works away from home while the mother spends virtually all her time at home rearing the children. Authority—in principle—is shared by the parents (a marked change from the patriarchal structure of the past), but clearly, it is exercised far more intensively and continuously by the mother than by the father. Ideally, the mother (if she is modern) is less concerned with efforts to repress and restrict the expressive, impulsive behavior of her children than she was in the past, just as she is less likely to emphasize obedient, submissive behavior as desirable. Instead, she is expected to facilitate the child's desires to explore, to test the environment, and to encourage self-reliant and autonomous behavior. What is now "good" is not so much the obedient, quiet, clean cautious child, but rather the child who acquires verbal and motor skills early, who is precocious in his understanding, who can do things for himself, and who relates well to strangers and to other children. Mother attempts to instill such qualities by use of so-called "psychological" techniques of discipline—giving and withdrawing her love. She tries to avoid the traditional, more "physical" forms of punishment, trying instead to convey a nondomineering attitude, nurturing nonauthoritarian style. Father, relatively a part of the background, strives for a generally warm, nonauthoritarian and supportive approach.

This mode of childrearing has become ascendant in American culture in this century, especially in the last three decades. It relies, then, on a high degree of exclusive dependence on the mother coupled with strong demands on the child for cognitive mastery and a will to strive and achieve. Research suggests that this family situation is a superior one for generating precisely those characteristics that enable successful participation in a culture that stresses individual achievement, formal education, rationality, and flexibility.

The culturally desired outcome of this family (and my emphasis here is on *male* character) is a child who achieves masculine identity and independence by fulfilling his mother's expectations that he will be independent and striving, whose guilt and anxiety is focused on achievement of internal standards of excellence, who enjoys testing and is capable of being tested, and who is able to handle sexual, aggressive, and other impulses and emotions by expressing them at the appropriate times and places while not letting them seriously interfere with his capacity for work, rational action, and self-reliance. Thus, impulses are not denied (as the traditional Protestant Ethic demanded) but managed. This process is greatly facilitated by the delicately balanced combination of demand and freedom, dependence and independence, and mothering and autonomy that ideally characterizes the suburban family.

How often such an "ideal" outcome actually results from this family situation is questionable. Although the mother-centered nuclear family meshes nicely with crucial *official values* embodied in the educational and occupational system, it appears to be highly vulnerable to a variety of severe contradictions that occur in the course of actual day-to-day life in the society. These contradictions are readily derivable from the general crisis of the culture I have been trying to sketch.

PARENTAL VALUE CONFLICT AND CONFUSION

Undoubtedly, parents experience a great deal of strain when they permit freedom and encourage autonomy on the part of their children. One source of such strain is the difference between the comparatively strict atmosphere in which most middle class parents were raised and the atmosphere they try to create in their own homes. Another is that many parents continue to be emotionally committed to the traditional virtues of cleanliness, obedience, emotional control, and the like. Undoubtedly, then, many mothers and fathers are quite inconsistent with respect to discipline and demands; sometimes they punish their children for infraction of their rules and at other times they do not; sometimes they insist on traditional "good habits" while sometimes they are more relaxed. Frequently such parental inconsistency may result in what has been called "absorption" of the child's personality. Rather than molding a flexible, striving, self-sufficient character, the result is a character who fears failure *and* success, experiences deep anxiety about his acceptance by others, finds it difficult to establish his own autonomy, and is, consequently, far more driven toward conformity and "security" than toward independence and personal achievement. Indeed, some social critics have argued that this "other-directed" character type is becoming ascendant and that the achievement-oriented, "inner-directed" type is fading. Whether or not this is true, it seems plain that parental confusion over the nature of discipline and virtue is widespread and seriously undermines cultural goals rooted in achievement motivation.

Many parents are clearly committed to providing opportunities for free expression and autonomy for their children. They favor a life of fulfillment, experiential richness, and less self-denial. They may desire such a life for *themselves*, but find it difficult to consistently and wholeheartedly treat their children in this manner. Clearly, parents in a small nuclear family revolving around the mother as the exclusive childcare specialist must expend a tremendous investment of patience and energy, especially if they exercise permissiveness. To permit children to wander, experiment, and test requires constant vigilance to protect their physical safety. To provide children intellectual stimulation and sensory variety requires intensive involvement in the quality of their activities. But if parents are to provide the quantities of time, energy, and patience required to achieve these goals they must limit their *own* recreation and pursuits and get enough sleep so that they will have sufficient energy and patience to allow their offspring to be the central focus of attention whenever the children are awake and around. Undoubtedly, this is a source of strain even for parents with articulate commitment to "liberated" values— perhaps especially for them, since they themselves want freedom, autonomy, and the like. This conflict between the demands of childrearing and the personal needs of the parents constitutes another source of parental inconsistency that undermines the "ideal" character of the modern middle class family.

A third source of parental confusion is the conflict between effort and indulgence. Typical middle class parents expect their offspring to strive and achieve and to understand the necessity for self-discipline and effort in attaining goals. Very often, however, such families have surplus incomes and try to provide their children with a sense of being well taken care of. Indeed, in many families, parents indulge their children in order to demonstrate their love and care. Many fathers assuage the guilt they feel because of their absence from the home by showering their children with presents; many rationalize their own self-sacrifice by averring that anything that frees their kids from suffering is worthwhile. In any case, such parental indulgence (which is undoubtedly functional for the consumer goods sector of the economy) tends to weaken the offsprings' sense of necessity for self-discipline, sacrifice, and toil. Indeed, many children of affluence sense that as heirs of their parents' material property, they are likely to have some degree of permanent lifelong economic security. Under these circumstances, effort and achievement lose much of their motivational potency and moral meaning. This is especially so if fathers suggest to their sons (which they often do) that they can afford to enjoy life in ways that previous generations could not.

Thus, it seems plausible that incoherence and confusion are virtually inevitable features of the modern middle class family and the suburban style of life. As we shall see, the consequences for the general culture and for the youths who will inherit it contribute to the sense of crisis.

MATERNAL AMBIVALENCE

In addition to such value confusion, there are other sources of childrearing imbalance and parental inconsistency. One of the most significant is the ambivalence and discontent that many women experience as they try to play the new maternal roles dictated by the family structure and childraising ideology we have been depicting. These discontents revolve around the fact that the woman who becomes a mother is expected to be a full-time mother and housewife in a situation in which she is highly isolated from adult social relations and must perform tasks that are menial and meaningless. She is expected to accept this role even though her formal education before marriage and motherhood has made her qualified to perform other roles and despite her aspirations for independence and self-fulfillment. Understandably, such a women finds it difficult to narrow her interests to the world of her three-year-old child and even more difficult not to feel guilty because she is discontent and hostile to her children and to her husband.

The ways in which women have adapted to this situation are diverse. Most adaptations that have been recorded, however, have been condemned as culturally dysfunctional and/or psychologically damaging to the child. For instance, there is the smothering, overprotective mother (whose protectiveness is said to be a screen for her unconscious hostility toward the child); the "seductive" mother (who becomes extremely close to her son as a displacement for her more general interpersonal and sexual frustrations); the mother who subtly, and often unconsciously, denigrates her husband to her children as an expression of her jealous resentment of his privilege and his abandonment of her; the mother who attempts to live vicariously through her children (hoping that they will achieve goals that she herself has been blocked from achieving); and the working mother (who, according to some childrearing experts, intensifies the child's fears of separation and abandonment).

All of these compensations are seen as damaging to the child's ability to manage and overcome his dependence on the mother, prolonging that dependency or forcing him to identify with her (instead of with the father) and weakening the male child's ability to accept culturally approved definitions of masculine identity. All of these patterns may weaken achievement motivation and damage the child's capacity for self-reliance.

Although many psychologists characterize such maternal behavior as "neurotic," a sociological perspective emphasizes the fact that such behavior is *socially determined—it is built into the maternal role* as it is now structured, especially considering the manner in which young women have been socialized and the increasing cultural support for the equality of women. More specifically, the discontent of middle class mothers is an inevitable consequence of the fact that they are forced into roles that do not match their aspirations and self-conceptions—aspirations and self-conceptions they have been taught are their right. Such a fundamental contradiction in women's roles is a further consequence and determinant of the general cultural crisis.

PATERNAL AMBIVALENCE

The paternal role contains its own built-in contradictions. This is so because fathers, as effective models of adult achievement, self-reliance, and rationality that they are expected to be, must be available for the psychological benefit of their children. At the same time, the middle class male who is striving or is already successful is likely to have a range of responsibilities and commitments outside the home. The highly career-oriented father may be available to his children hardly at all, partly from "necessity" and partly because he finds that life in the family is mundane when compared with life outside the home, where the responsibility and the power he can command are exciting.

Other fathers experience considerable regret and discontent with their work; they have ended up in positions that do not fulfill their earlier aspirations, they find their work unfulfilling or morally dubious, and they find work itself increasingly onerous. Many such fathers undoubtedly communicate their self-doubts and their skepticism to their sons. Still other men experience themselves as failures—as impotent and second rate in their work. The family, for them, becomes an arena for the exercise of power, aggression and self-importance which they cannot find elsewhere.

Like contradictions in the mothers' role, such paternal ambivalence is derived from fundamental cultural contradictions. These contradictions revolve around cultural demands for continuous striving and simultaneous demands for endless consumption—demands that men be dedicated careerists and, at the same time, good fathers, and that they compartmentalize the public and private worlds, reserving personal warmth, intimacy, and expressiveness for the latter.

A second source of strain for the middle class male is that the cultural measure of his worth (as well as his own sense of self-esteem) is based on his occupational success, but that success is a limitless goal on the one hand and is denied most men on the other. To the extent that the male accepts the cultural definition of his value, his self-esteem suffers. This inadequacy is communicated to his children; to the extent that he rejects the cultural standard, he communicates to his children a certain skepticism about the cultural framework.

As a result the developing child is exposed to another source of confusion. To the extent that the father embodies any of these contradictions, he is lacking in his effectiveness as a model, and since the typical suburban family is nuclear and isolated, the male child finds few alternatives to serve as effective models.

THE PACE OF SOCIAL CHANGE

A final source of parental confusion derives from the sense perhaps shared by most people in the culture—that the world in which children will be adults will be substantially different from the world in which they are children, in ways that are considerably obscure. Parents generally conceive of themselves—perhaps more than at any time in history—as inadequate models for their children because they are already obsolete. In this situation, the parental tone of voice lacks conviction, parental guidance has overtones of fatuousness, and parental authority is undermined by the parents' own lack of confidence. This particular source of cultural incoherence may not be directly related to the structure of the nuclear family itself, but it is a rather obvious consequence of a culture that values technological change and development as one of its central priorities. Presumably, a childrearing program that emphasizes independence, flexibility, and openmindedness meshes with a culture that values change. But as we have seen, such virtues are more easily espoused than instilled in a culture that places such heavy reliance on isolated and morally confused mothers and fathers to implement such a program.

It should not be hard to envision from our depiction of the built-in "strains" associated with the middle class nuclear family some idea of the consequences for young people. Briefly, such a family situation is likely to generate considerable confusion over values, goals, roles, and aspirations for the youth who experience it. More specifically, we can suggest that the "new" family is likely to impart a number of dispositions and personality "trends" in its offspring—traits or potentialities that predispose such youth to be restless with, skeptical of, or alienated from certain crucial aspects of conventional culture and, consequently, ready for certain kinds of cultural change.

A listing of some hypotheses concerning certain tendencies that the middle class family situation seems to generate in its offspring follows (I term them hypotheses, which await persuasive empirical tests, because for the most part, there is little direct evidence that these tendencies are clearly linked to childhood socialization):

1. Confusion and restlessness with conventional definitions of success. Such feelings would derive from the types of paternal ambivalence we have described, from the psychological distance of the father's work role from those

of his sons', from the parental value confusions we have called attention to, and from the pattern of maternal domination. Even youths who have strong motivations to achieve and who may act these out in school would be likely to entertain doubts about whether material success, status-striving and careerism constitute appropriate avenues for expressing their desires to "do well." But neither conventional parents nor the conventional culture provide very many clues about how one can achieve in ways other than the economic. The consequences of this combination of predispositions to question material success coupled with predispositions to achieve include profound indecisiveness about vocation (what Erik Erikson has called "role confusion"), vague yearnings for recognition and fame, and a restless search for alternative vocations and life styles.

2. Restlessness under conditions of imposed discipline. These derive from such features of the family as parental indulgence and permissiveness and are related to feelings of discontent with conventional definitions of vocation and achievement. Some consequences are discontent with classroom drill and learning situations requiring rote memorization; tendencies to feel bored and restless when concentration is required; avoidance of school subjects requiring discipline and attention to detail; and a generalized resistance to tasks that do not appear to be personally rewarding or are set without reference to goals determined by the self. These feelings are accompanied by intense desires for immediate experience, often coupled with guilt.

3. Restlessness with conditions of arbitrary or coercive authority. Such feelings might derive from expectations developed in the family for authority structures based on egalitarianism—expectations derived from parental fostering of participation, independence and autonomy and parental refusal to use physical punishment or coercion. Children raised in this way, we can speculate, may grow to expect that authority *outside* the family will be similarly responsive, democratic, nonpunitive and permissive. A consequence of such dispositions and expectations about authority is the tendency to be unusually trusting of teachers and other adults, but vociferously and unusually upset, angry and rebellious when such authority figures betray expectations that they will be egalitarian, democratic, and so forth. Or one might expect such children to be capable of more active expression of opposition and resistance to authority when it appears arbitrary, more skeptical of its claims in general, more likely to ask embarrassing questions, and more ready to systematically test the limits of its tolerance.

4. Discomfort with conventional sex-role definitions. Boys who have ambivalent fathers or who tend to identify with their mothers and have accepting, nonpunitive parents are likely to define masculinity in ways that are quite untraditional. They are likely to be less motivated for dominance, less physically aggressive and tough, less physically competitive, and more emotionally expressive and aesthetically inclined. Presumably, many girls raised in these

ways are likely to be less submissive, more assertive, and more self-assured and independent. Insofar as parents continue to expect conventional sex-role performance on the part of their children—and insofar as such performance is expected by the schools and by peers—confusion and feelings of inadequacy can be the result.

Speculation on the kinds of traits, dispositions, and feelings that might be expected to be patterned outcomes of the family structure and childrearing practices we have been discussing could go on indefinitely, but the main line of our argument should be clear: certain major changes in social structure and economy have had a direct impact on the structure of the family, especially in the "middle class." These changes have also had a profound impact on the values and practices of parents. The result is a mixed one: on the one hand, the "new" family appears eminently suitable as an instrument for creating the "right" kinds of people for technological society; on the other hand, inherent in the same family situation are tendencies to generate profound feelings of dislocation and discontent with established values, institutions and roles. Thus, the American family, especially the middle class, suburban American family with its confusions and ambivalences, reflects the general crisis of American culture. At the same time, it contributes to that crisis by generating in the next generation aspirations, expectations, and impulses that are not compatible with established norms and institutionalized patterns. It creates the psychic grounds for new identities in a society that provides no models, roles, or life styles around which such new identities can crystallize.

The middle class family is *necessary* in advanced industrial capitalism. Nevertheless, it *necessarily* creates many youths who have trouble accepting the society. When the key institutions of socialization inherently generate tendencies toward nonconformity, there surely is a cultural crisis. This seems to be the situation that has developed in the United States during the last three decades, as families have had to come to grips with a cultural framework that no longer fits social reality.

Meanwhile, a similar pattern of incoherence is played out in all the other institutions responsible for socialization and cultural indoctrination. In the schools, the media and the churches, such contradictory values as self-denial and self-expression, discipline and indulgence, and striving and being are preached, dramatized, fostered, and practiced all at once. On the one hand, television and magazines advocate hedonism, consumption, and living it up, while schools and churches continue, uneasily, to embody the Protestant Ethic. The economy demands discipline and self-control in order to *make* a living and spending and self-indulgence as a *way* of living. Political leaders tend to espouse the old virtues, while pop culture celebrities systematically flout them. Incentives to strive, compete, and become disciplined are systematically undermined by affluence, but all institutionalized means to be creative and productive (as in high-level professional work) continue to be linked with demands to be competitive, striving and self-denying. An incredible number and variety of means are provided for hedonistic pursuit and sensuality, yet all such experience is heavily laden with guilt, is often defined as illegal or immoral, is prohibited to minors, or is so highly commercialized as to lose its authentically expressive character.

The incoherence of the general culture thus interacts with the confusion of the individual family. It seems probable that virtually all American youth experience cultural incoherence and "anomie" as an integral feature of their growing up. The argument we are making, however, would lead us to predict that the youth who experience this situation most acutely are those for whom conventional values have been most weakened or irrelevant.

Bibliographical Notes

1. The "decline" of the "Protestant Ethic" has been discussed in many ways by people. Weber's classic definition of the culture of capitalism appears, of course, in his *The Protestant Ethic and the Spirit of Capitalism* (New York: Scribner's, 1958). Joseph Schumpeter prophesied the decline of entrepreneurial values in *Capitalism, Socialism and Democracy* (New York: Harper, 1942). An influential work describing changes in the American character was David Riesman's *The Lonely Crowd* (New York: Doubleday-Anchor, 1953). Seymour Martin Lipset and Leo Lowenthal, *Culture and Social Character* (Glencoe, Ill.: Free Press, 1961) contains important commentary on Riesman's work, especially an essay by Talcott Parsons and Winston White.

2. My discussion of the American middle class family is heavily indebted to the following: Kenneth Keniston, *The Uncommitted* (New York: Harcourt, Brace and World, 1962); Riesman, *The Lonely Crowd*; A. W. Green, "The Middle Class Male Child and Neurosis," *American Sociological Review*, 11 (1946): 31–41; Talcott Parsons and Robert F. Bales, *Family, Socialization and Interaction Process* (Glencoe, Ill.: Free Press, 1955); Daniel Miller and Guy Swanson, *The Changing American Parent* (New York: Wiley, 1958); Betty Friedan, *The Feminine Mystique* (New York: Norton, 1963); David C. McClelland, *The Achieving Society* (Princeton, N.J.: Van Nostrand, 1961); and Philip Slater, *The Pursuit of Loneliness* (Boston: Beacon, 1970). In addition, I have relied on impressions gathered from my research on families of activist and nonactivist students and from my own experience as a parent.

When you were a child, did you ever build a secret fort, set up a club room, or retreat to a neighbor's treehouse with your friends? Robert Paul Smith did.

In his delightful book of childhood reminiscences "Where Did You Go?" "Out" "What Did You Do?" "Nothing." *Smith describes the important role peers play in teaching many things adults never talk about. Although this excerpt from Smith's book is light-hearted and funny, it offers a touching reminder of our own childhoods and of how necessary peers are as agents of socialization.*

As you read Robert Paul Smith's account, keep in mind the special role of friends in the socialization process.

Kids, Clubs, and Special Places

ROBERT PAUL SMITH

The trouble with the treehouse was that, little though we were, we could not for long convince ourselves that it was a house. It wasn't, and we knew it after what may have been days or weeks or months—time is a very flexible thing with kids. I know today that I could not possibly have stared at my first cricket for more than minutes, and yet today in that length of time I could write a whole first act. The treehouse after a certain length of time was only a couple of boards and a piece of awning loosely attached to a tree.

But the hut; well, that was a place where we could live. I have been trying hard to remember just how we started to build it. Certainly there was no foundation. I seem to remember building the first wall in one piece, boards and tarpaper hammered onto a couple of two-by-fours, and the two-by-fours extending below, the whole structure raised and the extensions going into holes, and rocks being jammed around. I imagine we got the second wall up the same way, and ran roof beams across the top so that it stood up. The roof, if memory serves, and I am getting pretty dubious about that, was something that was lying around the lot. An abandoned cellar door, perhaps.

I am lying a little now—hell, I am lying a lot. I don't really remember building the hut. I remember repairing it, and expanding it, and putting a better door in it, a hasp and a lock. I remember packing rocks from the rock-

33

pile around the perimeter, to strengthen the hut—it was by then a fortress—against any attack. I remember tamping down the dirt floor, and finding a piece of linoleum and a gunny sack to brighten the corner which was mine.

I suppose, when I come right down to it, none of us could stand upright in the hut, and I have a kind of notion that when there were more than two of us in it, no one of us could move.

This is a hell of a note, on an August afternoon in my declining years to realize that really, that hut, that shining palace, that home away from home, that most secure of all habitations, was not much bigger than a big doghouse, and could have been pushed over by an angered Shetland pony. (Which any of us were going to get any moment, or a magic lantern, as soon as we had sold thirty-four million packages of blueing.)

No matter. It was ours. It belonged to us. And if you were not one of us, you could not come in. We had rules, oh Lord, how we had rules. We had passwords. We had oaths. We had conclaves.

It was a pitiful wreck of a tarpaper hut, and in it I learned the difference between boys and girls, I learned that all fathers did that, I learned to swear, to play with myself, to sleep in the afternoon, I learned that some people were Catholics and some people were Protestants and some people were Jews, that people came from different places. I learned that other kids wondered, too, who they would have been if their fathers had not married their mothers, wondered if you could dig a hole right to the center of the earth, wondered if you could kill yourself by holding your breath.(None of us could.)

I learned that with three people assembled, it was only for the briefest interludes that all three liked each other. Mitch and I were leagued against Simon. And then Simon and I against Mitch. And then—but you remember. I didn't know then just how to handle that situation. I still don't. It is my coldly comforting feeling that nobody still does, including nations, and that's what the trouble with the world is. That's what the trouble with the world was then—when Mitch and Simon were the two and I was the one.

What else did I learn in the hut? That if two nails will not hold a board in place, three will probably not either, but the third nail will split the board. I think kids still do that. I think objects made of wood by children, left to their own devices, if such there be, will assay ten percent wood, ninety percent nails.

I learned that I could lift things, rocks mostly, that my mother would have thought too heavy for me.

I learned to smoke, first, cornsilk wrapped in newspaper. I can taste it to this day. We never had the patience to let the cornsilk really dry. I don't imagine kids do that very much any more, mostly because they've never heard of it. What you do is take the cornsilk, spread it out in the sun until it is brown, like the little beard you find in the husk. Wrap it in a spill of newspaper—it'll look more like a very small ice-cream cone than anything else—

set fire to the end, being careful not to torch off your eyebrows. My recollection is that it bore no relationship to tobacco, but it wasn't bad at all. It had one big virtue. When caught, you had not committed a sin, as you did later when you smoked real cigarettes. Real cigarettes stunted your growth, we knew that. What that meant to us was that your growth stopped, right there. It was not impeded. You just plain stopped growing, as if you were frozen. You would be three feet tall when you were sixty years old. It was in no way contradictory that we never saw a grownup three feet tall. They had never smoked as children, and certainly the ones who had were not going to walk around in the daylight letting everybody know what *they* had done.

And to make this intellectual adjustment absolutely complete, we were able to hold this certain knowledge, this fact, intact and at the same time, as soon as possible, start smoking cigarettes.

Before that we smoked scribblage, like cigars. That was pretty bad.

Getting cigarettes was quite a problem. Most of the fathers on our block smoked cigars or pipes, and so far as we knew, no woman smoked. There were no vending machines. Getting cigarettes involved suborning some kid between childhood and adulthood, and the blackmail he thereafter commanded was too expensive. You could then buy cigarettes in little cardboard boxes of ten. You could theoretically, but the man in the store would not sell them to us, no matter how earnestly we told him a father, an uncle, some man on the corner, had asked, nay, commanded us to purchase them. Kids on the wrong side of the tracks could buy them, one at a time, from an open box that storekeepers used to keep on their counters. Three for a penny, was it, or a penny apiece?

It didn't matter. We were on the right side of the tracks. We could not buy, borrow, or beg them. So we stole them.

In this selection, Norman Denzin discusses the school as a social system. To Denzin, school is "a tangled web of interactions based on competing ideologies, rhetorics, intents and purposes." Schools are involved in much more than simply teaching the "three r's"—reading, 'riting, and 'rithmetic. Among other things they are asked to prepare children to be good citizens and to assume certain roles in life.

According to Denzin, schools reflect the society and the community in which they are located. In the United States, most schools emphasize middle-class values and treat children who are lacking them as deficient, even deviant, persons.

As you examine Denzin's selection, be sure you understand what he means when he says that schools are moral agencies and implies that they are critical transmitters of certain cultural norms and values.

Children and Their Caretakers

NORMAN K. DENZIN

Schools are held together by intersecting moral, political and social orders. What occurs inside their walls must be viewed as a product of what the participants in this arena bring to it, be they children, parents, instructors, administrators, psychologists, social workers, counselors or politicians. A tangled web of interactions—based on competing ideologies, rhetorics, intents and purposes—characterizes everyday life in the school. Cliques, factions, pressure groups and circles of enemies daily compete for power and fate in these social worlds.

Children and their caretakers are not passive organisms. Their conduct reflects more than responses to the pressures of social systems, roles, value structures or political ideologies. Nor is their behavior the sole product of internal needs, drives, impulses or wishes. The human actively constructs lines of conduct in the face of these forces and as such stands over and against the external world. The human is self-conscious. Such variables as role prescription, value configurations or hierarchies of needs have relevance only when they are acted on by the human. Observers of human behavior are obliged to enter the subject's world and grasp the shifting definitions that give rise to orderly social behavior. Failing to do so justifies the fallacy of objectivism: the imputing of motive from observer to subject. Too many architects of schools and education programs have stood outside the interactional worlds of children and adults and attempted to legislate their own interpretation of right and proper conduct.

Such objectivistic stances have given schools a basic characteristic that constitutes a major theme of this essay. Schools are presently organized so as to effectively remove fate control from those persons whose fate is at issue, that is, students. This loss of fate control, coupled with a conception of the child which is based on the "underestimation fallacy" gives rise to an ideology that judges the child as incompetent and places in the hands of the adult primary responsibility for child-caretaking.

SCHOOLS AS MORAL AGENCIES

Schools are best seen, not as educational settings, but as places where fate, morality and personal careers are created and shaped. Schools are moral institutions. They have assumed the responsibility of shaping children, of whatever race or income level, into right and proper participants in American society, pursuing with equal vigor the abstract goals of that society.

At one level schools function, as Willard Waller argued in 1937, to Americanize the young. At the everyday level, however, abstract goals disappear, whether they be beliefs in democracy and equal opportunity or myths concerning the value of education for upward mobility. In their place appears a massive normative order that judges the child's development along such dimensions as poise, character, integrity, politeness, deference, demeanor, emotional control, respect for authority and serious commitment to classroom protocol. Good students are those who reaffirm through their daily actions the moral order of home, school and community.

To the extent that schools assume moral responsibility for producing social beings, they can be seen as agencies of fate or career control. In a variety of ways schools remind students who they are and where they stand in the school's hierarchy. The school institutionalizes ritual turning points to fill this function: graduations, promotions, tests, meetings with parents, open-houses, rallies and sessions with counselors. These significant encounters serve to keep students in place. Schools function to sort and filter social selves and to set these selves on the proper moral track, which may include recycling to a lower grade, busing to an integrated school or informing a student that he has no chance to pursue a college preparatory program. In many respects schools give students their major sense of moral worth—they shape vocabularies, images of self, reward certain actions and not others, set the stage for students to be thrown together as friends or enemies.

Any institution that assumes control over the fate of others might be expected to be accountable for its actions toward those who are shaped and manipulated. Within the cultures of fate-controlling institutions, however, there appears a vocabulary, a rhetoric, a set of workable excuses and a division of labor to remove and reassign responsibility. For example, we might expect that the division of labor typically parallels the moral hierarchy of the people within the institution, that is, the people assigned the greatest moral worth are ultimately most blameworthy, or most accountable. Usually, however, moral responsibility is reversed. When a teacher in a Head Start program fails to raise the verbal skills of her class to the appropriate level she and the project director might blame each other. But it is more likely that the children, the families of the children or the culture from which the children come will be held responsible. Such is the typical rhetorical device employed in compensatory education programs where the low performances of black children on white middle-class tests is explained by assigning blame to black family culture and family arrangements. Research on the alleged genetic deficiencies of black and brown children is another example of this strategy. Here the scientist acts as a moral entrepreneur, presenting his findings under the guise of objectivity.

WHAT IS A CHILD?

Any analysis of the education and socialization process must begin with the basic question, "what is a child?" My focus is on the contemporary meanings assigned children, especially as these meanings are revealed in preschool and compensatory education programs.

In addressing this question it must be recognized that social objects (such as children) carry no intrinsic meaning. Rather, meaning is conferred by processes of social interaction—by people.

Such is the case with children. Each generation, each social group, every family and each individual develops different interpretations of what a child is. Children find themselves defined in shifting, often contradictory ways. But as a sense of self is acquired, the child learns to transport from situation to situation a relatively stable set of definitions concerning his personal and social identity. Indeed most of the struggles he will encounter in the educational arena fundamentally derive from conflicting definitions of selfhood and childhood.

CHILD PRODUCTION AS STATUS PASSAGE

The movement of an infant to the status of child is a socially constructed event that for most middle-class Americans is seen as desirable, inevitable, irreversible, permanent, long term in effect and accomplished in the presence of "experts" and significant others such as teachers, parents, peers and siblings.

For the white middle income American the child is seen as an extension of the adult's self, usually the family's collective self. Parents are continually reminded that the way their child turns out is a direct reflection of their competence as socializing agents. These reminders have been made for some time; consider this exhortation of 1849:

> Yes, mothers, in a certain sense, the destiny of a redeemed world is put into your hands; it is for you to say whether your children shall be respectable and happy here, and prepared for a glorious immortality, or whether they shall dishonor you, and perhaps bring you grey hairs in sorrow to the grave, and sink down themselves at last to eternal despair!

If the child's conduct reflects upon the parent's moral worth, new parents are told by Benjamin Spock that this job of producing a child is hard work, a serious enterprise. He remarks in *Baby and Child Care*:

> There is an enormous amount of hard work in child care—preparing the proper diet, washing diapers and clothes, cleaning up messes that an infant makes with his food . . . stopping fights and drying tears, listening to stories that are hard to understand, joining in games and reading stories that aren't very exciting to an adult, trudging around zoos and museums and carnivals . . . being slowed down in housework. . . . Children keep parents from parties, trips, theaters, meetings, games, friends. . . . Of course, parents don't have children because they want to be martyrs, or at least they shouldn't. They have them because they love children and want some of their very own. . . . Taking care of their children, seeing them grow and develop into fine people, gives most parents— despite the hard work—their greatest satisfaction in life. This is creation. This is our visible immortality. Pride in other worldly accomplishments is usually weak in comparison.

Spock's account of the parent-child relationship reveals several interrelated definitions that together serve to set off the contemporary view of children. The child is a possession of the adult, an extension of self, an incompetent object that must be cared for at great cost and is a necessary obligation one must incur if he or she desires visible immortality.

These several definitions of childhood are obviously at work in current educational programs. More importantly, they are grounded in a theory of development and learning that reinforces the view that children are incompetent selves. Like Spock's theory of growth, which is not unlike the earlier proposals of Gesell, contemporary psychological theories see the child in organic terms. The child grows like a stalk of corn. The strength of the stalk is a function of its environment. If that environment is healthy, if the plant is properly cared for, a suitable product will be produced. This is a "container" theory of development: "What you put in determines what comes out." At the same time, however, conventional wisdom holds that the child is an unreliable product. It cannot be trusted with its own moral development. Nor can parents. This business of producing a child is serious and it must be placed in the hands of experts who are skilled in child production. Mortal mothers and fathers lack these skills. Pressures are quickly set in force to move the child out of the family into a more "professional" setting—the preschool, the Head Start program.

CARETAKING FOR THE MIDDLE CLASSES

Preschools, whether based on "free school" principles, the Montessori theory, or modern findings in child development, display one basic feature. They are moral caretaking agencies that undertake the fine task of shaping social beings.

Recently, after the enormous publicity attendant to the Head Start program for the poor, middle income Americans have been aroused to the importance of preschool education for their children. "Discovery Centers" are appearing in various sections of the country and several competing national franchises have been established. Given names such as We Sit Better, Mary Moppit, Pied Piper Schools, Les Petites Academies, Kinder Care Nursery and American Child Centers, these schools remind parents (as did the Universal Education Corporation in the *New York Times*) that:

> Evaluating children in the 43 basic skills is part of what the Discovery Center can do for your child. The 43 skills embrace all the hundreds of things your child has to learn before he reaches school age. Fortunately preschoolers have a special genius for learning. But it disappears at the age of seven. During this short-lived period of genius, the Discovery Center helps your child develop his skills to the Advanced Level.

Caretaking for the middle classes is a moral test. The parent's self is judged by the quality of the product. If the product is faulty, the producer is judged inadequaté, also faulty. This feature of the socialization process best explains why middle-class parents are so concerned about the moral, spiritual, psychological and social development of their children. It also explains (if only partially) why schools have assumed so much fate control over children; educators are the socially defined experts on children.

The children of lower income families are often assumed to be deprived, depressed and emotionally handicapped. To offset these effects, current theory holds that the child must be "educated and treated" before entrance into kindergarten. If middle income groups have the luxury of withholding preschool from their children, low income, third-world parents are quickly learning they have no such right. Whether they like it or not, their children are going to be educated. When formal education begins, the culturally deprived child will be ready to compete with his white peers.

WHAT IS CULTURAL DEPRIVATION?

The term "culturally deprived" is still the catchall phrase which at once explains and describes the inability (failure, refusal) of the child in question to display appropriate conduct on I.Q. tests, street corners, playgrounds and classrooms. There are a number of problems with this formulation. The first is conceptual and involves the meanings one gives to the terms *culture* and *deprived*. Contemporary politicians and educators have ignored the controversy surrounding what the word *culture* means and have apparently assumed that everyone knows what a culture is. Be that as it may, the critical empirical indicator seems to be contained in the term *deprived*. People who are deprived, that is, people who fail to act like white, middle income groups, belong to a culture characterized by such features as divorce, deviance, premarital pregnancies, extended families, drug addiction and alcoholism. Such persons are easily identified: they tend to live in ghettos or public housing units, and they tend to occupy the lower rungs of the occupation ladder. They are there because they are deprived. Their culture keeps them deprived. It is difficult to tell whether these theorists feel that deprivation precedes or follows being in a deprived culture. The causal links are neither logically or empirically analyzed.

The second problem with this formulation is moral and ideological. The children and adults who are labeled culturally deprived are those people in American society who embarrass and cause trouble for middle income moralists, scientists, teachers, politicians and social workers. They fail to display proper social behavior. The fact that people in low income groups are under continual surveillance by police and social workers seems to go unnoticed. The result is that members of the middle class keep their indelicacies behind closed doors, inside the private worlds of home, office, club and neighborhood. Low income people lack such privileges. Their misconduct is everybody's business.

The notion of cultural deprivation is class based. Its recurrent invocation, and its contemporary institutionalization in compensatory education programs reveals an inability or refusal to look seriously at the problems of the middle and upper classes, and it directs attention away from schools which are at the heart of the problem.

Herbert Gans has noted another flaw in these programs. This is the failure of social scientists to take seriously the fact that many lower income people simply do not share the same aspirations as the middle class. Despite this fact antipoverty programs and experiments in compensatory education proceed as if such were the case.

Schools are morally bounded units of social organization. Within and from them students, parents, teachers and administrators derive their fundamental sense of self. Any career through a school is necessarily moral; one's self-image is continually being evaluated, shaped and molded. These careers are interactionally interdependent. What a teacher does affects what a child does and vice versa. To the extent that schools have become the dominant socializing institution in Western society it can be argued that experiences in them furnish everyday interactants with their basic vocabularies for evaluating self and others. Persons can mask, hide or fabricate their educational biography, but at some point they will be obliged to paint a picture of how well educated they are. They will also be obliged to explain why they are not better educated (or why they are too well educated), and why their present circumstances do not better reflect their capabilities (e.g., unemployed space engineers). One's educational experiences furnish the rhetorical devices necessary to get off the hook and supply the basic clues that will shore up a sad or happy tale.

THE SCHOOL'S FUNCTIONS

I have already noted two broad functions served by the schools: they Americanize students, and they sort, filter and accredit social selves. To these basic functions must be added the following. Ostensibly, instruction or teaching should take precedence over political socialization. And indeed teaching becomes the dominant activity through which the school is presented to the child. But if schools function to instruct, they also function to entertain and divert students into "worthwhile" ends. Trips to zoos, beaches, operas, neighboring towns, ice cream parlors and athletic fields reveal an attempt on the part of the school to teach the child what range of entertaining activities he or she can engage in. Moreover, these trips place the school directly in the public's eye and at least on these excursions teachers are truly held accountable for their class's conduct.

Caretaking and babysitting constitute another basic function of schools. This babysitting function is quite evident in church oriented summer programs where preschools and day-care centers are explicitly oriented so as to sell themselves as competent babysitters. Such schools compete for scarce resources (parents who can afford their services), and the federal government has elaborated this service through grants-in-aid to low income children.

Formal instruction in the classroom is filtered through a series of interconnected acts that involve teacher and student presenting different social selves to one another. Instruction cannot be separated from social interaction, and teachers spend a large amount of time teaching students how to be proper social participants. Coaching in the rules and rituals of polite etiquette thus constitutes another basic function of the school. Students must be taught how to take turns, how to drink out of cups and clean up messes, how to say please and thank you, how to take leave of a teacher's presence, how to handle mood, how to dress for appropriate occasions, how to be rude, polite, attentive, evasive, docile, aggressive, deceitful; in short, they must learn to act like adults. Teachers share this responsibility with parents, often having to take over where parents fail or abdicate, though, again, parents are held accountable for not producing polite children. Because a child's progress through the school's social structure is contingent on how his or her self is formally defined, parents stand to lose much if their children do not conform to the school's version of good conduct. When teachers and parents both fail, an explanation will be sought to relieve each party of responsibility. The child may be diagnosed as hyperactive, or his culture may have been so repressive in its effects that nothing better can be accomplished. Career tracks for these students often lead to the trade school or the reformatory.

Another function of the schools is socialization into age-sex roles. Girls must be taught how to be girls and boys must learn what a boy is. In preschool and daycare centers this is often difficult to accomplish because bathrooms are not sex segregated. But while they are open territories, many preschools make an effort to hire at least one male instructor who can serve as male caretaker and entertainer of boys. He handles their toilet problems among other things. Preschool instructors can often be observed to reinterpret stories to fit their conception of the male or female role, usually attempting to place the female on an equal footing with the male. In these ways the sexual component of self-identity is transmitted and presented to the young child. Problem children become those who switch sex roles or accentuate to an unacceptable degree maleness or femaleness.

Age-grading is accomplished through organization of classes on a biological age basis. Three-year-olds quickly learn that they cannot do the same things as four-year-olds do, and so on. High schools are deliberately organized so as to convey to freshmen and sophomore how important it is to be a junior or senior. Homecoming queens, student body presidents and athletic leaders come from the two top classes. The message is direct: work hard, be a good student and you too can be a leader and enjoy the fruits of age.

It has been suggested by many that most schools centrally function to socialize children into racial roles, stressing skin color as the dominant variable in social relationships. Depictions of American history and favored symbolic leaders stress the three variables of age, sex and race. The favored role model becomes the 20 to 25-year-old, white, university-educated male who has had an outstanding career in athletics. Implicitly and explicitly students are taught that Western culture is a male oriented, white-based enterprise.

Shifting from the school as a collectivity to the classroom, we find that teachers attempt to construct their own versions of appropriate conduct. Students are likely to find great discrepancies between a school's formal codes of conduct and the specific rules they encounter in each of their courses and classes. They will find some teachers who are openly critical of the school's formal policies, while at the same time they are forced to interact with teachers who take harsh lines toward misconduct. They will encounter some teachers who enforce dress standards and some who do not. Some teachers use first names, others do not, and so on. The variations are endless.

The importance of these variations for the student's career and self-conception should be clear. It is difficult managing self in a social world that continually changes its demands, rewards and rules of conduct. But students are obliged to do just that. Consequently the self–conception of the student emerges as a complex and variegated object. He or she is tied into competing and complementary worlds of influence and experience. Depending on where students stand with respect to the school's dominant moral order, they will find their self-conception complemented or derogated and sometimes both. But for the most part schools are organized so as to complement the self-conception of the child most like the teacher and to derogate those most unlike him or her. And, needless to say, the moral career of the nonwhite, low income student is quite different from the career of his white peer.

I have spelled out the dimensions around which a student comes to evaluate himself in school. Classrooms, however, are the most vivid stage on which students confront the school, and it is here that the teacher at some level must emerge as a negative or positive force on his career. While the underlife of schools reflects attempts to "beat" or "make–out" in the school, in large degree the student learns to submit to the system. The ultimate fact of life is that unless he gets through school with some diploma he is doomed to failure. Not only is he doomed to failure, but he is socially defined as a failure. His career opportunities and self-conceptions are immediately tied to his success in school.

Schools, then, inevitably turn some amount of their attention to the problem of socializing students for failure. Indeed, the school's success as a socializing agent in part depends on its ability to teach students to accept failure. A complex rhetoric and set of beliefs must be instilled in the students. Children must come to see themselves as the school defines them. They are taught that certain classes of selves do better than other classes, but the classes referred to are not sociological but moral. A variation of the Protestant ethic is communicated and the fiction of equality in education and politics is stressed. Students must grasp the fact that all that separates them from a classmate who goes to Harvard (when they are admitted to a junior college) are grades and hard work, not class, race, money or prestige. Schools, then, function as complex, cooling out agencies.

Two problems are created. School officials must communicate their judgments, usually cast as diagnoses, prescriptions, treatments and prognoses, to students and parents. And second, they must establish social arrangements that maximize the likelihood that their judgments will be accepted, that is, submission to fate control is maximized, and scenes between parents and students are minimized.

FATE CONTROL

The most obvious cooling out agents in schools are teachers and counselors. It is they who administer and evaluate tests. It is they who see the student most frequently. In concert these two classes of functionaries fulfill the schools' functions of sorting out and cooling out children. Their basic assignment is to take imperfect selves and fit those selves to the best possible moral career. They are, then, moral entrepreneurs. They design career programs and define the basic contours around which a student's self will be shaped.

A basic strategy of the moral entrepreneur in schools is co-optation. He attempts to win a child's peers and parents over to his side. If this can be accomplished, the job is relatively easy. For now everyone significant in the child's world agrees that he is a failure or a partial success. They agree that a trade school or a junior college is the best career track to be followed.

Another strategy is to select exemplary students who epitomize the various tracks open to a student. Former graduates may be brought back and asked to reflect on their careers. In selecting types of students to follow these various paths, schools conduct talent searches and develop operating perspectives that classify good and bad prospects. Like the academic theorist of social stratification, these officials work with an implicit image of qualified beings. They know that students from middle and upper income groups perform better than those from lesser backgrounds. They know that students who have college educated parents do better than those whose parents dropped out of high school. They learn to mistrust nonwhites. In these respects schools differ only slightly from medical practitioners, especially the psychiatrist who has learned that his trade works best on persons like him in background. Teachers too per-perpetuate the system of stratification found in the outside world.

STUDENT TYPES

Schools can cool out the failures in their midst. They have more difficulty with another type of student, the troublemakers or militants. Troublemakers, as would be predicted, typically come from low income white and nonwhite ethnic groups. Forced to process these children, school systems developed their own system of stratification, making low status schools teach trouble-makers. This has become the fate of the trade school or the continuation high school. Here those who have high truancy or arrest records, are pregnant, hy-peractive or on probation are thrown together. And here they are presented with white middle-class curriculums.

Militants and troublemakers refuse to accept the school's operating per-spective. To the extent that they can band together and form a common world view, they challenge the school's legitimacy as a socializing agent. They make trouble. They represent, from the middle-class point of view, failures of the socializing system.

In response to this, schools tend to adopt a strategy of denial. Denial can take several forms, each revealing a separate attempt to avoid accountability. Denial of responsibility takes the form of a claim that " we recognize your problem, but the solution is outside our province." The need for alternative educational arrangements is recognized, but denied because of reasons be-yond control. Private and public guilt is neutralized by denying responsibility and placing blame on some external force or variable such as the state of the economy.

When some resource is denied to a social group, explanations will be devel-oped to justify that denial. My earlier discussion has suggested that one ex-planation places blame on the shoulders of the denied victim. Thus the theory of cultural deprivation removes blame, by blaming the victim. Scientific theory thus operates as one paradigm of responsibility.

Another form of strategy is to deny the challengers' essential moral worth. Here the victim is shown to be socially unworthy and thereby not de-serving of special attention. This has been the classic argument for segregation in the South, but it works only so long as the victim can be kept in place, which has lately in that part of the world involved insuring that the challenger or victim is not presented with alternative self models. Shipping black instruc-tors out of the South into northern urban ghettos represents an attempt to re-move alternative self models for the southern black child.

THE VICTIM'S RESPONSE

Insofar as they can organize themselves socially, victims and challengers may assume one of three interrelated stances. They may condemn the condemner, make appeals to higher authorities or deny the perspective that has brought injury. In so doing they will seek and develop alternative scientific doctrines that support their stance.

Condemning the condemner reverses the condemner's denial of moral worth. Here the school or political and economic system is judged hypocritical, corrupt, stupid, brutal and racist. These evaluations attempt to reveal the underlying moral vulnerability of the institution in question. The victim and his cohort reverse the victimizer's vocabulary and hold him accountable for the failures they were originally charged with (for example, poor grades or attendance records).

These condemnations reveal a basic commitment to the present system. They are claims for a just place. They are a petition to higher authority. Democratic ideology is proclaimed as a worthy pursuit. The school is charged with failure to offer proper and acceptable means to reach those goals. Here the victims' perspective corresponds with dominant cultural ideologies.

Denial of perspective is another stance. Best seen in the Nation of Islam schools, the victim now states that he wants nothing the larger system can offer. He leaves the system and constructs his own educational arrangements. He develops his own standards of evaluation. He paints his own version of right and proper conduct. (Private educational academies in the South, partly a function of the Nixon administration, serve a similar function for whites.)

Denials of perspective thus lead to the substitution of a new point of view. If successfully executed, as in the case of the Nation of Islam, the victims build their own walls of protection and shut off the outside world. In such a setting, one's self-conception is neither daily denied nor derided. It is affirmed and defined in positive terms.

Lower self-conceptions would be predicted in those settings where the black or brown child is taught to normalize his deficiencies and to compensate for them. This is the setting offered by Head Start and Follow-Through. The victim accepts the victimizers' judgments and attempts to compensate for socially defined flaws.

Americans of all income levels and from all racial groups, including white, are troubled over the current educational system. They are demanding a greater say in the social organization of schools; they are challenging the tenure system now given teachers; they feel that schools should accept greater responsibilities for the failures of the system. (A Gallup Poll in late 1970 showed that 67 percent of those surveyed favor holding teachers and administrators more accountable for the progress of students.) Accordingly it is necessary to consider a series of proposals that would bring education more in line with cultural and social expectations.

From this perspective education must be grounded in principles that recognize the role of the self in everyday conduct. The child possesses multiple selves, each grounded in special situations and special circles of significant others. Possessing a self, the child is an active organism, not a passive object into which learning can be poured.

Conventional theories of learning define the child as a passive organism. An alternative view of the social act of learning must be developed. George Herbert Mead's analysis provides a good beginning. Creativity or learning occurred, Mead argued, when the individual was forced to act in a situation where conventional lines of conduct were no longer relevant. Following Dewey's discussion of the blocked act, Mead contended that schools and curricula must be organized in ways that challenge the child's view of the world. Standard curricula are based on an opposite view of the human. Redundancy, constant rewards and punishments, piecemeal presentation of materials, and defining the child as incompetent or unable to provoke his own acts best characterized these programs. Course work is planned carefully in advance and study programs are assiduously followed. The teacher, not the child, is defined as the ultimate educational resource. Parents and local community groups, because they tend to challenge the school's operating perspective, are treated only ritualistically at P.T.A. meetings, open houses, school plays, athletic contests. Their point of view, like the child's, is seldom taken seriously. They are too incompetent. Taking them seriously would force a shift in existing power arrangements in the school.

Mead's perspective proposes just the opposite view of parents, children and education. Education, he argued, is an unfolding, social process wherein the child comes to see himself in increasingly more complex ways. Education leads to self-understanding and to the acquistion of the basic skills. This principle suggests that schools must be socially relevant. They must incorporate the social world of child and community into curriculum arrangements. Cultural diversity must be stressed. Alternative symbolic leaders must be presented, and these must come from realistic worlds of experience. (Setting an astronaut as a preferred "self model" for seven-year-old males as a present text book does, can hardly be defined as realistic). Problematic situations from the child's everyday world must be brought into the classroom. Mead, for example, proposed as early as 1908 that schools teach sex education to children.

Children and parents, then, must be seen as resources around which education is developed and presented. They must be taken seriously. This presupposes a close working relationship between home and school. Parents must take responsibility for their children's education. They can no longer afford to shift accountability to the schools. This simple principle suggests that ethnic studies programs should have been central features of schools at least 50 years ago. Schools exist to serve their surrounding communities, not bend those communities to their perspective.

REDEFINING SCHOOLS

If this reciprocal service function is stressed, an important implication follows. Schools should educate children in ways that permit them to be contributing members in their chosen worlds. Such basics as reading, writing and counting will never be avoided. But their instruction can be made relevant within the worlds the child most directly experiences. This suggests, initially at least, that black and brown children be taught to respect their separate cultural heritages. Second, it suggests that they will probably learn best with materials drawn from those cultures. Third, it suggests that they must be presented with self models who know, respect and come from those cultures—black teachers must not be removed from southern schools.

To the extent that schools and teachers serve as referent points for the child's self-conception it can be argued that it is not the minority student who must change. But instead it is the white middle-class child who must be exposed to alternative cultural perspectives. Minority teachers must be made integral components of all phases of the educational act.

Mead's perspective suggests, as I have attempted to elaborate, that the classroom is an interactive world. Research by Roger G. Barker and Paul V. Gump on big schools and little schools supports this position and their findings suggest an additional set of proposals. Briefly, they learned that as class and school size increases student satisfaction decreases. Teaching becomes more mechanized, students become more irrelevant and activities not related to learning attain greater importance, social clubs, for example. In short, in big schools students are redundant.

Classroom size and school size must be evaluated from this perspective. If schools exist to serve children and their parents, then large schools are dysfunctional. They are knowledge factories, not places of learning or self-development. Culturally heterogeneous, small-sized classes must be experimented with. Students must have opportunities to know their teachers in personal, not institutional terms. Students must be taught to take one another seriously, not competitively. Small, ecologically intimate surroundings have a greater likelihood of promoting these arrangements than do large-scale, bureaucratically organized classes.

At present, standardized, state and nationally certified tests are given students to assess their psychological, emotional, intellectual and social development. Two problems restrict the effectivenesss of these methods, however.

With few exceptions they have been standardized on white middle-class populations. Second, they are the only measurement techniques routinely employed.

A number of proposals follow from these problems. First, open-ended tests which permit the child to express his or her perspective must be developed. These tests, such as the "Who Am I?" question, would be given to students to determine the major contours of their self-conceptions. With this information in hand teachers would be in a better position to tailor teaching programs to a child's specific needs, definitions, intentions and goals.

Second, tests such as "Who is Important to You?" could be given students on a regular basis to determine who their significant others are. It is near axiomatic that derogation of the people most important to one leads to alienation from the setting and spokesman doing the derogation. Teachers must learn to respect and present in respectful terms those persons most important to the child.

A third methodological proposal directs observers to link a student's utterances, wishes and self-images to his or her day-to-day conduct. Written test scores often fail to reflect what persons really take into account and value. In many social settings verbal ability, athletic skill, hustling aptitudes, money and even physical attractiveness serve as significant status locators. I.Q. tests often do not. Furthermore, a person's score on a test may not accurately reflect his ability to handle problematic situations, which is surely a goal of education. Observations of conduct (behavior) in concrete settings can provide the needed leads in this direction.

METHODOLOGICAL IMPLICATIONS

A critic of these proposals might remark that such measures are not standardized, that their validity is questionable, that they cannot be administered nationally, and that they have questionable degrees of reliability. In response I would cite the ability of Roger Barker and colleagues to execute such observations over time with high reliability (.80–.98 for many measures). But more to the point I would argue that conventional tests are simply not working and it is time to experiment with alternative techniques, perspectives and theories.

This defense suggests that schools of education must begin to consider teaching their students the methodologies of participant observation, unobtrusive analysis and life history construction. These softer methods have been the traditional province of sociologists and anthropologists. Members of these disciplines must consider offering cross-disciplinary courses in methodology, especially aimed for everyday practitioners in school settings. Graduate requirements for teaching credentials must also be reexamined and greater efforts must be made to recruit and train minority students in these different approaches.

These proposals reflect a basic commitment. Schools should be organized so as to maximize a child's self-development and they should permit maximum child-parent participation. It is evident that my discussion has not been limited to an analysis of compensatory education programs. This has been deliberate. It is my conviction that education, wherever it occurs, involves interactions between social selves. Taking the self as a point of departure I have attempted to show that what happens to a preschool child is not unlike the moral experiences of a black or brown 17-year-old senior. But most importantly, both should find themselves in schools that take them seriously and treat them with respect. Schools exist to serve children and the public. This charge must be also taken seriously.

Suggested Readings

Centuries of Childhood by Phillipe Aries (New York: Random House, 1962).

Big School and Small School by Roger Barker and Paul V. Gump (Stanford, California: Stanford University Press, 1964).

The Sociology of Teaching by Willard Waller (New York: John Wiley, 1967, originally published in 1937).

*Our "own" attitudes about ourselves and others are
learned—often unconsciously—from people around us.
We then internalize these attitudes by making them integral parts of our personalities and personal beliefs.
Such is the case with sexual stereotypes.*

*A number of social scientists have pointed out that
although sexual stereotyping is common in a sexist
society (a society which constantly relegates women to
second-class citizenship), it need not be that way. In
this essay Florence Howe indicates the depth of sexism
and suggests ways that parents and teachers might alter
this imbalance.*

*As you read Howe's essay, pay particular attention to
how teachers and authors of textbooks have established
a labeling process that assigns behavioral expectations
to both men and women.*

Sexual Stereotypes Start Early

FLORENCE HOWE

"I remember quite clearly a day in sixth grade," a college freshman told me a
year ago, "when the class was discussing an article from a weekly supplementary reader. The story was about a chef, and someone in the class ventured the
opinion that cooking was women's work, that a man was a 'sissy' to work in
the kitchen. The teacher's response surprised us all. She informed us calmly
that men make the best cooks, just as they make the best dress designers,
singers, and laundry workers. 'Yes', she said, 'anything a woman can do a
man can do better.' There were no male students present; my teacher was a
woman."

Children learn about sex roles very early in their lives, probably before they
are eighteen months old, certainly long before they enter school. They learn
these roles through relatively simple patterns that most of us take for granted.
We throw boy-babies up in the air and roughhouse with them. We coo over
girl-babies and handle them delicately. We choose sex-related colors and toys
for our children from their earliest days. We encourage the energy and physical activity of our sons, just as we expect girls to be quieter and more docile.

We love both our sons and daughters with equal fervor, we protest, and yet we are disappointed when there is no male child to carry on the family name.

A hundred fifty years ago, Elizabeth Cady Stanton learned to master a horse and the Greek language in an attempt to comfort her father who had lost his only son and heir. No matter what evidence of brilliance Cady Stanton displayed, her father could only shake his head and murmur, "If only you were a boy, Elizabeth," much to the bafflement of the girl who had discerned that riding horses and studying Greek were the activities that had distinguished her dead brother from her living sisters. Only thirty years ago, at family gatherings, I remember hearing whispers directed at my brother and me: "Isn't it a pity that he has all the looks while she has all the brains." Others could contribute similar anecdotes today.

The truth of it is that while we in the West have professed to believe in "liberty, equality, and fraternity," we have also taken quite literally the term "fraternity." We have continued to maintain, relatively undisturbed, all the ancient edicts about the superiority of males, the inferiority of females. Assumptions current today about woman's alleged "nature" are disguised psychological versions of physiological premises in the Old Testament, in the doctrines of the early church fathers, and in the thinking of male philosophers, writers, educators—including some who founded women's colleges or opened men's colleges to women. In short, what we today call the "women's liberation movement" is only the most recent aspect of the struggle that began with Mary Wollstonecraft's *Vindication of the Rights of Women* in 1795—a piece of theory that drew for courage and example on the fathers of the French and American revolutions. It is, of course, only one hundred years since higher education was really opened up to women in this country, and many people know how dismal is the record of progress for professional women, especially during the past fifty years.

How much blame should be placed on public education? A substantial portion, although it is true that schools reflect the society they serve. Indeed, schools function to reinforce the sexual stereotypes that children have been taught by their parents, friends, and the mass culture we live in. It is also perfectly understandable that sexual stereotypes demeaning to women are also perpetuated by women—mothers in the first place, and teachers in the second—as well as by men—fathers, the few male teachers in elementary schools, high school teachers, and many male administrators and educators at the top of the school's hierarchy.

Sexual stereotypes are not to be identified with sexual or innate differences, for we know nothing about these matters. John Stuart Mill was the first man (since Plato) to affirm that we could know nothing about innate sexual differences, since we have never known of a society in which either men or women lived wholly separately. Therefore, he reasoned, we can't "know" what the pure "nature" of either sex might be: What we see as female behavior, he maintained, is the result of what he called the education of "willing slaves." There is still no "hard" scientific evidence of innate sexual differences, though there are new experiments in progress on male hormones of mice and monkeys. Other hormonal experiments, especially those using adrenaline, have indicated that, for human beings at least, social factors and pressures are more important than physiological ones.

Sexual stereotypes are assumed differences, social conventions or norms, learned behavior, attitudes, and expectations. Most stereotypes are well-known to all of us, for they are simple—not to say simple-minded. Men are smart, women are dumb but beautiful, etc. A recent annotated catalogue of children's books (distributed by the National Council of Teachers of English to thousands of teachers and used for ordering books with federal funds) lists titles under the headings "Especially for Girls" and "Especially for Boys." Verbs and adjectives are remarkably predictable through the listings. Boys "decipher and discover," "earn and train," or "foil" someone; girls "struggle," "overcome difficulties," "feel lost," "help solve," or "help [someone] out." One boy's story has "strange power," another moves "from truancy to triumph." A girl, on the other hand, "learns to face the real world" or makes a "difficult adjustment." Late or early, in catalogues or on shelves, the boys of children's books are active and capable, the girls passive and in trouble. All studies of children's literature—and there have been many besides my own—support this conclusion.

Ask yourself whether you would be surprised to find the following social contexts in a fifth-grade arithmetic textbook:

1. girls playing marbles; boys sewing;
2. girls earning money, building things, and going places; boys buying ribbons for a sewing project;
3. girls working at physicial activities; boys babysitting and, you guessed it, sewing.

Of course you would be surprised—so would I. What I have done here is to reverse the sexes as found in a fifth-grade arithmetic text. I was not surprised, since several years ago an intrepid freshman offered to report on third-grade arithmetic texts for me and found similar types of sexual roles prescribed: Boys were generally making things or earning money; girls were cooking or spending money on such things as sewing equipment.

The verification of sexual stereotypes is a special area of interest to psychologists and sociologists. An important series of studies was done in 1968 by Inge K. Broverman and others at Worcester State Hospital in Massachusetts. These scientists established a "sex-stereotype questionnaire" consisting of "122 bipolar items"—characteristics socially known or socially tested as male or female. Studies by these scientists and others established what common sense will verify: that those traits "stereotypically masculine . . .are more often perceived as socially desirable" than those known to be feminine. Here are some "male-valued items" as listed on the questionnaire:

very aggressive
very independent
not at all emotional
very logical
very direct
very adventurous
very self-confident
very ambitious

These and other characteristics describe the stereotypic male. To describe the female, you need only reverse those traits and add "female-valued" ones, some of which follow:

very talkative
very tactful
very gentle
very aware of feelings of others
very religious
very quiet
very strong need for security

and the one I am particularly fond of citing to men who control my field—"enjoys art and literature very much."

The Worcester scientists used their 122 items to test the assumptions of clinical psychologists about mental health. Three matched groups of male and female clinical psychologists were given three identical lists of the 122 items unlabeled and printed in random order. Each group was given a different set of instructions: One was told to choose those traits that characterize the healthy adult male; another to choose those of the healthy adult female; the third, to choose those of the healthy adult—a person. The result: The clinically healthy male and the clinically healthy adult were identical—and totally divergent from the clinically healthy female. The authors of the study concluded that "a double standard of health exists for men and women." That is, the general standard of health applies only to men. Women are perceived as "less healthy" by those standards called "adult." At the same time, however, if a woman deviates from the sexual stereotypes prescribed for her—if she grows more "active" or "aggressive," for example—she doesn't grow healthier; she may, in fact, if her psychiatrist is a Freudian, be perceived as "sicker." Either way, therefore, women lose or fail, and so it is not surprising to find psychologist Phyllis Chesler reporting that proportionately many more women than men are declared "sick" by psychologists and psychiatrists.

The idea of a "double standard" for men and women is a familiar one and helps to clarify how severely sexual stereotypes constrict the personal and social development of women. Studies by child psychologists reveal that while boys of all ages clearly identify with male figures and activities, girls are less likely to make the same sort of identification with female stereotypes. With whom do girls and women identify? My guess is that there is a good deal of confusion in their heads and hearts in this respect, and that what develops is a pattern that might be compared to schizophrenia: The schoolgirl knows that, for her, life is one thing, learning another. This is like the Worcester study's "double standard"—the schoolgirl cannot find herself in history texts or as she would like to see herself in literature; yet she knows she is not a male. Many women may ultimately discount the question of female identity as unimportant, claiming other desciptions preferable—as a parent, for example, or a black person, or a college professor.

Children learn sexual stereotypes at an early age, and by the time they get to fifth grade, it may be terribly difficult, perhaps hardly possible by traditional means, to change their attitudes about sex roles—whether they are male or female. For more than a decade, Paul Torrance, a psychologist particularly interested in creativity, has been conducting interesting and useful experiments with young children. Using a Products Improvement Test, for example, Torrance asked first-grade boys and girls to "make toys more fun to play with." Many six-year-old boys refused to try the nurse's kit, "protesting," Torrance reports, "I'm a boy! I don't play with things like that." Several creative boys turned the nurse's kit into a doctor's kit and were then "quite free to think of improvements." By the third grade, however, "boys excelled girls even on the nurse's kit, probably because," Torrance explains, "girls have been conditioned by this time to accept toys as they are and not to manipulate or change them."

Later experiments with third, fourth, and fifth-graders using science toys further verify what Torrance calls "the inhibiting effects of sex-role conditioning." "Girls were quite reluctant," he reports, "to work with these science toys and frequently protested: 'I'm a girl; I'm not supposed to know anything about things like that!' " Boys, even in these early grades, were about twice as good as girls at explaining ideas about toys. In 1959, Torrance reported his findings to parents and teachers in one school and asked for their cooperation in attempting to change the attitudes of the girls. In 1960, when he retested them using similar science toys, the girls participated willingly and even with apparent enjoyment. And they performed as well as the boys. But in one significant respect nothing had changed: The boys' contributions were more highly valued—both by other boys and by girls— than the girls' contributions, regardless of the fact that, in terms of sex, boys and girls had scored equally. "Apparently," Torrance writes, "the school climate has helped to make it more acceptable for girls to play around with science things, but boys' ideas about science things are still supposed to be better than those of girls."

Torrance's experiments tell us both how useful and how limited education may be for women in a culture in which assumptions about their inferiority run deep in their own consciousness as well as in the consciousness of men. While it is encouraging to note that a year's effort had changed behavior patterns significantly, it is also clear that attitudes of nine-, ten-, and eleven-year-olds are not so easily modifiable, at least not through the means Torrance used.

Torrance's experiments also make clear that, whatever most of us have hitherto assumed, boys and girls are not treated alike in elementary school. If we consider those non-curricular aspects of the school environment that the late anthropologist Jules Henry labeled the ''noise'' of schools, chief among them is the general attitude of teachers, whatever their sex, that girls are likely to ''love'' reading and to ''hate'' mathematics and science. As we know from the Rosenthal study of teacher expectations, *Pygmalion in the Classroom*, such expectations significantly determine student behavior and attitudes. Girls are not expected to think logically or to understand scientific principles; they accept that estimate internally and give up on mathematics and science relatively early. And what encouragement awaits the interested few in high school? For example, in six high school science texts published since 1966 and used in the Baltimore city public schools—all of the books rich in illustrations—I found photographs of one female lab assistant, one woman doctor, one woman scientist, and Rachel Carson. It is no wonder that the percentage of women doctors and engineers in the United States has remained constant at 6 per cent and 1 per cent respectively for the past fifty years.

Though there is no evidence that their early physical needs are different from or less than boys', girls are offered fewer activities even in kindergarten. They may sit and watch while boys, at the request of the female teacher, change the seating arrangement in the room. Of course, it's not simply a matter of physical exercise or ability: Boys are learning how to behave as males, and girls are learning to be ''ladies'' who enjoy being ''waited on.'' If there are student-organized activities to be arranged, boys are typically in charge, with girls assisting, perhaps in the stereotyped role of secretary. Boys are allowed and expected to be noisy and aggressive, even on occasion to express anger; girls must learn ''to control themselves'' and behave like ''young ladies.'' On the other hand, boys are expected not to cry, though there are perfectly good reasons why children of both sexes ought to be allowed that avenue of expression. Surprisingly early, boys and girls are separated for physical education and hygiene, and all the reports now being published indicate preferential treatment for boys and nearly total neglect of girls.

In junior high schools, sexual stereotyping becomes, if anything, more overt. Curricular sex-typing continues and is extended to such ''shop'' subjects as cooking and sewing, on the one hand, and metal- and woodworking, printing, ceramics, on the other. In vocational high schools, the stereotyping becomes outright channeling, and here the legal battles have begun for equality of opportunity. Recently, the testimony of junior high and high school girls in New York has become available in a pamphlet prepared by the New York City chapter of NOW (*Report on Sex Bias in the Public Schools*, available from Anne Grant West, 453 Seventh St., Brooklyn, N.Y. 11215). Here are a few items:

> Well, within my physics class last year, our teacher asked if there was anybody interested in being a lab assistant, in the physics lab, and when I raised my hand, he told all the girls to put their hands down because he was only interested in working with the boys.

> There is an Honor Guard . . . students who, instead of participating in gym for the term, are monitors in the hall, and I asked my gym teacher if I could be on the Honor Guard Squad. She said it was only open to boys. I then went to the head of the Honor Guard . . . who said that he thought girls were much too nasty to be Honor Guards. He though they would be too mean in working on the job, and I left it at that.

> We asked for basketball. They said there wasn't enough equipment. The boys prefer to have it first. Then we will have what is left over. We haven't really gotten anywhere.

Finally, I quote more extensively from one case:

> MOTHER: I asked Miss Jonas if my daughter could take metalworking or mechanics, and she said there is no freedom of choice. That is what she said.
> THE COURT: That is it?
> ANSWER: I also asked her whose decision this was, that there was no freedom of choice. And she told me it was the decision of the board of education. I didn't ask her anything else because she clearly showed me that it was against the school policy for girls to be in the class. She said it was a board of education decision.
> QUESTION: Did she use the phrase, ''no freedom of choice''?
> ANSWER: Exactly that phrase—no freedom of choice. That is what made me so angry that I wanted to start this whole thing.

> • • •

> THE COURT: Now, after this lawsuit was filed, they then permitted you to take the course; is that correct?
> DAUGHTER: No, we had to fight about it for quite a while.
> QUESTION: But eventually they did let you in the second semester?
> ANSWER: They only let me in there.
> QUESTION: You are the only girl?
> ANSWER: Yes.
> QUESTION: How did you do in the course?
> ANSWER: I got the medal for it from all the boys there.
> QUESTION: Will you show the court?

ANSWER: Yes (indicating).

QUESTION: And what does the medal say?

ANSWER: Metal 1970 Van Wyck.

QUESTION: And why did they give you that medal?

ANSWER: Because I was the best one out of all the boys.

THE COURT: I do not want any giggling or noises in the courtroom. Just do the best you can to control yourself or else I will have to ask you to leave the courtroom. This is no picnic, you know. These are serious lawsuits.

Such "serious lawsuits" will, no doubt, continue, but they are not the only routes to change. There are others to be initiated by school systems themselves.

One route lies through the analysis of texts and attitudes. So long as those responsible for the education of children believe in the stereotypes as givens, rather than as hypothetical constructs that a patriarchal society has established as desired norms—so long as the belief continues, so will the condition. These beliefs are transmitted in the forms we call literature and history, either on the printed page or in other media.

Elementary school readers are meant for both sexes. Primers used in the first three grades offer children a view of a"typical" American family: a mother who does not work, a father who does, two children—a brother who is always older than a sister—and two pets—a dog and sometimes a cat—whose sexes and ages mirror those of the brother and sister. In these books, boys build or paint things; they also pull girls in wagons and push merry-go-rounds. Girls carry purses when they go shopping; they help mother cook or pretend that they are cooking; and they play with their dolls. When they are not making messes, they are cleaning up their rooms or other people's messes. Plots in which girls are involved usually depend on their inability to do something—to manage their own roller skates or to ride a pony. Or in another typical role, a girl named Sue admires a parachute jumper: "What á jump!" said Sue. "What a jump for a man to make!" When her brother puts on a show for the rest of the neighborhood, Sue, whose name appears as the title of the chapter, is part of his admiring audience.

The absence of adventurous heroines may shock the innocent; the absence of even a few stories about women doctors, lawyers, or professors thwarts reality; but the consistent presence of one female stereotype is the most troublesome matter:

Primrose was playing house. Just as she finished pouring tea for her dolls she began to think. She thought and thought and she thought some more. "Whom shall I marry? Whomever shall I marry?

"I think I shall marry a mailman. Then I could go over to everybody's house and give them their mail.

"Or I might marry a policeman. I could help him take the children across the street."

Primrose thinks her way through ten more categories of employment and concludes, "But now that I think it over, maybe I'll just marry somebody I love." Love is the opiate designated to help Primrose forget to think about what she would like to do or be. With love as reinforcer, she can imagine herself helping some man in his work. In another children's book, Johnny says, "I think I will be a dentist when I grow up," and later, to Betsy, he offers generously, "You can be a dentist's nurse." And, of course, Betsy accepts gratefully, since girls are not expected to have work identity other than as servants or helpers. In short, the books that schoolgirls read prepare them early for the goal of marriage, hardly ever for work, and never for independence.

If a child's reader can be pardoned for stereotyping because it is "only" fiction, a social studies text has no excuse for denying reality to its readers. After all, social studies texts ought to describe "what is," if not "what should be." And yet, such texts for the youngest grades are no different from readers. They focus on families and hence on sex roles and work. Sisters are still younger than brothers; brothers remain the doers, questioners, and knowers who explain things to their poor, timid sisters. In a study of five widely used texts, Jamie Kelem Frisof finds that energetic boys think about "working on a train or in a broom factory" or about being President. They grow up to be doctors or factory workers or (in five texts combined) to do some hundred different jobs, as opposed to thirty for women.

Consider for a moment the real work world of women. Most women (at least for some portion of their lives) work, and if we include "token" women—the occasional engineer, for instance—they probably do as many different kinds of work as men. Even without improving the status of working women, the reality is distinctly different from the content of school texts and literature written for children. Schools usually at least reflect the society they serve; but the treatment of working women is one clear instance in which the reflection is distorted by a patriarchal attitude about who *should* work and the maleness of work. For example, there are women doctors—there have been women doctors in this country, in fact, for a hundred years or so. And yet, until the publication this month of two new children's books by the Feminist Press (Box 334, Old Westbury, N.Y. 11568), there were no children's books about women doctors.

In a novel experiment conducted recently by an undergraduate at Towson State College in Maryland, fourth-grade students answered "yes" or "no" to a series of twenty questions, eight of which asked, in various ways, whether "girls were smarter than boys" or whether "daddies were smarter than mommies." The results indicated that boys and girls were agreed that 1) boys were not smarter than girls, nor girls smarter than boys; but 2) daddies were indeed smarter than mommies! One possible explanation of this finding depends on the knowledge that daddies, in school texts and on television (as well as in real life), work, and that people who work know things. Mommies, on the other hand, in books and on television rarely stir out of the house except to go to the store—and how can someone like that know anything? Of course, *we* know that half of all mothers in the United States work at some kind of job, but children whose mommies do work can only assume—on the basis of evidence offered in school books and on television—that their mommies must be "different," perhaps even not quite "real" mommies.

If children's readers deny the reality of working women, high school history texts deny women their full historical role. A recent study by Janice Law Trecker of thirteen popular texts concludes with what by now must seem a refrain: Women in such texts are "passive, incapable of sustained organization or work, satisfied with [their] role in society, and well supplied with material blessings." Women, in the grip of economic and political forces, rarely fighting for anything, occasionally receive some "rights," especially suffrage in 1920, which, of course, solves all *their* problems. There is no discussion of the struggle by women to gain entrance into higher education, of their efforts to organize or join labor unions, of other battles for working rights, or of the many different aspects of the hundred-year-long multi-issue effort that ended, temporarily, in the suffrage act of 1920. Here is Dr. Trecker's summary of the history and contributions of American women as garnered from the thirteen texts combined:

> Women arrived in 1619 (a curious choice if meant to be their first acquaintance with the New World). They held the Seneca Falls Convention on Women's Rights in 1848. During the rest of the nineteenth century, they participated in reform movements, chiefly temperance, and were exploited in factories. In 1920, they were given the vote. They joined the armed forces for the first time during the Second World War and thereafter have enjoyed the good life in America. Add the names of the women who are invariably mentioned: Harriet Beecher Stowe, Jane Addams, Dorothea Dix, and Frances Perkins, with perhaps Susan B. Anthony, Elizabeth Cady Stanton . . . [and you have the story].

Where efforts have been made in recent years to incorporate black history, again it is without attention to black women, either with respect to their role in abolitionist or civil rights movements, for example, or with respect to intellectual or cultural achievements.

Just as high school history texts rely on male spokesmen and rarely quote female leaders of the feminist movement—even when they were also articulate writers such as Charlotte Perkins Gilman, or speakers such as Sojourner Truth—so, too, literary anthologies will include Henry James or Stephen Crane rather than Edith Wharton or Kate Chopin. Students are offered James Joyce's *Portrait of the Artist as a Young Man* or the *Autobiography of Malcolm X*, rather than Doris Lessing's *Martha Quest* or Anne Moody's *Coming of Age in Mississippi*. As a number of studies have indicated, the literary curriculum, both in high school and college, is a male-centered one. That is, either male authors dominate the syllabus or the central characters of the books are consistently male. There is also usually no compensating effort to test the fictional portraits—of women and men—against the reality of life experience. Allegedly "relevant" textbooks for senior high school or freshman college composition courses continue to appear, such as Macmillan's *Representative Men: Heroes of Our Time*. There are two women featured in this book: Elizabeth Taylor, the actress, and Jacqueline Onassis, the Existential Heroine. Thirty-five or forty men—representing a range of racial, political, occupational, and intellectual interests—fill the bulk of a book meant, of course, for both men and women. And some teachers are still ordering such texts.

It's not a question of malice, I assume, but of thoughtfulness or ignorance. Six or seven years ago I too was teaching from a standard male-dominated curriculum—and at a women's college at that. But I speak from more than my own experience. Last fall at this time I knew of some fifty college courses in what has come to be known as women's studies. This fall, I know of more than 500, about half of which are in literature and history. I know also of many high school teachers who have already begun to invent comparable courses.

School systems can and should begin to encourage new curricular developments, especially in literature and social studies, and at the elementary as well as the high school level. Such changes, of course, must include the education and re-education of teachers, and I know of no better way to re-educate them than to ask for analyses of the texts they use, as well as of their assumptions and attitudes. The images we pick up, consciously or unconsciously, from literature and history significantly control our sense of identity, and our identity—our sense of ourselves as powerful or powerless, for example— controls our behavior. As teachers read new materials and organize and teach new courses, they will change their views. That is the story of most of the women I know who, like me, have become involved in women's studies. The images we have in our heads about ourselves come out of literature and history; before we can change those images, we must see them clearly enough to exorcise them and, in the process, to raise others from the past we are learning to see.

That is why black educators have grown insistent upon their students' learning black history—slave history, in fact. That is also why some religious groups, Jews for example, emphasize their history as a people, even though part of that history is also slave history. For slave history has two virtues: Not only does it offer a picture of servitude against which one can measure the present; it offers also a vision of struggle and courage. When I asked a group of young women at the University of Pittsburgh last year whether they were depressed by the early nineteenth-century women's history they were studying, their replies were instructive: "Certainly not," one woman said, "we're angry that we had to wait until now—after so many years of U.S. history in high school—to learn the truth about some things." And another added, "But it makes you feel good to read about those tremendous women way back then. They felt some of the same things we do now."

Will public education begin to change the images of women in texts and the lives of women students in schools? There will probably be some movement in this direction, at least in response to the pressures from students, parents, and individual teachers. I expect that parents, for example, will continue to win legal battles for their daughters' equal rights and opportunities. I expect that individual teachers will alter their courses and texts and grow more sensitive to stereotypic expectations and behavior in the classroom. But so far there are no signs of larger, more inclusive reforms: no remedial program for counselors, no major effort to destereotype vocational programs or kindergarten classrooms, no centers for curricular reform. Frankly, I don't expect this to happen without a struggle. I don't expect that public school systems will take the initiative here. There is too much at stake in a society as patriarchal as this one. And schools, after all, tend to follow society, not lead it.

As the well-known sociologists Robert MacIver and Charles Page once wrote: "the individual is not born with prejudices any more than he is born with sociological understanding. The way he thinks as a member of a group, especially about other groups, is at bottom the result of social indoctrination." In other words, just as people are taught to love so are they taught to hate. In order to overcome their prejudices people must undergo a process of relearning, of resocialization.

Sometimes resocialization is accomplished through formal teaching, sometimes (as we shall see in Part IV) through incarceration. Sometimes confrontation is used to make people aware that what they had learned about others may simply be untrue. This method is described in Thomas J. Cottle's selection about an experiment with black and white school children in Boston.

As you read about Cottle's experiment, which was conducted in the early 1960s, keep in mind the extent to which cultural values influence attitudes and the usefulness of the self-analytical techniques discussed by Cottle for reducing intergroup tensions and for resocializing prejudiced individuals.

Encounter in Color

THOMAS J. COTTLE

School-bussing integration programs normally proceed along fairly predictable lines. Students of both races are told simply that a merger soon will occur; automatically, whites are designated as the home team, the Negroes are the visitors. The outnumbered transients—and Negroes feel like transients—then are plopped into the middle of a familiar and well-rehearsed drama, one in which they are totally uncomfortable. And throughout the entire process, teachers must assume responsibility for making the merger work.

The sadness of the drama is that it takes place with almost no psychological preparation and with no time devoted to the resolution of human and institutional complications. Yet as though by some magic, students are supposed to live together peaceably and to learn something. The drama's irony is that where schools in the past have exulted in their socializing function, when

integration becomes a reality they hurriedly retreat to their fundamental di-
dactic activities. School boards try to combine the races in varying ratios—ad-
vantageous to the whites but justified by national or regional proportions—
with the hope that somehow the kids will work it out. Afterwards social scientists are employed to diagnose the existing exigencies and to present the
statistics on prior injustices and inequalities.

Social science methodology and sophistication hardly are required, however, to assess contemporary token integration programs, for anyone can observe the difficulties involved for students, teachers, and administrators. Anyone can vibrate to the currents of open and muffled prejudice and of hatreds.
And of the inevitable despair. Yet in the design of human environments
social science can make one important contribution which provides a workable
way in which integration and learning may evolve naturally.

For the past year, a groups of us at Harvard have been engaged in a small
project aimed at developing an experimental context which permits the observation of integration dynamics. At the same time we have offered an arena for
the confrontation of adolescents who bring to this most complex encounter
their conspicuous and well-rehearsed sentiments, and less well-understood,
newly discovered fears and fantasies.

Our intention was to transport integration to a laboratory setting modeled
after the real and often frightening world of contemporary high-school
students. Our participants were lower- and middle-class Negro and white boys
and girls, and their difficult task was to meet together and to speak directly
upon the issues of race and social relations.

But these were not simple seminars. They were self-analytic groups. In self-
analytic groups, an experienced leader "trains" group members to pursue the
personal expressions and interpersonal processes which arise "spontaneously." Group members are encouraged to analyze their feelings and verbalize
their attitudes, actions, and even fantasies. The emphasis in self-analytic
groups rests on the meaning of group interactions, as well as on private rev-
elations.

In such groups, the self-analytic procedures normally are not outlined fully
to group members; rather they are insinuated by the leader into the ongoing
group processes. The leader guides the group towards more expansive observation and analysis, and the mood generated is one of constrained freedom.
Anything can be said by anyone at any time, but the inferred rule is that expression and analysis must run contiguously.

This notion is borrowed from the psychoanalytic tradition which argues
that the ego must be "split" if one is to perform two requisite therapeutic
tasks. A second notion, taken from the same source, is that leaders (not unlike
classical analysts), by participating minimally, create in the minds of group
members a need to construct a viable social system with inherent institutional
arrangements and necessary role allocations. (In fact, taciturn leaders, by

creating social contracts which are seemingly devoid of normally evident sanctions, accentuate their own positions as the ultimate authority and render ever so complicated the nature of relationships between members.) The starkness of the self-analytic context, by compelling participants to develop for themselves a social order which they then must assess, brings to the laboratory a setting which some authors claim is suitable for studying the most primitive and complex forms of human behavior.

The greatness of such groups comes as they succeed in getting persons to confront both private and public issues normally avoided or not noticed.

The danger in the technique, as we employed it, was that innocent students inadvertently were transformed into cadres of miniature psychotherapists. And, untrained, they may have believed mistakenly that manifest content had little value. The balance fell into the very human hands of the leader, who in the safety of his role and with his dappled moments of real understanding, had the power to drive the group to either end. In the process he came to be perceived, at least by people of his own race, as father, mother, teacher, older brother, therapist, and—if he played it wrong—as God himself.

Three points should be made here about our perspectives on the self-analytic technique. First, we did not consider the groups as psychotherapy. The assumption was *not* illness and the intention was *not* treatment. (This is not to say that people enlisting in self-analytic groups may not have been seeking the therapy context.)

Second, it was expected that when problems were so complex that they could not be verbalized, groups would deal with them in fantasy terms, and thus provide both an outlet for their expression and a justification for direct interpretation. The open and direct line to their own fantasies held by adolescents actually increased the significance of this point.

Third, as in psychotherapy, every action of every moment was considered potentially significant. Thus, jokes, member absences, meeting time and place, physical appearance, and apparently casual topics assumed importance.

The applicaton of self-analytic groups to racial integration barely has been explored. But we selected such groups for our program because we believe this format is ideal and offers stimulating experiences which also can be observed carefully. Furthermore, because of their flexibility, such groups could be structured in at least two ways to simulate the paradigms for school-bussing operations.

The first school-bussing program, which may be called the "September plan," is the method by which reluctant administrators throw Negro and white students together in white schools, with instructions to get along. While the previous Summer has brought deep and searching thoughts and hopes for the impending merger, as well as pessimism and red hot antipathies, few professionals with the exception of men like Robert Coles, author of *Children of Crisis*, have concerned themselves with these, months before school integration, either in terms of research or as a time for support and guidance of the equally bewildered white and Negro students. Presumably a bit more humane, the "June plan" grants Negroes and whites a brief moment to discuss their fears and animosities in the privacy of their own academic and racial environments.

Accordingly, our groups were arranged to replicate these two alternative ways of handling school integration. Some of our groups consisted of Negroes and whites together from the start, with the size of groups limited to 10 or 12 students. Other groups of four to six youths each began in a segregated fashion and met thus for six sessions. After six meetings, we merged the groups for six more weeks. For these groups, announcement of approaching integration came at the beginning of the first segregated session. Students were asked to participate in 12 group meetings, one per week, with each lasting a little more than an hour. Because of the students' busy school and work programs, the sessions all were scheduled in the early evenings or on Saturday mornings. To avoid administrative complications, meeting rooms were reserved in a Harvard University building; and this meant, of course, that while the "turf" was unfamiliar to both races, it clearly was on the white side of neutral. To accentuate this, we arranged for groups to meet after merger at the same time and in the same room as did white students during the segregated sessions. A community's university of course is hardly a neutral stimulus for lower-class adolescents. And the structure symbolized by the university, forbidding to Negroes, may be even more upsetting to white students for whom the university and the very idea of research represent familiar but unattainable objects.

Some 45 students were selected from local high schools, church groups, and neighborhood youth clubs for our self-analytic group experiment. They volunteered for a project advertised as an experiment in human relations. Ironically Negro participants had to be reimbursed for taxi fare necessary to transport them from their homes—both distant from and inconvenient to the university. There was no other reimbursement for members because we felt that only would complicate things. Termination of "salaried" students could be interpreted as the firing of inferior employees. (As an incentive and a gesture of nurture, however, students were given beverages and snacks during each meeting.)

Strict obeying of bussing statistics would urge white-dominated groups, but the natural anxieties attending self-analytic experiments of this type dictated instead a goal of population equality. Students of about the same age— sophomores and juniors—were assigned to groups in random fashion but with the stipulation that sexes and races would be distributed evenly. Definitely to be avoided in the project (and in schools as well!) was a group with one Negro or only one boy, and other such dramatic imbalances.

As it turned out, several of the students knew each other from school, and though prior acquaintanceship often interferes with group progress, actually it proved beneficial in some instances. In one group for example, a Negro boy listened intently to a white girl's discussion and then told of his prior distaste for her, and of his newly formed admiration. Her performance in the group demonstrated a courage and intelligence he had never seen in the classroom, he said. It was with obvious joy that he announced his change of heart.

Just as important as group composition was the selection of group leaders. If leaders were overly specialized, the possible general applicability of the project's results would be greatly decreased. Certainly our resources were limited by the availability of people possessing similar kinds of group experience so that relatively uniform group structures could be set up.

Available to us in almost superabundance, however, was a population of university students, both graduate and undergraduate, who not only had taken part in self-analytic groups but had spent additional months observing groups other than their own. This then became the delicate minimum for leader credentials: one year as a group member, plus at least one semester of observation.

Schoolroom realities suggested using female leaders—for us a sadly rare commodity. Hence, acknowledging both reality guideposts and the characteristics of the university manpower pool, five white males—two graduate and three undergraduate students—were selected as group leaders. None of these young men had previous experience as leaders but each had been in groups and had worked in areas of race relations. It was through their mature insights and sensitivites, as well as through their natural apprehensions and reticence, that the project was conceived and launched.

It is always difficult to differentiate between rational calculations about what groups should be and the experimental designs drawn according to the less rational and invisible needs of those who direct them. The fact that the subtle expectancies of the experimenter influence the outcomes of research has been more than amply demonstrated by Robert Rosenthal in his book, *Experimental Effect in Behavioral Research*. Similarly, self-analytic groups all have expectations which drive members toward certain demarcated ends. Leaders—or therapists—do not create a vacuum with their ungainly silences and vocally bland penetrations; they build toward a discrete and peculiar atmosphere which often makes normal brain function difficult but putatively yields the desired and desirable ends.

We simply do not know the degree to which our own needs were met by project procedures. For example, our decision to substitute in-group observers and tape recorders for the frequently used one-way mirrors may be explained in several ways: while public-private, formal-informal dimensions exist naturally in groups, there also are nebulous realms of insecurity, intimacy, competence, and potency. On the other hand, private, closed rooms protect leaders and members from outside evaluation.

The influence of leaders on groups, furthermore, varies from man to man, session to session, and probably from moment to moment. Leader strategies and reactions could not possibly be uniform, or even consistent, except perhaps in cases where single leaders ran both the Negro and white segregated groups prior to merging.

At best, leaders could but listen intensely and predicate their utterances upon a concern for their group members and upon what in a word is history, namely that only months before, as group members themselves, they too had struggled with similar problems in similar fashion.

Assessments of our results certainly must be made not only in light of integration factors and more characteristic adolescent social phenomena but also with consideration for the reaction of human beings to the novel, seductive, and perhaps terrifying system offered by group structure and purpose. The early phase of all our groups, for instance, was characterized by a grappling at so-called reality levels with the proposed (white) authority and intimacy, and on fantasy levels with the actual or promised racial merger. The groups sidled into the authority problem by verbal attacks on the University, inquiries into whether Harvard's president, the governor of Massachusetts, and even Senator Robert Kennedy would learn of the project. The groups wanted to know: Would it be written up? Were they guinea pigs? Was all this really confidential? What might result from the excessive freedom and exposure of one's inner self?

Contained within these natural queries, of course, was the students' hope that if they would open up to one another, the leader in turn would approve of their efforts, reveal his involvement with them, and even reward them ironically by declaring negative sanctions.

The major problem in our early meetings was to establish a social order involving trust but also taking account of authority hierarchies and qualities of interpersonal attachment. Sample conversations were: "We're just like the United Nations and he (the leader) is like a silent Secretary General." "What would happen if he weren't here?" "There would be anarchy." "What would that mean?" "Probably free love for everyone." Every single group met and solved that problem: the transference of free minds and open discussions to free love and, to use a neologism often heard in groups, "orgification."

In his silence and manifest sureness, the self-analytic group leader perpetrates what at the beginning can be felt, if not perceived, as a legitimized seduction and human coalescence. If the coalescence is overly-sexual, group members must align their sex-role definitions and defenses in reaction to the aroused threats. If in his coalescing the leader appears overly paternalistic, an action not necessarily excluding Negroes, members must align their mutual associations in accordance with social codes appropriate in family and peer realms. Such alignments bring up unconscious interpretations of sexual prohibitions relating to patterns of incest, premarital intercourse, and ensuing illegitimate childbirth. "How many of us here are accidents?" one boy shouted as he attempted to discover a potentially uniting reality—and in so doing planted the seeds of an incestuous sibling rivalry.

No matter how he came across in our group, the leader was the unequivocal agent of integration and, in our segregated groups, he was also the sole person to share communications and histories of Negroes and whites alike. It became apparent that, whatever the source and strength of the leader-member tie might be, this bond necessarily transcended a pure racial identity. In fact, a form of "backlash" emerged as the neutrality of each group leader caused whites to see him often either as a turncoat or as a father abandoning his own children. Negroes began to perceive the leader as an inexplicably trustworthy person and perhaps even as a suitable stepfather. In the first session of one merged group, a Negro girl left her fellow Negroes and pulled her chair halfway around the room so that she might sit down next to (and a bit behind) the white leader.

Actual merger of the segregated groups naturally affected the quality of the transference to the leader. During segregated sessions, the approach of both whites and Negroes changed radically as the whites evidenced fear of abandonment and their disbelief that a member of their own race would lead them knowingly into such a predicament. Negroes tended to drift back to a more primitive self-perception and a stereotype ghetto behavior. Possibly because of this element in their shared group experience, the participants collectively returned to the leader during final sessions before merging in an almost childlike posture of dependence. We interpreted this as symbolizing their hopes that the leader would regulate their activities and thus bring the merger to its desired ending.

The transference, however, changed for a third time as group members gradually realized that they *alone* were the architects and inhabitants of this new community and that their prior real and fantasy histories—both with and without the leader—had to be reconciled or even altered to accommodate a still newer environment. Although less clear, similar transformations occurred in integrated groups as well.

Given these many complexities, how does one interpret one white girl's explosive response to the proposition of racial merger and the presence of white male authority: "Let's talk about premarital sexuality!" And how do we explain the exquisite associations of a slight Negro girl as she nervously wandered through fantasy descriptions: gypsy marriages, desire for racial equality, student demonstrations in Florida, life in her own ghetto, the crimes committed by police, her pleasure at the Boston Strangler's escape from prison (an escape from another kind of ghetto), her terror that the strangler would come to her home, and her subsequent and *real* preparations: boarding windows and doors and piling knives and scissors under her chair. Poignantly, she ended the verbal fantasy by revealing one more fear—that midst his seemingly uncontrollable psychosis, the Strangler still would discriminate against a Negro and reject her as a murder victim.

Our groups' remarks about premarital sexuality well may refer to what many participants saw as a "marriage" of the races, performed in the group by the integrating "ceremony" of the group leader who has "powers invested in him" and was equally associated with both white and Negro group members.

In one integrated group, an almost Quakerlike ceremony actually was performed as two boys, one Negro and the other white, gradually developed a closeness sufficiently strong and public to unite the entire group as a congregation. The presence of girls presumably kept the boys' intimacy from gaining the pejorative status.

In another experimental group composed of Negro and white gang boys, a similar intended marriage, if it can be called that, became aggressive and atavistic as each side designated one of its members as inferior and agreed to a contract of mutual denigration. Swelling with homosexual overtones, their project fizzled; a basketball game was proposed, with the leader acting as referee. The merger failed as the "bunch" of whites and "pile" of Negroes (their own description) never melded.

Much of the foregoing imagery seems to us related to the group's need for control particularly in spheres of authority and morality. In our groups, authority assumed heightened significance in light of the racial merger, either scheduled or already enacted. It was not surprising therefore that participants made strong pleas for refereeing and social policing; someone must define not only psychospatial limits of the group but the "legal" extent of the merger's penetration.

In one of our integrated groups, an eloquent Negro boy was able to contrive a medium for expressing the vertical intimacies inherent in good authority arrangements. Speaking of the microcosm which was his group, he spelled out the disparities of local and highway police: the former—slow, dark, dirty, irresponsible, inconsistent in their punishment, unavailable when needed; the latter—sleek, neat, tall, strong, quick to attend. And his poetry continued: "All of us are dark specks on a policeman's badge." Soon afterwards, he turned these descriptions into a comparison of Negro and white fathers, and then he concluded by expressing his distaste for his own father in what seemed to the group to be his wish to be ministered to or even adopted by the leader, a man no more than three years his senior.

Comparable feelings were equally prevalent among white group members, but the undeniable existence of the white authority figure must not be overlooked, for it may have inspired what Eric Erickson calls negative identity elements in Negroes in the group and, at the same time, have made statements of needs for parental-like gratifications more difficult for the whites.

In their attempt to sculpt a social identity it was expected our group members would turn to those aspects of family and peer-group subsystems which seemed sociologically appropriate and psychological congenial. The group thus provided an unanticipated opportunity to engineer if not a miniature social-psychological Utopia, then at least a stage for rehearsing ideal psychosocial identity. Flexibility and credulity in adolescent role playing made this rehearsal seem like the real thing, but the evolution of a Utopia was not without occasional racial and sexual clashes, replete with fantasies of violence, as the various interest groups bid to build their own special social structures.

One identity component which showed itself in our groups was the urge to become substantially more potent and to increase the felt sense of a free autonomy and naked power. Normal levels of potency and aggression just did not suffice when races and sexes saw themselves in public competiton. But how often their concerns were swathed in terror. From white male students in one segregated group came: "What are they? Colored? Older? Girls? They'll kill us. Make 'em younger . . . real small, pygmies with eyes like poison darts. Why are they coming? They'll want to fight! We'll talk and let them sit in the back of the room."

Then, with no apparent connecting thought: "Do you think there are people on the moon? No atmosphere . . . too low . . . too high . . . too many craters. No human could live there . . . We're not human as far as they're concerned."

From the Negro camp, though the groups were meeting separately, came the reciprocal posture of the aggressor. Negroes, too, spewed platitudes that revealed how deeply lodged the bigotry of ignorance was, and how clear the way in which their self-degradation was transformed into precarious esteem by the stereotyping of whites: "Whites aren't as good; you can't slick the slicker; you can't bullshit the bullshitter . . . The white people slide, we glide . . . We have natural-born rhythm. They can't dance. Can't sing soul . . . We're naturally strong. If you see a strong Whitey, you know he's been lifting weights . . . And we got better girls."

Clearly each side feared the devastation, and even total annihilation, of its own social fabric. In almost revolutionary terms, each group seemed to believe that one social order must be torn down before a new one could be installed. Evident throughout was the recurring disbelief of white students that a white leader could draft his own kind into such a battle; the Negroes, explicit acceptance of and preparation for battle; and in all the group participants, the primitive interweaving of both sexual and destructive fantasies.

The basic aggression and the uncertainty about the ultimately victorious and hence superior race came out in discussion about the war in Viet Nam, or school experiences involving teachers, which served as conversational starting points for almost every group. Typical talk went this way: "It's the good white against the bad colored . . . It's the pure and powerful stabilizers versus the vile and unclean troublemakers . . . It's racial violence . . . If the Negroes refused to fight, America would lose . . . Negroes are America's potency and the untapped potential for its continuing strength . . . Let's not confuse Negroes like us with the inferior types that come up from the South and in from Puerto Rico . . . You got to get immigration laws and keep the Puerto Ricans out . . . Who's better, Adam Clayton Powell or Edward Brooke? They're both no good. Powell doesn't help his own people and Brooke takes advantage of the white liberals and gets the rest of the vote by being a Republican. What's more they either marry white people or hire them as secretaries . . . You gotta crawl in and dig those Viet Cong out of their black tunnels . . . and either build a democracy for them or kill 'em!''

This concentration on defeat of the Viet Cong may have symbolized not only the eradication of Negroes, or racial integration. It also may have represented the Negroes' own destruction of existing stereotypes and their desire to be divorced from what they themselves labeled as "black trash."

Certainly Viet Nam represented aspects of white aggression, foreign invasion, and draft laws as both races encounter them. Like the war, conquest of the moon also provided a perfect medium for the embroidering of fantasies which ultimately were concerned with racial integration. "Aliens probably look like us," said one Negro boy, "Maybe they're a bit bigger with an extra finger . . . maybe just a glob of hair." Thus, intruders were Negroes from different communities, aliens from a different planet, or soldiers from a different country.

As important as the actual theme of fantasies was the fact that without suggestion, groups selected topics on which they could build elaborate fantasies serving the multifarious purposes and needs of *all* contributors. Perhaps the greatest impact of the self-analytic procedure is felt, not when the leader unraveled by interpretation the various intertwined fantasy threads and returned them to their originators, but when group members themselves recognized the various layers of implications as they were built up in the course of such embroidery sessions. Just such an experience was felt by one who tried to act out her unstated sense of a racial perspective by turning off the lights in the group room and leaving them on in the hall, and then reversing the procedure. Irrespective of the illumination or her own physical location, her point about skin-color permanence and the eye of the beholder was forcibly communicated. The more she went on with her fantasy, the more she realized what she was doing.

Typically, fantasy expression increased as experienced reality became more difficult to face head-on, but fantasies were not just alternative to so-called reality considerations. Rather they were less threatening detours to them, or rehearsals for them. Often resembling free-form behavior trials, collective fantasies mirrored the fears, wishes, and defenses of participants as the group attempted to mold new sentiments and action strategies. Nowhere is this more true than during adolescence, a period condoning fantasy experimentation as a way of tasting those public morsels which someday may become reality.

One notion stemming from our project was that effecting change in adolescent fantasies may alter more real perceptions and hence change the eventual behavior. And so a question to be answered in our experiements was: how does the evolution of fantasy vary within basic group structures?

In the integrated groups, change came gradually from so-called internal dynamics, because from the start both races contended with a fixed structure.

In those Negro and white groups which were merged after six sessions, the physical merger seemed to render invalid the members' previously constructed fantasies. Even with preparation, the change may have been so disrupting that adaptability could not easily take place. One virtue of such a disruption is that prior belief systems were seen to be inaccurate. Hence a second phase of adaption was required. A liability of the merger, of course, is that it may have communicated the necessity of relinquishing totally the familiar belief systems and a sense of competence within them.

In the long run as research continues, groups which merge after first meeting separately may prove the more effective paradigm, if only because actual social change becomes part of the process and history which lead to ongoing social engagements. Where the originally integrated groups should develop a sense of earlier-later, the merged groups might experience more of a sense of beforeness-afterness or even oldness—temporal feelings ideal for reinforcing the conception that something has, indeed, been accomplished.

Self-analytic groups do not provide *the* solution for all the tensions indigenous to school-integration programs, and the kinds of students volunteering for group membership and for leader roles in our project were not sufficiently representative to permit extensive generalization of any sort. Moreover, the self-analytic process, itself so idiosyncratic, cannot be alleged to work successfully in *all* school settings or in *all* community clubs. But the findings which came even from our small experiment are, to say the least, encouraging.

First, we have learned that the self-analytic technique can be fathomed and used by lower- and middle-class young adolescents. Second, we observed incredibly moving, deeply personal expressions and interpretations in groups which were led by nonprofessionals. The fact that leaders also were young and at times awkward may have helped to establish the trust so necessary for viable working groups.

The racial factor might have made the white leaders appear real and warm to white students while Negroes saw the leaders as the unfamiliar representatives of a hostile group. But our evidence did *not* show this at all.

Third, the procedure of keeping groups segregated at the start seemed to permit a direct and open confrontation of the realities and fantasies connected with integration, even—or especially—when the authority figure was white.

While it is obvious that Negroes cannot grow to their full height in a society incessantly demanding that right be equated with white, the Negroes in our project may have been spared some of the tensions inherent in the existing social comparison.

For different reasons, our university buildings and leaders may have been just as foreign to the whites as to the Negroes. A study of racial integration cannot neglect, therefore, the discrete concerns of white students and the eminent force of social-class differentiations.

Fourth, the power of our self-analytic group to a limited extent came from an ability to cut through the barriers that are built into the "September plan," in which Negro and white students are herded together with neither group knowing what to expect nor how to act.

Perhaps the study's outstanding finding is that, even temporarily encountered, the social structure demanded solutions to problems which in their form and intensity tended to blur racial issues. As always in nondirective groups, the dilemmas of intimacy (with threats of homosexuality and heterosexuality) and the definitions of existing and potential power hierarchies had to be resolved, and unequivocal action taken.

Yet these facts also might indicate that the net effect of the self-analytic device was symptom *substitution* rather than *resolution*. Perhaps our efforts did little more than arouse new and different threats which were met with new and different defenses. Perhaps we did a disservice in fact by creating a structure which linked racial integration with authority, and with sexuality. But what else is the reality?

It cannot be denied that while our intention was to explore integration, our procedures at times deflected the emphasis away from race. By putting boys and girls together in a relatively free culture, we evoked that essence of human beings from which come social facts like interaction norms, incest taboos, prejudicial projections.

But, even if the integration-sexuality-authority linkage does represent a phenomenon underlying racial mergers, a potentially liberating experience still was provided by the group environment and significant bits of information still were exposed. School integration is not simply a coming together of people. It is a merger of boys and girls, and it is the convergence of their pre-established realities and fantasies. And, while leader strategies certainly pushed our groups in easily-definable directions, authorship of group fantasies, contents, and associations still belonged for the most part to the members.

To some people, integration well may symbolize intermarriage or even illegitimate intercourse, and white authority may signify the slave master, Uncle Tom, or even white man (or strangler) looking for a Negro prostitute or victim. Though these images may seem absurd, no one can overlook the fantasies which are stimulated in high-school classrooms where teachers openly seduce some students, turn others into children or patients, and never bother at all with the rest. Talk in our groups pointed this up: ''What about the little child just breaking out of her shell? (whom the teacher rejects in favor of some newcomer) . . . I'll do all in my power to hate that girl. She's gonna take all the love and care out of that room . . . No, she (the teacher) don't have to be my friend if she's gonna be that way . . . I don't like teachers who stick to one person.''

We would invite the use of self-analytic techniques in schools, for not only could teachers and counselors learn to lead groups, but their participation as leaders could extricate them from restrictions normally placed on their expressive and integrating abilities.

Where groups seem to offer even greater natural implementations to the environment, however, is in the new concept of the educational park in which social scientists will have to prescribe ways to bring city and suburban populations together. In such environments the distinction between home team and visiting team will be lost, and the question about who is the aggressor or the intruder will be blurred. In the park plan, there will be no one to confront nor even to approach about the problems in bringing races together in schools. Thus, group encounters might well be built-in.

It may be that student-group encounters will offer direct roads to social and cultural problem areas. Such groups also can offer a radically new medium in which academic learning may take place. Social integration, after all, must be a part of all school activities, not just an hour a week of isolated research.

For the moment our own efforts are aimed at systematically assessing the value in both segregated and merged groups, as well as in evaluating the reactions to integration by sex, social class, and race. For us, the immediate future holds more groups with both female and Negro leaders and, hopefully, other groups in which parents will join their children in the self-analytic dialogue. Many participants in our first groups have expressed their desire to carry ''the thing home.'' As one girl projected: ''So maybe we can talk our problems out and they can go home and tell their parents, and we can go home and tell our parents . . .''

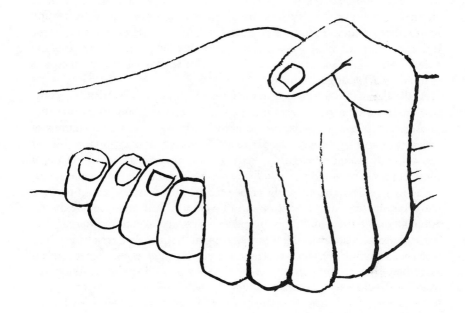

Ben Shahn

PART II
ESTABLISHING NEW RELATIONSHIPS

LIVING IS AN EVER-CHANGING EXPERIENCE. IT SEEMS THAT WE HAVE only just mastered a skill or accepted the importance of a particular idea when it is time to learn something new and to change our thoughts about this or that. How often young people are told, "It's o.k. for a child to do that, but, come now, you're not a baby anymore."

Parents of grown-up children will often say that, in retrospect, each period of child rearing was tougher than the one before. What they are really saying is that socializing others—teaching them language and etiquette, encouraging appropriate behavior and discouraging inappropriate behavior—is no easy task. But, as we all know, it is not easy to be socialized, either. It often seems that there are increasing pressures on people to move in one direction or another, increasing signals telling them what to do or not to do, increasing inducements to deviate from fixed patterns, and increasing constraints to toe the line. Many of these—especially as they pertain to the home and the school—were discussed in the first section. Here we move into certain aspects of the world of young adulthood.

As the ties that bind children to the family begin to be cut, friends become new models and peer-group culture becomes increasingly important. In time, pressures from parents and peers combine with the general expectations of society to encourage young people to find partners of the opposite sex, or "mates." Although the rating, dating, and mating game has changed considerably in recent years, it still exists and almost all young people are affected by its rules. The major difference today is the increasing acceptance of temporary liaisons and partnering out of wedlock. Still, most people marry, although one in three marriages these days is destined to end in divorce.

For those who are married, a power struggle frequently develops between traditional-minded husbands and increasingly liberated wives. This struggle is exacerbated when children arrive. Not only are children intruders on the dyadic husband-wife relationship, they are helpless entities in need of constant care and nurturing. And, curiously, most of us are ill-prepared for the major social responsibility of parenthood.

All of these subjects are topics considered in the pages to follow. Part Two picks up where Part One ended as we read about the importance of peers, the early moves toward establishing independence, marriage, parenting, and the problems of divorce and of being single in a partner-oriented society.

Each of these topics, in and of itself, is a mini-study in socialization, in learning new rules and new roles. No better example is to be found than in the last two selections, "The Six Stations of Divorce," and on "The Single Woman in Today's Society."

As we have seen in Part One, which discussed early socialization, many factors influence values, beliefs, and behavior. Parents and teachers are among the most significant others with whom young people come into contact. However, they are not the only ones with whom young people interact. Peers are important, too.

As Bensman and Rosenberg explain, peers are close friends who are often of the same age and background and have similar interests. Peers are more than casual acquaintances and peer groups often have their own codes of behavior—rules for conduct, speech, dress. As such, peer groups frequently provide alternative outlooks on various aspects of life as well as a sort of escape from the demands of the home situation. With one's peers one can engage in activities and actions that test independence and challenge adult authority in a spirit of cameraderie. Not suprisingly, the end result is not true independence but new forms of conformity.

As you read "The Peer Group," note the use and meaning of such terms as role segmentation, identity crisis, generation gap, age-grading, and youth culture, all of which relate to the transition from childhood to adolescence and young adulthood.

The Peer Group

JOSEPH BENSMAN AND BERNARD ROSENBERG

Historically, family organization is the matrix from which all other institutions arise. At first, these institutions are extensions of the family; in time, they are rivals. Conflict ensues, and it cuts across human existence at the cultural, societal, religious, economic, political, personal, and interpersonal levels. This conflict, which waxes more than it wanes, will not end in the calculable future. For harmony to prevail, the family would have to dissolve, and it is very much with us. Even now no other institution matches the family as an early instrument of socialization, as a catalyst of personality or as a conveyor of values, attitudes, loyalties, and orientations. Human beings cannot be wholly disentangled from family ties without losing all that is personal, warm, private, and intimate. "Out there" in the institutional maze of contemporary society, impersonal, cool, and "rational" rules apply. In that world we are expected to comply demonstratively with the segmental public demands of role playing. As they oppress us, we seek refuge in the family, but not only in the family. Another group beckons with promises of equivalent escape and gratification. It is the peer group.

By definition, such a group is an association of self-selected equals who coalesce around common interests, tastes, preferences, and beliefs. Peer groups use informal criteria for membership, confer informal rewards, and impose informal sanctions. Friendship, acceptance, and belongingness are staples of the peer group in which roles remain loosely defined to cover a wide range of attachments. Vaguely specified conventions include distinctive clothing and hair styles, shared jokes, games, speech patterns, songs, dances, heroes, and villains.

One kind of peer group that attracts members from within a large-scale organization is technically designated as the "informal group" by sociologists who wish to underscore its unplanned and unstructured qualities. Another kind of peer group originates in the community where it is known as a "social circle." Yet another derives from the neighborhood or school setting, and it is called a "youth group," a "clique" or a "gang." Despite their many common properties, it would be as absurd to equate these disparate peer groups as it is to lump all "small groups" or all "primary groups" together.

COMPETITION WITH THE FAMILY

And yet, every peer group offers satisfactions or meets needs comparable to those of the family—with which it competes and over which it sometimes triumphs. Similarities matter, for without them there would be no rivalry. Still, one dissimilarity is decisive: the family integrates, as the peer group segregates, individuals of different ages and different generations. Unlike peer-group emotions, family emotions bind children, parents, grandparents, and other relatives of both sexes to one another. And the mingling of generations makes for a further disparity between the family and the peer group. The family, for all our talk about its "democratic" makeup, is anything but an association of equals. Small children do not have the competence and are not accorded the authority of their elders. Adolescents with a certain amount of competence may be denied authority that oldsters without competence continue to exercise. Rights and responsibilities shift throughout the life cycle; bottom dogs become top dogs and vice versa; but family structure required that inequality be built into it. This type of inequality also implies a certain amount of instability. Children are on the upswing, as they attain physical maturity, just when their parents and grandparents are biologically on the downswing. A modified role reversal is now is order, but each generation is accustomed to a role that it should have "outgrown." Neither children long encouraged to be irresponsible nor adults long habituated to being responsible find it easy to switch roles. Switch they must, but not without pain on both sides. Here as elsewhere nature and culture are out of phase. The problem of family succession can never be completely solved. Train a child very well and very long to be a child, and you unfit him for being an adult. Train him with great effort to be an adult, and he will be repelled by the idea of a second childhood. The family succession, as a social sore spot, can be inflamed or assuaged, but it cannot be avoided.

This problem does not plague the peer group, in which members are either at an identical point in the life cycle or age itself is irrelevant to their activities. They come together as equals, but—in George Orwell's imperishable phrase—some of them are more equal than others. Some stand out as leaders or have visibly greater ability in the performance of a common task; others are more easily led and show less aptitude for the enterprise in which they are all engaged. This is simply to say that while members of a peer group are homogeneous, they are not identical. Their individuality is submerged; it is not extinguished. Just as peer groups are not completely egalitarian, so they are not totally isolated from the rest of society. If it is a question of more or less, then we may say that the peer group is more insulated than the family.

THE GENERATION GAP

We believe this to be the case most especially in periods of vertiginous social change. Ours is such a period. We see generations measured in fewer and fewer years, with the family incorporating more and more generations. Family culture draws its raw materials from a remote past, a recent past, an immediate past, and a multitude of sources located in the proximate present. Past experience is lodged in the memory of parents and grandparents. They have direct (although variously screened, censored, and distorted) access to the obsolete symbolic systems of their youth. Memory is defective, but man is after all preeminently the animal that remembers. What he remembers of his past is a tricky business, but any residue comprises a substantial part of the self that he now presents. His juniors are furthest removed from a side of his personality rooted in an era to which they can have access only insofar as he communicates it to them. We are unequally endowed in our capacity to communicate across generations. Some men get through to those chronologically removed from them because they are better communicators or better chameleons than other men. Much depends upon how swiftly and fully they are able to forget their past.

When the highly publicized generation gap is widest, people on each side of it find that they do not speak the same language. Nothing dates us faster than the antiquity of our slang (unless it is our taste for last year's popular music). Slang changes so fast the "now" language of high-school children is inaccessible to their slightly older or slightly younger siblings. By the time it is diffused to other generations, a new and similarly transitory argot will have emerged. Words gain and lose their meaning at such a rate that when we place the generations in very thin strata each is found to have its own universe of discourse. No component of culture is more important than a common language. The peer group generates a language common to its members but alien to its members' families. To increase understanding in one realm is to decrease it in the other.

Profoundly alike, and much at odds, these institutions can hardly fail to collide. Although many of the same needs can be met by either, each one characteristically calls for strong and exclusive loyalty. They could be, but in our time seldom are, complementary. This was not always so. In most preliterate and peasant societies, age groups divided by gender were organized into many separate centers. Warriors, members of totemic and other religious groups, and sexually segregated, unmarried youths formed clubs, sodalities, and the like in which they regularly interacted with their age mates. None of this posed a serious threat to the family, with which it meshed in a tightly knit system of tribal and rural village life.

The family was preeminent while man was a hunter and food gatherer; it remained preeminent after the agricultural revolution reduced nomadism to a minimum. The rural family, engaged in agriculture and horticulture—at first for its own consumption of foodstuffs and much later for the sale of cash crops—was socially and economically self-contained to a degree almost unimaginable in our time. Outside military service, formal education, and politics (all of them dominated until recently by a small, upper-class, male elite), the sustained contact of age mates was negligible. It was urbanism in ancient and medieval times, and increasingly from then to now, that really paved the way to age-graded sociability. Cities were always somewhat different, but they were also demographically, if not culturally, insignificant. Only a small percentage of the total population lived in cities. A spectacular, worldwide shift from country to city living is still in process. It has not yet been completed even in Western Europe and North America where (except for England) countrymen far outnumbered city people until approximately 1850.

AGE GRADING

Formal education, institutionalized in academies, seminaries, colleges, and universities, did separate the scholar from his family and from other age-graded groups. It also provided him with a special culture, an organizational base and a vested interest in his age mates. Generational conflict inheres in this situation, as is apparent in the ancient Athenian Academy, in medieval universities, and in today's institutions of higher learning. A similar specter haunts all human groups that are sharply divided along chronological lines. Always present to some extent, the generation gap widened noticeably in the nineteenth century. Only in our time has it become a major phenomenon.

In the Past

Philippe Ariès in his monumental social history of family life demonstrates convincingly that medieval and Renaissance society did not recognize the categories of age grading that we so often take for granted. To make his point, Ariès ransacked records, diaries, memoirs, books of etiquette, and even more impressively, paintings, tapestries, sculptures, tombs, clothes, mortuary decorations, engravings and woodcuts. Save for some particularization by period and class, the picture Ariès discovered in all his source material is much the same. For instance:

> Medieval art until the twelfth century did not know childhood or did not attempt to portray it. It is hard to believe that this neglect was due to incompetence or incapacity; it seems more probable that there was no place for childhood in the medieval world. An Ottonian miniature of the twelfth century provides us with a striking example of the deformation which an artist at that time would inflict on children's bodies. The subject is the scene in the Gospels in which Jesus asks that little children be allowed to come to Him. The Latin text is clear: *parvuli*. Yet the miniaturist has grouped around Jesus what are obviously eight men, without any of the characteristics of childhood; they have simply been depicted on a smaller scale. In a French miniature of the late eleventh century the three children brought to life by St. Nicholas are also reduced to a smaller scale than the adults, without any other difference of expression or features.[1]

In Psalters of the time, painters often gave the naked figures of children the musculature of adults. In St. Louis's Bible, Ariès notes, "Isaac is shown sitting between his two wives, surrounded by some fifteen little men who come up to the level of the grown-ups' waists: these are their children."[2] Nor was this just a matter of aesthetic transposition; Ariès establishes that the medieval child, once past infancy, "was dressed just like the other men and women of his class."[3] Not until the sixteenth century, and then more for boys than for girls, do we come to an approximation of specialized childhood costumes. Art works, even calendar illustrations, show children and adolescents taking part in the great seasonal and traditional festivals on an equal footing with all other members of society. People of all ages and sizes joined in communal celebrations: "Whatever the role allotted to childhood and youth, primordial on May Day, incidental on Twelfth Night, it always followed a traditional pattern and corresponded to the roles of a collective game which mobilized the whole of society and brought all age groups together."[4]

From an economic standpoint, the child as diminutive adult—quarter-man, half-woman—was an heir, a potential worker, a laborer with less than full capacity. He applied himself to adult tasks with the expectation that physical growth and skill would go hand in hand. Step by step boys and girls proceeded to their socially ordained occupations. In adolescence they were full-grown adult workers. Under the guild system master craftsmen took apprentices into their workshops and households for stipulated periods. The guild system, like the instruction of squires and kings, meant "on the job training," with a youth in the midst of other youths and a number of adults. Basically, the setting, whether workshop or castle, was that of a family, an unselfconscious mixture of age groups.

Ariès makes it sufficiently clear that childhood was an idea the West had to discover or to rediscover. As a criterion for classification, segregation, and education, it is foreshadowed in the writings of Jean Jacques Rousseau and his followers. We are the heirs of men from Rousseau to Montessori and beyond who have supplied us with something more than a child-centered philosophy of education. That philosophy, when mixed with developmental psychology, has also fostered an entirely new way of looking at society. Sensitivity to chronological gradations opens the floodgates to a novel but insular super-segmentation of society.

In Modern Society

The modern approach to thinking about the "ages of man" adds, divides, and multiplies—but seldom subtracts—categories. Our life cycle is analyzed into smaller and smaller units. If Freud thought psychosexual development was decisive, he was also willing to settle for an anal-oral-genital progression. Freud's successors have infinitely complicated each of the three stages that psychoanalysis originally postulated. In an "epigenetic chart" on which much of his fame rests, Erik H. Erikson, a Freudian deeply influenced by anthropology and sociology, offers us the "Eight Ages of Man." Each of these ages turns on a conflict, beginning with the baby's basic trust or basic mistrust. Then *ad seriatim* come seven more antinomies: autonomy versus shame and doubt, initiative versus guilt, industry versus inferiority, identity versus role confusion, intimacy versus isolation, generativity versus stagnation, and ego integrity versus despair. (See Erikson's works for an explication of these terms.[5]) The implication of conflict and crisis at every age is apparent. But, just as Freud stressed the formative effect of early childhood training, so Erikson is best known for his announcement of "the adolescent identity crisis."

When he advanced that concept in 1950, students felt a shock of recognition. They are now, we would judge, more given to putting it, and him, down as passé.

At present, adolescence *as such* is segmented and obscured by the socially supported recognition of subteenagers, teenyboppers, nymphets, jocks, straights, and a legion of pre- or postpubertal freaks. Somewhere these categories fade into "youth," which, however, breaks down into: the twenties, the mid- and late twenties, and the problematic thirties—similarly subdivided. A bit later there are, by their own or other lights, the middle aged, viewed as younger or older or middle-aged, on their way to becoming golden-aged senior citizens, senile psychotics, young and old retirees, a reserve army of impoverished supernumeries, and so on and on. Not long ago anthropologists spoke of seven human categories: baby, boy, girl, adult male, adult female, old man, and old woman. Today, seventeen seems closer to the mark than seven, and no end to the proliferation is in sight.

Philosophers such as Rousseau certainly gave some impetus to this proliferation, but it was the machine, the mine, and the factory that hatched an age-graded culture. Steam-powered mines and industrial factories initially employed children from the ages of four or five to work the same twelve- or fourteen-hour day imposed on adults. Small children probably put in as many hours on the farm or in the old workshop, but there they were employed by parents or parent substitutes. If they were badly treated, and no doubt many or most were, it was assumed that parents had the right to do what they liked with their progeny, and that love harnessed to self-interest would mitigate the severity of exploitation. Before the Industrial Revolution, in principle, and often in practice, the articles of apprenticeship (a contract between parent and guild master) protected minors from excessively oppressive work. Afterward, neither in law nor in fact did the early factory system afford such restraints. Nothing rings so true in the writings of Karl Marx and Friedrich Engels (notably in the latter's *Conditions of the Working Class in England*) as their strictures on the inhuman treatment of adult and juvenile workers. Reports of the Factory Commission, the impressions of such an acute observer as Alexis de Tocqueville, and the not so fanciful fiction of Victorian novelists—above all Charles Dickens in *Hard Times* and *Oliver Twist*—yield an identical portrait of merciless exploitation.

As the Elizabethan poor laws were designed to compensate indigents and orphans, so now as urban misery mounted did indignation and compassion prompt a collective cry for legislative relief of industrial workers. The relief eventually arrived. One of its incidental consequences, at least in the world of work, was to make youth a special category of helpless and needful people. Factory law enacted from humanitarian concern successively raised and further divided the formal ages of youth. Much later, social legislation defined and redefined the categories of old age—inconclusively. Except when keyed to medical assistance, pensions, and retirement, categories of the aged remain vague and uncertain.

Out of the same nineteenth-century impulse came public schools and mandatory education. Politics obscured the link between factory and school legislation. We now see that, as children were legally removed from gainful employment in a society that required their parents to work away from home, "day care" became a problem. Schools, whatever else they may be, are important custodial institutions that help to solve this problem. With a capital-intensive economy that had once been labor-intensive, children were transformed from little workers into perennial students. High schools and then colleges absorbed more and more of them for longer and longer. Adolescence, invented by Rousseau at the same time that Watt invented the steam engine, stretched from puberty well into the twenties. And with it throughout the century, but at an accelerated pace in the last several decades, enforced schooling has continuously expanded. Trade unions were eager to eliminate low-paid, youthful competition—as they were that of Orientals, blacks, browns, and women. Employers were pleased to have the state subsidize vocational and professional education, and educators could only applaud the extension of their domain.

None of these factors, and least of all the surplus labor force, is ordinarily cited to explain the enormous growth of formal education. Its commonest rationale is "the complexity of modern life." And yet, as Frank Musgrove, an English sociologist, remarks in a recent treatise on the subject:

Life in a "civilized" society is in many ways simpler and easier to learn than life in a non-literate tribe. The structure of the language may well be simpler; social forms and institutions less elaborate; areas of knowledge and understanding which are considered essential qualifications for adult life in the "simpler" societies of little or no importance. The kinship system is a comparatively light burden on the growing child's understanding and memory: he has a more limited range of behavior and attitudes to learn towards different kinsmen. Though he may require some understanding of machines, he can get by—and usually does—with a negligible understanding of animal behavior, psychology and anatomy; in our secular society he will be accorded adult status without proven competence in the orthodox theology (although a detailed knowledge of the organization and events of contemporary sports may be virtually obligatory). He lives in a society which, though far more populous, may have a much simpler social hierarchy than those of many African and Oceanic tribesfolk.[6]

It is evidently not "increasing complexity" that has caused the age-integrated family to be replaced at so many levels by the age-graded, age-segregated institution of learning. Rather this process is part of a larger development, with which we will deal in later chapters, that has led to the formation of new, formal, secondary, bureaucratic institutions.

Regardless of its origins, the legal, educational, and institutional age grading of whole populations has had farflung consequences. Among those we cannot fail to note are new methods of stratification and classification, greater frequency and intensity of interaction with peers, and growing isolation from others. The overall shift into differential association based upon age made it possible for those in each chronological category to conceive of themselves as a group. Preschoolers of two or three, fourth graders, Pony Leaguers (as distinct from Little Leaguers), Cubs (as distinct from Boy and Girl Scouts), teenagers, or young moderns were encouraged to be conscious of their special "identity." Today the young are not only subdivided but similarly subdivide adults. Across the generation gap, young people as a whole may look like a different species to adults who are in turn so defined by young people—and each is also likely to detect chronological subspecies.

Not that this outlook is at all fixed or constant. Since our society is exceptionally dynamic, its age classifications keep changing. At any one time, different people of different ages use different age classifications. If to the five-year-old boy his teenaged sister is a woman, then to the middle-aged mother her twenty-five-year-old son is a boy.

YOUTH AND ADULTHOOD

In the 1960's, a number of campus revolutionaries considered age thirty the threshold to adulthood, and "Don't trust anyone over thirty" was an often quoted rubric. They were then in their late teens or early twenties. As many approached the age not to be trusted, it became an unsatisfactory ceiling. One of their number half-humorously proposed raising it to forty, but most youths, as they grew ever less youthful, simply abandoned the idea of a specific threshold between youth and adulthood. However, it could be restored even as we write. Historically of course, thirty is a fairly advanced age for anyone still not to be adult. Alexander the Great was a world ruler by the age of twenty-one; Joan of Arc raised the siege of Orléans at sixteen; Elizabeth I was queen of England and Ireland when she was twenty-five; and at nineteen William Pitt was a prime minister.

To lengthen and segment the category of youth is in part simply to acknowledge the general prolongation of life. Adults do not so readily vacate positions that their early death would in times past have conferred on youthful successors. With greater life expectancy the old cling more tenaciously to power even as they undertake to relinquish it. Recent history offers no better example than that of the Great Chinese Revolution. In the 1960's Mao

Tse-tung sponsored a bureaucratic purge that lasted three years. Thitherto irreproachable party functionaries were "therapeutically" taunted, beaten, humiliated, decapitated, or otherwise deposed by "better," *viz* younger, Marxist-Leninist–Maoists who however were soon superseded once again by their "older and wiser" predecessors. The gerontocracy remained intact.

In economically developed societies, affluence itself delays the age at which youth begins to do adult work. So it comes to pass that the person who has matured biologically is still socially and economically immature. He is inexperienced in the performance of adult roles that his forefathers would already have assumed at his age. It is possible to make too much of this situation. Some sociologists declare that friction between generations is nothing more than a role conflict. They reason that the physiological adult when treated as an infant naturally rebels against his elders. He is then said to crave the pleasures of adulthood without its responsibilities. The situation seems to us to be much more complicated than that. We will consider it in a subsequent chapter.

YOUTH CULTURE

Here it is perhaps enough to suggest that the youth culture that surfaced some years ago, say at the University of California in 1964, did indeed provide an operational definition of youth and adulthood. Mario Savio spoke for campus rebels at large when he proclaimed that it was wrong to trust anyone over the age of thirty. Whatever Savio had in mind, his cut-off point *is* meaningful for the reason that adulthood is most definitively achieved when a young person no longer needs financial assistance from his parents. It is fully realized when he supplies such assistance to his parents and to his children. The provision of financial aid symbolizes a certain measure of self-sufficiency and social responsibility. The recipients of aid are typically compelled to be subservient. And they are obliged to accept advice. Nothing is more conducive to the emergence of resentment. Providers, on the other hand, are encouraged to be authoritarian, and if they feel resentful it is classically because their dependents defy or disobey them. Insofar as financial independence is a good indicator of the beginning of adulthood, late entry into the labor force severely retards it. Children who support their parents effect a role reversal that they themselves will experience at an even earlier age.

Age grades created by administrators or institutions isolate and intensify the social interaction of peers. This kind of stratification sets the stage for age-graded cultures and subcultures. Beyond the classroom with its chronological subculture are nationally and even internationally age-graded subcultures with jokes, songs, poems, and games exclusive to them. Teenage culture is the most widely publicized case in point, but by now preschool culture may be equally important. The world of "Sesame Street" and "Captain Kangaroo," of TV cartoons and commercials is as real as that of slightly older children who consume other fare that the media make just for them. High-school and campus cultures break down into subcultures. Just so, we find *inter alia*, post-college cultures of the young unmarried and the chic, of retirees drawn together by the tunes of Mitch Miller or Lawrence Welk, that is, the tunes of their youth. The young, when not nostalgic for a past they never knew, reject these tunes. They develop songs and sounds of their own, the better to be "with it," "in," and "now." Contemporary creations of youth culture to be sure include new lyric or rhythmic treatment of old music. That new treatment, however, is so distinctive as to repel most elders and to stamp it with a special style. This style suffices to identify even old music with youthful performers, purveyors, and enthusiasts.

Relation to the Mass Media

Such evidence suggests that youth culture, like so much else that is age-graded in our society, bears a complex relation to the mass media. While some of that culture may be viewed as a reaction to the media, a great deal of it is derived from the media. This point needs elaboration. . . . For the present, let us simply note that age grading has been steeply accentuated in mass culture. Disk jockeys, for example, disseminate youth music, pop, rock, blues, and bubblegum; television producers and other impresarios assemble musical combos, employ composers, arrange festivals, sponsor new groups, and select those "artists" they wish to record, market, and enrich. A similar flurry of activity surrounds every age group.

Supporters, promoters, and packagers of chronological culture need not belong to the same age group as those who perform, consume, listen, or watch. In this sense, age-graded culture is, so to speak, for the people (at whom it is aimed) but not by the people or of the people. Hence at one time such performers as Bob Hope, Bing Crosby, Frank Sinatra, and Liberace appealed to a generation different from their own. In some cases, pop culture emerges in one age group and is then appropriated by media men in another age group—who restore and disseminate it more thoroughly to the original group. The Beatles in their first incarnation seemed to embody a youth-centered rock 'n' roll style. Spectacular success led not only to their personal cooptation and transmutation by the mass media but to the cooptation and transmutation of their style. Multiple diffusion of that style through the mass media brought Beatlemania to a greatly enlarged audience. So for instance, the Music Corporation of America, a packaging outfit, hired a Beatle-style ensemble called The Monkees, saw to it that material was written for them by their elders, and that songs, programs, and promotion were duly provided.

Imitation followed imitation, each one projecting a Beatle-like image through the media. Some specimens of age-graded culture emanate spontaneously from within an age group, while others are manufactured and packaged in imitation of successful innovation, usually in the mass media by *older* agents of the mass media. But whatever its origins, all age-graded culture depends on the acceptance of its content by a rather narrow age group. This group comprises its essential audience or its basic constituency.

The interplay between age of sponsor or creator of age-graded culture and age of audience suggests several interesting possibilities. Pervading all age groups is a consciousness of kind that separates as it integrates audiences. Their self–consciousness is sealed in part by hostility to other age groups whose subcultures they sharply differentiate from their own.

Four Types

It is possible to look at youth culture by dividing it into pro-adult cultures and anti-adult cultures, or from another angle, into cultures sponsored by adults and cultures not sponsored by adults. With these as our variables, we can postulate four types of youth culture:

Attitude toward Adult Establishment

SPONSORED BY	PRO	ANTI
Adult	1	2
Youth	3	4

1. Adult-sponsored, pro-adult-establishment youth culture
2. Adult-sponsored, anti-adult-establishment youth culture
3. Youth-sponsored, pro-adult-establishment youth culture
4. Youth-sponsored, anti-adult-establishment youth culture

Type 1—adult-sponsored, pro-adult-establishment youth culture—seems so obvious that it is all but overlooked by most observers. Yet it is certainly the oldest and commonest type of youth culture involving the largest number of participants. It includes large organizations like the 4-H Clubs, the Girl Scouts and the Boy Scouts of America, as well as the Future Farmers of America, juvenile branches of every religious denomination and every political party, most extracurricular school clubs, the Little League, the Pony League, the Police Athletic League, sororities, fraternities, and summer camps. These organizations are financed and sustained by adults who rely heavily on printed and electronic media. They publish and fill the pages of *Scholastic Magazine* in all its many age-graded versions, of *American Boy, Seventeen, Mademoiselle, Charm*, and sectarian periodicals of every description. Theirs is a huge market in books, pamphlets, and periodicals aimed at every segment of the youth population. It is enhanced by the radio, record, and TV industries from within which adults manufacture material for their juniors that is not considered a threat to the status quo.

Type 4—youth-sponsored, anti-adult-establishment youth culture—is meant to be a threat, and a subversive or revolutionary threat at that. Its avatars have recently ranged from the narrowly political Maoists, Panthers (Black and White), Students for a Democratic Society, Weathermen and Weatherwomen, on campuses or underground, to hippies, yippies, runaways, communards and other residents of "collectives," street people (who for a moment in the sixties were "flower children"), aficionados of pop art, and psychedelic freaks who equate pot, acid, speed, and scag with the square, nicotine-and-alcohol culture of conventional society. Insofar as lower-class delinquent boys belong to the subculture of gangs described by Albert K. Cohen,[7] they also partake of Type 4 youth culture. The delinquency and youth crime of these boys and the girls who sometimes accompany them are characterized by "non-ulitarianism, negativism and maliciousness." In their own way, they too turn the adult middle-class code inside out and upside down. Such gangs are not to be confused with those that have such "rational" aims as theft for profit. The illicit traffic in forbidden goods and services is a bridge, not a gap, between the generations. Organized elements in the adult underworld and in the adult upperworld welcome old-fashioned delinquents to their ranks. For inclusion among those who personify Type 4 youth culture, we have the new-fashioned delinquents in mind.

Type 2 is adult-sponsored, anti-adult-establishment youth culture. Here we find an assortment of political offspring spawned by the Communist party, the Socialist Workers party, the Progressive Labor party. Sometimes these movements are homegrown; occasionally they enjoy the support of foreign governments. The Jewish Defense League, a militant, lower-class Jewish youth movement with adult sponsorship is an embarrassment not just to the middle-class Jewish establishment but apparently to the government of Israel as well. By contrast, pro-Arab youth movements on the American campus originate in organizations created by the Arab League. And Fidelista youth movements in the United States receive direct support from the Cuban government: *Venceremos* was both the slogan and the name assigned to Castroite students who, in defiance of their own government, made annual pilgrimages to Cuba. There they helped harvest sugarcane—to the consternation of authorities in this country and the delight of authorities in Cuba.

The young lead the young, and some continue to lead after they themselves have ceased to be young. In the 1960s a number of New Left leaders already in their late twenties came to prominence on American campuses as nonstudent firebrands. Latin America has its *cronicos*, or perennial students, who dabble in academic studies and grow gray while leading, politicizing, and indoctrinating one generation of matriculants after another. On or off the campus, men of this sort remain youth leaders by doggedly attaching themselves to youth movements. They are joined by other adults who feel rejuvenated in the effervescence of youth movements. Youth regained by association can at the same time signify redemption from the sin of growing up or growing old. Youth movements are irresistible to aging conformists touched by an unwonted excitement, by proximity to an "in" thing, to an ephemeral wave of the future. For a while, it is modish, chic, sophisticated, and possible, by identification and recognition, to be young once again. With age, experience, know-how, and intellectual ascendancy, such adults become youth leaders. They function as theorists, philosophers, lawyers, advisers, and planners. If they do but share the political premises of their comrades, they will often not be disqualified by reason of age. Timothy Leary and Alan Ginsberg in early or advanced middle age were perfectly acceptable gurus to young rebels. Nor, when their taste is more for radical politics than for transcendental meditation, do they spurn such oracular septuagenarians as Herbert Marcuse or octogenarians as Mao Tse-tung.

We have already alluded to certain mass media personalities, disk jockeys, impresarios, music programers, and packagers in their capacity as leaders, supporters, and purveyors of antiestablishment pop art forms. They are indispensable to one subdivision of Type 2 youth culture. So are those elders in partly or wholly organized criminal syndicates who attract susceptible youth to their antiestablishment activities.

Type 3—youth-sponsored, pro-adult-establishment youth culture—is most uncommon. If Gray Panthers attempt to organize aged people, they welcome their juniors as Panther Cubs, and not vice versa. The young who replicate adult recreational activity—card playing, dancing, bowling, swimming, and the like—do so precisely in a non-age-graded spirit.

Socialization to the Adult World

Does the virtual nonexistence of a separate Type 3 culture mean that youth has no resources to lend the adult establishment? Does youth acting on its own necessarily oppose adult culture? We think not. More probably, when youth affirms the adult society, it uses channels of self-expression no different from those sponsored and supported by adults. These educational, occupational, recreational, symbolic, and artistic channels are shared. They cut a wide swath across whole generations. And the vast majority of youth accept adult-controlled institutions. This is true in part because these institutions, however enervated, are still operating with a semblance of legitimacy. More to the point, adulthood, with its manifold burdens and responsibilities, is nearly ineluctable. Few indeed are the adolescents who can indefinitely postpone the assumption of adult roles. The remorselessness of biological and social change severely limits the roles youth can play. If adulthood is operationally determined by the balance of payments between parents and progeny, then when parents age and die, progeny cease to be children—the more so when they themselves become parents. Given at eighteen the franchise, the prospect of conscription, legal liability, permission to drink spirituous liquids and to buy contraceptive devices, even an adolescent reluctant to grow up is usually forced to think about it. Sensing the push that society gives him he more and more rehearses adult roles. His felt and perhaps acute reaction to the adult establishment may be negative, but even that reaction is most likely to be experienced in at least quasi-adult terms. Only some of the very rich can perpetuate a favorable balance of payments, and so forever delay their entry into the adult world. A small number of middle-class youngsters who drop out of society stay out of it for good. They are able to make a clean break by living at marginal economic levels and avoiding all but superficial contact with the square world. The price of such prolonged or perpetual youth, and the explanation for its rarity, is a sharp restriction of wants and needs. Otherwise, it is still the case that to remain a youth is to remain dependent upon others. For the most part, youthful independence is a delusion, if not a contradiction in terms. And this is the case no matter how we view it: economically, socially, or psychologically.

It should be clear from this analysis that not all youth culture is antiestablishment or antiadult. Nevertheless, much age-segregated culture, peer-group bearers and all, does stand in active opposition to the age-integrated family. Wherever it gains the upper hand we are in deep crisis. If the Western family was a major producer of "individuals," it is individuals who at present are most in jeopardy.

The cultural machinery that makes a human being always creaks a bit. Under stress it may break down completely. Between inevitable imperfections and total collapse there are intermediate states. An educated guess would place contemporary man in one of those states. Social forces that once converged on the individual in a family context now shoot off in different directions. The result is a fragmentation of personality. As Erich Kahler has pointed out, the word *atom* originally meant an indivisible object. In translating *atom* from Greek to Latin, Cicero used the word *individual*. Midway through the twentieth century, as Kahler puts it, man split the previously indivisible physical atom—and the human atom as well.[8] Age-centered peer groups in combat with family-centered cultures do much to foster the breeding of fragmented individuals.

THE FAMILY AND AGE-GRADED CULTURES

Western families used to be the principal source of youthful identification with elders through whom they absorbed assorted values and attitudes that ideally led to firmly internalized superegos—and to autonomy or individuality. So conceived, the individual would be more than an extension of the family. He would so fully internalize norms, and they would so strengthen him, that he could transcend the family from which they were transmitted. With maturation, he would no longer need a family model for his standards. Those standards would be incorporated in his own identity, equipping him with a measure of independence from the very same family that had so largely formed him, and fortifying his consciousness with the capacity to resist or oppose all other social groups no matter what rewards and sanctions they had to offer. In transcending the family one became an individual responding to one's own values and standards. Such an individual would be so much in possession of his own superego that its breach would occasion anxiety and guilt rather than shame or loss of face with others.

The widely heralded identity crisis of our time can be traced most substantially to the family's debilitation. Weak families do not produce individuals in the classic sense described above. They are not favorable to identification with or liberation from parents and other adults. Weak families produce neither a collective nor a personal superego and are not likely to foster a secure sense of self.

LARGE-SCALE ORGANIZATION AND AGE-GRADED CULTURES

Why the debilitation? Large-scale organizations, so-called secondary groups, impersonal institutions, surely have much to do with it. They project an alternative source of limited, segmental, and rational values that, however, leave the diffuse and emotional side of man unsatisfied. The incorporation of such values is bound to produce a certain lopsidedness, matched by the incorporation of peer-group values with their complementary stress on nonrational values. We suspect that peer groups offer more serious competition to the family than secondary groups. Peer groups promise exactly those rewards that the family is uniquely able to provide.

This is not to suggest that the peer group is just a psychological substitute for the family. Despite their structural similarities, there is a decisive difference between them. If the family in good working order ultimately rears individuals who transcend it, the peer group in equally good working order moves to no such end. Its norms are not meant to be deeply internalized. Nor are they designed to issue in self-judgment. The cultivation of individuality is not their objective. On the contrary, they stand in collective judgment of behavior controlled by group sanctions set in accordance with group standards. From first to last, they are sustained by joint acceptance and rejection. Irrespective of how volatile it may be, the peer group demands conformity. This cannot be said of the family that optimally imbues an individual with his own ethic. The ideal family points to inner-direction, the ideal peer group to other-direction.

Let us recapitulate and advance a bit. It is obvious that the growth of industrialism and urbanism gives rise to secondary institutions and that they undermine the family. A diminished superego and a doubtful identity followed from the shrunken family that in turn was partially replaced by secondary groups. Large, paternalistic, corporate bodies hatched Organization Men. Many found that their lives were instrumentalized. Lacking the warmth and spontaneity of a family system that could not be restored and unhappy about the corporate solution that swallowed them up, they were trapped in a double bind. Soon it was to be a triple bind.

When men half-consciously seek but do not find satisfaction in their private or their public roles, when family and job leave them deeply dissatisfied, they can then turn to peer groups. Large-scale urban and industrial society generates peer groups, especially those of the age-graded variety. And modern mass media circulate much of the culture for those groups. With them come a new focus of interests, amiable companions, a readymade hierarchy of likes and dislikes, and some hope of personal gratification. That hope is dashed for the socialized individual who is unwilling to surrender his personal autonomy or who, having yielded it, comes to regret his sacrifice. Peer groups turn out to be a mixed bag.

To the extent that youth peer groups are arrayed against the family and the establishment, they convey a feeling of liberation from the straight world inhabited by parents and other adults. But participation in these groups also involves a sacrifice. Often enough it involves submission to the peers and their tyranny. To the extent that peer groups are arrayed against corporate, secondary, educational and economic organizations—within which so much of life must currently be lived—they offer an alternative to segmental satisfaction. Academic recognition and incremental income follow from compliance with rules in a task imposed from above. They are rewards earned in a formal, bureaucratic environment whose antithesis is the peer group with its own range of rewards. Forsaking one, to be liberated from its constricted atmosphere, and then embracing the other with equal fervor is not to free oneself. Exchanging one primary group for another (peer group for family) is qualitatively no different from exchanging a secondary group (school or work) for a primary group (the peer group.) One master merely replaces his predecessor.

Suggested Readings

Philippe Ariès, *Centuries of Childhood: A Social History of Family Life.* Translated by Robert Baldick, New York: Alfred A. Knopf and Random House, Vintage Books, 1962. The seminal theory of the modern concepts of childhood and age-grading as new developments in the last four centuries, through a study of the "silent history" of dress, games, art, language, education.

Monica Wilson. *Good Company: A Study of Nyakyusa Age-Villages*. Boston: Beacon Press, 1963. An African culture in which age grading and its accompanying values are shown to be fundamental to that particular form of social organization.

August B. Hollingshead. *Elmtown's Youth*. New York: John Wiley & Sons, 1949. Cliques and class in the midwestern Corn Belt. Adolescent behavior is shown to be functionally related to class position of families.

Kingsley Davis. "The Sociology of Parent-Youth Conflict." *American Sociological Review* 5 (1940): 523–35. An early and still cogent sociological analysis of *"the generation gap"* as a universal area of social conflict.

Albert K. Cohen, *Delinquent Boys: The Culture of the Gang*. New York: Free Press, 1955. The classic study of the peer group as antisocial because it creates and sustains its own value system.

Harry Silverstein, ed. *The Sociology of Youth: Evolution and Revolution*. New York: Macmillan Publishing Co., 1973. An anthology of current work that reflects an increasing interest in the variety of behavior among today's young people.

David Riesman with Nathan Glazer and Reuel Denney. *The Lonely Crowd: A Study of the Changing American Character*. Abr. ed. New Haven, Conn.: Yale University Press, 1969. The famous debut of "other-direction" as an analytic concept. Still important for an understanding of pressures toward modern peer group proliferation.

Eda LeShan. *The Wonderful Crisis of Middle Age*. New York: David McKay Co., 1973; Warner Paperback Library, 1974. A current example of upbeat "how to" aimed at the "self-actualization" of an adult age-graded outgroup.

Notes

1. Philippe Ariès, *Centuries of Childhood* (New York: Alfred A. Knopf, 1962), p. 33.

2. Ibid.

3. Ibid., p. 50.

4. Ibid., p. 79.

5. Especially *Childhood and Society*, 2d ed. (New York: W.W. Norton & Co., 1963), pp. 247–74.

6. Frank Musgrove, *Youth and the Social Order* (Bloomington: Indiana University Press, 1965), p.27.

7. Albert K. Cohen, *Delinquent Boys: The Culture of the Gang* (Glencoe, Ill.: Free Press, 1955).

8. Erich Kahler, *The Tower and the Abyss* (New York: George Braziller, 1957), p. 4.

Finding and keeping friends of the same sex is very common in our society, but so is what Gail Sheehy calls "the urge to merge." She is referring, of course, to the desire to have a loving partner. As Sheehy shows, much of our early socialization is taken up with preparing individuals to assume marital roles, to be attentive, nurturing wives and responsible, hardworking husbands.

Focusing mainly on the perspectives and positions of women, Sheehy's essay echoes some of the ideas expressed in Florence Howe's article, "Sexual Stereotypes Start Early," presented in Part One.

As you read Sheehy's description and analysis, think about what is commonly called the double standard which permitted men far more freedom than women. Also note, as she does, the new morality which has altered some of our older "conventional wisdoms."

The Urge To Merge

GAIL SHEEHY

Until recently, seeking has been done primarily by boys and merging by girls. Girls could seek scholarship so long as it didn't interfere with popularity. It was fine to take a summer job, but not to embark on a serious career. They could train their talents in dance lessons, drama clubs, piano recitals, church choirs, any of which would suit them well for a lifetime of pleasing. Unless— and this apprehension lurked always in the back of the mind—they turned out to be gifted. For then they would be forced to make a painful choice: either marriage or mastery of their art. Most of them gave up the lessons.

Boys learn basic skills of teamwork and competition on the sports field, skills that later serve them well in business and political organizations. They are also introduced to buddyism in the locker room. In activities approved for girls, there has been little practice with competing and even less opportunity for comradeship. Girls rarely found themselves in situations comparable to a football game or military service, in which the adventure involved great-enough risk to demand interdependency. Sharing an apartment with a roommate was mild by comparison and usually perpetuated the competition for boyfriends.

ALL YOU NEED IS LOVE

The mass cult of songs, soaps, poems, pulp, flicks, scents, ads, art and miscellaneous hype extols LOVE as all a girl needs. This has a far broader impact than the most exquisite thinking of any social scientist, for instance Abraham Maslow.[1]

In his "hierarchy of needs" theory, love and belongingness follow right after food and shelter and safety. Yet there are two more rungs beyond love on the ladder of human needs. One is *esteem*, the desire for achievement, mastery, competence, and confidence, as well as for the respect and recognition of others. Beyond that is the need for eventual *self-actualization*.

Most theorists agree that more than anything else, it is successful work experience that helps a young person resolve the conflicts of dependency and establish an independent identity.[2] But while young men have been encouraged to make the search for a lifework their first priority, young women have been expected to be content with, and adjust to, a sense of identity bootlegged from their sex role. The message has been: You are who you marry and who you mother.

True, alternate models for girls now enliven children's books, magazines, the TV screen, even congressional hearings. But in the excitement over new heroines, it is easy to overlook one fact, as simple as its power is stunning: The very first image every girl identifies with, her model at the earliest and most penetrating stage of development, is mother—a woman who unmistakably had a child.

How does a young woman pull loose from her phantom parent and establish her own identity if the only occupation fully endorsed for her is to become her mother in her own married household? The answer is, of course, that most women up to recent times did not pull loose.

It was barely conceivable, before the 1960s, that a girl child could embark on Being Somebody before her father has escorted her to the altar under a fingertip illusion veil. The door to adulthood would be magically unlocked by wedlock, a piece of doublethink endlessly celebrated. This form will persist as the most favored route to female identity: the *"complete me" marriage*.

But if only mothers and fathers and society push young women into wedlock, how do we explain all the daughters of today's wiser parents who warn them to wait, but to no avail? An even subtler coercion works on young women: their own inner timidity.* They *want* to believe that a man will com-

---

*A distinction is intended between fear—of real and observable dangers (i.e., the streets are icy; is it safe to drive the car?)—and inner timidity, which I have used to mean the inner picture one has of a situation and the meaning one assigns to it.

plete them and keep them safe. Marriage is a half step, a way to leave home without losing home. Somehow a substitute world is going to materialize spontaneously out there, a playhouse, important friends, excitement. What such a marriage brings instead is a foreclosure of identity. The commitment to being a wife is made before the individual is allowed, or allows herself, to struggle with and select from the possible life choices. The pull is back toward safety and sameness, a highly seductive pull in the late teens and early twenties.

The problem has been that most young women wouldn't dare or weren't allowed to have an identity crisis. And so they never quite grew up.

THE PIGGYBACK PRINCIPLE

Throughout the film *American Graffiti,* the high school hero wavers about pulling away from his steady girl and the whole comfortable universe as he knows it to depart for college 2,000 miles away. The drag and thrust is punishing. The boy hesitates, falls back into the arms of his sweetheart; they cling. Throbbing through the soundtrack is a wishful theme song that repeats the romantic logic:

Only you make this change in me,
For it's true, you are my destinee. ©

The longing to merge with a lover is perfectly natural at this stage (as is the impetus, previously described, to seek a cause greater than oneself and people and ideas to put one's faith in). But particularly for young women, the natural impulse has grown into a full-blown assumption.

The assumption is: we can piggyback our development by attaching ourselves to a Stronger One.

Serena was a small-town girl who went away to college in Champaign, Illinois. She wanted to believe in the piggyback principle, too. How she craved in the formlessness of freshman year to have her hometown Jim beside her. Spinning through the library carrels, through the sex maze and value systems of people from practically everywhere, Serena was no longer the big-fish high school leader. She was one of 36,000 minnows swept along in the tides of a Big Ten university. "I desperately wanted somebody there to understand what I was going through."

Jim, apparently the strong, detached one, wrote back from his own distant university, "You can't keep hanging on to me."

Serena had a strong advantage over girls who are encouraged to lean. She was the eldest daughter, and firstborn daughters are often brought up with privileges and expectations no different from a son's. Their fathers are likely to emphasize abilities rather than sex role, to teach them sports, and to encourage them to seek excellence. They are given chores and often expected to earn their own way, as Serena was. Frequently, fathers seem to be seeking in a firstborn daughter the comradeship they can't have with their wives because their wives are always starting dinner. A phenomenon observed in some of the biographies I collected was also noted in a University of Michigan study of successful men. While their wives were definitely expected to be noncompetitive and nonachieving, the men took pride in a competitively successful daughter. She was often the favorite because she, unlike a son, could reflect well on her father without becoming a rival.[3]

The outstanding event of Serena's freshman year was this: all turned out in businesslike brown, even to the matched stockings and executive-height heels, Serena marched into the school newspaper to impress the editor. He, in his Bolshevik jeans, laughed but gave her the job. She was good at it, very good. The longing for Jim subsided (but not much). She wrote him fourteen-foot-long letters on the wire service rolls.

Love at 18 is largely an attempt to find out who we are by listening to our own echo in the words of another. To hear how special and wonderful we are is endlessly enthralling. That's why young lovers can talk the night away or write fourteen-foot-letters yet never seem to come to the end of a sentence.

Then the snapback. Home from the first year's stretching at college to the old ties of high school: the Indian summer of childhood.

"When Jim and I got back together that summer, we were suddenly bumping into each other, not fitting in." They slept together for the first time, but sex would not cement the gap between them. Serena and Jim spared themselves falling victims to the Piggyback Principle. The chafe of their uneven growth was too evident.

At a new coffeehouse in town, for instance: "Why can't you wear lower heels?" Jim was shorter than Serena, a discrepancy he had never mentioned before. Now he seemed determined to cut her down to size.

"I'm already in flats."

Like all the rest of their friends, Jim hadn't the first inkling of what he wanted to do. Serena was the exception; she knew. When she bounded across the coffeehouse to interview the manager, Jim blew up.

"Why do you have to look for a story on a date with me?"

"But I'm"—hateful words, envied identity—"a newspaper reporter."

Jim began taking an interest in another girl. He clearly resented the conversion of Serena from hanger-on to entity, and one who dared to match him intellectually.

"It was suddenly a snapping period," she says. "The puzzle pieces had all reshaped themselves, and we didn't fit together anymore. I decided that we both needed a lot more room."

And with more room, both of them flourished. From the vantage point of her mid-twenties, Serena can say, "Jim was probably the first person who helped me to grow up.'' She also acknowledges that every young girl she knows tried to smother her first love in possessiveness. Oh, what tears and rejection await the girl who imbues her first delicate match with fantasies of permanence, expecting that he at this gelatinous stage will fit with her in a finished puzzle for all the days. Serena was fortunate.

JAILBREAK MARRIAGE

Although the most commonplace reason women marry young is to "complete" themselves, a good many spirited young women gave another reason: "I did it to get away from my parents." Particularly for girls whose educations and privileges are limited a *jailbreak marriage* is the usual thing. What might appear to be an act of rebellion usually turns out to be a transfer of dependence.

A lifer: that is how it felt to be Simone at 17, how it often feels for girls in authoritarian homes. The last of six children, she was caught in the nest vacated by the others and expected to "keep the family together." Simone was the last domain where her mother could play out the maternal role and where her father could exercise full control. That meant good-bye to the university scholarship.

Although the family was not altogether poor, Simone has tried to make a point of her independence by earning her own money since the age of 14. Now she thrust out her bankbook. Would two thousand dollars in savings buy her freedom?

"We want you home until you're 21."

Work, her father insisted. But the job she got was another closed gate. It was in the knitting machine firm where her father worked, an extension of his control. Simone knuckled under for a year until she met Franz. A zero. An egocentric Hungarian of pointless aristocracy, a man for whom she had total disregard. Except for one attraction. He asked her to marry him. Franz would be the getaway vehicle in her jailbreak marriage scheme: "I decided the best way to get out was to get married and divorce him a year later. That was my whole program."

Anatomy, uncontrolled, sabotaged her program. Nine months after the honeymoon, Simone was a mother. Resigning herself, she was pregnant with her second child at 20.

One day, her husband called with the news, the marker event to blast her out of the drift. His firm had offered him a job in New York City.

"Then and there, I decided that before the month was out I would have the baby, find a lawyer, and start divorce proceedings. "The next five years were like twenty. It took every particle of her will and patience to defeat Franz, who wouldn't hear of a separation, and to ignore the ostracism of her family.

At the age of 25, on the seventh anniversary of her jailbreak marriage (revealed too late as just another form of entrapment), Simone finally escaped her parents. Describing the day of her decree, the divorcée sounds like so many women whose identity was foreclosed by marriage: "It was like having ten tons of chains removed from my mind, my body—the most exhilarating day of my life."

OPENINGS

Springing up from the multiple attitude revolutions in the last decade, a lively tolerance for diversity now supports more openings: pilgrimages and communes as a temporary way of life, living together, staying single, becoming a bachelor mother or remaining a childless couple, experimenting with bisexuality or homosexuality. People who can prolong their schooling or who qualify for tempting career apprenticeships are marrying later, having children later, having fewer children, or planning none at all.

Barbara, now 31 and still single, is of the first generation of women to be more relaxed about making such departures from the old mold. She also had five willful aunts and a family history that supported the idea of eccentricity. Although her mother wanted Barbara to be "gorgeous" and marry rich, her father took pleasure in explaining complicated information to the precocious little girl. "I think he wanted me to be a kid, and stay that way as long as possible and never ask him for money."

Very early on, Barbara had an important presentiment: "The great thing about being a kid is that you have a long apprenticeship—if you'll take the trouble to put yourself through it." She began at 18 teaching herself to write fiction. Her stories were terrible, naturally, but that bothered her not in the least. Craft is everything, she had been told by an older friend who was a writer, and once she got craft down, everything else would follow.

Her ideas about what she didn't want to be could not have been stronger. "I wasn't going to end up like the kids I knew in the suburbs, who were spoiled and dumb and whose parents' values were idiotic. I had no interest in being a normal, average kid." But she was typically foggy on how to go about getting what she wanted, "which was, I suppose, an apartment and a job."

And so she made the break with her family, at 19, by dropping out of college and running off with an older man. "I didn't want to live with him particularly, although I tried to talk myself into it, but I knew I didn't have any choice. I had no money, no job, no skills, nothing. To get those things through the normal channels, you go to college for four years. I just didn't see that for me." Of course, she did have a choice. What she saw was an older man who would be the vehicle to transport her into the adult world; once there, she broke off with this transitional figure and before the year was out, found her first official apartment, roommate, and job. "I got off pretty clean, though to this day I don't feel terribly honorable about it."

By the time Barbara was 25, she knew her craft and knew what was publishable. She had returned to school and was just now finishing up. She took a summer job as an office temporary and wrote up a storm. That fall, her first story was purchased by *The New Yorker*. Deliriously happy, she ran off with another man, thinking "this was a blazing love," and hit ground rather hard. At 29, she began to bring to her love life some of the discipline that had always characterized her writing life. She had met a wonderful man. "I was very glad I took a year to get to know him, a year in which my first book appeared and I fell in love." At present, Barbara and her beau are about to throw their possessions together. What she is feeling is terror—"I don't know if I'm fit to live with; who knows?"—but for the first time, she feels her emotional life is grounded.

For all her initiative and stick-to-itiveness, Barbara was not without ambivalence in her merging instincts. All along she wondered, "Why couldn't I have been the sort of person who just settles down and doesn't give anyone a moment's trouble, meaning, have a baby and the whole thing. I didn't want it. But I felt that I should have. In my happiest moments, I wouldn't have traded my life for anybody's. In my most unhappy moments, I would say, 'Well, it's clear that you're just nuts and no one will ever have you.' But I was always very smart, cold, clear, and uncomplicated about my own work. I love to write. I want to have everything. And I don't see why I can't."

Considerable support among young people of Barbara's generation has shifted away from being locked in and toward the pattern she chose. A person may keep his or her options open and move from one tentative commitment to another, actively seeking people, ideas, and some endeavor to believe in but maintaining a transient status.

Yet even today, sociologists report that many women between the ages of 18 and 24 live as if suspended. They can't bring themselves to make career commitments, or any extended plan for that matter, until they know whom they are going to marry.[4] And although today there are many trial marriages, as Gary Wills says, there is no such thing as a trial child.

THE COMPLETE-ME CHILD

When it becomes imperative in the late teens to prove that one can *do* something, make something work on one's own, the easiest place for a young woman to turn is to her uterus. The occupation of baby maker is always available. It gives her a clear identity. Motherhood may be a very satisfying occupation, but it is also one behind which all those fears about not measuring up in the outside world can be hidden.

Contemporary theories advanced to explain the desire of women to use their anatomy range from Erikson's controversial concept of a woman's "inner space" (a perpetual vacuum asserting her emptiness until it be filled) to a more varied list of reasons proposed by Edward H. Pohlman in *Psychology of Birth Planning*. A woman may wish through having a baby to prove her competency, to assert her gender, to compete with her mother, to ensnare a husband, to gain attention, to fill up her time, to punish herself or others, to become immortal.[5] Striking by its absence from this list is the universal wish to attach to another.

Great leaps of the last fifteen years in technology and ideology have given us the brand new "contracepted women" and a profound feminism, followed by antimotherhood books and even antifertility rites. The revolt against automatic motherhood has spread to all classes. In a 1973 survey by Daniel Yankelovich, only 35 percent of college women and an astoundingly low 50 percent of noncollege women agreed to the proposition that "having children is a very important value." How much of this is their heads talking? Career counselors say that young women students today may *know* that motherhood is no longer a lifetime career, but they still cannot feel that way about it.

The thrall of motherhood has subsided very little among girls from 15–19. The birthrate plummeted by one-third in the 1960s for girls between 20 and 24. Yet married teenage girls continued to turn out babies at an amazing and almost consistent rate over the same period. And nearly half the brides in this age group are rushed to the altar by shotgun.[6]

Girls from poor families aren't the only ones preoccupied with their reproductive powers, although for them the compulsion is all the more poignant for the literal lack of anything else to do with themselves. Once they leave high school, there is no job, no further schooling, no higher goal even suggested within their milieu than to carry a nice boy's child, preferably their husband's.

But things are definitely changing. After tonsillectomy, abortion is now the second most frequently performed operation in this country.

COMPULSORY GRAFFITI

What now is the story for Ms. Average American Girl? She is likely to be graduated from high school but not from college. She will find a tentative job, become a wife at the age of 21, and exit from the work world shortly thereafter to start a family. She will remain in this domestic setting until her mid-thirties. What girls aren't told is the plot of the second half of their lives.

The average American woman is likely to return to work at 35 when her last child enters school. She can then look forward to a career, or more probably clerk-work, for the next *quarter of a century*.[7] This paragraph should be written on the walls of the girls' washrooms in every high school in America.

Boys have the urge to merge, too. For almost every female identity foreclosed by early marriage and maternity, there is likely to be a young man tied into an occupational slot before he has had time to experiment with his latent talents. A study of 5,000 high school graduates found that those who went right to work or into full-time homemaking were more constricted, had less intellectual curiosity, and less interest in new experiences.[8]

At least temporarily, such young people surrender the battle to invent themselves and take on instead the form proffered by father, mother, teacher, religious leader, or the group. They find themselves in the position I describe as locked in. (This correlates with the "identity-foreclosed" status defined by Marcia.) Understandably, one of the most popular routes out of the locked-in position is divorce. Teen-age marriages are nearly twice as likely to end in dissolution as contracts made at later ages.[9]

THE COLLEGE WOMAN

Although it appeared the best chance to seek was to be had by those with advanced educations, that liberalized notion backfired on many college women. What a shock it was when the early instructions to be as bright and industrious as boys were reversed, at least implicitly, to read: Be pleasing, not competitive; be loved, not ambitious; find a man, not an occupation (unless it was teaching, because it was said, one could always combine teaching with raising a family).

Is it any wonder that most women came out of college with their identities diffused? Discouraged by the external world and debilitated by their inner fears, they gave up searching for their own form and commitments. They could not, therefore, have the crisis and growth that search provokes. Upon graduation, most college women were searching for a man and, if anything, had a "Why aren't I married?" crisis. Once that was resolved, their identities were usually foreclosed, at least for the time being.

In 1969, a study comparing male with female personality development in college finally broke the grantsmanship barrier. (Funding had been withdrawn from a previous such study because the foundation thought the results disturbing.) Anne Constantinople took a cross-sectional look at 952 undergraduates at the University of Rochester, using Erikson's measure of personality development to score each student. These were her findings:

Although the women seemed more mature when they entered college, only the men moved consistently over the four years toward a resolution of their identities. The academic environment supported and coaxed the male student toward making career choices and gaining assurance. The same pressures and opportunities led many female students to a prolonged sense of identity diffusion. (The identity-diffused, as described by Marcia, are unable to rebel against their parents, teachers or friends, who expect from them something other than what they want or how they feel; hence they perform well enough but always feel like misfits). Many of the young women felt that they had to choose between a career and being a parent, a choice no young man is asked to make. So long as the women students could not make this decision or put it off, they were unable to resolve their identities.[10]

FINDING MY "TRUE SELF"

Why can't we hurry up and find absolute truth at 21?

The notion of a true self embodying all real goodness is a romantic fiction. The best of all parents have not shielded us from wrestling with the problems of security, acceptance, control, jealousy, rivalry. The strategies for living that we develop, some causing us to be tender and loving and others egging us on to be competitive and cruel, form parts integral to our distinctive character by the end of childhood.

To "know theyself" in the full sense, one must eventually allow acquaintance with all these parts. This is the opportunity presented to us as we move through a series of critical passages. But although a writer finds it convenient to assemble a great variety of studies and biographies into a concept such as passages, the person moving through the steps one at a time is absorbed by the developmental tasks of whatever period he or she is in. And even as one part of us seeks the freedom to be an individual, another part is always searching for someone or something to surrender our freedom to.

Notes

1. Maslow presented his theory of the hierarchical structure of needs in *Motivation and Personality* (1954).

2. "In general, it is the inability to settle on an occupational identity which most disturbs young people," Erikson has proposed (1968). Stating the case even more strongly, Burt Schacter insists that occupational experiences which confirm a person's competence are the most important, even more important than finding a group role, a sex role, or a world view. See "Identity Crisis and Occupational Processes," *Child Welfare* 47:1 (1968), pp. 26–37.

3. Taken from the Bardwick study (1974), p. 88.

4. Jessie Bernard discusses career planning in *The Future of Marriage* (1972), p.165.

5. See Edward H. Pohlman's *Psychology of Birth Planning* (Schenkman, 1969), pp. 35–81, for a summary of reasons for wanting children.

6. In the year 1968, for example, HEW figures show that almost half (46 percent) of the married women ages 15 to 19 gave birth to a child, while only one-quarter of the married women aged 20 to 24—the group with the next highest birthrate—gave birth during that year. HEW also estimates that "somewhere in the neighborhood of 60 percent of the infants born to teenage mothers that year were conceived out of wedlock." From *Teenagers: Marriages, Divorces, Parenthood, and Mortality*. U.S. Department of Health, Education, and Welfare publication (August 1973), pp. 18–19.

7. Compulsory graffiti taken from U.S. census figures as reported in the Dept. of Labor's *Occupational Outlook Quarterly* (Spring 1973) by Gloria Stevenson. See also Paul Glick's updated report for U.S. Bureau of Census, "The Life Cycle of the Family" (in preparation at the time of writing).

8. Among nearly 5,000 high school graduates studied over a four-year period, those who "persisted in college were more likely to move toward an open-minded, flexible, and autonomous disposition [than] those who went to work or into full-time homemaking." This conclusion is from a study by Trent and Medsker in 1968 as reported by Stanley H. King (November 1972) in "Coping and Growth in Adolescence," *Seminars in Psychiatry*, p. 363.

9. Taken from the HEW report on *Teenagers: Marriages, Divorces, Parenthood, and Mortality* (1973).

10. Using 952 male and female subjects drawn from the four college classes, Anne Constantinople did a study entitled, "An Eriksonian Measure of Personality Development in College Students," published in the *Journal of Developmental Psychology* 1:4 (1969), pp. 357–372.

Marriage is rarely a romantic journey down the primrose path of life by two loving partners. It is a complex social relationship involving sexual, economic, and political interactions. Yes, political.

Unfortunately, sociologists of the family have largely ignored the question of differential physical, social, and economic power exercised by the modern American male over his wife and the rest of the family. In this essay, published in 1969, Dair Gillespie reviews some of the literature on the subject and tries to show that the idea of egalitarian marriage is a myth. As Gillespie says, "The best man is very seldom a woman." The essay, which was written before the progress toward sexual equality of the past few years and is based on material from the 1960s, is especially interesting as a "period piece."

As you read this essay, note the questions that the author poses while setting up measurements of power in the family and trying to ascertain the sources of decision making.

Who Has the Power? The Marital Struggle

DAIR L. GILLESPIE

Marriage is the destiny traditionally offered to women by society. It is still true that most women are married, or have been, or plan to be, or suffer from not being. The celibate [single] woman is to be explained and defined with reference to marriage whether she is frustrated, rebellious, or even indifferent in regard to that institution.

Simone deBeauvoir

THE CHANGING POWER STRUCTURE

Modern theorists of the family agree that the American family has evolved from a paternalistic to a much more democratic form. Before the Civil War married women had many duties, few rights. They were not permitted to control their property, even when it was theirs by inheritance or dower, or to make a will. To all intents and purposes they did not own property. The husband had the right to collect and use the wife's wages, to decide upon the education and religion of the children, and to punish his wife if she displeased him. The right to will children, even unborn, to other guardians was retained by the husband. In the case of divorce, when granted at all, the husband had the right to determine the control of the children. To a married woman, her husband was her superior, her companion, her master. In every sector of the social arena, women were in a subordinate position. The church was one of the most potent forces for maintaining them in this position. Within the church, women were segregated from men, were not allowed to sing, preach or take public action. There were no high schools for girls, and no college in the world admitted women. Unpropertied males, slaves, and all women were not allowed into the political process at all.

Today, as the textbooks never tire of telling us, couples are more free to choose partners than formerly, they are able to separate more easily, the differences in age and culture between husband and wife are less marked than formerly, the husband recognizes more willingly the independence of his wife's demands, they may share housekeeping and diversions, and the wife may even work. In fact, sociologists claim that the modern husband and wife are so nearly equal in power that marriage today can be termed "democratic," "equalitarian," or "egalitarian."

These changes in the form of marriage are generally attributed to the entrance of women into the economic structure and to the extension of an equalitarian ideology to cover women. This type of explanation is careful to emphasize socioeconomic conditions of the past and the "rise of women" in the American economy. However, socioeconomic conditions of the present are no longer examined, for it is assumed that women have won their rights in all social arenas, and if they haven't—well, ideology takes a while to filter down to the masses. New egalitarian ideals, they tell us, will bring about further socioeconomic changes and a better position for women.

In a major research project on the modern American family, Blood and Wolfe state:

> Under former historical circumstances, the husband's economic and social role almost automatically gave him pre-eminence. Under modern conditions, the roles of men and women have changed so much that husbands and wives are potential equals—with the balance of power tipped sometimes one way, sometimes the other. It is no longer possible to assume that just because a man is a man, he is the boss. Once upon a time, the function of culture was to rationalize the predominance of the male sex. Today the function of culture is to develop a philosophy of equal

rights under which the saying goes, "May the best man win!"—and the best man is sometimes a woman. The role of culture has shifted from sanctioning a competent sex over an incompetent sex to sanctioning the competent marriage partner over the incompetent one, regardless of sex (1960:29–30).

There is good evidence, however, that the balance of power is tipped the same way it always was, and that the best man is very seldom a woman. I am arguing, then, against the *personal* resource theory and am positing that, in fact, this is still a caste/class system rationalizing the preponderance of the male sex.

THE MEASUREMENT OF POWER

Before examining the causes of male dominance in marital power, I would like to examine first how Blood and Wolfe[1] conceive of power and how they measure it. Operationally, power is restricted to who makes the final decision in each of eight areas, ranging from those traditionally held entirely by the husband to those held entirely by the wife. These eight areas include:

1. What job the husband should take.
2. What car to get.
3. Whether or not to buy life insurance.
4. Where to go on a vacation.
5. What house or apartment to take.
6. Whether or not the wife should go to work or quit work.
7. What doctor to have when someone is sick.
8. How much money the family can afford to spend per week on food.

These questions were asked because (a) they are all relatively important, (b) they are questions which nearly all couples have to face, and (c) they range from typically masculine to typically feminine decisions, but affect the family as a whole (1960: 19–20).

This measurement of power leaves much to be desired. Safilios-Rothschild has made probably the most telling criticisms of such studies. She points out that all decisions are given equal weight even though not all decisions have "objectively" the same degree of importance for the entire life of the family. Which job the husband would take (with important consequences in terms of time to be spent away from home, location of job, salary level, amount of

---

[1] Blood and Wolfe's work plays a major part in this paper because it has been one of the most influential studies of marriage in the last 10 years.

leisure available, etc.) and which doctor to call were considered decisions equally affecting the family and the balance of power within the family. Further, some decisions are made less frequently than others; thus, while a decision such as "what food to buy" requires a daily or weekly enactment, a decision such as "what car to buy" is only made every few years. In addition, some decisions are "important" and frequent, others frequent but not "important,"others "important" and not frequent, and still others not important and not frequent. Thus, the familial power structure may not be solely determined on the number of areas of decisions that one can appropriate for himself/herself. She also mentioned the multidimensionality of some of the decision-making areas and suggested that it is possible that one spouse decides which make of car to buy and the other specifies color (1969:297–298).

It seems, then, that the conception and measurement of power is already biased in that it does not expose certain kinds of power which automatically accrue to the husband by virtue of his work; and second, that it takes no account of the differential importance of the eight decisions in the power structure of the marriage. Further, there is good evidence that even if we accepted Blood and Wolfe's measures as being true measures of power, the husband still controls most of the power decisions in the family (Figure 1). I must conclude, then, that the husband has much more power than he appears to have according to Blood and Wolfe's analysis.

Their discussion of "who decides" is even more convincing that there are power differentials which are being overlooked. For example, they explain:

> That the husband should be more involved in his wife's job decisions than she with his is understandable. For one thing, her work is seldom her major preoccupation in life the way it is for a man. Even if she works just as many hours a week, she does not usually make the same lifelong commitment to the world of work. Nor is her pay-check indispensable to the family finances (if only because it is smaller). In such ways the choice of whether to work or not is less vital to a woman than to a man.
>
> In addition, the wife's decisions about working have repercussions on the husband. If his wife goes to work, he will have to help out more around the house. If he is a business executive, he may prefer to have her concentrate her energy on entertaining prospective clients at home. As a small businessman or independent professional, he may need her services in his own enterprise. On the other hand, regardless of his own occupation, he may want her to work in order to help him buy a house or a business or pay for the children's education.
>
> It may be, then the work role is so much the responsibility of the husband in marriage that even the wife's work is but an adjunct of his instrumental leadership, leaving this decision in his hands (p. 22).

FIGURE 1. *Husband's Mean Power in Family Decision Making Areas*

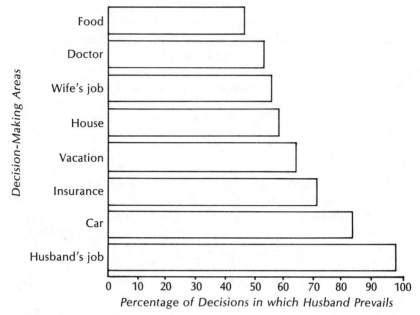

SOURCE: Plotted from data contained in Robert O. Blood, Jr., and Donald M. Wolfe, *Husbands and Wives: The Dynamics of Married Living* (New York: Free Press, 1960).

In these *justifications* of the division of power, Blood and Wolfe use the device of examining why a husband would want more power in particular areas. The basic assumption is, of course, that he can have it if he wants it. I think a more pertinent question would be not who wants power, since there are always myriad reasons why anyone would want power, but why he is able to get it if he wants it. This question is not even broached.

William Goode in *World Revolution and Family Patterns* comments on this aspect of power and authority:

> After evaluating the conflicting comments and data published by Shaff-ner, Rodnick, Schelski and Wruzbacher, Baumert comes to the conclusion which seems eminently reasonable, that claims of fundamental equalitarianism in the German family (or in any other European family) are not correct and that an unequivocally equalitarian family is rarely to be found. In the final analysis, only a few family relations are not determined by the male. It is not possible at present to state just how well such a statement could be applied to other countries. In reality, in all

countries there are many women who manage to dominate the man, but it seems likely that in most countries, when the husband tries to dominate he can still do this. Even when the husband performs the household chores, his participation means that he gains power—the household becoming a further domain for the exercise of prerogatives for making decisions.

Perhaps the crucial qualitative difference is to be found in the extent to which, in one country or another, the male can still dominate *without* a definite effort to do so (1963:70).

In *The Family,* Goode calls this "negative authority—the right to prevent others from doing what they want" (1964:75).

I must conclude, then, that the power structure is much more lopsided than Blood and Wolfe lead us to believe, and that it is the husband who holds this hidden power. Why does the husband have all this power? How does he obtain it? How does he maintain it?

It is assumed that most marriages begin with partners at a somewhat egalitarian level. All evidence points to homogamous marriage, i.e., that the woman's *husband* and *father* occupy similar positions in the socioeconomic structure. However, regardless of her background, "her future rank is mainly determined by the future job achievement of the man she marries, rather than by the class position of his family,"[2] or hers, needless to say. In discussing differentials in power which emerge in marriage, most social scientists use an individualistic perspective as do Blood and Wolfe in *Husbands and Wives.* They remark:

> The balance of power is, after all, an interpersonal affair, and the wife's own characteristics cannot long be disregarded if we are to understand who makes the decisions. Whenever possible it is desirable to compare the wife and the husband on the same characteristics, for then the comparative resourcefulness and competence of the two partners can be discovered. Once we know which partner has more education, more organizational experience, a higher status background, etc. we will know who tends to make the most decisions (p. 37).

The major error made by Blood and Wolfe (and others who use this perspective) is in assuming that this control of competence and resources occurs in individual couples by chance rather than being structurally predetermined (in a statistical sense) in favor of the male. To state it more clearly, I am arguing that it is still a caste/class system, rationalizing the preponderance of males. The distribution of power is not an interpersonal affair, but a class affair. Blood and Wolfe continue:

[2] Goode, 1964:87.

Some husbands today are just as powerful as their grandfathers were—
but they can no longer take for granted the authority held by older
generations of men. No longer is the husband able to exercise power just
because he is the "man of the house." Rather, he must prove his right to
power, or win power by virtue of his own skills and accomplishments *in
competition with his wife* (p. 29). (emphasis mine)

I am arguing that in the competition with his wife, the man has most of the
advantages. If we assume that the marriage contract is a mutual mobility bet
for gaining ascendancy in power, personal autonomy, and self-realization, we
will find that the opportunity for winning the bet is very slim for the woman.
She is already at a disadvantage when she signs the contract. For further self-
realization, for further gains in status and experience as compared with her
husband, the cards are already stacked against her, for women are *structurally*
deprived of equal opportunities to develop their capacities, resources, and
competence in competition with males.

Since theorists of marriage have a quite notable tendency to disregard the
psychological, legal, and social blocks put in the way of women as a class when
they are discussing power differentials and their sources, I would like to examine some of these differences.

SOURCES OF MARITAL POWER

Socialization

Men and women are differentially socialized. By the time women reach mar-
riageable age, we have already been damaged by the socialization process. We
have been systematically trained to accept second best, not to strive, and to accept the "fact" that we are unworthy of more. Naomi Weisstein's "Kinde,
Kuche, Kirche as Scientific Law" states this process clearly:

How are women characterized in our culture, and in psychology? They
are inconsistent, emotionally unstable, lacking in strong conscience or
superego, weaker, "nurturant" rather than productive, "intuitive"
rather than intelligent, and if they are at all "normal," suited to the
home and family. In short, the list adds up to a typical minority group
stereotype of inferiority; if they know their place, which is in the home,
they are really quite loveable, happy, childlike, loving creatures. In a
review of the intellectual differences between little boys and little girls,
Eleanor Maccoby has shown that there are no intellectual differences until about high school, or if there are, girls are slightly ahead of boys. At
high school, the achievement of women now measured in terms of pro-
ductivity and accomplishment, drops off even more rapidly. There are a

number of other, non-intellectual tests which show sex differences; I chose the intellectual differences since it is seen clearly that women start becoming inferior. It is no use to talk about women being different but equal; all of the tests I can think of have a "good" outcome and a "bad" outcome. Women usually end up at the "bad" outcome. In light of social expectations about women, what is surprising is not that women end up where society expects they will; what is surprising is that little girls don't get the message that they are supposed to be stupid until high school, and what is even more remarkable is that some women resist this message even after high school, college, and graduate school (1969:7).

Thus, women begin at a psychological disadvantage when we sign the marriage contract, for we have differential training and expectations.

Marriage: A Free Contract Between Equals

Sociologists universally fail to discuss legal differences in power when the marriage contract is signed.[3] Marriage is ordinarily considered a contract freely entered into by both partners, and the partners are assumed to stand on common footing of equal rights and duties. Sheila Cronan (1969:2–4) examined this "free" contract between equals and found a few unlisted terms.

SEX. She found that the husband can legally force his wife to have sexual intercourse with him against her will, an act which if committed against any other woman would constitute the crime of rape. By definition, a husband cannot be guilty of raping his own wife, for "the crime (of rape) is ordinarily that of forcing intercourse on someone other than the wife of the person accused" (Gallen 1967:6). Women are well aware of the "right" of the husband to "insist" and the "duty" of the wife to submit to sexual intercourse. The compulsory nature of sex in marriage operates to the advantage of the male, for though the husband theoretically has the duty to have intercourse with his wife, this normally cannot occur against his will. (Both partners are protected in that a marriage can be annulled by either party if the marriage has not been consummated.)

OTHER MARITAL RESPONSIBILITIES. Women believe that we are voluntarily giving our household services, but the courts hold that the husband is legally entitled to his wife's services, and further, that *she cannot be paid for her work*. In *Your Marriage and the Law*, Pilpel and Zavin state:

[3] It should be made clear that legality is not necessarily a basis for decision making. It merely reflects the position of society as to how the power is to be distributed when such distributions are contested in the courts. This normally occurs upon dissolution of marriage and not in an ongoing relationship.

As part of the rights of consortium, the husband is entitled to the services of his wife. If the wife works outside the home for strangers, she is usually entitled to her own earnings. But domestic services or assistances which she gives her husband are generally considered part of her wifely duties. The wife's services and society are so essential a part of what the law considers the husband is entitled to as part of the marriage that it will not recognize any agreement between spouses which provides that the husband is to pay for such services or society.

In a Texas case David promised his wife, Fannie, that he would give her $5000 if she would stay with him while he lived and continue taking care of the house and farm accounts, selling his butter and doing all the other tasks which she had done since their marriage. After David's death, Fannie sued his estate for the money which had been promised her. The court held that the contract was unenforceable since Fannie had agreed to do nothing which she was not already legally and morally bound to do as David's wife (1967:65).

The legal responsibilities of a wife are to live in the home established by her husband, to perform the domestic chores (cleaning, cooking, washing, etc.) necessary to help maintain that home, and to care for her husband and children (Gallen 1967:4). The husband, in return, is obligated to provide her with basic maintenance which includes "necessities" such as food, clothing, medical care, and a place to live, in accordance with his income. She has no legal right to any part of his cash income, nor any legal voice in spending it ("Know Your Rights," Women's Bureau, Department of Labor, 1965:1). Were he to employ a live-in servant in place of a wife, he would have to pay the servant a salary, provide her with her own room (as opposed to "bed"), food, and the necessary equipment for doing her job. She would get at least one day a week off and probably would be required to do considerably less work than a wife and would not be required to provide sexual services.

Thus, being a wife is a full-time job for which one is not entitled to pay. (Chase Manhattan Bank estimates a woman's overall work week at 99.6 hours.) Furthermore, the wife is not entitled to freedom of movement. The husband has the right to decide where the family will live. If he decides to move, his wife is obliged to go with him. If she refuses, he can charge her with desertion. This has been upheld by the courts even in cases where the wife could be required to change her citizenship. In states where desertion is grounds for divorce (47 states plus the District of Columbia), the wife would be the "guilty party" and would therefore be entitled to no monetary settlement (Gallen 1967:6).

A MARRIED WOMAN'S NAME. Leo Kanowitz in *Women and the Law* found that the change in a woman's name upon marriage is not only consistent with social custom; it also appears to be generally required by law.

The probable effects of this unilateral name change upon the relations between the sexes, though subtle in character, are profound. In a very real sense, the loss of a woman's surname represents the destruction of an important part of her personality and its submersion in that of her husband. . . . This name change is consistent with the characterization of coverture as "the old common-law fiction that the husband and wife are one. . . [which] has worked out in reality to mean that the one is the husband (1969:41).

THE LAW OF SUPPORT. The universal rule is that it is the primary obligation of the husband to provide financial support for the family. Kanowitz explored some of the legal ramifications of this general rule.

The effects of the basic rule upon the marital relationship itself are complex. In common law marital property jurisdictions, the husband's legal obligation to support the family is not an unmixed blessing for the wife. That obligation has been cited, for example, as justifying his right to choose the family home. It has no doubt also played an important part in solidifying his legal role as head and master of the family. For in according the husband this position within the family, the law often seems to be applying on a grand scale the modest principle that "he who pays the piper calls the tune." However, even in the community property states, in which a wife's services in the home are theoretically viewed as being equal to or exceeding in monetary value the husband's earnings outside of the home, husbands have generally been given the rights to manage and control the community property, along with other superior rights and interests in it (1969:69).

Thus, it is clear that husbands have access to legal advantages which wives do not have. True, the wife does gain legal protection against capricious action by the male, but in exchange, she becomes his vassal. He is the economic head of the joint household, and hence, represents it in view of society. She takes his name and belongs to his class. She follows where his work calls to determine their place of residence. Their lives are geared to the daily, weekly, annual rhythms of his life. She gives him her person and her private labor, but he wants more.

THE "WHITE MAN'S BURDEN." In today's "love match," the husband does not merely require an obedient and efficient worker, he wants something more. He wants his wife to love him, that is, to freely choose over and over again to be subjected to the control of the other, to make his welfare the center of her being.[4] This very demand is the crux of what husbands term their "oppression" as Simone de Beauvoir has so clearly observed:

[4] Conversation with Ann Leffler, 1969.

Her very devotion seems annoying, importunate; it is transformed for the husband into a tyranny from which he tries to escape; and yet he it is who imposes it upon his wife as her supreme, her unique justification. In marrying her, he obliges her to give herself entirely to him; but he does not assume the corresponding obligation, which is to accept this gift and all its consequences.

It is the duplicity of the husband that dooms his wife to a misfortune of which he complains that he is himself the victim. Just as he wants her to be at once warm and cool in bed, he requires her to be wholly his and yet no burden; he wishes her to establish him in a fixed place on earth and to leave him free; to assume the monotonous daily round and not to bore him; to be always at hand and never importunate; he wants to have her all to himself and not to belong to her, to live as one of a couple, and to remain alone. Thus she is betrayed from the day he marries her. Her life through, she measures the extent of that betrayal (1968:H51).

Throughout their lives together, she attempts to wrest back from him some measure of her independence. Surely, it is not entirely an accident that divorce rates are highest at this early phase of the marriage cycle and drop with the birth of children, when women are most dependent upon the husband economically and emotionally.

Economic Sources of Power

It is clear that an economic base of power is important in marriage, for the higher the husband on the social scale, the greater his decision-making in the family. Using three indices of success in the community, Blood and Wolfe found that all three affected power differentials in the family.

1) The higher the husband's occupational prestige, the greater his voice in marital decisions.

2) Income was an even more sensitive indicator of power than his occupation. The higher the husband's income, the greater his power.

3) The higher the husband's status (based on occupation, income, education, and ethnic background), the more power he had to make decisions.

The major break in power fell between white-collar occupations and blue-collar occupations, the middle-class husbands having much more power than working-class husbands. The increment to power by income was steady. By social status, there is a curvilinear relationship to power. The low-blue collar workers had more power than high blue-collar workers, and power for the husband increased again at the low white-collar level and the high white-collar level. Middle class husbands, then, are generally more powerful than blue-collar husbands, but in the blue-collar marriages, the low blue-collar worker has more power than the high blue-collar worker. I will discuss some of the possible causes of this in the section on education.

The material bases of power were operant despite the fact that middle-class husbands espouse a more egalitarian ideology than do working-class husbands. William Goode commented on this tension between the ideal and the real distributions of power.

> Since at present this philosophy [of equalitarianism in the family] is most strongly held among better educated segments of the population, and among women more than among men, two interesting tensions may be seen: Lower-class men concede fewer rights *ideologically* than their women in fact *obtain*, and the more educated men are more likely to concede *more* rights ideologically than they in fact grant (1963:21).

He then supplies us with excellent example of how ideology may be modified to justify the current distribution of power:

> One partial resolution of the latter tension is to be found in the frequent assertion from families of professional men that they should not make demands which would interfere with his *work*: He takes preference as a *professional*, not as a family head or as a male; nevertheless, the precedence is his. By contrast, lower-class men demand deference as *men*, as heads of families.

As we can see, marital power is a function of income to a large extent, and egalitarian philosophies have very little impact on the actual distribution of power. It seems clear that the authority of the male is used as a justification of power where it is useful (working-class), and new justifications will arise as they are useful, as in the case of professional men who demand deference because of their work, thus enabling them to accept the doctrine of equality while at the same time undermining it for their own benefit as males. If this is the effect of that much touted egalitarian ideology which will bring about better conditions for women and racial and ethnic minorities as soon as it filters down to the masses, it seems we will have a long, long wait for cosmic justice.

Blood and Wolfe claim that this superior power of high-status husbands is not due to coercion, but to the recognition by both partners that the husband is the one eminently qualified to make the decisions in the family. This argument is reminiscent of arguments in labor relations. The labor contract is assumed to be freely entered into by both partners. The power conferred on the one party by the difference in class position—the real economic position of both—is not taken into account. That economic relations compel the worker to surrender even the last semblance of equal rights is of no concern. Coercion (however subtle) based on economic power is still coercion, whether it involves wife-beating or not.

As further evidence that individual competence and resourcefulness (regardless of sex) are not the real issues, we must examine Blood and Wolfe's discussion of the *deviant* case—wife dominance. In these cases, they claim that wives who have superior power acquire it, not because they have access to pragmatic sources of power or because they are more competent than their husbands (heaven forbid!), but by default.

> We will find throughout this study dissatisfaction associated with wife-dominance. This is not, however, simply a reflection of the breaking of social rules. Rather, the circumstances which lead to the wife's dominance involve corresponding inadequacies on the husband's part. An inadequate husband is by definition unable to make a satisfactory marriage partner. So the dominant wife is not exultant over her "victory" but exercises power regretfully by default of her "no good" or incapacitated husband (p. 45).

For Blood and Wolfe, wives can never gain dominance legitimately; it falls in our unhappy laps and is accepted only unwillingly and with much bitterness.

Despite the superior power gained by the husband because of his economic position, there are conditions under which wives do erode that power to some extent. Not surprisingly, the wife's participation in the work force is an important variable. Women who work have more power vis-a-vis their husbands than do non-working wives, regardless of race or class. The number of years the wife has worked also affects the balance of power—the longer she has worked, the more power she is able to obtain. This, to some extent, explains why blue-collar wives have more power than white-collar wives (in comparison to their husbands), since their participation in the work force is much higher than for the wives of high-status, high-income husbands (Blood and Wolfe, 1960:40–41).

Organizational Participation

Organizational participation, too, is a factor which affects marital decision making as shown by Blood and Wolfe's data. Women with much more organizational participation than their husbands alter the balance of power in the wife's direction. In those cases where the participation is equal or in which the husband is superior (by far the most frequent), the balance of power increases in the husband's direction (p. 39).

Education

Education was also influential in the distribution of power. The more education the husband has, the greater his power. High white-collar husbands continue to gain power if they exceed their wives' education (and chances are good that they do, in fact, exceed), and they lose it if they fall short of the wife. The same trend holds within the low white-collar and high blue-collar groups, leaving a low blue-collar reversal, i.e., low blue-collar husbands have more power even when their wives have superior educations (p. 28, 38).

Mirra Komarovsky in *Blue Collar Marriage* has drawn attention to the fact that education is a much more important variable when the husband's income and social status are relatively low. In working-class families, the less educated and unskilled husbands have more power than do those with higher incomes. She attempted to explain some of the causes of this power anomaly. First, patriarchal attitudes are more prevalent among the less educated and hence, a source of power in some families. High school graduates, because of a social milieu which does not sanction patriarchal authority (though it does sanction male privilege), tend to lose power. Second, among the less-educated, the husband is more likely to excel in personal resources for the exercise of influence, and this margin of male superiority narrows among the high school graduates. Among the less-educated, the husband has wider contacts in the community than his wife. He represents the world to his family, and he is the family's "secretary of state." In contrast, a few of the more educated wives enjoy wider contacts and higher status outside the home than their husbands. Third, the education of the spouses was found to affect their degrees of power because of mating patterns. The effect of educational inequality appears to explain the lower power of skilled workers in comparison with the semiskilled. The skilled worker is more likely than the semi-skilled worker to marry a high school graduate. By virtue of their relatively high earnings, skilled workers may be able to marry better-educated women, but by marrying "upward" they lose the degree of power enjoyed by the semi-skilled over their less-educated wives. Fourth, male prestige or social rank was a source of power in low blue-collar families (1967:226–229).

Physical Coercion

Komarovsky is one of the few sociologists who has mentioned physical coercion as a source of power in the family. In her discussion of the low blue-collar family, she found that the use of physical violence was a source of masculine power. However, not only the use of physical violence, but its *threat* can be an effective form of control. She reports that one woman said of her husband: "He is a big man and terribly strong. One time when he got sore at me, he pulled off the banister and he ripped up three steps." With the evidence of this damage in view, this woman realized, as she put it, what her husband could do to her if he should decide to strike her (1967: 227).

Lynn O'Connor has suggested that threats of violence (in gestures of dominance) are not limited to any particular class, but are a universal source of male power and control. After discussing dominance gestures in primates, she states:

> Although there have been no systematic studies of the gestures of dominance and submission in human groups, the most casual observation will show their crucial role in the day to day mechanics of oppression. An example should clarify.

A husband and wife are at a party. The wife says something that the husband does not want her to say (perhaps it reveals something about him that might threaten his ranking with other men). He quickly tightens the muscles around his jaw and gives her a rapid but intense direct stare. Outsiders don't notice the interaction, though they may have a vaguely uncomfortable feeling that they are intruding on something private. The wife, who is acutely sensitive to the gestures of the man on whom she is dependent, immediately stops the conversation, lowers or turns her head slightly, averts her eyes, or gives off some other gestures of submission which communicate acquiescence to her husband and reduce his aggression. Peace is restored; the wife has been put in her place. If the wife does not respond with submission, she can expect to be punished. When gestures of dominance fail, the dominant animal usually resorts to violence. We all know stories about husbands beating up their wives after the party when they have reached the privacy of their home. Many of us have experienced at least a few blows from husbands or lovers when we refuse to submit to them. It is difficult to assess the frequency of physical attacks within so called love relationships, because women rarely tell even one another when they have taken place. By developing a complicated ethic of loyalty (described above in terms of privacy), men have protected themselves from such reports leaking out and becoming public information. Having already been punished for stepping out of role, the woman is more than a little reluctant to tell anyone of the punishment because it would mean violating the loyalty code, which is an even worse infraction of the rules and most likely would result in further and perhaps more severe punishment (1970:9).

That violence or the threat of violence may be more widespread than is currently admitted is also suggested by complaints made by wives in divorce. Goode in *Women in Divorce* found that almost one-third (32 percent) of the wives reported "authority-cruelty" as the reason for divorce. Authority problems are defined as being disagreements concerning permissible degree of dominance over wife and include cruelty, beating, jealousy, and "wanted to have own way" (1956:120, 123). Since Goode did not code cruelty or beating separately, we have no definitie evidence as to the frequency of such behavior, but there is evidence that problems with male dominance are widespread in the population. Goode comments:

. . . In different strata and groups, the husband may be permitted different control techniques. For example, the middle-class male will very likely be censured more if he uses force to control his wife than if he uses techniques of nagging, jealousy, or sulking. On the other hand, there is a strong reservoir of attitude on the part of the American male generally, that he has a *right* to tell his wife what to do. This attitude is given more overt expression, and is more frequently backed by force, in the lower strata. It is not so much that beating and cruelty are viewed as an obvious male right in marriage, but only that this is one of the techniques used from time to time, and with little or no subsequent guilt, for keeping control of the wife. . . . In our society, the husband who successfully asserts his dominance does enjoy some approval and even a modicum of envy from other males. Male dominance is to some extent actually approved (1956:122).

Suburbanization

Blood and Wolfe also found that families living in the suburbs were more husband-dominant than those which live in the central city. This directly contradicts the popular image of suburban life as being dominated by women and therefore, oriented toward the satisfaction of women's needs. The data showed that suburban families were more husband-dominant at every status level than their urban peers (p. 36). They then speculated that suburban husbands were more powerful "because suburban wives feel more indebted to their husbands for providing them with a place to live which is more attractive than the industrial city of Detroit. If so, this fits the theory that power accrues to those husbands who are able to provide for their wives especially well" (p. 36).

In a recent study on the working class in suburbia, Tallman has suggested that other factors than the wife's gratitude might be working to build up the husband's power. He constructed a profile of the working-class marriage which indicated consistently that wives tend to maintain close ties with relatives and old girl friends while husbands continue their premarital peer group associations. Social and psychological support emanates, then, not from marriage partners, but from same-sex friends, and kin from long standing and tight-knit social networks. As a consequence, there is a relatively high degree of conjugal role segmentation which is characterized in part by a lack of communication between the spouses. In general the experiences of working class women are more localized and circumscribed than their male counterparts. Since their security and identity depend upon their position vis-a-vis a small group of intimates, their opinions and beliefs are both dependent upon and in accord with this group. Blue-collar women have minimal experience in the external world and tend to view it fearfully. Men, on the other hand, have more frequent social contacts, in part for occupational reasons, but also because they have been socialized into male roles which define them as family representatives to the outside world.

Tallman concluded that suburban women are more isolated because of disruptions in the primary group relations. The disruption of friendship and kinship ties are not only personally disintegrating for the wife but also demand fundamental changes in the role allocations in the family. Suburban wives are more dependent upon their husbands for a variety of services previously provided by members of tight-knit networks. In brief, he found that moving to the suburbs was experienced as a disintegrative force in the lives of many working class women, leading to a greater isolation and dependence upon the husband (1969: 66–69). This partial explanation of the husband's increased power in the suburbs as being due to the wife's increased isolation and dependence seems eminently more reaonsable than Blood and Wolfe's explanation that it is due to gratitude on the part of the wife. Tallman's data also indicates that the wife frequently regrets the move to the suburbs, despite more pleasant living conditions, because of its disruption of the kinship and friendship network.

Race

Blood and Wolfe report very little on black families, except to say that Negro husbands have unusually low power. Their data show that white husbands are always more powerful than their Negro status equals and that this is true within each occupational stratum, each income bracket, and each social level.[5] They concede that "the label 'black' is almost a synonym for low status in our society—and Detroit Negroes are no exception in having less education, lower incomes, inferior jobs, and lower prestige generally than whites. Since low status white husbands make relatively few decisions, we would expect Negro husbands to exercise little power, too" (p. 34).

What they fail to take into account (among other things) is that black women, too, are discriminated against in this society. They, too, have less education, lower incomes, inferior jobs, and lower prestige generally than whites. The fact that blacks are discriminated against does not explain power differentials within black families. To explain power differentials in black families, just as for white families, the sources of power for black men and black women must be examined and compared. Blood and Wolfe fail to do this.

Their primary purpose seems to be to demonstrate gross differences between black and white families, without bothering to report differences with-

---

[5] Blood and Wolfe's report of the data is so skimpy that it makes interpretation difficult. For example, they say that the 35 high income husbands (over $4000) have lower mean power (4.09) than their 68 less affluent colleagues (4.56). This is possibly analogous to the distribution in the white blue-collar class, where low blue-collar husbands have more power than the high blue-collar husbands. Comparisons are difficult because, for the general population, income was broken into five groups, while for black families they used only two—over $4000 and below $4000. They reported that "the generalization that the husband's power is correlated with occupational status also holds within the Negro race" (4.31, 4.60, no cases, and 5.00 respectively). The only mention of Negro husbands and social status was that the few white husbands in the lowest status groups differ sharply from their powerless negro counterparts (no figure reported).

in black families. Andrew Billingsley in *Black Families in White America* has criticized just this approach used in sociological studies. He draws attention to the fact that class variables are as important in black families as in white families. "Negro families are not only Negroes to be compared and contrasted with white families, they may also be upper-class (10 percent), middle-class (40 percent), or lower-class (50 percent), with urban or rural moorings, with southern or northern residence, and most importantly, they may be meaningfully compared and contrasted with each other" (1968:8).

Billingsley accounts to some extent for what may be part of the white/black differentials in overall power. He notes that Negro samples are dominated by low-income families and points out that even where income levels between whites and blacks are similar, the groups are not truly comparable, for the Negro group reflects not only its income level but its experience with prejudice and subjugation as well.

Because both black husbands and black wives are discriminated against in this society, it is absurd to explain power differentials between them as being due to race (as Blood and Wolfe do), unless there are mitigating factors brought about by racial discrimination which operate in favor of one sex's access to sources of marital power. Since data on the black family are so sadly inadequate, I can at this point only examine some demographic data which have possible implications for power distributions in black families.

Black women comprised 40 percent of all black workers in 1960. They earned considerably less than black men. The median earnings of full-time year round black women in 1959 was two-fifths that of black men.[6] (In 1964, it was 64.2 percent.)[7] The unemployment rate for black women is higher than for black men. In 1967, for Negro men aged 20–64, the unemployment rate was 3.7. For Negro women it was 6.0. The unemployment rates for black women under 20 were also higher than for Negro men.[8] Clearly, then, black women are not superior to black men in income.

In occupational status, we find that Negro women are most frequently in service jobs while Negro men are predominantly blue-collar workers. However, relatively more Negro women than men had professional or technical jobs, this being due primarily to their extensive employment as teachers and nurses. Of all full-time year round Negro workers in 1960, Negro women constituted nearly all the private household workers. They were more than half the number of Negroes employed as professional workers (61 percent) and other service workers (51 percent). Except for the clerical group in which the numbers were about equal, the remaining occupational groups (sales, man-

[6] Negro Women Workers, Women's Bureau, Department of Labor, 1964:23–25.

[7] Fact Sheet on the Relative Position of Women and Men Workers in the Economy, U.S. Department of Labor, Women's Bureau, 1965, p. 3.

[8] U.S.Department of Labor, Bureau of Labor Statistics, Employment and Earnings, Vol. 16, No. 7, January 1970, Table A-1 (Data under Negro heading is for "Negro and Other Races").

agers, operatives, crafts, laborers, and farmers) had fewer Negro women than men.[9]

Negro women in general had a higher median education than Negro men. (This is also true in the white population.) The median educational level of nonwhite women was 8.5 years in 1960, but for men it was 7.9. However, at the top of the educational ladder, just as for the white population, men are more numerous.[10]

Though there are differences, we find that the relations *between the sexes* for both Negroes and whites are similar. Obviously, black men have suffered from discrimination in this society. This is evident in the figures of income, occupation, and education. However, it is also evident that Negro women have suffered discrimination, not only because of race, but also because of their sex. Thus, they are doubly oppressed. This, too, is evident in figures of income, occupation, and education.

Jesse Bernard in *Marriage and Family Among Negroes* has suggested still another variable which must be taken into account in Negro family patterns. She reports that there is an extraordinarily low sex ratio (number of males per 100 females) among urban Negroes as compared to whites. The ratio is especially low (88.4) in the critical years of marriageability. Bernard conjectures that the low sex ratio means that Negro women are competing for a relatively scarce "good" when they look forward to marriage, being buyers in a sellers' market (1966:69). While this is certainly not the cause of power distributions in the black family, it does suggest a source of male power.[11] Delores Mack, in a study of black and white families, supports this contention (1969).

What these findings suggest is that researchers have not carefully evaluated the logic of the assumptions of their hypotheses. They have looked at the white community; there they have observed that education, occupation, and income are important sources of power. . . . They have ignored the possibility that the sources of power in the Black community may be different from that in the white community. In fact, they have ignored one of the most potent forms of power in any marriage, but particularly sex power in Black marriages. Certainly researchers have noted the preoccupation of the Black male with sex. Some have viewed this preoccupation with sex as a form of escapism, failing to realize that this concentration on sexual activities may be a main source of power.

[9] Negro Women Workers, pp. 23–25.
[10] Negro Women Workers, pp. 13–14.
[11] This has also been suggested in several articles in *The Black Woman*, edited by Toni Cade (1970), particularly "Dear Black Man," Fran Sanders; "Who Will Revere the Black Woman?," Abbey Lincoln; "The Black Woman as Woman," Kay Lindsey; "Double Jeopardy: To Be Black and Female," Frances Beale; "On the Issue of Roles," Toni Cade; "Black Man, My Man, Listen!," Gail Stokes; "Is the Black Man Castrated?," Jean Carey Bond and Pat Peery.

The Black male is well aware, as Eldridge Cleaver notes, that he is the desired sex object for both the white and the Black female. He may use this power in his marriage, much as the white male uses his education and earning power as a lever in his marriage.

The threat or use of physical violence (as discussed above) is another factor which must be taken into account to explain power distributions in black as well as in white families. Obviously, a great deal of research on the differences within black families is needed, as Billingsley has suggested.

Life Cycle

The stages of the family life cycle also affect the marital power distribution. In the early (childless) stage of marriage, the wife is frequently working, but the pressure of social discrimination against women is already beginning to be exerted. Women are unable to procure anything but low paying, low status jobs as compared with their husbands. Already status background and autonomous experiences are being eroded. Though the married childless woman maintains some sort of independent social and economic status if she works, it is below that of her husband. During this period, the power of the husband is moderate.

With the birth of children, there is a substantial jump in power differentials, the husband universally gaining (Blood and Wolfe, 1960:41–44). There is more than a little truth in the old saw that the best way to control a woman is to "keep her barefoot and pregnant," for there is evidence that the power of the wife declines as the number of children grows (Heer, 1958:341–347). At this period after the first child is born, but before the oldest child is in school, the power of the husband reaches its maximum. Many women stop working during this stage and in doing so, become isolated and almost totally socially, economically, and emotionally dependent upon their husbands, further eroding any strength they may have gained due to earning power or participation in organizations. She loses her position, cannot keep up with developments in her field, does not build up seniority. Further, she loses that precious "organizational" experience, the growth of competence and resources in the outside world, the community positions which contribute to power in the marriage. The boundaries of her world contract, the possibilities of growth diminish. If she returns to work, and most women do, she must begin again at a low status job and she stays there—underemployed and underpaid. As her children grow up, she gradually regains some power in the family.

These data again call into question the theory of individual resources as the source of power in marriage. As David Heer pointed out, there is no reason, according to Blood and Wolfe's theory, for the power of the wife to be greater before she has borne children than when her children are pre-school age.

Surely the wife with pre-school children is contributing more resources to the marriage than she did before their children were born (1963:138). Power, then, is clearly not the result of individual contributions and resources in the marriage, but is related to questions of social worth; and the value of women and women's work, as viewed by society, is obviously very low. The contributions of women in the home are of little concern and are consequently little valued, as Margaret Benston explained in "The Political Economy of Women's Liberation" (1969:3–4).

In sheer quantity, household labor, including child care, constitutes a huge amount of socially necessary production. Nevertheless, in a society based on commodity production, it is not usually considered "real work" since it is outside of trade and market place. It is pre-capitalist in a very real sense. The assignment of household work as the function of a special category "women" meant that this group *does* stand in a different relation to the production than the group "men." We will tentatively define women, then, as that group of people who are responsible for the production of simple use-values in those activities associated with the home and the family.

Since men carry no responsibility for such production, the difference between the two groups lies here. Notice that women are not excluded from commodity production. Their participation in wage labor occurs, but as a group, they have no structural responsibility in this area and such participation is ordinarily regarded as transient. Men, on the other hand, are responsible for commodity production; they are not, in principle, given any role in househod labor. . . . The material basis for the inferior status of women is to be found in just this definition of women. In a society in which money determines value, women are a group who work outside the money economy. Their work is not worth money, is therefore valueless, is therefore not even real work. And women themselves, who do this valueless work, can hardly be expected to be worth as much as men, who work for money. In structural terms, the closest thing to the condition of women is the condition of others who are or were outside of commodity production, i.e., peasants or serfs.

THE HUSBAND: MOST LIKELY TO SUCCEED

Thus, it is clear that for a wife to gain even a modicum of power in the marital relationship, she must obtain it from external sources, i.e., she must participate in the work force, her education must be superior to that of her husband, and her participation in organizations must excel his. Equality of resources leaves the power in the hands of the husband. Access to these sources of power are structurally blocked for women, however.

In the general population, women are unable to procure anything but low-status, low-paying, dead end jobs as compared with their husbands, be it factory or university.[12] Partly as a result of unequal pay for the same work, partly as a consequence of channeling women into low-paying jobs, the median income of women is far less than that of men workers. Black women tend to fare slightly better in relation to black men, but make only two-thirds as much as white women.

Median Income of Year-Round Full Time Workers
by Sex and Color, 1964.[13]

	MEN	WOMEN	WOMEN AS % OF MEN
White	$6,497	$3,859	59.4
Nonwhite	4,285	2,674	62.2

In higher socioeconomic classes, the husband is more likely to excel his wife in formal education than he is among blue-collar workers. Men predominate among college graduates, regardless of race, but adult women have a higher median of education (12.1 for women, 12.0 for men in 1964).[14] (We have already seen that the educational attainment of the non-white population is lower [8.5 for women, 7.9 for men], reflecting discrimination on the basis of race.)

All of these areas are sources of power in the marital relationship, and in all of these areas women are structurally blocked from realizing our capacities. It is not because of individual resources or personal competence, then, that husbands obtain power in marriage, but because of the discrimination against women in the larger society. Men gain resources as a class, not as individuals, and women are blocked as a class, not as individuals.

In our mutual mobility bet the woman (as a class) always loses in the fight for power within the marital relationship. We live in a system of institutionalized male supremacy, and the cards are systematically stacked against women in all areas—occupational, political, educational, legal, as well as within the institution of the family. As long as the structure of society remains the same, as long as categorical discrimination against women is carried out,

[12] Handbook on Women Workers, U.S. Department of Labor, Woman's Bureau, 1965, pp. 34–35.
[13] Fact Sheet on the Relative Position of Women and Men Workers in the Economy, U.S. Department of Labor, Women's Bureau, 1965, p. 3.
[14] Handbook on Women Workers, 1965, p. 172.

there is relatively little chance for the woman to gain autonomy, *regardless* of how much good will there is on the part of her husband.

The equalitarian marriage as a norm is a myth. Under some conditions, women can gain power vis-a-vis their husbands, i.e., working women, women with higher educations than their husbands have more power than housewives or women with lesser or identical education as their husbands, but more power is not equal power. Equal power we will never get so long as the present socioeconomic system remains.

References

deBeauvoir, Simone
  1968   The Second Sex, New York: Bantam Books.
Benston, Margaret
  1969   "The political economy of women's liberation," Monthly Review, September.
Bernard, Jesse
  1966   Marriage and Family Among Negroes. Englewood Cliffs, N.J.: Prentice Hall.
Billingsley, Andrew and Amy Tate Billingsley
  1968   Black Families in White America. Englewood Cliffs, N.J.: Prentice Hall.
Blood, Robert O., Jr. and Donald M. Wolfe
  1960   Husbands and Wives, the Dynamics of Married Living. New York: Free Press.
Cade, Toni
  1970   The Black Woman, an Anthology. New York: New American Library.
Cronan, Sheila
  1969   "Marriage," The Feminist. New York.
Gallen, Richard T.
  1967   Wives' Legal Rights. New York: Dell Publishing Co.
Goode, William
  1956   Women in Divorce. New York: The Free Press.
  1963   World Revolution and Family Patterns. New York: The Free Press.
  1964   The Family. Englewood Cliffs, N.J.: Prentice Hall.
Heer, David M.
  1958   "Dominance and the working wife," Social Forces 36 (May): 341–347.
  1963   "The measurement and bases of family power: An overview," Marriage and Family Living 25 (May): 133–139.
Kanowitz, Leo
  1969   Women and the Law, the Unfinished Revolution. Albuquerque: The University of New Mexico Press.
Komarovsky, Mirra
  1967   Blue Collar Marriage. New York: Vintage Books.
Mack, Delores
  1969   The Husband-Wife Power Relationship in Black Families and White Families. Ph. D. Dissertation, Stanford University.

O'Connor, Lynn
   1970   "Male dominance, the nitty-gritty of oppression." It Ain't Me, Babe, Vol. 1, No. 8, June 11–July 1: 9–11.
Pilpel, Harriet F. and Theodora Zavin
   1964   Your Marriage and the Law. New York: Collier Books.
Safilios-Rothschild, Constantia
   1969   "Family sociology or wives' family sociology? A cross-cultural examination of decision making," Journal of Marriage and the Family 31 (2) (May): 290–301.
Tallman, Irving
   1969   "Working class wives in suburbia: Fulfillment or crisis?" Journal of Marriage and the Family 31 (1) (February): 65–72.
Weisstein, Naomi
   1969   Kinde, Kuche, Kirche as Scientific Law: Psychology Constructs the Female. Boston: New England Free Press.

GOVERNMENT PUBLICATIONS

Fact Sheet on the Relative Position of Women and Men Workers in the Economy, U.S. Department of Labor, Women's Bureau, 1965.

1965 Handbook on Women Workers, U.S. Department of Labor, Women's Bureau.

Negro Women Workers in 1960, U.S. Department of Labor, Women's Bureau.

U.S. Department of Labor, Bureau of Statistics, Employment and Earnings, Vol. 16, No. 7, January 1970.

Know Your Rights: What a Working Wife Should Know About Her Legal Rights, U.S. Department of Labor, Women's Bureau, 1965.

*One of the roles for which Americans seem least pre-
pared is that of parent. Somehow even anticipatory socialization—playing "daddy" and "mommy" during
childhood years, caring for younger siblings, baby-sitting, and other presumably preparatory experiences—
does not adequately prepare most of us for the encum-
bering status of parenthood and its attendant social and
financial responsibilities that are not easily renounced.
As sociologist Alice Rossi shows, becoming a parent is
more or less irrevocable. A child presents a parent with
a new set of obligations—and satisfactions. Although
many have written about parental influence on children, Rossi's article is one of the first to deal with
parental responsibility.*

*As you read Rossi's selection, keep in mind what you
already know about socialization to new roles and consider carefully what is so special about the mystique of
parenthood.*

Transition to Parenthood

ALICE S. ROSSI

FROM CHILD TO PARENT: AN EXAMPLE

What is unique about [the] perspective on parenthood [in this article] is the
focus on the adult parent rather than the child. Until quite recent years, concern in the behavioral sciences with the parent-child relationship has been
confined almost exclusively to the child. . . .

The very different order of questions which emerge when the parent replaces the child as the primary focus of analytic attention can best be shown
with an illustration. Let us take, as our example, the point Benedek makes
that the child's need for mothering is *absolute* while the need of an adult
woman to mother is *relative*.[1] From a concern for the child, this discrepancy in

[1] Therese Benedek, "Parenthood as a Developmental Phase," *Journal of American Psychoanalytic
Association*, 7:8 (1959), pp. 389–417.

need leads to an analysis of the impact on the child of separation from the mother or inadequacy of mothering. Family systems that provide numerous adults to care for the young child can make up for this discrepancy in need between mother and child, which may be why ethnographic accounts give little evidence of postpartum depression following childbirth in simpler societies. Yet our family system of isolated households, increasingly distant from kinswomen to assist in mothering, requires that new mothers shoulder total responsibility for the infant precisely for that stage of the child's life when his need for mothering is far in excess of the mother's need for the child.

From the perspective of the mother, the question has therefore become: what does maternity deprive her of? Are the intrinsic gratifications of maternity sufficient to compensate for shelving or reducing a woman's involvement in non-family interests and social roles? The literature on maternal deprivation cannot answer such questions, because the concept, even in the careful specification Yarrow has given it,[2] has never meant anything but the effect on the child of various kinds of insufficient mothering. Yet what has been seen as a failure or inadequacy of individual women may in fact be a failure of the society to provide institutionalized substitutes for the extended kin to assist in the care of infants and young children. It may be that the role requirements of maternity in the American family system extract too high a price of deprivation for young adult women reared with highly diversified interests and social expectations concerning adult life. Here, as at several points in the course of this paper, familiar problems take on a new and suggestive research dimension when the focus is on the parent rather than the child. . . .

Parsons' analysis of the experience of parenthood as a step in maturation and personality growth does not allow for negative outcome. In this view either parents show little or no positive impact upon themselves of their parental role experiences, or they show a new level of maturity. Yet many women, whose interests and values made a congenial combination of wifehood and work role, may find that the addition of maternal responsibilities has the consequence of a fundamental and undesired change in both their relationships to their husbands and their involvements outside the family. Still other women, who might have kept a precarious hold on adequate functioning as adults had they *not* become parents, suffer severe retrogression with pregnancy and childbearing, because the reactivation of older unresolved conflicts with their own mothers is not favorably resolved but in fact leads to personality deterioration[3] and the transmission of pathology to their children.[4]

---

[2] Yarrow, *op. cit.*

[3] Mabel Blake Cohen, "Personal Identity and Sexual Identity," *Psychiatry*, 29:1 (1966), pp. 1–14; Joseph C. Rheingold, *The Fear of Being a Woman: A Theory of Maternal Destructiveness*, New York: Grune and Stratton, 1964.

[4] Theodore Lidz, S. Fleck, and A. Cornelison, *Schizophrenia and the Family*, New York: International Universities Press, Inc., 1963; Rheingold, *op. cit.*

Where cultural pressure is very great to assume a particular adult role, as it is for American women to bear and rear children, latent desire and psychological readiness for parenthood may often be at odds with manifest desire and actual ability to perform adequately as parents. Clinicians and therapists are aware, as perhaps many sociologists are not, that failure, hostility, and destructiveness are as much a part of the family system and the relationships among family members as success, love, and solidarity are. . . .[5]

ROLE CYCLE STAGES

A discussion of the impact of parenthood upon the parent will be assisted by two analytic devices. One is to follow a comparative approach, by asking in what basic structural ways the parental role differs from other primary adult roles. The marital and occupational roles will be used for this comparison. A second device is to specify the phases in the development of a social role. If the total life span may be said to have a cycle, each stage with its unique tasks, then by analogy a role may be said to have a cycle and each stage in that role cycle, to have its unique tasks and problems of adjustment. Four broad stages of a role cycle may be specified:

1. Anticipatory Stage

All major adult roles have a long history of anticipatory training for them, since parental and school socialization of children is dedicated precisely to this task of producing the kind of competent adult valued by the culture. For our present purposes, however, a narrower conception of the anticipatory stage is preferable: the engagement period in the case of the marital role, pregnancy in the case of the parental role, and the last stages of highly vocationally oriented schooling or on-the-job apprenticeship in the case of an occupational role.

2. Honeymoon Stage

This is the time period immediately following the full assumption of the adult role. The inception of this stage is more easily defined than its termination. In the case of the marital role, the honeymoon stage extends from the marriage ceremony itself through the literal honeymoon and on through an unspecified and individually varying period of time. Raush[6] has caught this stage of the marital role in his description of the "psychic honeymoon": that extended postmarital period when, through close intimacy and joint activity,

[5] Cf. the long review of studies Rheingold covers in his book on maternal destructiveness, *op. cit.*
[6] Raush *et al., op. cit.*

the couple can explore each other's capacities and limitations. I shall arbitrarily consider the onset of pregnancy as marking the end of the honeymoon stage of the marital role. This stage of the parental role may involve an equivalent psychic honeymoon, that post-childbirth period during which, through intimacy and prolonged contact, an attachment between parent and child is laid down. There is a crucial difference, however, from the marital role in this stage. A woman knows her husband as a unique real person when she enters the honeymoon stage of marriage. A good deal of preparatory adjustment on a firm reality-base is possible during the engagement period which is not possible in the equivalent pregnancy period. Fantasy is not corrected by the reality of a specific individual child until the birth of the child. The "quickening" is psychologically of special significance to women precisely because it marks the first evidence of a real baby rather than a purely fantasized one. On this basis alone there is greater interpersonal adjustment and learning during the honeymoon stage of the parental role than of the marital role.

3. Plateau Stage

This is the protracted middle period of a role cycle during which the role is fully exercised. Depending on the specific problem under analysis, one would obviously subdivide this large plateau stage further. For my present purposes it is not necessary to do so, since my focus is on the earlier anticipatory and honeymoon stages of the parental role and the overall impact of parenthood on adults.

4. Disengagement-Termination Stage

This period immediately precedes and includes the actual termination of the role. Marriage ends with the death of the spouse or, just as definitively, with separation and divorce. A unique characteristic of parental role termination is the fact that it is not clearly marked by any specific act but is an attenuated process of termination with little cultural prescription about when the authority and obligations of a parent end. Many parents, however, experience the marriage of the child as a psychological termination of the active parental role.

UNIQUE FEATURES OF PARENTAL ROLE

With this role cycle suggestion as a broader framework, we can narrow our focus to what are the unique and most salient features of the parental role. In doing so, special attention will be given to two further questions: (1) the impact of social changes over the past few decades in facilitating or complicating the transition to and experience of parenthood and (2) the new interpretations of new research suggested by the focus on the parent rather than the child.

1. Cultural Pressure to Assume the Role

On the level of cultural values, men have no freedom of choice where work is concerned: They must work to secure their status as adult men. The equivalent for women has been maternity. There is considerable pressure upon the growing girl and young woman to consider maternity necessary for a woman's fulfillment as an individual and to secure her status as an adult.[7]

This is not to say there are no fluctuations over time in the intensity of the cultural pressure to parenthood. During the depression years of the 1930's, there was more widespread awareness of the economic hardships parenthood can entail, and many demographic experts believe there was a great increase in illegal abortions during those years. Bird has discussed the dread with which a suspected pregnancy was viewed by many American women in the 1930's.[8] Quite a different set of pressures were at work during the 1950's, when the general societal tendency was toward withdrawal from active engagement with the issues of the larger society and a turning in to the gratifications of the private sphere of home and family life. Important in the background were the general affluence of the period and the expanded room and ease of child rearing that go with suburban living. For the past five years, there has been a drop in the birth rate in general, fourth and higher-order births in particular. During this same period there has been increased concern and debate about women's participation in politics and work, with more women now returning to work rather than conceiving the third or fourth child.[9]

2. Inception of the Parental Role

The decision to marry and the choice of a mate are voluntary acts of individuals in our family system. Engagements are therefore consciously considered, freely entered, and freely terminated if increased familiarity de-

[7] The greater the cultural pressure to assume a given adult social role, the greater will be the tendency for individual negative feelings toward that role to be expressed covertly. Men may complain about a given job but not about working per se, and hence their work dissatisfactions are often displaced to the non-work sphere, as psychosomatic complaints of irritation and dominance at home. An equivalent displacement for women of the ambivalence many may feel toward maternity is to dissatisfactions with the homemaker role.

[8] Caroline Bird, *The Invisible Scar*, New York: David McKay Company, 1966.

[9] When it is realized that a mean family size of 3.5 would double the population in 40 years, while a mean of 2.5 would yield a stable population in the same period, the social importance of withholding praise for procreative prowess is clear. At the same time, a drop in the birth rate may reduce the number of unwanted babies born, for such a drop would mean more efficient contraceptive usage and a closer correspondence between desired and attained family size.

creases, rather than increases, intimacy and commitment to the choice. The inception of a pregnancy, unlike the engagement, is not always a voluntary decision, for it may be the unintended consequence of a sexual act that was recreative in intent rather than procreative. Secondly, and again unlike the engagement, the termination of a pregnancy is not socially sanctioned, as shown by current resistance to abortion-law reform.

The implication of this difference is a much higher probability of unwanted pregnancies than of unwanted marriages in our family system. Coupled with the ample clinical evidence of parental rejection and sometimes cruelty to children, it is all the more surprising that there has not been more consistent research attention to the problem of *parental satisfaction,* as there has for long been on *marital satisfaction* or *work satisfaction.* Only the extreme iceberg tip of the parental satisfaction continuum is clearly demarcated and researched, as in the growing concern with "battered babies." Cultural and psychological resistance to the image of a nonnurturant woman may afflict social scientists as well as the American public.

The timing of a first pregnancy is critical to the manner in which parental responsibilities are joined to the marital relationship. The single most important change over the past few decades is extensive and efficient contraceptive usage, since this has meant for a growing proportion of new marriages, the possibility of and increasing preference for some postponement of childbearing after marriage. When pregnancy was likely to follow shortly after marriage, the major transition point in a woman's life was marriage itself. *This transition point is increasingly the first pregnancy rather than marriage.* It is accepted and increasingly expected that women will work after marriage, while household furnishings are acquired and spouses complete their advanced training or gain a foothold in their work.[10] This provides an early marriage period in which the fact of a wife's employment presses for a greater egalitarian relationship between husband and wife in decision-making, commonality of experience, and sharing of household responsibilities.

The balance between individual autonomy and couple mutuality that develops during the honeymoon stage of such a marriage may be important in establishing a pattern that will later affect the quality of the parent-child relationship and the extent of sex-role segregation of duties between the parents. It is only in the context of a growing egalitarian base to the marital relationship that one could find, as Gavron has,[11] a tendency for parents to establish some barriers between themselves and their children, a marital defense against the institution of parenthood as she describes it. This may eventually replace the typical coalition in more traditional families of mother and children against husband-father. . . .

[10] James A. Davis, *Stipends and Spouses: The Finances of American Arts and Sciences Graduate Students,* Chicago: University of Chicago Press, 1962.
[11] Hannah Gavron, *The Captive Wife,* London: Routledge & Kegan Paul, 1966.

There is one further significant social change that has important implications for the changed relationship between husband and wife: the increasing departure from an old pattern of role-inception phasing in which the young person first completed his schooling, then established himself in the world of work, then married and began his family. Marriage and parenthood are increasingly taking place *before* the schooling of the husband, and often of the wife, has been completed.[12] An important reason for this trend lies in the fact that, during the same decades in which the average age of physical-sexual maturation has dropped, the average amount of education which young people obtain has been on the increase. Particularly for the college and graduate or professional school population, family roles are often assumed before the degrees needed to enter careers have been obtained . . . .

The major implication of this change is that more men and women are achieving full adult status in family roles while they are still less than fully adult in status terms in the occupational system. Graduate students are, increasingly, men and women with full family responsibilities. Within the family many more husbands and fathers are still students, often quite dependent on the earnings of their wives to see them through their advanced training.[13] No matter what the couple's desires and preferences are, this fact alone presses for more egalitarian relations between husband and wife, just as the adult family status of graduate students presses for more egalitarian relations between students and faculty.

3. Irrevocability

If marriages do not work out, there is now widespread acceptance of divorce and remarriage as a solution. The same point applies to the work world: we are free to leave an unsatisfactory job and seek another. But once a pregnancy occurs, there is little possibility of undoing the commitment to parenthood implicit in conception except in the rare instance of placing children for adoption. We can have ex-spouses and ex-jobs but not ex-children. This being so, it is scarcely surprising to find marked differences between the relationship of a parent and one child and the relationship of the same parent with another child. If the culture does not permit pregnancy termination, the equivalent to giving up a child is psychological withdrawal on the part of the parent.

This taps an important area in which a focus on the parent rather than the

[12] James A. Davis, *Stipends and Spouses: The Finances of American Arts and Sciences Graduate Students, op. cit.*; James A.Davis, *Great Aspirations*, Chicago: Aldine Publishing Company, 1964; Eli Ginsberg, *Life Styles of Educated Women*, New York: Columbia University Press, 1966; Ginsberg, *Educated American Women: Self Portraits*, New York: Columbia University Press, 1967; National Science Foundation, *Two Years After the College Degree—Work and Further Study Patterns*, Washington, D.C.: Government Printing Office, NSF 63-26, 1963.
[13] Davis, *Stipends and Spouses, The Finances of American Arts and Sciences Graduate Students, op. cit.*

child may contribute a new interpretive dimension to an old problem: the long history of interest, in the social sciences, in differences among children associated with their sex-birth-order position in their sibling set. Research has largely been based on data gathered about and/or from the children, and interpretations make inferences back to the "probable" quality of the child's relation to a parent and how a parent might differ in relating to a first-born compared to a last-born child. The relevant research, directed at the parents (mothers in particular), remains to be done, but at least a few examples can be suggested of the different order of interpretation that flows from a focus on the parent.

Some birth-order research stresses the influence of sibs upon other sibs, as in Koch's finding that second-born boys with an older sister are more feminine than second-born boys with an older brother.[14] A similar sib-influence interpretation is offered in the major common finding of birth-order correlates, that sociability is greater among last-borns[15] and achievement among first-borns.[16] It has been suggested that last-borns use social skills to increase acceptance by their older sibs or are more peer-oriented because they receive less adult stimulation from parents. The tendency of first-borns to greater achievement has been interpreted in a corollary way, as a reflection of early assumption of responsibility for younger sibs, greater adult stimulation during the time the oldest was the only child in the family,[17] and the greater significance of the first-born for the larger kinship network of the family.[18]

Sociologists have shown increasing interest in structural family variables in recent years, a primary variable being family size[19]. . . . The question posed is: what is the effect of growing up in a small family, compared with a large family, that is attributable to this group-size variable? Unfortunately, the theoretical point of departure for sociologists' expectations of the effect of the family-size variables is the Durkheim-Simmel tradition of the differential effect of group size or population density upon members or inhabitants.[19] In the case

[14] Orville G. Brim, "Family Structure and Sex-Role Learning by Chilren," *Sociometry*, 21 (1958), pp. 1–16; H.L. Koch, "Sissiness and Tomboyishness in Relation to Sibling Characteristics," *Journal of Genetic Psychology*, 88 (1956), pp. 231–244.
[15] Charles MacArthur, "Personalities of First and Second Children," *Psychiatry*, 19 (1956), pp. 47–54; S. Schachter, "Birth Order and Sociometric Choice," *Journal of Abnormal and Social Psychology*, 68 (1964), pp. 453–456.
[16] Irving Harris, *The Promised Seed*, New York: The Free Press, a division of the Macmillan Co., 1964; Bernard Rosen, "Family Structure and Achievement Motivation," *American Sociological Review*, 26 (1961), pp. 574–585; Alice S. Rossi, "Naming Children in Middle-Class Families," *American Sociological Review*, 30:4 (1965), pp. 499–513; Stanley Schachter, "Birth Order, Eminence and Higher Education," *American Sociological Review*, 28 (1963), pp. 757–768.
[17] Harris, *op. cit.*
[18] Rossi, "Naming Children in Middle-Class Families," *op. cit.*
[19] Thus Rosen writes: "Considering the sociologist's traditional and continuing concern with group size as an independent variable (from Simmel and Durkheim to the recent experimental studies of small groups), there have been surprisingly few studies of the influence of group size upon the nature of interaction in the family," *op. cit.*, p. 576.

of the family, however, this overlooks the very important fact that family size is determined by the key figures *within* the group, i.e., the parents. To find that children in small families differ from children in large families is not simply due to the impact of group size upon individual members but to the very different involvement of the parent with the children and to relations between the parents themselves in small versus large families.

An important clue to a new interpretation can be gained by examining family size from the perspective of parental motivation toward having children. A small family is small for one of two primary reasons: either the parents wanted a small family and achieved their desired size, or they wanted a large family but were not able to attain it. In either case, there is a low probability of unwanted children. Indeed, in the latter eventuality they may take particularly great interest in the children they do have. Small families are therefore most likely to contain parents with a strong and positive orientation to each of the children they have. A large family, by contrast, is large either because the parents achieved the size they desired or because they have more children than they in fact wanted. Large families therefore have a higher probability than small families of including unwanted and unloved children. Consistent with this are Nye's finding that adolescents in small families have better relations with their parents than those in large families[20] and Sears and Maccoby's finding that mothers of large families are more restrictive toward their children than mothers of small families.[21]

This also means that last-born children are more likely to be unwanted than first- or middle-born children, particularly in large families. This is consistent with what is known of abortion patterns among married women, who typically resort to abortion only when they have achieved the number of children they want or feel they can afford to have. Only a small proportion of women faced with such unwanted pregnancies actually resort to abortion. *This suggests the possibility that the last-born child's reliance on social skills may be his device for securing the attention and loving involvement of a parent less positively predisposed to him than to his older siblings.*

In developing this interpretation, rather extreme cases have been stressed. Closer to the normal range, of families in which even the last-born child was desired and planned for, there is still another element which may contribute to the greater sociability of the last-born child. Most parents are themselves aware of the greater ease with which they face the care of a third fragile newborn than the first; clearly, parental skills and confidence are greater with last-born children that with first-born children. But this does not mean that the attitude of the parent is more positive toward the care of the third child than

---

[20] Ivan Nye, "Adolescent-Parent Adjustment: Age, Sex, Sibling, Number, Broken Homes, and Employed Mothers as Variables," *Marriage and Family Living*, 14 (1952), pp. 327–332.
[21] Sears *et al., op. cit.*

the first. There is no necessary correlation between skills in an area and enjoyment of that area. Searls[22] found that older homemakers are *more* skillful in domestic tasks but experience *less* enjoyment of them than younger homemakers, pointing to a declining euphoria for a particular role with the passage of time. In the same way, older people rate their marriages as "very happy" less often than younger people do.[23] It is pehaps culturally and psychologically more difficult to face the possibility that women may find less enjoyment of the maternal role with the passage of time, though women themselves know the difference between the romantic expectation concerning child care and the incorporation of the first baby into the household and the more realistic expectation and sharper assessment of their own abilities to do an adequate job of mothering as they face a third confinement. Last-born children may experience not only less verbal stimulation from their parents than first-born children but also less prompt and enthusiastic response to their demands—from feeding and diaper-change as infants to requests for stories read at three or a college education at eighteen—simply because the parents experience less intense gratification from the parent role with the third child than they did with the first. The child's response to this might well be to cultivate winning, pleasing manners in early childhood that blossom as charm and sociability in later life, showing both a greater need to be loved and greater pressure to seek approval.

One last point may be appropriately developed at this juncture. Mention was made earlier that for many women the personal outcome of experience in the parent role is not a higher level of maturation but the negative outcome of a depressed sense of self-worth, if not actual personality deterioration. There is considerable evidence that this is more prevalent than we recognize. On a qualitative level, a close reading of the portrait of the working-class wife in Rainwater,[24] Newsom,[25] Komarovsky,[26] Gavron,[27] or Zweig[28] gives little suggestion that maternity has provided these women with opportunities for personal growth and development. So too, Cohen[29] notes with some surprise that in her sample of middle-class educated couples, as in Pavenstadt's study of lower-income women in Boston, there were more emotional difficulty and

[22] Laura G. Searls, "Leisure Role Emphasis of College Graduate Homemakers," *Journal of Marriage and the Family*, 28:1 (1966), pp. 77–82.
[23] Norman Bradburn and D. Caplovitz, *Reports on Happiness*, Chicago: Aldine Publishing, 1965.
[24] Lee Rainwater, R. Coleman, and G. Handel, *Workingman's Wife*, New York: Oceana Publications, 1959.
[25] John Newsom and E. Newsom, *Infant Care in an Urban Community*, New York: International Universities Press, 1963
[26] Mirra Komarovsky, *Blue Collar Marriage*, New York: Random House, 1962.
[27] Gavron, *op. cit.*
[28] Ferdinand Zweig, *Woman's Life and Labor*, London: Camelot Press, 1952.
[29] Cohen, *op. cit.*

lower levels of maturation among multiparous women than primiparous women. On a more extensive sample basis, in Gurin's survey of Americans viewing their mental health,[30] as in Bradburn's reports on happiness,[31] single men are less happy and less active than single women, but among the married respondents the women are unhappier, have more problems, feel inadequate as parents, have a more negative and passive outlook on life, and show a more negative self-image. All of these characteristics increase with age among married women but show no relationship to age among men. While it may be true, as Gurin argues, that women are more introspective and hence more attuned to the psychological facets of experience than men are, this point does not account for the fact that the things which the women report are all on the negative side; few are on the positive side, indicative of euphoric sensitivity and pleasure. The possibility must be faced, and at some point researched, that women lose ground in personal development and self-esteem during the early and middle years of adulthood, whereas men gain ground in these respects during the same years. The retention of a high level of self-esteem may depend upon the adequacy of earlier preparation for major adult roles: men's training adequately prepares them for their primary adult roles in the occupational system, as it does for those women who opt to participate significantly in the work world. Training in the qualities and skills needed for family roles in contemporary society may be inadequate for both sexes, but the lowering of self-esteem occurs only among women because their primary adult roles are within the family system.

4. Preparation for Parenthood

Four factors may be given special attention on the question of what preparation American couples bring to parenthood.

A. PAUCITY OF PREPARATION. Our educational system is dedicated to the cognitive development of the young, and our primary teaching approach is the pragmatic one of learning by doing. How much one knows and how well he can apply what he knows are the standards by which the child is judged in school, as the employee is judged at work. The child can learn by doing in such subjects as science, mathematics, art work, or shop, but not in the subjects most relevant to successful family life: sex, home maintenance, child care, interpersonal competence, and empathy. If the home is deficient in training in these areas, the child is left with no preparation for a major segment of his adult life. A doctor facing his first patient in private practice has

---

[30] Gerald Gurin, J. Veroff, and S. Feld, *Americans View Their Mental Health*, New York: Basic Books, Monograph Series No. 4, Joint Commission on Mental Illness and Health, 1960.
[31] Bradburn and Caplovitz, *op. cit.*

treated numerous patients under close supervision during his internship, but probably a majority of American mothers approach maternity with no previous child-care experience beyond sporadic baby-sitting, perhaps a course in child psychology, or occasional care of younger siblings.

B. LIMITED LEARNING DURING PREGNANCY. A second important point makes adjustment to parenthood potentially more stressful than marital adjustment. This is the lack of any realistic training for parenthood during the anticipatory stage of pregnancy. By contrast, during the engagement period preceding marriage, an individual has opportunities to develop the skills and make the adjustments which ease the transition to marriage. Through discussions of values and life goals, through sexual experimentation, shared social experiences as an engaged couple with friends and relatives, and planning and furnishing an apartment, the engaged couple can make considerable progress in developing mutuality in advance of the marriage itself.[32] No such headstart is possible in the case of pregnancy. What preparation exists is confined to reading, consultation with friends and parents, discussions between husband and wife, and a minor nesting phase in which a place and the equipment for a baby are prepared in the household.[33]

C. ABRUPTNESS OF TRANSITION. Thirdly, the birth of a child is not followed by any gradual taking on of responsibility, as in the case of a professional work role. It is as if the woman shifted from a graduate student to a full professor with little intervening apprenticeship experience of slowly increasing responsibility. The new mother starts out immediately on 24-hour duty, with responsibility for a fragile and mysterious infant totally dependent on her care.

If marital adjustment is more difficult for very young brides than more mature ones,[34] adjustment to motherhood may be even more difficult. A woman can adapt a passive dependence on a husband and still have a successful marriage, but a young mother with strong dependency needs is in for difficulty in maternal adjustment, because the role precludes such dependency. This situation was well described in Cohen's study[35] in a case of a young wife with a

---

[32] Rapoport, "The Transition from Engagement to Marriage," *op. cit.*; Raush *et al.*, *op. cit.*

[33] During the period when marriage was the critical transition in the adult woman's life rather than pregnancy, a good deal of anticipatory "nesting" behavior took place from the time of conception. Now more women work through a considerable portion of the first pregnancy, and such nesting behavior as exists may be confined to a few shopping expeditions or baby showers, thus adding to the abruptness of the transition and the difficulty of adjustment following the birth of a first child.

[34] Lee G. Burchinal, "Adolescent Role Deprivation and High School Marriage," *Marriage and Family Living*, 21 (1959), pp. 378–384; Floyd M. Martinson, "Ego Deficiency as a Factor in Marriage," *American Sociological Review*, 22 (1955), pp. 161–164; J. Joel Moss and Ruby Gingles, "The Relationship of Personality to the Incidence of Early Marriage," *Marriage and Family Living*, 21 (1959), pp. 373–377.

[35] Cohen, *op. cit.*

background of co-ed popularity and a passive dependent relationship to her admired and admiring husband, who collapsed into restricted incapacity when faced with the responsibilities of maintaining a home and caring for a child.

D. LACK OF GUIDELINES TO SUCCESSFUL PARENTHOOD. If the central task of parenthood is the rearing of children to become the kind of competent adults valued by the society, then an important question facing any parent is what he or she specifically can do to create such a competent adult. This is where the parent is left with few or no guidelines from the expert. Parents can readily inform themselves concerning the young infant's nutritional, clothing, and medical needs and follow the general prescription that a child needs loving physical contact and emotional support. Such advice may be sufficient to produce a healthy, happy, and well-adjusted preschooler, but adult competency is quite another matter.

In fact, the adults who do "succeed" in American society show a complex of characteristics as children that current experts in child-care would evaluate as "poor" to "bad." Biographies of leading authors and artists, as well as the more rigorous research inquiries of creativity among architects[36] or scientists,[37] do not portray childhoods with characteristics currently endorsed by mental health and child-care authorities. Indeed, there is often a predominance of tension in childhood family relations and traumatic loss rather than loving parental support, intense channeling of energy in one area of interest rather than an all-round profile of diverse interests, and social withdrawal and preference for loner activities rather than gregarious sociability. Thus, the stress in current child-rearing advice on a high level of loving support but a low level of discipline or restriction on the behavior of the child—the "developmental" family type as Duvall calls it[38]—is a profile consistent with the focus on mental health, sociability, and adjustment. Yet the combination of both high support and high authority on the part of parents is most strongly related to the child's sense of responsibility, leadership quality, and achievement level, as found in Bronfenbrenner's studies[39] and that of Mussen and Distler.[40]

[36] Donald W. MacKinnon, "Creativity and Images of the Self," in *The Study of Lives*, ed. by Robert W. White, New York: Atherton Press, 1963.
[37] Anne Roe, *A Psychological Study of Eminent Biologists*, *Psychological Monographs*, 65:14 (1951), 68 pages; Anne Roe, "A Psychological Study of Physical Scientists," *Genetic Psychology Monographs*, 43 (1951), pp. 121–239; Anne Roe, "Crucial Life Experiences in the Development of Scientists," in *Talent and Education*, ed. by E. P. Torrance, Minneapolis: University of Minnesota Press, 1960.
[38] Evelyn M. Duvall, "Conceptions of Parenthood," *American Journal of Sociology*, 52 (1946), pp. 193–203.
[39] Urie Bronfenbrenner, "Some Familial Antecedents of Responsibility and Leadership in Adolescents," in *Studies in Leadership*, ed. by L. Petrullo and B. Bass, New York: Holt, Rinehart, and Winston, 1960.
[40] Paul Mussen and L. Distler, "Masculinity, Identification and Father-Son Relationships," *Journal of Abnormal and Social Psychology*, 59 (1959), pp. 350–356.

Brim points out[41] that we are a long way from being able to say just what parent role prescriptions have what effect on the adult characteristics of the child. We know even less about how such parental prescriptions should be changed to adapt to changed conceptions of competency in adulthood. In such an ambiguous context, the great interest parents take in school reports on their children or the pediatrician's assessment of the child's developmental progress should be seen as among the few indices parents have of how well *they* are doing as parents.

[41] Orville G. Brim, "The Parent-Child Relation as a Social System: I. Parent and Child Roles," *Child Development*, 28:3 (1957), pp. 343–364.

"By tradition," Margaret Adams states, "the term single has been applied to women who have never been married, and until recently it carried the official, if not de facto, connotation of sexual abstinence." In recent years this view is no longer appropriate or accurate. The designation "single woman" includes those who were married and have been divorced or widowed as well as those who never have married, both celibate and not.

In the following essay, Adams discusses single women aged thirty and over and their problems in a society which increasingly recognizes but does not entirely accept their desire to maintain an existence which combines autonomy with sexual equality.

As you read "The Single Woman in Today's Society," note both the traditional attitudes about the disadvantages of being without a husband and what Adams sees as the two-fold advantages of being single today.

The Single Woman in Today's Society

MARGARET ADAMS

Writing on a theme of major societal significance today—such as the changing role of women—resembles a natural history exercise in which the student starts out to study a particular species, only to find that its ecological status and respondent characteristics have altered beyond recognition. So it is with the topic of single women. This article was planned on the basis of my own life experience as a middle-aged professional single woman, augmented by friends and colleagues of different ages, and reinforced by the model of three maiden aunts who functioned as significant social figures in my English west-country childhood. However, considering the subject more carefully, I realized that these seemingly stable and clearly delineated models are to a large extent an anachronistic figment of a bygone—or at least swiftly passing—social era, and that a fresh definition of what constitutes the single woman today must precede any discussion of her social role.

By tradition, the term single has been applied to women who have never been married, and until recently it carried the official, if not de facto, connotation of sexual abstinence. In this way the phenomenon of singleness was the antithesis of marriage, and its clearly defined social status was dependent on marriage being a stable social institution only ruptured by the death of one partner. Today, a different set of variables is needed to identify the single woman category because earlier marriages and easier divorce practices have robbed marriage of its permanence, while easily available and safe contraceptive techniques have made extramarital sex a commonplace. Within this article, then, singleness will apply not only to the numerically restricted group of never-marrieds but will also embrace widows and divorced women who fit other criteria that I am putting forward as the basis for a more relevant concept of singleness by today's social standards.

The primary criterion—or vital prerequisite—of being single is the capacity and opportunity to be economically self-supporting. This basic condition provides the elementary social independence from which most of the other features of singleness derive, and it relates this social status to broader societal issues. Thus the incidence of single women as a defined category within any given society is closely connected with its economic and political system and the roles that devolve on women. A society that engages in periodic bouts of violent warfare will have a surplus of women, so that, unless polygamy is the approved marital pattern, some will be without husbands and have to maintain themselves. In the Middle Ages, for example, lower-class single women found a livelihood on the land, in domestic service, and as alewives or spinners (hence the term spinster) while their upper-class counterparts were absorbed in the religious system as anchorites or nuns (Power, 1926). These arrangements came into being to counteract the decimation and absence of the male population occasioned by the Crusades.

A second essential criterion of singleness is social and psychological autonomy. The single woman's basic lifestyle is emotionally independent of relationships that carry with them long term commitment and a subjugation of personal or individual claims for their maintenance. This means she does not recognize a core relationship with a man as the primary or exclusive source of emotional satisfaction or social identity, neither is she encumbered by direct and statutorily defined dependents such as children. Single women, however, often have to assume some less direct, informal family responsibilities, such as contributing substantially to the financial support of aging, sick, or otherwise needy relatives, taking direct care of them on a temporary or protracted basis, and being available for emotional support and advice at times of crisis. My definition deliberately excludes the many unmarried, divorced, and widowed women who are female heads of families, on the grounds that their situation contains many features not pertinent to the life style of the single woman, and merits a discussion of its own.

The third criterion is a clearly thought through intent to remain single by preference rather than by default of being requested in marriage, either as first venture or following widowhood and divorce. It is important to stress this factor because marriage is invested with such a high premium in American society that very little credence is given to the idea that some women remain unmarried on purpose. Even when the choice seems arbitrarily imposed by a shortage of men, the failure of some personable women to secure a husband may be explained by their selective standards, set so high that they have not been met by the males available. In such cases, it may be inferred that the basic often unconscious, intention has been realized, though some of these women may be so hitched to the prevailing societal norms as to cherish the belief that they would have liked to have married.

Age is another significant factor and I have selected 30 and upwards as the chronological boundary delimiting the single state, on the grounds that the talk of unmarried girls in their twenties concentrate their energies on remedying their condition. This assumption is supported by statistics of March 1969, which show the following age distribution (in thousands) for single women—20–24 years, 2850; 25–29 years, 726; 30–34 years, 345; with the three successive decades showing a relatively stable figure between 560 and 600 (Department of Commerce, 1970). Thus we see that in the latter half of the 20 age group, the numbers of single women have declined to nearly a quarter of the figure reported in the 20–24 age group, and that this attenuated number is halved in the next five-year period. On the basis of these figures, one can infer that by 30 most women who are still unmarried are beginning to build up economic independence, and investment in work, and a viable value system that allows them to identify and exploit major sources of personal and social satisfaction in other areas than marriage and family. Even those whose first preference is marriage are compelled to readjust their social sights and relationships because the number of eligible men will have thinned out and their married peers will be caught up in a web of social and domestic activities with which they cannot identify and that do not meet their needs. At this juncture the unmarried woman, if she is not to be plagued by a constant sense of dissatisfaction, must take stock of her situation and carefully evaluate both its negative features and its assets. The remainder of this paper will try to define some of these social issues, and suggest solutions that will enable single women to realize a more viable and socially sanctioned identity.

The problems of unattached women range from the practical mechanics of day-to-day existence, such as a job and living accommodations, to the more subtle but equally vital questions of social role, acceptability, and personal self-esteem. Most of the intangible difficulties stem from one major core disadvantage, namely that single women constitute a clearly defined minority group* that demonstrates a conspicuously deviant pattern of functioning in terms of the dominant value system and the organizational goals of American society.

Although the world population crisis is fast turning the nuclear family into an obsolete and negatively redundant system, the myth of the sanctity of family life still has such a tenacious hold on the American imagination that women who eschew this modus vivendi are subject to a subtle array of social sanctions that erode their self-esteem, distort their relationships and disturb their sense of homeostasis in the shifting world scene. Single women, for example, are still the victims of quite outrageous stereotyping in regard to their ascribed characteristics, and their unmarried status is popularly attributed to personal failings, such as lack of sexual attractiveness (whatever that elusive quality may be), unresolved early psychosexual conflicts, narcissistic unwillingness to be closely committed to another individual, latent lesbianism. These characteristics may often be present, but if being single was not defined in terms of social deviance they would carry a less pathological connotation.

In this connection it is interesting to note the greater frequency with which psychological reasons have been adduced to explain singleness, rather than equally cogent sociological causes. While women today (except for the very poor and uneducated) have access to an increasingly broad repertoire of interesting opportunities in both work and social spheres, these factors are rarely put forward as serious reasons for not being married; if considered at all they are usually dismissed as second-best sublimated options. We have already mentioned the questionable value of the family as a useful social unit, but no one openly commends the decision of the unattached woman not to ally herself with this dinosaurlike social pattern.

Many of the less flattering qualities traditionally associated with unattached women—rigidity, overpreoccupation with minutiae, lack of self-confidence, excessive diffidence, or the overcompensatory quality of brazen hostility—are invariably attributed to poor ego-functioning, but very little thought is given to the extreme social insecurity within which the single woman has to operate. In a society that grants her sex the semblance of protection and economic support in exchange for subordinate obedience to male supremacy, the single woman who fends for herself is fair game for any exploitation the male-dominated working world chooses to exact. The fact that *all* women are in a relatively powerless position in most significant spheres of life—as demonstrated by salary differentials, sex discrimination in the more prestigious and powerful professional jobs, and numbers of women holding real executive power (Hedges, 1970)—means that the single ones have to be highly sensitive to potential exploitation and forearmed with defensive tactics. This social predicament is a more likely reason for aggressive behavior towards men than is the more personal psychological explanation of sexual frustration or defensive

---

*In the age range 30–74, the combined total (in thousands) of single, widowed, and divorced was 10,856, as against 35,279 married women, and in what might be termed the age span of greatest social activity, *i.e.,* between 30 and 54, the unmarried were 4,294 as against 25,218 (Department of Commerce, 1970).

denial of forbidden wishes. Furthermore, survival in today's highly competitive society demands a high level of self-assertiveness from both sexes; therefore this characteristic in single women must be seen as part of a societal mode of interaction rather than a personal idiosyncracy of sexual status.

The accusation that single women are malicious or lacking in generosity towards each other also requires a sociological as well as psychological interpretation. The emotional frustration that results from any devalued minority status tends to be turned inwards upon the group, rather than outwards to the social forces responsible: this is the same type of defense mechanism manifested by socially respectable members of racial minorities who castigate the social inadequacy of welfare recipients.

This devalued social definition of single women and the distorted selfimage of inferiority that it creates can exert a subtly damaging effect on the quality of social relationships with peers, the opposite sex, and married couples. The insidious conviction of being only second best makes it hard for single women to put a proper value on themselves; they tend to approach relationships in an over-diffident, if not apologetic, frame of mind, and perceive them as bestowing something of value on themselves rather than as of reciprocal benefit. In relationships with men this attitude has been particularly destructive, making women over-susceptible to exploitation and often ending in an abandonment that serves to reinforce the latent conviction of failure.

The more aware single woman, who is becoming liberated from this fettering self-concept of inadequacy, still has some residual uncertainty about her own identity, and in her heterosexual relationships is liable to be caught in a double bind of trying to decide what priority in time and emotional energy to devote to serious involvement with a man, while raising anew the question of how sincerely she is committed to the freedom of being single. For the man in question, there is confusion about the woman's newly emerging identity and the ambiguous and unclear goals of the relationship. The old exploitative options of "getting trapped" or "ditching the girl" no longer seem valid, which evokes anxiety—particularly when it involves redefining the beggar maid in more equitable terms.

Friendships with other single women are prone to a similar kind of problem, particularly if both still believe in the inferior status of women and suspect that each is only using the other's companionship and emotional support as a stopgap to ward off loneliness and fill in the time, pending a more rewarding relationship with a man. Further, the overwhelming importance attached to this latter objective introduces a frustration and desperation heightened by the fear that one may succeed, thus abandoning the other to loneliness and a reinforced sense of underachievement. This ambiguous and destructive situation will improve only when marriage or long-term involvement with the other sex is seen as a matter of personal choice and not of social prestige and obligation.

Relationships with married friends are also invested with hazards, although they offer the best scope for the single woman to be herself, because she is not being measured solely for her sexual viability. She may even lose her poor-relation status and be welcomed as someone whose broader range of work experience and more varied social and cultural contacts can introduce a note of novelty into a family situation. To the children, she presents a different facet of the adult world from the familiar one they experience in their own mother and those of their friends. Through this contact the wife is kept aware of roles open to women other than the strictly homemaking one she is momentarily absorbed in; this sort of unobtrusive psychological reinforcement to the fuller personality and identity of the housebound woman is an important liberating factor. For the husband, the relationship with the single friend supplies a fresh dimension to the absorbing model of domesticity with which he and his wife have become saddled, as well as the prospect of other more varied facets of life that both can resume in the future. It also provides opportunity for enjoying additional feminine company in the safe confines of a family friendship.

Here, a comment is needed on the word "safe," which is used deliberately to illustrate another unconscious social and psychological belittlement of the single woman, through its implication of the wife's superior sexual attractiveness, her impregnable sense of security in possession, or implicit reliance on the friend's loyalty. This dilemma of the "friendly threesome," and the underpull of tensions that sustain the relationship, is rarely acknowledged, while almost universal recognition is given to its more pronounced version, the eternal triangle. If she is not careful, the single woman can often unwittingly find herself in the position of being a stand-in spouse, even to being consigned the future care of the husband should he survive his wife. Such situations are reminiscent of Biblical parables, of tribal customs for ensuring the care of dependent survivors, and even suttees—the common factor to all these practices being the testimentary disposition of socially vulnerable women for society's convenience.

I have been concentrating on the more subtle aspects of personal relationships because these are closely tied to the emerging social identity of women and, being less obtrusive, have been overshadowed by more obvious problems. Up till recently, scope for sexual experience presented a major difficulty for single women because of narrow penalizing sexual mores and the actual danger of becoming pregnant. The development of effective and reliable contraceptive techniques that are within women's control has, to a large extent, removed both these obstacles and provided single women with opportunity for sexual relationships equal to those hitherto available to legally married women and *all* men. This end to the double standard of sexual behavior is having an influence on the quality of sexual relationships in that the activity is developing a more strongly social character with less heavy psychological weighting than when it was precarious and taboo. One result seems to be a tendency for sexual liaisons to be more numerous and frequent, with much shorter-term commitment. (This is also reflected in the divorce rate [Department of Commerce, 1970], an institutionalized version of the same phenomenon.)

In this context I should like to mention the psychological myth that women are more inherently faithful than men in sexual relationships, are inclined to invest more emotion over a longer time span, and feel proportionately traumatized when the relationship terminates. My feeling is that this psychological attribute has been developed over time to rationalize and make bearable a situation into which women were trapped by marriage or recurrent childbearing, and that when these fettering external circumstances open up there will be accompanying internal flexibility and freedom. The freewheeling single woman should be among the first to be emancipated from this misconception and to invest the pejorative term, *promiscuity* (an exclusively female epithet), with the adventurous insouciance evoked by the phrase, *wild oats*. The revelation that women have greater and more sustained capacity for sexual activity than hitherto suspected will add grist to this notion once the prim ideas of monogamous loyalty and irrevocable emotional investment have been exploded (Masters and Johnson, 1966, 1970).

The social relationships of unattached women also present practical difficulties, particularly the question of how to develop a pattern of life that satisfies the need for day-to-day ongoing social intercourse. Apart from a relatively small number of women who have exceptional inner resources of their own or are involved in creative projects that require a good deal of solitary leisure, most single women have to cope with recurrent problems of personal loneliness. To counteract these social lacunae the single woman has to organize a deliberately structured social life for herself and invest a good deal of time and energy in maintaining its momentum.

Establishing a satisfying and stimulating social life bears especially hard on single women when they move to a new community because they have fewer introductory lines of communication than their married counterparts, whose husband and children provide a contact with other families or individuals. Also, as long as single women are regarded as a tiresome surplus, there is a reluctance to co-opt new members of the species into an extant social circle lest they disturb the balance of the sexes. For this same reason, single women are often denied admission to more formal social groups, such as country clubs.

A significant lack in the single woman's life is a congenial, trustworthy, and accessible person to serve as a sounding-board and provide the requisite feedback. To meet this need and to offset potential loneliness many single women are beginning to develop informal, loosely-knit communes of unattached individuals who are not close and intimate friends but operate among each other on the basis of shared needs and reciprocal services. Such a group can provide casual and ad hoc entertainment and an exchange of small but vital homemaking services in times of illness or emergency.

Living accommodation is another problem area for single women, though there has been a substantial development of accommodation suitable for single occupants over the last 40 years. In the 1930s, for example, unmarried professional or white collar women workers frequently had to live at home in the ambiguous role of adult child of the family or in a carefully selected private hotel or woman's residence (often euphemistically termed a "club," as in Muriel Spark's novel, *The Girls of Slender Means),* a bed-sitting room with shared cooking facilities, or, more rarely, a private apartment. Today, efficiency apartments and cooperatives offer a range of independent options. However, the lower salaries earned by women at all levels place an economic bar on their taking advantage of these opportunities (considerable savings are needed to purchase an even modest cooperative) and they are often forced into the compromise of rooming with one or two others in order to meet the rent and maintenance bills. While this may sometimes be a deliberate choice, it is more often an expediency involving a sacrifice of standards—in space or privacy—that diminishes the single woman's social self-sufficiency and autonomy. There is also a subtle prestige factor in that a certain level of social sophistication is associated with having your own menage (vide Helen Gurley Brown!), whereas a household shared by several women has a slightly comic undertone, calling up a residual picture of a college dormitory and adolescence.

Single women are also very vulnerable to harassment and intimidation by unscrupulous landlords, particularly in areas where there is heavy competition for housing, such as the larger cities to which unattached women tend to migrate because of the greater choice of work and social, educational, and cultural opportunities. Where there is a large financial investment at stake, such as purchasing a house in a socially desirable area, single women are liable to encounter prejudice of the same order experienced by blacks, in which realtors operate on the basis of a preconceived stereotype about the applicant rather than on whether the applicant earns enough money to be an effective purchaser, and to maintain the property at the level demanded by the community. All these problems—major and minor—represent an accumulative discrimination that keeps single women in a chronically second-grade living situation, reduces their social status, and saps their individual and corporate self-respect.

If this has been a rather dismal catalogue of complaints about the social condition of single women, I want to end with a brief account of what I consider to be some of the invaluable assets that also attach to this status. My intent in delineating the disadvantages has been to help identify the negative social forces that stand in the way of these assets being fully realized. By making explicit the severe psychological and social devaluation that has settled like an accretion around the concept of singleness, I mean to imply that this attitude is a societal product capable of being changed once its destructive potential is understood. By pointing up the practical difficulties single women face in everyday living, I hope to set in motion ingenious ideas and innovative experiments that will develop more efficient social arrangements to minimize these hazards.

The advantages of being single are two-fold—those that redound directly upon the single woman and those that accrue to the corporate good of society. To start with individual benefits, the unmarried woman has greater freedom to take advantage of the exceptional opportunities for new experiences offered by today's rapidly changing world. This can mean moving to work in a different city, country, or continent; it can mean leaving one type of employment for another. For the well-paid professional woman who has been able to save, this freedom from personal commitment allows her to purchase time and involve herself in some different creative activity such as traveling, writing a book, or continuing her education. Because her psychic energy is not primarily invested in the emotionally absorbing task of maintaining a home, a family, or a partner whose needs have to take precedence, the single woman can be more receptive to fresh experience and new ideas, and is able to develop the heightened capacity for social analysis and commentary so vital in today's swiftly evolving pre-revolutionary society. She also has greater freedom to involve herself in social action and reform movements, including activities that involve a high degree of risk-taking, such as being fired from employment, arrested for civil disobedience or physically assaulted by today's violently repressive process of law and order.

Having examined the social entity of the single woman and the debits and assets of the role she has been allotted in today's society, we must now consider how her societal characteristics relate to the radical women's movement, whether she has a special contribution to make to this dynamic social trend, and what impact its changes will have upon her modus vivendi.

The radical feminist movement has three major goals. First, to help women free themselves from the socially restrictive and psychologically enervating roles into which they have been forced by the exigencies of a male-dominated social system. Second, to demonstrate the connection between the tyranny imposed upon women as a sex and the exploitation of all powerless groups, both of which are an inevitable outcome of a capitalist economy. Third, to tap and channel the constructive social energy of women—currently dissipated in many futile, if not destructive, activities—as a motive force for propelling the basic social changes needed to bring about a more equitable and functional distribution of power.

In brief, the aim of women's liberation is to change the prevailing ideas about women—their rights, their potentialities, their aspirations; to change the social structure that has created and still supports this impotent definition; and to offer women, along with other oppressed groups, the opportunity to assume a more viable and satisfying social role with corresponding different functions and life styles.

How does the single woman fit into this scheme? Two areas immediately suggest themselves: psychological emancipation, and radical redefinition with altered social status and functioning.

The single woman, as we have seen, has been a particular victim of the psychological enslavement to which all women have been subjected. Feminist writing has frequently focused on the plight of married women, emphasizing the psychological seduction that has enmeshed them in the spider-web belief that their domesticated condition represents physical, mental, and cultural fulfillment. Less is said about the other side of the coin by which those outside of marriage are saddled with a sense of deprivation, deficit, and alienation. By defining women as sound, whole, viable beings in their own right the radical movement has restored the single woman's sense of self-esteem and put her into the mainstream of social acceptability and importance. Single women, if they can recognize the assets attaching to their status, are in a position to offer a more sharply defined model for the emerging social identity of their sex and the new societal roles that may devolve upon women.

Because of the stringent necessity to be economically self-supporting single women have also had to develop a greater sense of personal independence and some practical expertise in fending for themselves in a discriminating economic sphere. Women in the working and professional world have been conspicuously lacking in executive power, but involvement in this masculine arena, even at a lower social level, has given them an intimate familiarity with the habits of the male and the ecology of his power system. Such knowledge can be turned to good diagnostic account when the time comes for invading that system and instituting radical change. This knowledge is shared by all the female work force but the greater investment that single women are likely to have in their work, which is not only their economic mainstay but also a major force in defining their social identity, probably gives them sharper insights. The business executive's indefatigable secretary, the loyal nurse-receptionist who is privy to her doctor-employer's professional commitments, the woman faculty member, if they do not have a domestic male figure on which to exercise these observational skills, become very adept at sizing up the quirks, weaknesses, strengths and Achilles' heels of their male colleagues, much as potential revolutionaries study the characteristics of the regime they plan to overthrow. What may start as an intuitive diversion becomes a self-conscious exercise with important educational significance.

In terms of purposeful intent, single women are also likely to have a greater capacity for hardheaded, clear-thinking judgment because they are not influenced by the same conflicts and ambivalences that necessarily afflict women who are in a relationship of affectionate amity with a husband or long-term equivalent. This is not to say that the radical feminist movement is the work of single women alone, since the facts suggest quite the opposite, but merely that some of the burdens fall more heavily on their married counterparts.

Finally, what effect will radical change have on the small coterie of women I have designated as single? First, they are likely to be rendered obsolete as a specifically defined group, and far from being in a deviant minority may find that their situation has been transformed into the popular norm. This corresponds with the position that is currently predicted and advocated by many radical feminist writers. The threat of overpopulation and diminishing food supply has already begun to rob marriage of its vital rationale—*i.e.,* the procreation of children and maintenance of a stable family setting for their nurturance—and as more attention is focused on the importance of restricting population growth, marriage will come to be seen as a societal liability perpetuating an outmoded dysfunctional social system. Once women become disabused of the notion that marriage and rearing a family represent the most rewarding way of life, and can choose the sort of life they want to lead and where to invest their social energies and skills, there will be a much smaller drift towards this goal. I arbitrarily imposed the lower age limit of 30 on my definition of singleness to highlight its antithetical stance to marriage; when the lure of the latter has receded, singleness may become the more widely sought option and some of the characteristics and interactive patterns that I have described as pertaining to the present-day single woman may be assumed by women in the younger age bracket.

What effect this change of focus will have on women's social objectives and opportunities remains to be seen, but we can speculate that there will be greater and more visible scope for individuals to develop what Ruth Benedict terms their "congenial responses" instead of the contorted antics preordained by society. Those for whom pursuit of knowledge, exploration of ideas, and wider range of experience have a greater appeal than do close interpersonal relationships will be freer to follow this bent without having to pay lip service to the other, more socially dominating, objective of securing a lifelong male companion. Others for whom emotional involvement has higher priority will be able to rechannel their nurturing and protective impulses into public activities that foster the common weal rather than the private family unit. The diminished few who mate and produce children will be the minority, and their pattern of life will approximate more to that of their working counterparts who are unencumbered by dependents. Day care and other socially contrived family supports will be essential pieces of equipment for child-rearing, as the vacuum cleaner is for housework, and mothers—with or without attendant spouses—will be expected and encouraged to develop a wider sphere of interest than the narrow unit of the family within which most of them are currently confined. This trend has already been set in motion. When it attains its full momentum the more obvious differences between the officially single and officially married woman will be absorbed in a new common life pattern.

References

Hedges, J. "Women Workers and Manpower Demands in the 1970s. In *Women at Work: Monthly Labor Review*. U.S. Department of Labor, Bureau of Labor Statistics, Washington, D.C.: Government Printing Office, 1970.

Masters, W., and Johnson, V. *Human Sexual Response*. Boston: Little, Brown, 1966.

Masters, W., and Johnson, V. *Human Sexual Inadequacy*. Boston: Little, Brown, 1970.

Power, E. "The Position of Women." In *The Legacy of the Middle Ages*, edited by C. Crump and E. Jacob. Oxford: Clarendon Press, 1926.

U.S. Department of Commerce. *Statistical Abstracts of the United States*. Washington, D.C.: Government Printing Office, 1970.

Recent figures suggest that one in three of today's marriages will end in divorce. No longer an exceptional phenomenon, divorce has become a widespread means of resolving marital difficulties although, as anthropologist Paul Bohannon explains, new problems are often created in the process.

In his book After Divorce, *Bohannan examines the complex character of divorce in our society and in others. The following excerpt describes what he calls "The Six Stations of Divorce" (emotional, legal, economic, coparental, community, and psychic)— stages that begin with emotional turmoil and end, hopefully, with reintegration.*

As you read Bohannan's summary, ask yourself what he means when he says that preparation for divorce involves deselection, why divorce itself involves a form of grief (a term usually reserved for bereavement), and why psychic divorce is the last stage and the first step toward reintegration.

The Six Stations of Divorce

PAUL BOHANNAN

Divorce is a complex social phenomenon as well as a complex personal experience. Because most of us are ignorant of what it requires of us, divorce is likely to be traumatic: emotional stimulation is so great that accustomed ways of acting are inadequate. The usual way for the healthy mind to deal with trauma is to block it out, then let it reappear slowly, so it is easier to manage. The blocking may appear as memory lapses or as general apathy.

On a social level we do something analogous, not allowing ourselves to think fully about divorce as a social problem. Our personal distrust of the emotions that surround it leads us to consider it only with traditional cultural defenses. Our ignorance masquerades as approval or disapproval, as enlightenment or moral conviction.[1]

The complexity of divorce arises because at least six things are happening at once. They may come in a different order and with varying intensities, but there are at least these six different experiences of separation. They are the more painful and puzzling as personal experiences because society is not yet equipped to handle any of them well, and some of them we do not handle at all.

I have called these six overlapping experiences (1) the emotional divorce; which centers around the problem of the deteriorating marriage; (2) the legal divorce, based on grounds; (3) the economic divorce, which deals with money and property; (4) the coparental divorce, which deals with custody, single-parent homes, and visitation; (5) the community divorce, surrounding the changes of friends and community that every divorcee experiences; and (6) the psychic divorce, with the problem of regaining individual autonomy.

The first visible stage of a deteriorating marriage is likely to be what psychiatrists call emotional divorce. This occurs when the spouses withhold emotion from their relationship because they dislike the intensity or ambivalence of their feelings. They may continue to work together as a social team, but their attraction and trust for one another have disappeared. The self-regard of each is no longer reinforced by love for the other. The emotional divorce is experienced as an unsavory choice between giving in and hating oneself and domineering and hating one self. The natural and healthy "growing apart" of a married couple is very different. As marriages mature, the partners grow in new directions, but also establish bonds of ever greater interdependence. With emotional divorce, people do not grow together as they grow apart—they become, instead, mutually antagonistic and imprisoned, hating the vestiges of their dependence. Two people in emotional divorce grate on each other because each is disappointed.

In American society, we have turned over to the courts the responsibility for formalizing the dissolution of such a marriage. The legislature (which in early English law usurped the responsibility from the church, and then in the American colonies turned it over to the courts) makes the statutes and defines the categories into which every marital dispute must be thrust if legal divorce is possible. Divorce is not "legalized" in many societies but may be done by a church or even by contract. Even in our own society, there is only one thing that a divorce court can do that cannot be done more effectively some other way—establish the right to remarry.

The economic divorce must occur because in Western countries husband and wife are an economic unit. Their unity is recognized by the law. They can—and in some states must—own property as a single "legal person." While technically the couple is not a corporation, they certainly have many of the characteristics of a legal corporation. At the time the household is broken up by divorce, an economic settlement must be made, separating the assets of the "corporation" into two sets of assets, each belonging to one person. This is the property settlement.

All divorced persons suffer more or less because their community is altered. Friends necessarily take a different view of a person during and after divorce—

he ceases to be a part of a couple. Their own inadequacies, therefore, will be projected in a new way. Their fantasies are likely to change as they focus on the changing situation. In many cases, the change in community attitude—and perhaps people too—is experienced by a divorcee as ostracism and disapproval. For many divorcing people, the divorce from community may make it seem that nothing in the world is stable.

Finally comes the psychic divorce. It is almost always last, and always the most difficult. Indeed, I have not found a word strong or precise enough to describe the difficulty or the process. Each partner to the ex-marriage, either before or after the legal divorce—usually after, and sometimes years after—must turn himself or herself again into an autonomous social individual. People who have been long married tend to have become socially part of a couple or a family; they lose the habit of seeing themselves as individuals. This is worse for people who married in order to avoid becoming autonomous individuals in the first place.

To become an individual again, at the center of a new community, requires developing new facets of character. Some people have forgotten how to do it—some never learned. The most potent argument against teen-age marriages is that they are likely to occur between people who are searching for independence but avoiding autonomy. The most potent argument against hurried remarriage is the same: avoidance of the responsibilities of autonomy.

Divorce is an institution that nobody enters without great trepidation. In the emotional divorce, people are likely to feel hurt and angry. In the legal divorce, people often feel bewildered—they have lost control, and events sweep them along. In the economic divorce, the reassignment of property and the division of money (there is *never* enough) may make them feel cheated. In the parental divorce they worry about what is going to happen to the children; they feel guilty for what they have done. With the community divorce, they may get angry with their friends and perhaps suffer despair because there seems to be no fidelity in friendship. In the psychic divorce, in which they have to become autonomous again, they are probably afraid and are certainly lonely. However, the resolution of any or all of these various six divorces may provide an elation of victory that comes from having accomplished something that had to be done and having done it well. There may be ultimate satisfactions in it.

THE EMOTIONAL DIVORCE AND THE PROBLEM OF GRIEF

One of the reasons it feels so good to be engaged and newly married is the rewarding sensation that, out of the whole world, you have been selected. One of the reasons that divorce feels so awful is that you have been de-selected. It punishes almost as much as the engagement and the wedding are rewarding.

The chain of events and feelings that lead up to divorce are as long and as varied as the chain of events that lead up to being selected for marriage. The difference is that the feelings are concentrated in the area of the weak points in the personality rather than the growing points of the personality.

Almost no two people who have been married, even for a short time, can help knowing where to hit each other if they want to wound. On the other hand, any two people—no matter who they are—who are locked together in conflict have to be very perceptive to figure out what the strain is really all about. Marital fights occur in every healthy marriage. The fact of health is indicated when marital disputes lead to a clarification of issues and to successful extension of the relationship into new areas. Difficulties arise only when marital conflict is sidetracked to false issues (and sometimes the discovery of just what issue is at stake may be, in itself, an adequate conclusion to the conflict), or when the emotional pressures are shunted to other areas. When a couple are afraid to fight over the real issue, they fight over something else— and perhaps never discover what the real issue was.

Two of the areas of life that are most ready to accept such displacement are the areas of sex and money. Both sex and money are considered worthwhile fighting over in American culture. If it is impossible to know or admit what a fight is all about, then the embattled couple may cast about for areas of displacement, and they come up with money and sex, because both can be used as weapons. Often these are not the basis of the difficulties, which lie in unconscious or inadmissible areas.

These facts lead a lot of people to think that emotional divorce occurs over money or over sexual incompatibility just because that is where the overt strife is allowed to come out. Often, however, these are only camouflage.

Money and the Emotional Divorce

One of the most tenacious ideas from our early training is "the value of a dollar." When in the larger society the self is reflected in possessions, and when money becomes one mode of enhancing the self—then we have difficulty with anybody who either spends it too lavishly or sits on it more tightly then we do.

Money is a subject about which talk is possible. Most middle-class couples do talk about money; most of them, in fact, make compromises more or less adequate to both. But in all cases, money management and budgeting are endlessly discussed in the American household. If communication becomes difficult, one of the first places that it shows up is in absence of knowledge about the other person's expenditures.

I interviewed one divorced woman who blamed her ex-husband's spending practices and attitude toward money as a major factor in their divorce. She said that he bought her an expensive car and asked her to leave it sitting outside the house when she was not driving it. *She* announced that *he* could not afford it. He asked her to join a golf club. She refused, although she was a good golfer and liked to play—because *she* told him *he* could not afford it. Whenever he wanted to use her considerable beauty and accomplishments to reflect a little credit on himself for being able to have captured and kept such a wife, she announced that he could not afford it. After the divorce, it continued. Then one day, in anger, she telephoned him to say that she was tired of making sacrifices—this year she was going to take the children on a transcontinental vacation and that he would simply have to pay for the trip. He did not explode; he only thought for a minute and said that he guessed that would be all right, and that he would whittle down his plans for the children's vacation with him, so that it would come within the budget.

This woman told this story without realizing what she had revealed: that her husband was not going to push himself or them into bankruptcy; that he did indeed know how much things cost, and that he could either afford or otherwise manage what he wanted to give her. There was doubtless a difference of opinion about money—she, it appears, preferred to save and then spend; he preferred, perhaps, to spend and then pay. She, for reasons I cannot know from one extended interview, did not recognize his feelings. She *did* announce to him, every time that he wanted to spend money on her, that he was inadequate. I suspect it was her own fear that she would let him down. Without knowing it, she was attacking him where it hurt him and where her housewifely virtue could be kept intact, while she did not have to expose herself or take a chance.

I am not saying that there are not spendthrift husbands or wives. I am saying that if differences that lie beyond money cannot be discussed, then money is a likely battleground for the emotional divorce.

Sex and the Emotional Divorce

Among the hundreds of divorcees I have talked to, there is a wide range of sexual attitudes. There were marriages in which sexual symptoms were the first difficulties to be recognized by the couple. There were a few in which the sexual association seemed the only strong bond. I know of several instances in which the couple met for a ceremonial bout of sexual intercourse as the last legitimate act before their divorce. I have a newspaper clipping that tells of a man who, after such a "last legal assignation," murdered his wife before she became his ex-wife. And I know one divorce that was denied because, as the judge put it, he could not condone "litigation by day and copulation by night."

Usually, when communication between the spouses becomes strained, sexual rapport is the first thing to go. There are many aspects to this problem: sexual intercourse is the most intimate of social relationships, and reservations or ambivalences in the emotions are likely to show up there (with unconscious conflicts added to conscious ones). The conflicts may take the extreme form of frigidity in women, impotence in men. They may take the form of adultery, which may be an attempt to communicate something, an unconscious effort to improve the marriage itself. It may be an attempt to humiliate the spouse into leaving. Adultery cannot sensibly be judged without knowing what it means to a specific person and to his spouse in a specific situation. Adultery is a legal ground for divorce in every jurisdiction in the United States, and indeed in most of the record-keeping world.

Because sexuality is closely associated with integration of the personality, it is not surprising that disturbance in the relationship of the spouses may be exposed in sexual symptoms. Except in some cases in which the marriage breaks up within a few weeks or months, however, sexual difficulties are a mode of expression as often as they provide the basic difficulty.

Growing Apart

Married people, like any other people, must continue to grow as individuals if they are not to stagnate. Only by extending themselves to new experiences and overcoming new conflicts can they participate fully in new social relationships and learn new culture. That means that no one, at the time of marriage, can know what the spouse is going to become. Moreover, it means that he cannot know what he himself may become.

Some of this growth of individuals must necessarily take place outside of the marriage. If the two people are willing and able to perceive and tolerate the changes in one another, and overcome them by a growing relationship directly with the other person, then the mutual rewards are very great, and conflicts can be resolved.

Inability to tolerate change in the partner (or to see him as he is) always lies, I think, at the root of emotional divorce. All marriages become constantly more attenuated from the end of the honeymoon period probably until the retirement of the husband from the world of affairs. That is to say, the proportion of the total concern of one individual that can be given to the other individual in the marriage decreases, even though the precise quantity (supposing there were a way to measure it) might become greater. But the ties may become tougher, even as they become thinner.

When this growing apart and concomitant increase in the toughness of the bonds does *not* happen, then people feel the marriage bonds as fetters and become disappointed or angry with each other. They feel cramped by the marriage and cheated by their partner. A break may be the only salvation for some couples.

In America today, our emotional lives are made diffuse by the very nature of the culture with which we are surrounded. Family life, business or professional demands, community pressures—today all are in competition with one another for our time and energies. When that happens, the social stage is set for emotional divorce of individual couples, because the marriage relationship becomes just another competing institution. Sometimes emotional divorce seems scarcely more than another symptom of the diffuseness.

Emotional Divorce and Grief

Emotional divorce results in the loss of a loved object just as fully—but by quite a different route of experience—as does the death of a spouse. Divorce is difficult because it involves a purposeful and active rejection by another person, who merely by living, is a daily symbol of the rejection. It is also made difficult because the community helps even less in divorce than it does in bereavement.

The natural reaction to the loss of a loved object or person (and sometimes a hated one as well) is grief. The distribution of emotional energy is changed significantly; new frustration must be borne until new arrangements can be worked out. Human beings mourn every loss of meaningful relationship. The degree depends on the amount of emotional involvement. Mourning may be traumatic—and it may, like any other trauma, have to be blocked and only slowly allowed into awareness. Mourning may take several months or years.

Divorce is even more threatening than death to some people, because they have thought about it more, perhaps wished for it more consciously. But most importantly—there is no recognized way to mourn a divorce. The grief has to be worked out alone and without benefit of traditional rites, because few people recognize it for what it is.

When grief gets entangled with all the other emotions that are evoked in a divorce, the emotional working through becomes complicated—in a divorce one is very much on his own.

THE LEGAL DIVORCE AND THE PROBLEM OF GROUNDS

Judicial divorce, as it is practiced in the United States today, is a legal postmortem on the demise of an intimate relationship. It originated in Massachusetts in the early 1700s as a means for dealing with the problems that emotional divorce caused in families, at the same time that all going households could continue to be based on holy matrimony. Legal divorce has been discovered and used many times in the history of the world, but this particular institution has no precursors in European history. The historical period in which it developed is important. In those days it was considered necessary that the state could profess its interest in the marriage and the family only in the guise of punishing one of the spouses for misconduct. Thus, the divorce itself was proclaimed to be the punishment of the guilty party. Whether divorce as a punishment was ever a commonsensical idea is a moot point—certainly it is not so today. Yet, our law still reflects this idea.

Thus, if the state is to grant divorces to "innocent" spouses as punishment to offending spouses, it must legalize certain aspects of the family—must, in fact, establish minimal standards of performance in family roles. Marriages break down in all societies; we have come, by state intervention, to solve some of these breakdowns with the legal institution of divorce. Until very recently, no country granted its citizens the clear right to divorce, as they have the clear right to marry. The right is always conditional on acts of misbehavior of the spouse, as misbehavior has been legally defined and called "grounds." Whatever the spouse does must be thrust into the categories that the law recognizes before it can be grounds for divorce.

Divorce lawyers are forced, in the nature of the law, to put the "real situation," as they learn it from their clients, into language that the law will accept. If a divorce action is to go to court, it must first be couched in language that the courts are legally permitted to accept. Both marriage counselors and lawyers have assured me that reconciliation is always more difficult after grounds have been discussed and legal papers written than when it is still in the language of "reasons" and personal emotion. Legal language and choice of grounds are the first positive steps toward a new type of relationship with the person one of my informants called "my ex-to-be." Discussion of grounds often amounts, from the point of view of the divorcing person, to listing all the faults that the spouse ever committed, then picking one.

We all know that grounds and reasons may be quite different. The divorcing person usually feels that he should not "tattle" and selects the "mildest" ground. Yet, every person who institutes a suit for divorce must wonder whether to use "adultery" if in fact it occurred, or to settle for the more noncommittal "mental cruelty." Does one use drunkenness when divorcing an alcoholic? Or desertion? Or does one settle for "incompatibility"?

One of the reasons that the divorce institution is so hard on people is that the legal processes do not provide an orderly and socially approved discharge of emotions that are elicited during the emotional divorce and during the early parts of preparation for the legal processes. Divorces are "cranked out" but divorcees are not "cooled out."

THE ECONOMIC DIVORCE AND THE PROBLEM OF PROPERTY

The family household is the unit of economic consumption in the United States. As such, middle-class households must have a certain amount of domestic-capital equipment besides personal property such as cars and television sets. In most households, these items "belong to the family," even though they may be legally owned in the name of one of the spouses.

Behind the idea of fair settlement of property at the time of divorce is the assumption that a man cannot earn money to support his family if he does not have the moral assistance and domestic services of his wife. The wife, if she works, does so in order to "enhance" the family income (no matter how much she makes or what the "psychic income" to her might be). Therefore, every salary dollar, every patent, every investment, is joint property.

In most states, the property settlement is not recorded in the public records of divorce, so precise information is lacking. However, in most settlements, the wife receives from one-third to one-half of the property.

Many wives voluntarily give up their rights to property at the time they become ex-wives. Some are quite irrational about it—"I won't take *anything* from *him!*" Sometimes they think (perhaps quite justly) that they have no moral right to it. Others, of course, attempt to use the property settlement as a means of retaliation. The comment from one of my informants was, "Boy, did I make that bastard pay." It seems to me that irrational motives such as revenge or self-abnegation are more often in evidence than the facts of relative need, in spite of all that judges and lawyers can do.

Alimony

The word "alimony" is derived from the Latin word for sustenance, and ultimately from the verb which means "to nourish" or "to give food to." The prevailing idea behind alimony in America is that the husband, as head of the family, has an obligation to support his wife and children, no matter how wealthy the wife and children may be independently.

At the time of divorce, the alimony rights of the wife are considered to be an extension of the husband's duty to support, undertaken at the time of marriage. Therefore, alimony means the money paid during and after the divorce by the ex-husband to the ex-wife (rarely the other way around).

There is, however, another basis on which some courts in some American jurisdictions have looked on alimony—it can be seen as punishment of the husband for his mistreatment of the wife. Where this idea is found, the wife cannot be entitled to alimony if she is the "guilty party" to the divorce. In most states, the amount of alimony is more or less directly dependent on whatever moral or immoral conduct of the wife may come to the attention of the court. A woman known to be guilty of anything the court considers to be moral misconduct is likely to be awarded less than an "innocent" wife. The law varies widely on these matters; practice varies even more.

The most important thing about the award and payment of alimony is that it is done on the basis of a court order. Therefore, if it is not paid, the offending husband is in contempt of court. The institution of divorce is provided, as we have seen before, with only one formal sanction to insure the compliance of its various parties. And that is the court.

Child Support

Courts and citizens are both much clearer about child support than they are about alimony. The principle is obvious to all; as long as he is able to do so, the responsibility for supporting children lies with their father. Whether a man is morally and legally obligated to support his children depends only on one factor: his ability to do so. In assessing child support payments, the court looks simply at his ability to pay, including his health, and to the needs of the child. The amount may be set by the court; it is always ratified by the court.

THE COPARENTAL DIVORCE AND THE PROBLEM OF CUSTODY

The most enduring pain of divorce is likely to come from the coparental divorce. This odd word is useful because it indicates that the child's parents are divorced from each other—not from the child. Children do not always understand this: they may ask, "Can Father divorce *me?*" This is not a silly or naïve question; from the standpoint of the child what was a failure in marriage to the parents is the shattering of his kinship circle.

The children have to go somewhere. And even when both parents share joint legal custody of the child, one parent or other gets "physical custody"— the right to have the child living with him.

The word "custody" is a double-edged sword. It means "responsibility for the care of" somebody. It also means "imprisonment." The child is in the custody of his parents—the criminal is in the custody of the law. When we deal with the custody of children in divorces, we must see to it that they are "in the care of" somebody, and that the care is adequate—we must also see that the custody is not punitive or restricting.

Legal custody of children entitles the custodial parent to make decisions about their life-styles and the things they can do which are developmentally important to them—educational and recreational and cultural choices. In the common law, the father had absolute property rights over the child—the mother had none, unless she inherited them at the death of the father. About the time judicial divorce was established in America, custody preferences shifted until the two parents were about equal. With the vast increase in the divorce rate in the early third of the twentieth century, the shift continued, giving the mother preference in both legal and physical custody. We rationalize this practice by such ideas as mother love, masculine nature, or the exigencies of making a living.

Custody of the children, once granted to the mother, will be taken away from her by the courts *only* if she can be shown to be seriously delinquent in her behavior *as a mother*. Her behavior *as a wife* may be at stake in granting the divorce or in fixing the amount of the alimony—but not in granting custody. A woman cannot be denied her rights as a mother on the basis of having performed badly as a wife, or even on the basis of her behavior as a divorcee if the children were not threatened physically or morally. Similarly, a man cannot be penalized as a father for his shortcomings as a husband.

The overriding consideration in all cases is that the court takes what action it considers to be "in the best interests of the child." The rights of children as human beings override, in our morality and hence in our law, all rights of the parents as parents, and certainly their rights as spouses. We have absolutely inverted the old common law.

A man is always, either by statute law or by common law, obliged to take financial responsibility for his minor children. If there are overriding circumstances that make it impossible for him to work, then that responsibility devolves on the mother. Sometimes a mother refuses her ex-husband the right to support his children as a means to deny him the right to see them—some men accept this, but few would be forced by a court to accept it if they chose to question its legality.

The rights of the parent who has neither legal nor physical custody of the child are generally limited to his right of visiting the child at reasonable times. This right stems from parenthood and is not dependent on decrees issued by a court. The court may, of course, condition the rights of visitation, again in the best interest of the child.

Children and One-Parent Households

Children grow up. The association between parent and child and the association between the parents change with each new attainment of the child. The child grows, parents respond—and their response has subtle overtones in their own relationship. In divorce, their responses must necessarily be of a different nature from what it is in marriage. In divorce, with communication reduced, the goals of the spouses are less likely to be congruent—the child is observed at different times and from different vantage points by the separated parents, each with his own set of concerns and worries.

Coparental divorce created lasting pain for many divorcees I interviewed— particularly if the ex-spouses differed greatly on what they wanted their children to become, morally, spiritually, professionally, even physically. This very difference of opinion about the goals of living may have lain behind the divorce. It continues through the children.

The good ex-husband/father feels, "My son is being brought up by his mother so that he is not my son." A divorced man almost always feels that his boy is being made into a different kind of man from what he himself is. Often, of course, he is right. The good ex-wife/mother may be tempted to refuse her ex-husband his visitation rights because, from her point of view, "He is bad for the children." This statement may mean no more than that the children are emotionally higher strung before and after a visit, and therefore upset her calm. But the mother may think the father wants something else for the children than she does, thus putting a strain on her own efforts to instill her own ideals and regulations.

It is difficult for a man to watch his children develop traits similar, if not identical, to those he found objectionable in their mother and which were among those qualities that led to the emotional divorce. The child becomes the living embodiment of the differences in basic values. A man may feel that "she" is bad for the children even when he has the objectivity to see also that the children will not necessarily develop unwholesome personalities, but only different personalities from those they might have developed through being with him.

The problem for the mother of the children is different—she has to deal with the single-parent household, making by herself decisions, which she almost surely feels should be shared. She does not want somebody to tell her what to do, as much as somebody to tell her she is right and make "sensible suggestions." Like most mothers, she wants support, not direction.

There is a traditional and popular belief that divorce is "bad for children." Actually, we do not know very much about it. Children in divorce must pick up by instruction what they would have learned by habituation or osmosis in an unbroken healthy home.

The children must learn how to deal with the "broken orbit" of models for the roles they will play in life. A boy cannot become fully a man—or a girl a woman—if they model themselves only on the cues they pick up from one sex alone. A woman cannot teach a boy to be a man, or a girl a woman, without the help of men. And a man cannot teach either a boy to be a man or a girl to be a woman without help of women.

All of us interact with members of both sexes. Our cues about the behavior of men come from the responses of women, as well as from the responses of men. Children—like the rest of us—must have significant members of both sexes around them.

Obviously, children of even the most successful homes do not model themselves solely on their parents, in spite of the importance parents have as models. There are television models (boys walk like athletes or crime busters); there are teachers, friends, storekeepers, bus drivers, and all the rest. But the child who lives in a one-parent home has to adjust to a different mixture of sex-role models. The big danger may be not so much that a boy has no father model in his home, but that his mother stops his walking like Willie Mays or a television cowboy because she doesn't like it. And worst of all, she may, without knowing it, try to extinguish in him the very behavior patterns he has learned from his father: especially if she does not want to be reminded of his father.

Children who live in one-parent homes must learn what a husband/father is and what he does in the home—and they have to learn it in a different context from children of replete homes. They must learn what a wife/mother is in such a home. Children are taught to be husbands and wives while they are still children. In the one-parent home the children have to be taught actively and realistically the companionship, sexual coparenting, and domestic aspects of marriage.

A noted psychoanalyst has told me that in her opinion there are only two things children learn in two-parent homes that cannot be taught in one-parent homes; one is the undertone of healthy sexuality that is present in a healthy home. Nothing appears on the surface save love—but the sexual tone of married love permeates everything. Even in the most loving one-parent home this is something that can, perhaps, be explained to children, but something that they will have trouble feeling unless they experience it elsewhere. The other thing that is difficult to teach, she says, is the ambivalence of the child toward both parents. When the relationship of father-child is none of the business of the child's mother, or the relationship of mother-child outside the ken and responsibility of the child's father, then the illusion can be maintained by the child that father is wholly right and mother wholly wrong, or father wholly unjustified and mother completely innocent. It is seldom true.

In short, the ex-family must do many of the things that the family ordinarily does, but it does them with even more difficulty than the family. It is in the coparental aspects of the divorce that the problems are so long-lasting—and so difficult. And the reason, as we have seen, is that a child's mother and father are, through the child, kinsmen to one another, but the scope of activities in their relationship has been vastly curtailed.

THE COMMUNITY DIVORCE AND
THE PROBLEM OF LONELINESS

Changes in civil status or "stages of life" almost invariably mark changes in friends and in significant communities. We go to school, and go away to college. We join special-interest groups. When we are married, we change communities—sometimes almost completely except for a few relatives and two or three faithful friends from childhood or from college.

When we divorce, we also change communities. Divorce means "forsaking all others" just as much as marriage does, and in about the same degree.

Many divorcees complain bitterly about their "ex-friends." "Friends?"

one woman replied to my question during an interview, "They drop you like a hot potato. The exceptions are those real ones you made before marriage, those who are unmarried, and your husband's men friends who want to make a pass at you."

The biggest complaint is that divorcees are made to feel uncomfortable by their married friends.

Like newly marrieds, new divorcees have to find new communities. They tend to find them among the divorced. Morton Hunt's book, *The World of the Formerly Married*, provides a good concise report on these new communities. Divorcees find—if they will let themselves—that there is a group ready to welcome them as soon as they announce their separations. There are people to explain the lore that will help them in being a divorcee, people to support them emotionally, people to give them information, people to date and perhaps love as soon as they are able to love.

The community divorce is an almost universal experience of divorcees in America. And although there are many individuals who are puzzled and hurt until they find their way into it, it is probably the aspect of divorce that Americans handle best.

THE PSYCHIC DIVORCE AND THE PROBLEM OF AUTONOMY

Psychic divorce means the separation of self from the personality and the influence of the ex-spouse—to wash that man right out of your hair. To distance yourself from the loved portion that ultimately became disappointing, from the hated portion, from the baleful presence that led to depression and loss of self-esteem.

The most difficult of the six divorces is the psychic divorce, but it is also the one that can be personally most constructive. The psychic divorce involves becoming a whole, complete, and autonomous individual again—learning to live without somebody to lean on—but also without somebody to support. There is nobody on whom to blame one's difficulties (except oneself), nobody to shortstop one's growth, nobody to grow with.

Each must regain—if he ever had it—the dependence on self and faith in one's own capacity to cope with the environment, with people, with thoughts and emotions.

Why Did I Marry?

To learn anything from divorce, one must ask himself why he married. Marriage, it seems to me, should be an act of desperation—a last resort. It should not be used as a means of solving one's problems. Ultimately, of course, most people in our society can bring their lives to a high point of satisfaction and usefulness only through marriage. The more reason, indeed, we should not enter it unless it supplies the means for coping with our healthy needs and our desires to give and grow.

All too often, marriage is used as a shield against becoming whole or autonomous individuals. People too often marry to their weaknesses. We all carry the family of our youth within ourselves—our muscles, our emotions, our unconscious minds. And we all project it again into the families we form as adults. The path of every marriage is strewn with yesterday's unresolved conflicts, of both spouses. Every divorce is beset by yesterday's unresolved conflicts, compounded by today's.

So the question becomes: How do I resolve the conflicts that ruined my marriage? And what were the complementary conflicts in the spouse I married?

Probably all of us marry, at least in part, to defend old solutions to old conflicts. The difficulty comes when two people so interlock their old conflicts and solutions that they cannot become aware of them, and hence cannot solve them. Ironically, being a divorced person has built-in advantages in terms of working out these conflicts, making them conscious, and overcoming them.

Why Was I Divorced?

Presumably the fundamental cause of divorce is that people find themselves in situations in which they cannot become autonomous individuals and are unwilling to settle for a *folie à deux*. Divorcees are people who have not achieved a good marriage—they are also people who would not settle for a bad one.

A "successful" divorce begins with the realization by two people that they do not have any constructive future together. That decision itself is a recognition of the emotional divorce. It proceeds through the legal channels of undoing the wedding, through the economic division of property and arrangement for alimony and support. The successful divorce involves determining ways in which children can be informed, educated in their new roles, loved and provided for. It involves finding a new community. Finally, it involves finding your own autonomy as a person and as a personality.

Autonomy

The greatest difficulty comes from those people who cannot tell autonomy from independence. Nobody is independent in the sense that he does not depend on people. Life is with people. But if you wither and die without specific people doing specific things for you, then you have lost your autonomy. You enter into social relationships—and we are all more or less dependent in social relationships—in order to enhance your own freedom and growth, as well as to find somebody to provide for your needs and to provide good company in the process. Although, in a good marriage, you would never choose to do so, you *could* withdraw. You could grieve, and go on.

These are six of the stations of divorce. "The undivorced," as they are sometimes called in the circles of divorcees, almost never understand the great achievement that mastering them may represent.

Notes

1. The parts of this book that were written by Paul Bohannan are based on research carried out between 1963 and 1966 under grants MH 06551-01A1 and MH 11544-01 of the National Institute of Mental Health, and grant No. GS-61 from the National Science Foundation.

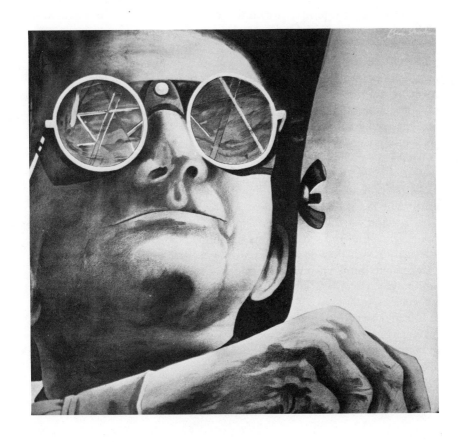

PART III
WORKING

In Japan it is said that "people are known by the companies that keep them." In the United States many of those who acknowledge that socialization is a life-long process fail to note the special significance of working, of the "labeling effect" of occupational choice, and of the workplace as arena of both formal and informal resocialization. Yet in our country most male adults and increasing numbers of females spend more time during the years from eighteen to sixty-five on the job than in the home and more time with colleagues than with family members.

The shops, factories, offices, or other "places of business" to which we repair each morning, day in, day out, year in, year out, often become homes away from home. They have their own rules, regulations, and special requirements. From the production line to the board room trainers and supervisors often become surrogate parents, especially in their capacities as rewarders and punishers. Not surprisingly, workmates often become like siblings, with all the tensions and rivalries attendant upon such close relationships.

Sometimes occupational duties are simple, requiring little skill; other times they are highly complex. Outsiders have vague notions of relative complexity and often rank occupations according to culturally defined ideas of job significance. The fact is that "Occupation" is frequently as important as any other "background variable"—such as "Name," "Age," and "Sex"—cited in sociological studies and statistical reports. Individuals are assessed by the labels attached to what they do for a living. We need only think of the differences that come to mind when we are introduced to "John Smith, janitor," "John Smith, electrician," "John Smith, teacher," and "John Smith, brain surgeon."

In Part Three we consider working in its broadest sense. Included are commentaries and analyses of routine factory work, careers in law enforcement, military service, and surgery, and the corporate life of big business. Part Three also sets the stage for the examination of certain mid-life problems and other changes that indicate that for many the life cycle is not one smooth transition after another but a series of steps and stages.

Ever since the publication of William H. Whyte, Jr.'s
The Organization Man *in 1956, sociologists and jour-*
nalists have had a label for those who, like most
Americans today, work for large organizations. Some,
like Charlie Chaplin in the classic film Modern Times,
are very small cogs in the great machinery; others are
high-ranking managers who wield considerable influ-
ence. Still, there is a commonality among all members
of the corporate hierarchy: they are all participants in
bureaucratic structures with fixed rules and roles and
often impersonal relationships.

This essay is a general introduction to the subject of
"working," that aspect of life which engages most of
our waking hours during the adult years. Here and in
succeeding selections, we will examine routinized work,
training for careers, and professional socialization and
its consequences.

As you read through this essay, note the varieties of
organizational styles as well as the basic structural
similarities of large scale organizations.

A Cog in the Machinery

RAFAEL STEINBERG AND
THE EDITORS OF TIME-LIFE BOOKS

A century ago Alfred Krupp, the German munitions maker, spelled out the principle underlying every large organization. He put it quite baldly: "What I shall attempt to bring about is that nothing of importance shall be dependent upon the life or existence of any particular person; that nothing of importance shall happen . . . without the foreknowledge and approval of the management; that the past and the determinable future of the establishment can be learned in the files of the management without asking a question of any mortal."

Such inhuman efficiency can never be achieved—fortunately so, in the view of most people—not even by tyrants as unfeeling and single-minded as Krupp. But his general goal, interpreted more humanely, has been shared by planners before his time and since: to create an organizational structure that would be self-perpetuating, flourishing independently of the human beings who come and go to make it operate. If one man on a Krupp furnace crew quit or was retired or fired, he could be replaced quickly without disrupting work. So, too, could every other laborer, clerk, foreman, engineer and manager—right up to the Krupp family members who, in succession, owned the firm. To accomplish this end, Krupp drew up a *Generalregulativ* that specified the duties and relationships of everyone from managers to office boys. If anyone had complaints he was to go through channels. And there must have been complaints. To arrive late at work by five minutes was punished by the loss of one hour's pay; impudence was punished by immediate dismissal. At one point Krupp even tried to persuade his workmen to wear uniforms—he himself would have been dressed as a field marshal—but he was talked out of it.

Even without uniforms, Krupp established a dynasty that accumulated Europe's largest family fortune and ruled Europe's largest industrial combine until 1967, when the firm became publicly owned. He succeeded because he understood that an organization must be more than a group of human beings; it is a structure of positions that human beings occupy. Even in the simplest organization—a Boy Scout patrol, a sailboat crew—activities have to be coordinated to achieve a common purpose. This coordination requires work to be planned and divided among the members; each must be given a definite position that calls for specific conduct, so that all can predict and respond to the behavior of everybody else. When one man throws a ball, another must be there to catch it; when the boss gives an order, a subordinate must carry it out.

In larger organizations, where co-workers may never meet, the survival of the entire establishment depends on maximum predictability, which only formally structured positions can assure. Each position must be defined and maintained not only in terms of its own functions but also in its relationship to other positions. In such a system individuals—from chairman of the board to night watchman—are replaceable; only the positions are vital and permanent. It is all very much like a play: the characters fill roles, and not in dress, speech nor action are the performers to be confused; the leading lady does not speak the housemaid's lines.

A play must be cast. And the roles in the organization must be filled also— with people. Theoretically, at least, a candidate is selected in terms of how well he will fit the opening, on the basis of what he is rather than who he is. Cleveland Amory underscores in *The Proper Bostonians* the generally impersonal standards involved. He tells of a Chicago firm that wrote to a Boston businessman asking for references for a job applicant. When the reference letter arrived full of praise for the applicant's family tree and fine manners, the Chicagoans answered it with thanks, but noted that the man in question was being considered only for a junior executive position, not for breeding purposes.

Somehow the requirements of the role have to be defined and human beings found who meet the needs, or, in time, can be trained to do so. They have to be identified with their roles in an obvious way—by title, badge, salary or subtler sign of status—so that other people recognize which human has custody of which role; confusion is inevitable if the only indication of power is an imposing bearing and an authoritative voice. Movement from role to role must be allowed for. There has to be a way to find superior individuals so that their talents can be put to use in more demanding roles, just as there must be a way to remove incompetents from roles they cannot handle.

This interaction between individual and role might be simpler than it is if people could be tailored to roles or vice versa, but a precise fit is impossible. The most admirable human qualities often get in the way. What is more, each individual has to fill several roles even on the job, and his personal life involves still others. Conflict is inevitable, and the kinds of conflicts that arise as well as the ways in which they are resolved vary surprisingly, not only from role to role and person to person but also from culture to culture.

Role playing, of course, is not something new in society, nor is it confined to large, complex organizations. A role is simply the behavior that is expected of an individual because of the position he holds in relation to other persons. The word person, in fact, is derived from the Latin for mask, suggesting that even the ancients understood that everyone, everywhere is always playing a role. The necessity of role playing underlies a scene in *Being and Nothingness*, in which Jean-Paul Sartre describes the complicated activities of a waiter in a café: his too-quick step, his solicitous voice, his stiff walk, the reckless, unstable way he carries his tray. "All his behavior seems to us a game," Sartre wrote. "He is playing, he is amusing himself. But what is he playing? . . . He is playing at being a waiter in a café. . . . [He] plays with his condition in order to *realize* it."

Yet complete realization of one role—or one part of a role—may interfere with others. A person's job may demand loyalties to more than one group, as in the case of a factory foreman who is expected to boss his men and yet behave like their buddy. Emotions are not supposed to have a place in organizational life, writes sociologist Wilbert Moore in *Conduct of the Corporation*, because they "interfere with duty, encourage slovenly performance, and provide protection for friendly fools." What the corporation needs instead, he says, is behavior by the book and SOP (Standard Operating Procedure).

There may be conflict between the various roles an individual is called upon to play—the common problem faced by a hard-driving, ambitious executive who does not have enough time or energy left over to be a good father or husband. A diplomat continually finds himself in this kind of dilemma: while abroad, and in public, he must defend the policies of his own country, but in dealing with his home government he must often become an advocate for the country in which he is stationed.

The best role players, paradoxically, face the worst conflicts of all. As a successful individual moves upward to more prestigious positions he may repeatedly have to shed familiar old statuses, along with the friends and social activities they permit. Any change, whether due to a reshuffling of responsibility within the organization or to an individual promotion, requires a certain amount of personal readjustment. But repeated changes upward are harder to cope with because the higher an executive rises in an organization the fewer equals he has, and consequently the fewer are his social opportunities to relax and be himself—to step out of his role.

What can happen to those who do mistakenly abandon role behavior was described by Chester Burger, a New York management consultant. He tells the story of a company vice president, successful and rising fast, who for some reason was anxious about his future. When he ingenuously revealed his worries to a colleague at lunch one day, he instantly destroyed his image of self-confident, invulnerable comer. The other man promptly set out to steal his job—and succeeded. Burger concludes: "If you're not sure whether to say something, don't. Share your anxieties with your wife, or with your personal friends, but never, never to a colleague on the job." A colleague can often be a competitor.

For the individual who can follow the rules and accommodate readily to his role, it provides welcome self-fulfillment and a comfortable life. Even before he joins the organization, the recruit can measure its needs against his. Because organizational positions tend to be permanent, he may be able to plan education to match the qualifications succeeding roles require. Once on the inside, his role can afford safety, security and status. If a person is content with his job, good role playing relieves him of worry about whether he is doing things right and eliminates the need to make difficult judgments. As William H. Whyte Jr. pointed out in *The Organization Man*, "The mere playing of the role of the well-adjusted team player can help quiet the inner worries."

Roles can also insulate an individual from unpleasantness when dealing or working with someone he dislikes, and they can spare him embarrassment when taking orders from those he considers his social or intellectual inferiors. It is not the person he is obeying, but the position that person holds. "You salute the uniform, not the man," is the Army's way of explaining that the military signal of obedience and respect is not subservience. How useful this depersonalization of authority can be was suggested by a 1940s study of restaurant workers. Some male cooks and pantrymen seemed to mix up—almost intentionally—the waitresses' orders. Apparently the men resented being told what to do by a woman. But the trouble disappeared once the waitresses were ordered to stop relaying orders verbally and instead to put written slips on a spike. There was no problem so long as the men could pick up the order, impersonally, from the spike where an impersonal hand had put it. By eliminating direct contact between the men and women, the spike enabled them to take refuge in their roles and to deal with one another in a way they would not have tolerated as individuals.

Such tricks for depersonalizing authority are seldom necessary because the role itself usually serves this function. Position in a chain of command comes with the role, determining who its bearer takes orders from and who takes orders from him. This specification of rank is, of course, essential to the smooth operation of the organization, since it enables decisions to be made and carried out with a minimum of confusion. But rank is also one of the chief benefits (or drawbacks, depending on the position and point of view) that a role brings to an individual. It establishes his status in society—explicitly within the organization and very often implicitly outside it.

Although the concept of rank is fundamental to organized life, its application varies widely. Rank may be obvious—in the military services or the Roman Catholic Church—or so concealed that it can be perceived only by a few insiders, as it is among behind-the-scenes power brokers who influence governmental actions. In Western societies—particularly in the United States—its signs may be subtle and its use flexible. In Japan, on the other hand, public and private business is rigidly regulated by protocol based on rank.

In a Japanese corporation or government bureau everyone addresses his superior by title or rank, Honorable Section Chief, Honorable Managing Director. Names are used only when talking to subordinates or equals, and equals rate more polite verbs and pronouns than subordinates do. Every Japanese corporate employee, down to the level of factory foreman, carries name cards bearing his company name and address and, most important, his rank. The cards serve a vital purpose: Japanese cannot talk properly or politely to one another unless everyone involved knows his relative rank and status.

Watch two Japanese businessmen meeting as strangers in circumstances where neither knows which of them takes precedence—at a corporation reception, for instance. If no one introduces them, they will try to avoid conversation. If forced to converse, they will immediately whip out their name cards for exchange, murmuring their company names and their own names, and bowing slightly. Within a second or two each will have read the other's card, noted the rank and calculated the value of the rank in terms of the size and importance of the company. Then, unless they judge their status to be approximately equal, the tableau will swiftly change. One of them will bow again, more deeply; his voice will soften and he will shift to a politer syntax. If both are waiting for something, to get to the bar, for instance, and if the junior is profoundly outranked, he may insist the other man go first. Meanwhile, the superior will have acknowledged the deep bow with a shallow one, or perhaps just a nod; his voice and phrasing will shift too, to a harder, more direct manner and his sentences will get shorter. He accepts the deference, for it is his due.

For a Westerner, there are two fascinating aspects to this performance. First of all, there never seems to be any doubt, once the cards are exchanged, about who outranks whom, and by how deep and how long a bow. Second, the recognition of their differing statuses, far from inhibiting discourse, actually encourages it. Only when a relationship is clear, with uncertainty and the possibility of a social gaffe removed, can significant conversation take place. The two unequals will never become buddies, but as long as the forms are observed, as long as both play their roles properly, they can conduct business or pass the time of day or even share a ride home in a taxicab.

The egalitarian tradition of the United States protects Americans from such naked flaunting of rank and status, but it gets them into other kinds of trouble. Because Americans feel that they are just as good as those set above them, they connive and angle for prestige in a way that would not only be considered bad form but would be futile in Japan, where status is clearly established. An American often suspects that his subordinates feel equal to him—and fears that they may be right. Thus he sometimes guards his status and privileges so jealously that he may fail to perform his duties rationally and effectively. Paradoxically, the egalitarian society's half-suppressed concern with rank undermines bureaucratic efficiency in a way early writers failed to foresee.

The United States represents the extreme opposite of the Japanese practice. But in many countries there is an ambivalence toward rank, most apparent in the way status is publicly identified. In military, church and academic organizations, titles are routine forms of address, and badges signifying rank may be worn on clothing. The Pope's red velvet and ermine cape, the cardinal's red hat, the bishop's purple cassock, jeweled ring and silver crosier are accepted and familiar insignia of the Catholic hierarchy. Like an admiral's gold braid, they proclaim status and authority in a way no member of the organization can miss.

With this open acknowledgment of rank goes a willingness to accept appropriate perquisites. Particularly in the military establishment—where discipline requires that everyone be able to tell at a glance whom to obey, and be prepared to obey automatically—exaggerated trappings and panoply are taken for granted. The private jets and honor guards for generals; the British Army officer's batman serving as valet and houseboy; the separate clubs for officers, noncoms and enlisted men; the deference the wives of officers expect from the wives of lower ranks—all are part of normal routine and tradition.

The Western organizations that encourage the display of status are mainly ancient ones, following traditional customs. More generally the flaunting of rank is discouraged in the West. Business cards may be exchanged, but as a convenient notation of name and address rather than to establish title. A bank clerk's clothes look exactly like the managing director's, from a distance, differing only in the quality of material and tailoring. Titles are used in formal address on the Continent, particularly in Germany—where an important man may be referred to as *Herr Verwaltungsgerichtoberinspektor* (senior court inspector)—but less often in England and still less in the United States. Many American executives insist on being called by their first names and take pride in working in shirt sleeves. Yet such modesty is to a great extent a screen. In every organization in every culture, badges of rank exist, proudly displayed and even fought over, as clear a sign of prestige and authority as the stripes on a Naval officer's sleeve—to those who know where to look.

Whether insignia are officially ordained—as, for example, the fresh flowers in the president's office—or emerge unofficially as do the differences in hair styling among different ranks of workers, these status symbols reinforce the prestige of the organization role both within the group and outside. Like the military and the Church, other organizations distribute such symbols most generously to the top echelons.

"A Title on the Door Rates a Bigelow on the Floor," an American carpet company advertised some years ago; by now so many offices have carpets that the color and thickness of the rug are the key to status. For many years the carpeting in the office of the U.S. Secretary of State was blue. One floor below, the assistant secretaries had green carpets and a floor below that, the office directors worked in offices with gray rugs. In every gray-rug office hung a black-and-white photograph of the President, but the pictures in the offices of the Secretary of State and assistant secretaries were in color.

Every executive's office at the New York headquarters of the Chase Manhattan Bank displays a fine original oil painting provided by the bank but selected by the occupant to reflect his personal taste. The value of the painting, however, is precisely determined according to the executive's rank. The practice has been that when he gets a promotion, he is taken to the bank's private collection and allowed to choose a work from the appropriate price range. If he already has one painting, he does not have to give it up for a new and costlier one, but he cannot add a second—unless his new role and rank allow for the value of both.

A more common symbol of rank is the desk, which gets bigger and fancier as its occupant goes up the line, changing from utilitarian steel to walnut and chrome, to mahogany, to Chippendale—until at the highest levels are the executives for whom no desk is big enough and who therefore use no desk at all. They let their secretaries and executive assistants take care of the documents and the paper clips, and they seem to be saying, "This whole establishment is my desk."

Rank can also be ascertained by the presence or absence of a secretary, by whether the secretary shares the boss's office or sits outside it in her own workspace, by how elegantly the secretary dresses or speaks. In New York City, some years back, a secretary with a cultured English accent was almost a requirement in the executive suite—while at the same time one-up Japanese executives were insisting on being chauffeured around Tokyo by female drivers.

The place an employee parks his car, whether he washes his hands in the common lavatory or in the executive washroom or in a private bathroom attached to his own office, whether his visitors sit on an upholstered couch or hard chairs, the number of telephone extensions assigned to him, and how far down the table from the top man he sits during staff meetings—all of these announce rank. If the official organization tries to eliminate such symbols, its members may invent unofficial ones. When a Boston publishing house put all its employees in one big room, the size of each desk, and the spaces between desks were meticulously graded by the staff itself. After someone was transferred or promoted, the desks would be quietly shifted a few inches in one direction or another in order to reflect the revised pecking order.

Like Army insignia, these informal badges must be jealously guarded by their owners. In sociologist Robert Merton's words, an official's "emotional dependence upon bureaucratic symbols and status" leads him to defend those symbols as if they possessed moral value. One reason is that they are subject to depreciation as the corporation spawns new divisions and dispenses titles and other symbols more widely. (At one time Firestone Tire and Rubber had 72 presidents, IBM had seven, and Borg-Warner had 40 presidents or chairmen.) When that kind of proliferation occurs, new and more luxurious badges have to be invented. And of course such badge currency can be devalued as well as inflated. After one promoted executive declined to exchange his low-rank company Buick for a high-rank company Cadillac, the firm's entire system of automotive promotion slipped down one notch; no one under him in the hierarchy could expect a promotion to bring a larger car either.

The most important badge of rank, however, would seem to be the paycheck—at least in a system of free competition for jobs. Presumably an individual's salary ought to reflect his importance to the organization and thus status within it. Yet this simple relationship does not always exist. People doing the same work and filling identical roles may get different pay, and many a supervisor earns less than some of his subordinates. There are a number of reasons for salary disparities. One of them is secrecy.

Why corporate white-collar salaries are generally discussed behind closed doors is a fascinating question. In government bureaucracies and in the military, pay generally coincides with grade and is a matter of public record. The hourly wage rate of millions of factory workers is determined by union negotiations and reported in the newspapers. But within management ranks, and in fact for nearly everyone who works in an office, salary is discussed only among the employee, his supervisor and the personnel department. Few people will volunteer their salaries, and it is considered impolite to ask.

Wilbert Moore takes a cynical view of this secrecy. He believes it is "designed to obscure an inequitable system of rewards and to protect those who determine salaries from the crude force of competition among subordinates. The man who is given a salary raise or bonus that is not given to his peers is commonly sworn to secrecy or at least told that 'this is confidential.' There is no reason at all for this if the difference in rewards reflects differences in merit by commonly accepted criteria. It is the uncertainty of the criteria of merit or the patent unfairness of increase differences that prompts deliberate concealment or obfuscation. . . . ''

But among executives, and indeed among many lesser white-collar workers, no ''commonly accepted criteria'' will apply with justice to all cases except where job proficiency can be measured in numbers, as is the case with a salesman or an investment analyst. There are too many unmeasurable factors involved, ranging from the diligence of a lowly telephone operator in tracking down a traveling executive to the ability of that executive—by a web of subtle gestures and phrases and minor decisions—to inspire the best work from his staff. Two people doing the same job, apparently playing the same sort of role, may earn different salaries because management has decided that one of them is abler or of greater potential value to the company. New recruits from outside the organization or from other divisions within it often may be attracted with higher salaries than those of the old hands alongside whom they will work. And an employee who is promoted rapidly through several ranks may have to wait a while before his salary catches up with his title. The secret salary therefore, although it undoubtedly redounds to the benefit of the organization, also seems to be a clear sign that individuals still count for something at certain levels of the corporate structure.

Seen in that light, the visible badges of role take on a new meaning. They are bestowed not only to broadcast an employee's worth but, when given instead of raises, may conceal the fact that an employee is not worth all that much. British sociologist David Lockwood points out that elegant sounding titles are recognized by those expert in human relations as an inexpensive way to keep a staff content; who would not prefer to be called a secretary rather than a shorthand-typist, an analyst rather than a clerk. The individual who knows he is well paid can be confident that the whole world sees how good he is; and the fellow who feels underpaid can at least take comfort from the fact that the new paintings hanging in his office seem to impress his visitors and his staff.

Status symbols, even raises, may represent no more than the icing on the cake to many organizational role players. For them the most important incentive is the power that a role bestows on its incumbent, and they struggle for promotion to ever more exalted status, not to enjoy the richer trappings but to exercise its greater power. This drive for advancement serves the organization's purpose, too, for its survival depends on the talent at the top, and the highest positions are the most difficult to fill. Relatively simple tests of skill and evaluations of personality may serve to select good production workers and clerks, and an occasional misfit is easily removed. But deciding who should get an opportunity to manage a factory or direct a governmental department involves fine judgment, grave risks and considerable planning.

In recent years a number of forward-looking organizations have developed ingenious methods of deciding who will get high executive roles. Instead of using psychological tests to find supposedly suitable personality types, as was the vogue after World War II, the new techniques set up situations simulating the real-life operations of an organization and test would-be executives for their ability to make the right decisions. In one of these "games," a group of five or six candidates is told to manage a fictitious toy company and increase its profits. Facts on the company and its market are presented to the group, but no one is put in charge and no procedural rules are laid down. Every few minutes the testers raise the pressure by announcing a change in costs or in competitors' prices. The assessors observe who takes charge of the group, who cooperates, who panics or gets confused as time runs out, and who operates cooly and flexibly under pressure.

In an even more grueling assessment game, an individual plays at filling in for a supervisor in an emergency. He is handed an in-basket full of memos and letters and given a fixed time to answer them all. The testers look for the candidate who sets priorities, spots connections between related items, seeks expert advice when necessary and delegates lesser matters to his staff. Sometimes, buried near the bottom of the pile, lies a note from the supervisor's secretary reminding him she has left on vacation; the candidate, who may already have delegated certain matters to her, must then decide whether to spoil her vacation and call her back, thus testing still another facet of his judgment.

Such testing games can be used either to select employees to be hired from outside the organization or to be promoted from within. When a role is to be filled only by promotion, simulation is not necessary. The test can be real. Sometimes the competition between those striving for advancement has nothing to do with the real aims of the company, and this approach may be dangerous. Cornered, fighting for survival, the individual may not compete merely by doing the best job he knows how; he may use every trick he can think of, including deceit and sabotage, to defeat his rival—and that might harm the organization. As Moore has noted, "The large corporation is spending some portion of its man-hour resources in internal war and its containment rather than in furthering its various stated objectives." Moreover, Chester Burger, the management consultant, views such power displays as potentially destructive. He believes that intense internal rivalry almost always begins at the top. The boss encourages competition in the belief that he will get the best work out of his employees by forcing them to struggle against one another.

Burger cites the example of a fierce and counterproductive rivalry between a production manager and a plant manager at a New England shoe factory. The senior man, Thea, had little to do besides supervising his very competent junior, Weiner. Thea, anxious to hold on to his job until he reached retirement age, made it his business to find fault with Weiner, and he tried to convince corporate headquarters that the younger man needed his expert help. Since Weiner was actually doing a good job, Thea invented problems, compounded minor ones and constantly criticized his subordinate, who of course had to counterattack. When the chief executive, in another city, was asked why he permitted such a clash to continue, he laughed. He admitted he had planned it that way. "We don't need two men there anyway," he told Burger. "Thea's got two years to go until retirement and I don't want to fire him now without a good reason. Weiner is a good man, but I decided it wouldn't hurt if I threw him into the pit with Thea and let the two of them fight it out. If Weiner isn't tough enough to handle himself, he doesn't deserve the top job. Either way, the company will come out ahead. I'll have a good excuse to force out Thea two years early and get rid of dead wood. Or I'll discover that Weiner is too weak to head up the plant, and I'd rather discover that *before* I give him the job instead of afterwards."

The competition that results from situations like this, according to corporate ideology, "divides the men from the boys." It also produces some other divisions. At one extreme are what Wilbert Moore calls the strainers, the ambitious young organization men "who keep alert, look smart, avoid missteps, and attempt to show up well on assignments or in group policy discussion. They have ideas if requested and otherwise find cogent reasons for supporting the wisdom of the boss's ideas. They learn golf, join the right clubs, think the right thoughts. Their wives are attractive but not brazen, entertain the right people, and suggest that John is brilliant as well as hard-working, a dedicated corporate servant but also a wonderful husband and father."

If the strainers are climbing a ladder, others whom Moore calls secure mobiles are on an escalator. They may not reach the heights that some strainers attain, but with considerably less struggle and fewer tensions they rise fairly high in their organizations, "not by doing nothing but also not by doing anything exceptional." Usually they can be found among the ranks of the professionals within management. "They may be ambitious," Moore relates, "but generally not for the power. . . . They do not spurn money, but [accept it] as payment for doing what they are doing and not for something else."

One problem for the escalator rider, or for anyone who enters an organization vowing just to do a good job and not get involved in the rat race, is that industrialized society brands anyone who doesn't aim for the top as a quitter. He is likely to be passed over repeatedly. And when bright young people press from below for promotion, his superiors may decide he is not the best person for his role. Then he is simply removed. There are now as many ways of getting the wrong people out of roles as there are of trying to get the right ones in.

No matter how it is accomplished, the experience of losing a job is traumatic. To relieve the pain some organizations have developed firing techniques to devious art. Chester Burger counsels managers never to use the word fired, suggesting "relieved of duty" or "terminated" as better terms. With similar tact, an American civil servant is not discharged but is "selected out." Most corporate executive firings are presented publicly as resignations or early retirements to save face for all. The victim may be permitted to keep a desk and secretary and to receive calls at the office for many weeks so that he can preserve the façade of employment while he seeks another job. Some managers find it so difficult to fire a subordinate that they hire consultants to wield the ax for them. One company president who could not face up to the task of firing a vice president directly sent him a memo instead. The vice president simply ignored the memo and his boss was too embarrassed to bring up the ugly matter again; the vice president remained in his job.

Undoubtedly the most uncivilized firing technique was dreamed up by a firm that announced it was moving corporate headquarters from New York to Texas. The notice declared that everyone would be informed by the following Monday whether he was being invited to move or would be left behind to wind up affairs at the old headquarters. It also stated, almost as an afterthought, that executives wanting to know which group they were in could call a special telephone number on Saturday. Naturally everyone phoned, and the unlucky ones got the final word from an impersonal answering-service operator, who reported that not only were they not going to Texas but read a message saying, "The personnel department will be in touch with you by mail; you won't have to go into your office on Monday. They'll make arrangements to deliver all your personal effects. I'm sorry. Thank you for calling. Goodbye."

The opposite extreme, however, can be nearly as dehumanizing for the individual who feels trapped in an organizational role. In corporations where incompetent executives are not fired but kicked upstairs, where good will and camaraderie are the order of the day, the individuals can become in the words of writer Alan Harrington, "trapped in a labyrinth of benevolence." Eloquently describing his short career in one such establishment, which he calls The Crystal Palace, Harrington writes:

"A mighty fortress is our Palace; I will not want for anything. I must live my days without humiliation. I will not be fired. It nourishes my respect. I am led along the paths of righteousness for my own good. I am protected from tyrants. It guards me against tension and fragmentation of my self. It anoints me with benefits. Though we pass through hard times I will be preserved. These strong walls will surely embrace all the days of my life, if I remain a corporation man forever."

Harrington eventually quit the labyrinth of The Palace because he did not want to follow the "clearly defined arrows [that] mark the corporate route that has been laid out for us by our superiors and by the Executive Development Committee." He wanted to follow his own way, rather than play a role and risk ending up like the "wayside zombies who have gone as far as they can go, performing the same duties over and over again."

Harrington was a rare case, even in America. Few workers there abandon the organized life once they have entered it, for their anointed benefits—pay, insurance, pensions, annuities, credit unions, expense accounts and many more—often add up to a private welfare state and they come to depend on it. In other countries, Harrington's defiance would seem stranger than it does in the United States, and in Japan it would probably be considered bizarre. For the aspects of organizational life that Harrington found repellent, the Japanese find attractive.

In Japan, it has been said, a man is known by the company that keeps him. To a degree that many Westerners consider ridiculous—or frightening—the Japanese have transferred their loyalties from their old feudal masters to the large corporations and government bureaucracies of today. And the loyalty flows both ways. Joining a large corporation upon leaving school, the Japanese youth expects to stay with the firm for his entire working life, never to be fired except for criminal acts or on grounds of insanity. In return he is expected to work loyally, to identify with the corporation, to follow the rules and wait his turn—and so he does, with very little of the kind of *angst* that caused Alan Harrington to quit his Crystal Palace. From his corporation the Japanese derives not only livelihood and security, but health care, further education and social life. Every large corporation also has a semiformal system to ensure that the employee's assignments match his personal needs and career desires as much as possible. If he is a young man seeking to marry, the company stands ready to help him find a bride and to provide a priest and a hall for the wedding ceremony. Later he and his family are likely to spend their vacations in the company of fellow employees of the same general rank at mountain or seashore resorts owned and operated by the firm.

That kind of lifelong dependence on a single organization clearly does not fit Western traditions of mobility and diversity. (And in fact there are signs that a new mobility is fraying the Japanese pattern around the edges, too.) It is true that IBM has a company song, that it is still possible to walk along Bond Street in London and see men wearing their old school ties, that at the Watergate hearings in 1973 one young man explained that he committed what he knew were improper acts because of "the fear . . . of not being a team player." But it is unlikely that America or Europe will ever match Japan, where all corporation employees, even lowly broom wielders and delivery boys, proudly wear company emblems in their lapels and announce that "I'm a Mitsubishi man," or "I work for Sony."

In a highly descriptive and useful volume entitled All the Livelong Day, *Barbara Garson—playwright, commentator, and journalist—presents her inquiries into the character of routine work in America. Her research led to visits and interviews with all sorts of people in all sorts of occupations, from tunafish packers to insurance company receptionists, from lumberjacks to lipstick manufacturers.*

The following selection consists of three vignettes from Garson's book. The first is about life in a Ping-Pong factory. The second concerns keypunching. The third is about the famous Lordstown Chevrolet plant and the men and women who work there.

As you read these selections from All the Livelong Day, *ask yourself why Garson says in her preface that "It was the positive things I saw that touched me the most. Not that people are beaten down (which they are) but that they almost always pop up. Not that people are bored (which they are) but the ways they find to make it interesting." Think about how people learn to get around routinization. Who teaches them?*

Routine Work

BARBARA GARSON

PING-PONG

I met a girl named Cindy who worked for a while in a Ping-Pong factory.

"My job was stacking the Ping-Pong paddles into piles of fifty. Actually I didn't have to count all the way up to fifty. To make it a little easier they told me to stack 'em in circles of four with the first handle facing me. When there got to be thirteen handles on the second one from the front, then I'd know I had fifty. After a while of stacking I didn't have to count anyway. I could tell fifty just by looking at the pile.

"I had to work real fast. I had to keep three labelers and three packers supplied all the time.

"After I stacked 'em, the women would take 'em off the stacks and put labels on the handles—for whatever brand it was. After that they got packed into table tennis sets, four paddles, two balls and a net.

"Sometimes I got ahead building up these barricades of stacks. I would have liked to have finished three full walls all around myself but I never got that far ahead. As soon as I'd stack 'em, they'd unstack 'em.

"Maybe it wouldn't have been so bad if I could have seen all the piles I stacked at the end of the day. But they were taking them down as fast as I was piling them up. That was the worst part of the job.

"No," she corrected herself. "That wasn't the worst part of the job. The worst part was you had to stand up all day doing it."

"Why did you have to stand up?" I asked.

"I don't know," Cindy answered. "All I know is you weren't allowed to sit. Even between orders.

"There were a couple of retards they hired to shove the stuff around and sometimes you'd have to wait for them to bring you more paddles. Even then if I sat down the forelady, Alma, would come screaming at me.

"You couldn't talk either. You wouldn't want to anyway because it was too noisy and the way we were all spaced apart, you'd have to lean over and shout. But if you ever tried to talk Alma would come running over with a lot more paddles or she'd yell, 'Why aren't you finished yet?' So you were alone with your head all day.

"I once had a job stuffing envelopes and then I didn't mind daydreaming all day. But at the time I was working in the Ping-Pong factory I was having domestic problems with the man I was living with. So I didn't want to be alone with my head all day. And I didn't want to be standing on my feet all day. And I didn't want to be hearing Alma yell at me all day. And at $1.85 an hour, I figured I could afford to quit."

About four and a half million Americans work for small manufacturing firms that hire less than 100 people.* The Paragon Table Top Sports Corporation, with around fifty factory workers, sounded pretty typical of this sort of industry. So I decided to interview the workers that stayed on at the Ping-Pong factory.

I asked Cindy for some names, but she didn't know any. Oh yes, the people had been friendly to her, especially the older women, but after all there were only those two ten-minute breaks and then at noon forty minutes to rush to the deli, make phone calls, get to the bank, and then eat your sandwich, if you could fit that in.

Cindy could remember some first names. "There was this one little old lady, Lilly, sat at a bench screwing the screws on the wing nuts. She was a gas! . . . A couple of black women looked like they'd been there a long time. . . . The young people? They're probably all gone by now. Listen, if you do it and you talk to Lilly, find out for me how she managed to stay so cheerful all the

---

* Compiled from *Country Business Patterns, U.S. Summary*, 1971. Published by the U.S. Bureau of the Census.

time. I mean she was always carrying on or chuckling and I'm sure she wasn't still enjoying the two great jokes."

"Jokes?"

"Yeah. The foremen had their favorite jokes when they dumped some more paddles or balls on you. 'O.K. ladies, make a racket. Here girls, have a ball!' "

The Paragon Table Top Sports Corporation is located in the factory-warehouse section of town. There is no way to take a casual look around. A paneled office enclosure at the front blocks any view of the factory. The windows along the alley are high and their lower panes are painted over so no one can look in, or out.

Cindy told me about a side door where the canteen truck parked during breaks. She thought I could meet people there when they came out for coffee. She was certain I would be ejected immediately if I tried to get in. "You can't just stroll around you know. I mean I worked there and they'd still chase me out if I wandered into shipping or sewing or some other section. It's hard to get to know anyone there."

If I wanted to meet the workers at Paragon Table Top I would have to stand outside their factory and introduce myself. And that is just what I did. I waited in front of the Ping-Pong plant at ten o'clock, three o'clock and five-thirty every day of the rainy week before Christmas.

First one out at quitting time on Monday was a lad with a big broad grin and beautiful long hair, washed and brushed and shining like a Breck commercial.

I told him I was writing articles about work. "Do you think I could interview you sometime?"

"I'm not a worker," he said. "I just work here."

I could see his point. But so far he was the only one there. I felt I could spend a little time talking to a hippy till the "real workers" started coming out.

"Well, but what do you do here?" I asked.

"Ping-Pong paddles."

"Oh, you do paddles. Well how does that work . . . I mean . . ."

"You wanna know what I do. I'll give you my whole day. Here it is. They ring a buzzer at seven-forty. Seven forty-five they ring another. You clock in after the first buzzer. If you're not in by the second you're late. And that's the end of your life till break. Around ten o'clock they give you ten minutes' break. They ring it when the canteen truck gets out back.

"The buzzer is right on the clock and Frank the foreman he rings it. Man I stare at that clock all day and I have such an urge. Someday I'm gonna push that buzzer myself. Wait'll you see Alma and Frank tearing down at me. 'What the hell are you doing?' I swear I'm gonna do it. I'm gonna do it the day I quit.

"Anyway, lunch is the same deal as the morning. Two buzzers in, two buzzers out and forty minutes between 'em. Then death till three when the canteen comes back. Then you go out of your head till the last buzzer. Then quittin' then splittin'. Out of here—whish." And he split. But he called back from the corner.

"You be out here tomorrow?"

"Yeah."

"You should talk to Lilly. I'll tell a couple of the old people about you. They're the ones ought to be complaining to the papers."

The real workers came out in clumps. They were no particular sex or type. There was a large number of hippies—which is to say young people—a lot of colors of colored people, West Indian, Latin, Portuguese, a couple of fat white women and a couple of white women not so fat but older. A pair of young black men with bright-colored hats broke the over-all brown-gray tone.

I stopped a black woman with no afro, no dress style and no particular expression. Here name was Ina, she was large and plain and she appeared to be in her thirties.

I walked a few steps with her and said, "I'm writing an article about a Ping-Pong factory. Could you tell me something about your job?"

"It's a bitch."

She seemed to think the interview was over and she continued down the street.

"Ah yes, but what do you do in the factory?" I asked.

"Oh a million people do different things."

"What do *you* do?"

"I put the rubber on the bats."

Ina explained her job to me as we walked to the bus station in the drizzle.

"My job is sittin' and standin'. Sittin' is for puttin' the rubber on the paddle—you got to get it just in the center. Standin' is for puttin' it through the machine that holds it on. It starts with a big piece of wood, see, and the boys cut 'em into bats. All along the way everyone is doing different things to the bats. One guy sands it, one guy shellacs it, one lady she inspects the bat. Then it comes to me. A hundred in a box. I run the rubber through the roller that puts the glue on; then I set the rubber on the bat—that's the part you got to be careful; and then I put it through these other rollers that press it on.

"It's not such a difficult job but you have to know what you're doing 'cause there's three different kinds of rubber. You can tell by the number on the bat if it's a 925 a 765 or a 57X."

I asked about pay.

"I work by piecework. I get $1.10 a box. [One hundred to a box.] I can do eighteen, nineteen, twenty boxes a day, depending on the kind of bat. Say I make $20.95 a day."

When we got to the bus station Ina said she had half an hour to wait so we went into her deli for tea.

"Lemon, you want lemon in your tea," balked Sam the deli man. "You think this is some kind of high-class place? Hey Ina, who's your high-class friend here?"

"She's writin' a book about me."

"Hey, ya hear that?" he shouted to someone out in back somewhere. "She's writin' Ina's autobiography. Hey why don't you write about me? Or Joe here—" And he turned from us to harass a truck driver while Ina and I settled down with our tea.

"It's not such a bad job," she began, answering her own question. "It's steady. And if you ask them for overtime they'll always give it to you if they got the work."

I wrote it down.

"I bet this book will be a big thing for Waxman."

"Who's Waxman?" I asked.

"He's the owner, the boss. He's down in Florida now. When he's here he just walks around with the other big bosses saying 'Why aren't you working?' Then he goes back to his plush office and sits. And we stay down in the dirt. It's a terrible greasy dirty place! But it's not a bad job. I guess it's like any other job. There's a month's vacation. Two weeks in the summer and a week at Christmas, unless they ask you to do inventory. The young girls they come and go real fast. They stay two hours, twenty-four hours. I been here five years.

"Yeah, it gets boring sometimes but it's kind of interesting. The wood for the bats comes from Russia and the rubber comes from Hong Kong. Sometimes I get to do samples. When you do samples you got to be perfect. The other work you got to be good but for samples you got to be perfect."

I asked Ina if she wouldn't like to switch jobs sometime with somebody else, perhaps learn to operate one of the machines.

"The machines is mostly the men's work. Anyway there's no promotion here. This Mr. Waxman he owns the business. When they assign you a place that's it. The only time you get to do something different is if your work is all caught up and they send you to somewhere else.

"Anyway if they switch me I wouldn't be making my piecework. Also they could switch me to Alma. I got men bosses. I'd rather work for a man than a woman any day. My bosses they're patient. They'll explain things to new people. You can go to the bathroom. Alma she gets on a person's back. They up and leave on her side. Lots of people leave. My side too." And she drifted into thought. "I wonder why they come here. They could go to college. Especially the young ones." Then returning: "It's an allright job for me though."

It was almost time for her bus and so Ina began summing up.

"This job, I guess it's good in one way, bad in another. I'd like it better if the place was cleaner and it paid more.

"One thing, when I leave my work is turned off. I don't see no [Ping-Pong] bats in my dreams like some people. I have a house in the country. Takes me three quarters of an hour then I'm home. So it's really not such a bad job." And she left the deli to catch the bus. . . .

KEYPUNCHING

I once read about an "isolation" experiment where people were suspended in tepid water. The subjects floated somewhere between up and down with nothing to see but the gray walls of their containers. The idea was to see what happens when people are isolated from changing inputs.

Very quickly they started fantasizing. And within a few hours they were all hallucinating and showing signs of severe schizophrenia.

I can't remember whether or not everyone got better after they were taken out. I do remember that the hallucinations and fantasies were very uniform. The authors pointed out that the fantasies of most crazy people are very much the same.

You might think that going off into yourself would bring out the unique ideas and idiosyncrasies. But it's not so. People in dungeons, solitary confinement, floating boxes, and assembly lines tend to come up with fairly stereotyped fantasies, mutterings, and diversions.

Of all the jobs I've observed, keypunching comes closest to the floating box. For the worker it's a lot like typing forms—only more routine.

Irene Ryan worked at Metropolitan Life and then at Columbia Teacher's College. She was a puncher, a supervisor, and eventually an administrator. Irene described the job to me:

"Take a payroll for example. You have a form with an employee's name, address, salary, tax info. You have a board like a typewriter except that the numbers are on the right like an adding machine. And you have the cards set up to accept the payroll information.

"Essentially you are typing on IBM cards.

"Now the card is divided into fields. Six digits might be left for salary and that information will always be in the same six columns for each person.

"You start in columns one to six with the salary—that's a field. The drum is all set up. It moves over to the next field for the next piece of information. You type again. Then it moves over to the next field. You don't have to do any of the spacing yourself, it's automatic. If you have to type something over you may have to press 'dupe.' If you're working on a payroll where the same date will be duplicated on each card you don't have to press 'dupe.' It dupes itself.

"When you finish a form the next card comes up automatically.

"A drum can be set up in many different ways. For instance it can do different things on alternating cards. Or be set to do half the job one way and half another.

"It sounds interesting but when you do it you don't have to know any of this. It's all set on the drum and you just type seven hours a day. If it's all numbers then you can do it with one hand all day.

"When you punch, your hands are occupied, your eyes are occupied, you can't move your body. Sometimes people used to try to talk and punch at the same time. When I was a supervisor and I saw it I'd say, 'Just stop and talk for ten minutes. You'll enjoy it more.' That was at Columbia. I don't think you could do that at Met Life.

"I felt you had to let them stop, smoke, go to the bathroom, anything. Otherwise it's just too constant, just gray for hours at a time. No way to break it.

"One thing Aida and I used to do is have races. [Aida Acevedo is a friend of Irene's. They both moved from Met Life to Columbia Teacher's College.] On the older machines you had to hit harder and they made a louder noise. So we could hear each other and when we were doing the same job we could race. Sometimes we'd synchronize—adjust so that you'd move into the next field exactly together. But you're always pressured to go the fastest with the least errors. They all keep track of your monthly production and per cent of errors.* So we'd synchronize for a while but it always turned into races.

"We didn't plan the races but we found ourselves listening to how fast the other person was going and doing it a little faster. At first we didn't know that the other one was racing. We were both doing it but we didn't know.

"Aida and I are very good, high performers—bored, but still high performers. So we thought racing might be our special thing. Then a girl, Janet, told us she did the same thing. I guess it was the only kind of entertainment you could have. Like I said, your hands were occupied, your eyes were occupied, you couldn't move your body, couldn't talk. You only had the numbers on the sheets and the sounds of the other machines."

I talked to five other keypunchers. None of them were as articulate as Irene or Aida. When I asked what a keypuncher does, the best I could get was, "You punch the information. Whatever they give you."

When I asked if they played games to keep their minds occupied I drew a blank.

* In some keypunching departments each machine is wired to the supervisor's board. By watching the lights on her board the supervisor can tell immediately when any operator in the room stops punching.

But when I asked about racing and described what Irene and Aida did, they recognized the act. The laughed and they were embarrassed. It was very difficult for them to talk about that peculiar secret that each one thought was her own private pleasure.

As it turned out, among the five there was one racer, one synchronizer and, most inarticulate of all, a complex syncopater.

"This'll sound crazy," she said, "but I like to keep a certain rhythm . . . sound going. I mean I'd move forward when the woman next to me was halfway through another field and then she'd move in when I was halfway through the next. So you'd get a constant—like, bum, bum, bum, zing; bum, bum, bum, babum, zing. You could only do that with certain jobs.

". . . No, no, she didn't know what I was doing. If she slowed down I'd sort of slow down, but if she made a mistake or stopped I'd just have to go on.

"Sometimes I had it going with three people, so we'd all be doing it exactly together. I don't think the others noticed it. It's like sometimes you notice that three friends will be walking in the street and their footsteps are all the same. It'll last for a while and then it'll get broken up with nobody noticing. We never planned it. I never mentioned it to the other girls. I don't think they noticed it. Everybody just does their work. I never knew anyone else was listening to my sounds."

It was difficult at first to talk about racing. But in the end it was like those wonderful conversations that sometimes happen in the park when mothers who hardly know each other start talking about sex, or children, or men. And everyone goes away saying, "Oh, then you mean it's not just me? I'm not crazy!"

In light of the "isolation" experiment, it shouldn't be surprising that so many keypunchers come up with the same game to play.

The wonder is how much of our own real selves remain no matter how uniform and gray the inputs. That's the indomitable human spirit, I guess. The one they're always rediscovering in concentration camps. I too have always professed faith in its absolute endurance.

Still, when I hear about automatic typing, word-processing centers, and the tape punching that's replacing keypunching, I worry. There are limits. . . .

LORDSTOWN

"Is it true," an auto worker asked wistfully, "that you get to do fifteen different jobs on a Cadillac?"

"I heard," said another, "that with Volvos you follow one car all the way down the line."

Such are the yearnings of young auto workers at the Vega plant in Lordstown, Ohio. Their average age is twenty-four and they work on the fastest auto assembly line in the world. Their jobs are so subdivided that few workers can feel they are making a car.

The assembly line carries 101 cars past each worker every hour. Most GM lines run under sixty. At 101 cars an hour, a worker has thirty-six seconds to perform his assigned snaps, knocks, twists or squirts on each car. The line was running at this speed in October when a new management group, General Motors Assembly Division (GMAD or Gee-Mad) took over the plant. Within four months they fired five hundred to eight hundred workers. Their jobs were divided among the remaining workers, adding a few more snaps, knocks, twists or squirts to each man's task. The job had been boring and unbearable before. When it remained boring and became a bit more unbearable there was a 97 per cent vote to strike. More amazing—85 per cent went down to the union hall to vote. *

One could give a broad or narrow interpretation of what the Lordstown workers want. Broadly they want to reorganize industry so that each worker plays a significant role in turning out a fine product, without enduring degrading supervision. Narrowly, they want more time in each thirty-six-second cycle to sneeze or to scratch.

John Grix, who handles public relations at Lordstown, and Andy O'Keefe for GMAD in Detroit both assured me that work at Lordstown is no different than at the older assembly plants. The line moves faster, they say, but then the parts are lighter and easier to install. I think this may be true. It is also true of the workers. These young people are not basically different from the older men. But they are faster and lighter. Because they are young they are economically freer to strike and temperamentally quicker to act. But their yearnings are not new. The Vega workers are echoing a rank-and-file demand that has been suppressed by both union and management for the past twenty years: *Humanize working conditions.*

Hanging around the parking lot between shifts, I learned immediately that to these young workers:

It's Not the Money

"It pays good," said one, "but it's driving me crazy."

"I don't want more money," said another. "None of us do."

---

* The union membership voted to settle the twenty-two-day strike in late March, but the agreement appeared to be somewhat reluctant; less than half of the members showed up for the vote, and 30 per cent of those voted against the settlement. The union won a number of concessions, among them full back pay for anybody who had been disciplined in the past few months for failure to meet work standards. But nothing was settled that affected the pace of the work. Meanwhile, UAW locals at over ten other GM plants around the country have struck on grounds similar to those established at Lordstown.

"I do," said his friend, "so I can quit quicker."

"The only money I want is my union dues back—if they don't let us out on strike soon."

It's the Job

It's not the money, it's the job," everyone says. But they find it hard to describe the job itself.

"My father worked in auto for thirty-five years," said a clean-cut lad, "and he never talked about the job. What's there to say? A car comes, I weld it; a car comes, I weld it; a car comes, I weld it. One hundred and one times an hour."

I asked a young wife, "What does your husband tell you about his work?"

"He doesn't say what he does. Only if something happened like 'My hair caught on fire' or 'Something fell in my face.' "

"There's a lot of variety in the paint shop," says a dapper twenty-two-year-old, up from West Virginia. "You clip on the color hose, bleed out the old color, and squirt. Clip, bleed, squirt, think; clip, bleed, squirt, yawn; clip, bleed, squirt, scratch your nose. Only now the Gee-Mads have taken away the time to scratch your nose."

A long-hair reminisced, "Before the Gee-Mads, when I was on door handles, I could get a couple of cars ahead and get myself a whole minute to relax."

I asked about diversions. "What do you do to keep from going crazy?"

"Well, certain jobs like the pit you can light up a cigarette without them seeing."

"I go to the wastepaper basket. I wait a certain number of cars then find a piece of paper to throw away."

"I have fantasies. You know what I keep imagining? I see a car coming down. It's red. So I know it's gonna have a black seat, black dash, black interiors. But I keep thinking what if somebody up there sends down the wrong color interiors—like orange, and me putting in yellow cushions, bright yellow!"

"There's always water fights, paint fights, or laugh, talk, tell jokes. Anything so you don't feel like a machine."

"I don't do anything any more," says an old-timer (twenty-four with four years seniority, counting nineteen months in the Army). "I think the time passes fastest if you let your mind just phase out and blend in with the speed of the line."

But everyone has the same hope: "You're always waiting for the line to break down."

The Vega plant hires about seven thousand assembly-line workers. They commute to Lordstown from Akron, Youngstown, Cleveland, even as far as

Pittsburgh. Actually, there is no Lordstown—just a plant and some trailer camps set among farmhouses. When the workers leave, they disperse throughout northern Ohio. GM presumably hoped that this location would help minimize labor troubles.

I took the guided tour of the plant. It's new, it's clean, it's well lit without windows and it's noisy. Hanging car bodies move past at the speed of a Coney Island ride slowing down. Most men work alongside the line but some stand in a man-sized pit craning their necks to work on the undersides of the cars.

I stopped to shout at a worker drinking coffee, "*Is there any quiet place to take a break?*" He shouted back, "*Can't hear you, ma'am. Too noisy to chat on a break.*" As a plant guard rushed over to separate us I spotted Duane, from Fort Lewis, shooting radios into cars with an air gun. Duane had been in the Army while I was working at a GI coffeehouse. He slipped me a note with his address.

When I left the plant there were leafleteers at the gate distributing *Worker's Power*. Guards with binocular cameras closed in, snapping pictures; another guard checked everyone's ID. He copied down the names of leafleteers and workers who took papers. He took my name too.

That evening I visited Duane. He had rented a two-bedroom bungalow on the outskirts of a town that had no center. He had grown his hair a bit but, in fact, he looked neater and trimmer than when he'd been in the Army.

I told him about the incident at the gate. "Just like the Army," he said. He summarized life since his discharge: "Remember you guys gave me a giant banana split the day I ETSed [got out on schedule]? Well, it's been downhill since then. I came back to Cleveland; stayed with my dad, who was unemployed. Man, was that ever a downer. But I figured things would pick up if I got wheels, so I got a car. But it turned out the car wasn't human and that was a problem. So I figured, 'What I need is a girl.' But it turned out the girl *was* human and *that* was a problem. So I wound up working at GM to pay off the car and the girl." And he introduced me to his lovely pregnant wife, of whom he seemed much fonder than it sounds.

A couple of Duane's high school friends, Stan and Eddie, wound up at Lordstown too. Stan at twenty-one was composed and placid, a married man with a child. Eddie at twenty-two was an excitable youth. Duane had invited them over to tell me what it's like working at the plant.

"I'll tell you what it's like," said Duane. "It's like the Army. They even use the same words, like *direct order*. Supposedly you have a contract so there's some things they just can't make you do. Except, if the foreman gives you a direct order, you do it, or you're out."

"Out?" I asked.

"Yeah, fired or else they give you a DLO—disciplinary layoff. Which means you're out without pay for however long they say. Like maybe it'll be a three-day DLO or a week DLO."

Eddie explained it further. "Like this new foreman comes up to me and says, 'Pick up that piece of paper.' Only he says it a little nastier with a few references to my race, creed, and length of hair. So I says, 'That's not my job.' He says, 'I'm giving you a direct order to pick up that piece of paper.' Finally he takes me up to the office. My committeeman comes over and tells me I could of lost my job because you can't refuse a direct order. You do it, and then you put in a grievance—HA!"

"Calling your committeeman," says Duane, "that's just like the Army too. If your CO [commanding officer] is harassing you, you can file a complaint with the IG [inspector general]. Only thing is you gotta go up to your CO and say, 'Sir, request permission to see the inspector general to tell him my commanding officer is a shit.' Same thing here. Before you can get your committeeman you got to tell the foreman exactly what your grievance is in detail. So meantime he's working out ways to tell the story different."

Here Stan took out an actual DLO form from his wallet. "Last week someone up the line put a stink bomb in a car. I do rear cushions and the foreman says, 'You get in that car.' We said, 'If you can put your head in that car we'll do the job.' So the foreman says, 'I'm giving you a direct order.' So I hold my breath and do it. My job is every other car so I let the next one pass. He gets on me and I say, 'Jack, it ain't my car. Please, I done your dirty work and the other one wasn't mine.' But he keeps at me and I wind up with a week off. Now, I got a hot committeeman who really stuck up for me. So you know what? They sent *him* home too. Gave the committeeman a DLO!

"Guy next to me, this boob Larry, he puts in alternators and they changed it to a one-man job. So he lets half the cars get away. Then he calls the committeeman and files a seventy-eight [a grievance claiming that the job can't be done in the allotted time]. I walk up to him afterwards and say, 'Look at you! Now you're smiling and you're doing the goddamn job. You can wipe your ass with that grievance.' Two months later he's still doing the job just like GM wants him to. The union is saying, 'Hang on fellah, we'll help you,' and he's still on the line like a fucking machine.

"See, just like the Army," Duane repeats. "No, it's worse cause you're welded to the line. You just about need a pass to piss."

"That ain't no joke," says Eddie. "You raise your little hand if you want to go wee-wee. Then wait maybe half an hour till they find a relief man. And they write it down every time too. 'Cause you're supposed to do it on your own time, not theirs. Try if too often and you'll get a week off."

"I'd rather work in a gas station," said Stan, wistfully. "That way you pump gas, then you patch a tire, then you go to the bathroom. You do what needs doing."

"Why don't you work in a gas station?" I asked.

"You know what they pay in a gas station? I got a kid. Besides, I couldn't even get a job in a gas station. Before I got in here I was so hard up I wound up selling vacuum cleaners—$297 door to door. In a month I earned exactly

$10 selling one vacuum cleaner to a laid-off steel worker, for which I'll never forgive myself."

"No worse than making cars," Eddie comforted him. "Cars are your real trap, not vacuum cleaners. You need the car to keep the job and you need the job to keep the car. And don't think they don't know it. They give you just enough to keep up the payments. They got it planned exactly, so you can't quit."

"He's a little paranoid," Duane cautioned me.

"Look-it," says the paranoid reasonably. "They give you fifty, fifty-five hours' work for a couple of weeks. So your typical boob buys a color TV. Then they cut you back to thirty hours. There's not a married man who doesn't have bills. And the company keeps it like that so there's no way out. You're stuck for life."

I asked about future plans.

Eddie was getting out as soon as he saved enough money to travel. He thought he might work for three more months. He'd said three months when he started and it was nine months already but, "Things came up."

Duane figured he'd stay till his wife had the baby. That way he could use the hospital plan. After that? "Maybe we'll go live on the land. I don't know. I wish someone would hand me a discharge."

Stan was a reasonable man . . . or a boob, as Eddie might have it. He knew he was going to stay. "If I'm gonna do some dumb job the rest of my life, I might as well do one that pays."

Though none of them could afford to quit, they were all eager for a strike. They'd manage somehow. For Stan it was a good investment in his future job. The others just like the idea of giving GM a kick in the ass from the inside.

An Auto Workers' Commune

Later in the week I stayed at an auto workers' commune. Like so many other young people, they were trying to make a one generational family—a homestead. Life centered, as of old, around the hearth, which was a water pipe bubbling through Bourbon. The family Bibles were the Books of the Dead—both Tibetan and Egyptian. Throughout the evening six to ten people drifted through the old house waiting for Indian Nut (out working night shift at Lordstown) and his wife, Jane (out baby-sitting).

Jane returned at midnight to prepare dinner for her husband. By 2 A.M. she complained, "They can keep them two, three, four hours over." (Overtime is mandatory for auto workers and it's not as popular at Lordstown as it is among older workers at other plants.)

At two-thirty the Nut burst in, wild-haired, wild-eyed, and sweet-smiled. He had a mildly maniacal look because his glasses were speckled with welding spatter.

"New foreman, a real Gee-mad-man. Sent a guy home for farting in a car. And another for yodeling."

"Yodeling?" I asked.

"Yeah, you know—" And he yodeled.

(It's common in auto plants for men to break the monotony with noise, like the banging of tin cans in jail. Someone will drop something, his partner will yell "Whaa" and then "Whaa" gets transmitted all along the line.)

"I bet there's no shop rule against farting." the Nut conjectured. "You know those porkers have been getting their 101 off the line again, and not that many of them need repairs. It's the hillbillies. Those cats have no stamina. The union calls them to a meeting, says, 'Now don't you sabotage, but don't you run. Don't do more than you can do.' And everybody cheers. But in a few days it's back to where it was. Hillbillies working so fast they ain't got time to scratch their balls. Meantime those porkers is making money even faster than they're making cars."

I ask who he means by the hillbillies. "Hillbillies is the general Ohio term for assholes, except if you happen to be a hillbilly. Then you say Polack. Fact is everybody is a hillbilly out here except me and two other guys. And they must work day shift 'cause I never see them.

"Sabotage?" says the Nut. "Just a way of letting off steam. You can't keep up with the car so you scratch it on the way past. I once saw a hillbilly drop an ignition key down the gas tank. Last week I watched a guy light a glove and lock it in the trunk. We all waited to see how far down the line they'd discover it. If you miss a car they call that sabotage. They expect the sixty-second minute. Even a machine has to sneeze. Look how they call us in weekends, hold us extra, send us home early, give us layoffs. You'd think we were machines the way they turn us on and off."

I apologized for getting Indian Nut so steamed up and keeping him awake late. "No," sighed Jane. "It always takes a couple of hours to calm him down. We never get to bed before four."

The next morning, about 1 P.M., Indian Nut cooked breakfast for all of us (about ten). One nice thing about a working-class commune—bacon and eggs and potatoes for breakfast—no Granola.

It took about an hour and a half to do the day's errands— mostly dope shopping and car repair. Then Indian Nut relaxed for an hour around the hearth.

As we talked some people listened to Firesign Theater while others played Masterpiece or Monopoly. Everyone sucked at the pipe from time to time.

A college kid came by to borrow records. He was the editor of the defunct local underground paper called *Anonymity*. (It had lived up to its title before folding.)

"I've been trying to get Indian Nut to quit working there," he said.

"Why?" I asked.

"Don't you know?" GM makes M-16s.

"Yeah, well you live with your folks," said one of the Monopolists.

"You can always work some kind of rip-off," replied the ex-editor.

Everyone joined the ensuing philosophical inquiry about where it was moral to work and who it was moral to rip off.

"Shit," sighed Indian Nut. "It's four-thirty. Someone help Jane with the dishes." Taking a last toke, the Nut split for the plant.

*It may be surprising to learn that blue-collar workers,
such as those who make ping-pong paddles and auto-
mobiles, are more ulcer-prone than those who work in
executive suites. Tensions and conflicts between co-
workers and between workers and their families all contribute to the stresses that accompany "shift work."
This stress is the subject of Robert Kahn's report on
some imaginative research conducted several years ago
by the Institute of Social Research at the University of
Michigan.*

*As you read this selection, pay particular attention to
two concepts he mentions: "role set" and "role conflict"; they are crucial to the understanding of the
analysis of "Stress: From 9 to 5."*

Stress: From 9 to 5

ROBERT L. KAHN

A man's job and his health are closely related. The lower his position, the
more likely it is that he is unhealthy. If he is promoted, his health will tend to
improve; if he is demoted, he will tend to become ill. The blue-collar worker
is more likely to have ulcers than the executive. But even if his job status indicates that his health should be good, conflict and tension within a man's
job-role can affect his well-being.

These findings emerged from a broad research program into mental health
in industry. The goal of our latest research at the Institute for Social Research
of the University of Michigan is to learn more about the human costs and
benefits of industrial production, about the meaning of work and about the
mental and physical consequences of organizational life. My colleagues in this
research include Sidney Cobb, John R. P. French Jr., Stanislav Kasl (now at
Yale), George Brooks, Jerald Bachman, Robert P. Quinn, Willard Rodgers,
John Lillibridge, and Ki-Taek Chun, and their work provided much of the
material for this article.

Among the most potent aspects of status for health are incompatibilities
between two roles simultaneously occupied by the same person, or between
two or more behaviors required in a single role. We have called such incompatibilities *role conflict*, and it has been a major theme in our research.

We began by thinking of the environment of any individual as consisting largely of formal organizations or groups. These groups and organizations—company, union, church, family, etc.—affect a person's physical and emotional state and are major determinants of his behavior.

In order to link the individual and the organization, we must locate the individual in his organizational relationships. The key concept for doing this is the office, the person's unique point in organizational space. Associated with each office is a set of activities or potential behaviors that constitutes the role to be performed by any person who occupies that office. Every member of every corporate organization is associated with others, most of whom are occupants of offices that are adjacent to his in the chart that mimics the work flow and the direction of authority. These other persons constitute that individual's *role set*.

The role set usually includes his supervisor, immediate supervisor, subordinates and some colleagues of equal rank. But his role set may also include close friends, family, respected models and any others who are concerned with his job behavior. All members of a person's role set depend in some way upon his performance: they are rewarded by it, or they require it in order to perform their own tasks. Because they have a stake in his performance, they develop attitudes and expectations about what he should and should not do in his role. And they communicate these role expectations—sometimes directly as when a supervisor instructs a subordinate; sometimes indirectly, as when a colleague expresses admiration or disappointment.

It is apparent that various members of a person's role set may hold quite different role expectations, and that these would imply different behaviors for the focal person. Members of the role set may impose conflicting pressures, and the man will experience psychological conflict. For example, a man's superior may make it clear that he is expected to hold his subordinates strictly to company rules and to high production schedules. At the same time, his subordinates make it clear that they want loose, informal supervision and that they will slow down and make things difficult if they are pushed too hard. He is thus confronted with an unacceptable choice; neither supervisory style will satisfy both his superior and his subordinates, and neither will increase production. The pressures are clearly incompatible and cannot be resolved merely by the use of authority. As the man in the middle, he must fall back on more personal reserves of influence, persuasion and tact with both superiors and subordinates.

We can identify several types of role conflict. The man caught between demands for close and loose supervision is a victim of *inter-sender* conflict. His superior and his subordinates are sending incompatible messages. In *intra-sender* conflict, a single member of the role set places incompatible pressures on a person. For example, a supervisor may request a man to get material that is unavailable through normal channels and at the same time forbid violation of those channels.

In *inter-role* conflict, pressures connected with membership in one group conflict with pressures that stem from membership in another group. Overtime work may conflict with family affairs. A man's role as worker then conflicts with his role as husband and father.

Other types of conflict come from clashes between environmental pressure and internal forces—these we call *person-role* conflict. Such conflict occurs when a person's role requirements violate his ethical values. For example, an executive may be pressured to join a price-fixing conspiracy that violates his personal code of ethics. In other cases, a person's needs and aspirations may lead to behavior that is unacceptable to members of his role set. For example, an ambitious young man might tread on his associates when he attempts to advance in the organization.

Common to all role conflicts is pressure exerted by members of a role set to change the man's behavior—new forces that threaten the equilibrium he already has worked out. And the stronger the pressure is, the greater the internal conflict.

The degree to which a person's behavior conforms to expectations will affect those expectations in the future. If his response is a hostile counterattack, members of his role set will behave one way toward him; if he is submissively compliant, they will behave in another manner. If he partially complies under pressure, they may increase the pressure; if he is overcome with tension and anxiety, they may lay off.

When we studied intensively 54 role sets in a number of different industries and surveyed 1,500 households across the nation, we discovered that role conflict is common. Almost half of our respondents reported being caught between conflicting persons or factions. These conflicts are usually hierarchical; 88 per cent of those involved report that at least one party to the conflict ranks above them in the organization. Fewer than half report that one of the conflicting parties is outside the organization. A dominant form of role conflict is overload, which can be thought of as a conflict among legitimate tasks, manageable singly but not simultaneously. Almost half of all respondents who reported role conflict described it in these terms.

The emotional costs of role conflict include low job satisfaction, low confidence in the organization and high tension. The most frequent response to role conflict is to avoid those seen as creating the conflict. The focal person may reduce communication with his co-workers and assert—sometimes unrealistically—that they lack power over him. Such withdrawal, which is a mechanism of defense, often reduces the possibility of arriving at later cooperative solutions to the conflict.

Going outside one's company in the line of duty is associated with role conflict, as salesmen and labor negotiators can attest. Moreover, the conflict increases with the frequency and importance of the trips. Crossing the company boundary is also associated with tension, but the greatest tension is felt by those who have frequent but not continuous outside contacts. Positions that require continuous extra-company contacts apparently are provided with special facilities or some other organization acknowledgement of boundary difficulties that render them less painful.

It appears that a worker who must deal with people outside his company usually has limited control over these outsiders. He cannot strongly influence their demands or the resources they supply. Moreover, a man in a boundary position is likely to be blamed by his co-workers for failures or errors by his outside contacts. And the outsiders may blame him for shortcomings in his own company. If the boundary-dweller must coordinate his outside activities with people in other departments of his own company, his difficulties are intensified. In general, working near a departmental boundary creates conflict and tension very like that found at the external boundaries of the organization.

Roles that demand creative problem-solving also carry high role conflict and tension. Holders of such roles appear to engage in conflict primarily with older and often more powerful employees, who want to maintain the status quo. People in innovative jobs complain of conflict between their nonroutine creative activities and their routine administrative duties. Paper work, they say, is time-consuming, disrupts their creative work, and is generally unpalatable.

Organizations appear to be selective in choosing people for innovative positions, and the people who are chosen tend to have high self-confidence, high mobility aspirations, high job-involvement and low apathy, and to rate their job extremely high in relation to other areas of their lives.

Supervisory responsibility emerges as a major organizational cause of role conflict, whether a man supervises rank-and-file employees or people who are themselves supervisors. Combined direct and indirect supervisory duties produce substantial role conflict and tension. There is a systematic relationship between rank and role conflict. Maximum conflict occurs at the upper-middle levels of management. We see this as coming partly from unfulfilled mobility aspirations of the middle management; the top management tends to have fulfilled aspirations.

The greatest pressure on a worker comes from his superiors in his own department who are dependent on his performance. They care about his adequacy, but they are not so dependent on him that they must inhibit their demands. Least pressure comes from a worker's peers and from role senders outside his department.

The kind and degree of pressure that people apply varies considerably with their formal relationship to the worker. Supervisors seem to refrain from forms of coercion that might impede the worker's performance and perhaps reflect upon the supervisor himself. On the other hand, subordinates apply coercive power in ways that threaten the efficiency of the organization. These include the withholding of aid and information.

When he is surrounded by people who depend heavily on him, have power over him and exert high pressure on him, a worker typically responds with apathy and withdrawal. He experiences a sense of futility. In such circumstances, his feeling of role conflict is very high and his job satisfaction is low.

There is significant evidence that close and positive relations between a worker and members of his role set can ease the effects of role conflict. In such cases, a given degree of role conflict produces less sense of stress. However, sustained role conflict can reduce a man's trust, respect and liking for his co-workers. If he feels conflict or ambiguity, he tends to weaken his relations with others. This is self-defeating, for the worker withdraws from the very persons from whom he requires information.

The effects of role conflict are also modified or intensified by the personality of the individual. Unsociable, independent persons report greater strain on interpersonal bonds and greater tension under role conflict than persons who are less independent. The independent person's social relations are often congenial and trusting but they are easily undermined by stress. Their taste for autonomy shows up when others exert strong pressures and create conflict. Similarly, emotionally sensitive persons show substantially higher tension scores for any given degree of conflict. Role senders tend to match pressure to personality, but not always in ways that make things easier for the individual. Thus, persons who are relatively flexible get stronger pressures than those who have the rigidity to resist them.

A recent study of 823 workers by Allen Kraut extended our research on role conflict. Kraut conducted his study in the sales department of a large corporation. In each of the department's 151 sales offices, the manager and a sample of salesmen participated. In general, Kraut confirmed our earlier research.

He also found that a salesman tends to perceive the expectations of his supervisor in a distorted manner, to see them as nearer his own than is actually the case. The effect is to understate conflict, which is perhaps one way of attempting to cope with it.

Kraut also related conflict to individual and office performance. In this respect, his research brought under empirical consideration an issue that traditionally has been handled by assumptions. Georg Simmel, in his classic essay, comes very near to making conflict an unvarying organizational benefit. Kenneth Boulding, on the other hand, asserts that "conflict in its nonsport aspect is usually felt as too much." Managers show similar differences of opinion. Some insist on "keeping the animals stirred up," as they put it, and others see any sign of conflict as a personal failure and an organizational threat.

Kraut's findings give little support to the single-minded proponents of either organizational peace or war. His statistics show that conflict affects performance negatively, but the extent is too small to be really significant for the organization.

We expected that shift work would create a kind of role conflict we had not previously studied: conflict between the life roles of the individual, rather than conflict between expectations of a single role. Floyd Mann and his colleagues studied shift-work patterns in five plants that included 950 employees working day, afternoon, night and rotating shifts. Both husbands and wives were interviewed.

Shift work apparently increases the individual's difficulty with his major life roles. Shift workers reported greater strain and tension in marriage than did day workers. Men working the afternoon shift reported difficulty with their roles as fathers and with miscellaneous household duties. Men working the night shift reported difficulty with their roles as protectors and as husbands, including the sexual relationship. Men who worked rotating shift patterns had all these difficulties and reported also that rotating shifts interfered with their friendships. The shift worker was less likely than the day worker to be a member of community organizations, less likely to be active in the organizations in which he was a member, and still less likely to be a leader in these same organizations.

Shift workers who reported difficulty with the shift-work pattern were commonly bothered by problems of the time-oriented body functions—sleep, appetite and elimination. They were also more likely to report colds, headaches, infectious diseases, ulcers and rheumatoid arthritis.

When the shift worker felt that the shift-work pattern interfered with his other activities, he was likely to experience low self-esteem and high anxiety. Personality, family relations and background also mediated the effects of shift work, although not always in an obvious manner. People whose test scores indicated some tendency toward neuroticism seemed less bothered by shift work than people whose scores were more nearly average.

The attitudes and behavior of the wives of shift workers appear to be particularly important. For example, those workers whose wives arrange meals, sleep, quiet and social life to harmonize with the work pattern were much less adversely affected. It seems that shift work gives the wife additional household power. She can, if she chooses, exclude the worker from much of the family and marital relationship, in ways that do not expose her to social criticism. Some of the interviews suggest also that wives and husbands use shift work to avoid each other. People can hide from each other in time as well as in space.

Our investigations of the link between job status and health began with a study of the relationship between job status and frequency of illness among employees of a large public utility. Illness was defined on the basis of voluntary visits to the company infirmary. Kasl and French, who had conducted this study, then repeated it in a quite different industry. The results in the two studies were substantially the same: the lower the status of the job, the higher the index of illness, whether among workers or among supervisors.

It could be argued, however, that such research shows only that management selects and promotes those employees with better physical and mental health. French and Kasl therefore conducted another study comparing the same persons over time, before and after status changes. The data confirmed our earlier studies: those who were promoted became "healthier," even though they had aged.

These preliminary studies indicated that low status generated illness, but they left a large theoretical gap between status and illness. On the assumption that what a person thinks of himself will reflect what others think of him and will influence his health, French and his colleagues measured, through questionnaires, the relationships between a man's self-esteem and his notion of what people think of his job. They found that workers ascribe the attribute of the job to the job holder. For instance, people were asked to rate two unknown men; the only information given was the kind of job each man held—a third-level management job and a low-skill craft job. The manager was consistently rated higher on things like ambition, education, hard work and administrative skill. Our raters found no difference between the two men on nonoccupational characteristics like honesty, sense of humor or helpfulness.

This attribution of job characterisitcs to job holders applies when a man evaluates himself. Since people ascribe to themselves the qualities that they and others consider necessary for their jobs, objective signs of job status like pay and number of subordinates are positively related to self-esteem. That is, if certain jobs are connected with certain pay levels, and are seen as requiring certain qualities of judgment and skill, the individual holding such a job and receiving such pay is evaluated by himself and by others as possessing these skills and qualities of judgment. High job status is related to esteem from others and to self-esteem.

Additional tests of these relationships were made in sensitivity training groups at a human relations conference. These T-groups were somewhat like encounter groups, where communication about the self and others was especially frank.

Measurements were taken at the beginning and the end of the two-week session, in order to show any changes in the way in which each person was actually evaluated by the others, the way in which he thought others were evaluating him, and the way in which he evaluated himself. The findings showed that, during the two weeks, a person's notion of how others were evaluating him came to resemble their actual evaluation more closely, particularly if he liked them. Moreover, his own evaluation of himself—self-esteem—increased or decreased to conform to his sense of his evaluation by other members of the group. For instance, if a man entered the T-group with the idea that he was a strong leader but found that others did not regard him that way, he would tend to change his self-evaluation to agree with this less enthusiastic public rating. Finally, this convergence of evaluation of self with the evaluation by others is strengthened by the amount of direct relevant communication from group members to the individual.

Next we looked at the effects of public esteem as communicated to one individual by another single person. French and Meyer studied the effects of the appraisal system in a large company. They interviewed 92 members of management before and after their annual appraisals. During each appraisal, trained observers recorded the behavior of both the boss and the subordinate. The number of criticisms made by the boss and the frequency of his praise were used to define communicated public esteem. Ten weeks later both the boss and the employee were interviewed again. The appraisals had indeed threatened self-esteem; 82 per cent of the employees reported that their ratings by the boss were lower than their self-evaluations.

Contrary to the usual assumptions of performance appraisal, French and Meyer had predicted that threats to self-esteem would be demoralizing, would inhibit rather than improve subsequent performance, especially for persons already low in self-esteem. They were right. If a person was low in occupational self-esteem, and his self-esteem was threatened further by a negative appraisal, his performance got worse.

On the other hand, threat or negative appraisal had no such effect for those high in occupational self-esteem. This study showed that while self-esteem is influenced by the work environment, it can also be a more-or-less stable characteristic of a person.

Research on the effects of organizational requirements on individual health is still at a very early stage, but it is already adding new facts and calling into question old beliefs. For example, in a study of 132 male shift workers we found that self-esteem, the causes of which we had been searching out in the studies already described, was related to the incidence of peptic ulcer. The lower the self-esteem, the greater the likelihood of ulcer. This fact does not fit the myth of executive ulcer, but earlier research had already called that into question. When Cobb compared craftsmen, foremen and executives, he found that foremen had the most ulcers and executives the fewest.

The research links that explain the impact of organization on the individual are thus slowly formed; the slowness reminds us that the aim of understanding the stressful characterisitcs of large organization is both grand and necessary. The stakes are too high for researchers to refuse the game. Man will live increasingly in large organizations, and if we wish to make these organizations livable, we must first understand them.

Again we consider the unique and often second-class position of women—not in the home this time but in the world of work. Louise Kapp Howe discusses the self-doubt that plagues many women, the sources of tension in a male-oriented, male-dominated job market, the personal, social, and economic meaning of work to women in different social classes, and the changes that many women are seeking in order to bring true equality of opportunity to the workplace.

As you read "Women in the Workplace," notice the repeated examples of labeling and categorizing of women in our society. Consider the consequences for both women and men of such socialized role ascription.

Women in the Workplace

Louise Kapp Howe

I

On the wall (reports the *Wall Street Journal*) is a picture of Israeli Premier Golda Meir captioned "But Can She Type?" There are other feminist posters, too. Seated around the room are forty women—all employees of Westinghouse, all invited to this "motivational" workshop because the company says it is interested in helping them to advance to higher positions within the corporation.

Actually Westinghouse is under the gun to help them do so. Like all major corporations with a history of sex discrimination—in short, *all* major corporations—it could be declared ineligible for federal contracts if it doesn't comply with new regulations to show "affirmative action" (which now means specific goals and timetables) to recruit and promote women to all levels of its job structure.

That is, of course, why every other week or so we hear of new company plans and programs and occasionally statistical progress such as IBM's announcement of a 35 per cent increase in its female managerial staff over the previous year. Though sounding impressive it was never made clear exactly what *numbers* were involved. More impressive are the recent strides in open-ing higher-level jobs and awarding back pay to thousands of women working for Ma Bell.

In any case, the Westinghouse workshop takes place in a motel conference room in Pittsburgh. For two days the invited employees debate whether it has been sex discrimination or women's own inadequacies that have kept us from the nation's top ranks of management. Because of the attention given to the Feminist Movement in the past few years, the women respond instantly that it has been the fault of our lousy male chauvinist occupational system—or do they?

Not here, not yet. Doubts and self-doubts instead. The women worry openly about their abilities, or rather their lack of them. They also express concern about losing their femininity or damaging their relationships with men by concentrating on careers. Although less than a quarter of the women present are married and living with their husbands, most still foresee and fear a future conflict between home and career. "Remember," one woman says, "it's more socially acceptable for a man to sacrifice his home for a career than it is for a woman."

Finally, according to *Wall Street Journal* reporter Ellen Graham, they decide to put the question of sex discrimination to a vote. At this point a woman named Janet pulls out a book of statistics showing that women college graduates earn on the average more than $5,000 a year less than their male counterparts. "Now won't you agree women have been discriminated against?" she asks. "Men are making more money because they're more qualified," Irene retorts. "If you're held back, it isn't because you're a woman, it's because of your own inadequacies." The vote is taken. Doubts and self-doubts. Irene wins.

Nevertheless, by the time it's over, the workshop seems to have made a dif-ference in the way the participants feel about themselves. There was only one avowed feminist when they began and now their consciousness has been raised for the future. Bring on the promotions! The workshop is praised.

II

Doubts and self-doubts still chip away at the potential abilities of how many women? *What should I be, what can I do, what will I have to give up to get there?* Spurred by the Feminist Movement, many thousands of women are refusing to give yesterday's ritual reply: wife-and-mother, period. Many who wouldn't have done so 10 years ago are now seeking careers instead, or careers *as well*, if they can manage it all.

But, as the Westinghouse workshop showed, for other women, for no doubt the vast majority of other women, the old conditioning about sex roles—that a man is your basic security, that his work always comes before your own—has not lost its power in a few short years. How could it? For most women the objective conditions that would breach the doubts have yet to arrive.

On the same day in April, 1973, that the *Wall Street Journal* reported the steps Westinghouse and other corporations were taking to help women advance in work, another item tabulated the latest rate of unemployment among married men (2.5 per cent). Washington experts will tell you that this is the one rate that matters the most. Although the rate is far lower than the overall jobless figure that encompasses us all, officials look at it first when unemployment start to climb. The overall figure isn't really that critical, John B. Connally announced definitively a couple of years ago. At that time it was 6 per cent and he was Secretary of the Treasury; after all, "it includes so many women and teenagers."

Our employment policies have always been based on the male breadwinner's needs first. During depressions, recessions, recurring periods of high unemployment, his prior right to available work, the *best* available work, has never been seriously questioned. It was he about whom the government worried to the extent it bothered to worry about its job-reduction policies to stem inflation at the beginning of this decade. And of course that was far from a frivolous concern. Nothing could have been more memorable than some of the shocked and saddened faces we saw on television at that time, white, middle-aged breadwinners who had thought they and their families were secure for life; after all, unemployment was something reserved for "lazy kids and blacks." The irony of their past bigotry, in some few instances an awakening to the inequities facing others for so long, came through on the tube as we watched them. But what the television cameras failed to show, what goverment officials failed to consider, in addition to the then deepening problems among the poor and the black, were the faces of the women who were also being laid off, women who needed work just as badly.

We keep hearing the statistics, but that doesn't mean they are taken seriously. Forty per cent of all women who work are dependent on neither a husband nor a father for their support. Of the 33 million women now in the labor force, more than 20 per cent are single; another 20 per cent are widowed, divorced, or separated; and about 15 per cent more have husbands who are earning less than $5,000 a year. Thirteen million American women who maintain their own households are responsible for the welfare of about 10 million children. The rate of unemployment is consistently higher for women looking for work than it is for men—more than two times higher for female heads of households than male—and the gap has widened in the past decade. Despite the Equal Pay Act of 1964, the disparity in pay has widened. Far from working for pin money, there is evidence, as the *Washington Post* put it, that the "working woman is to some extent doing in this country what the US

Government seems incapable of doing. Increasingly, she provides the essentials of life for the poorest of families and is pulling a very substantial number up the ladder into middle class life.''

Yet, when we hear about the plight of the unemployed, when we read about the problems of workers in general, for that matter, when the subject of "the worker" comes up in almost any context, what picture is being drawn for us? Yes, most always it is the picture of a man—although 40 per cent of the labor force is now female. Pick up a book about "sex roles" and you will spend most of your time reading about women. Pick up a book about work (the meaning of work, the alienation from work, the value of work) and you will mainly be reading about men. Workers are men. Women are, well, *sometimes*, women workers.

These attitudes obviously did not start with, nor are they confined to, the current administration we have all come to know and love so well. Paradoxically, Nixon and Company appear to have done more to advance and to retard the cause of working women than any adminsistration in recent history. On the one hand he giveth (through enforcement of equal-employment opportunity codes) while on the other he taketh away (by vetoing major child care legislation that would have made it possible or less difficult for working mothers to take advantage of the new opportunities).

Surely, politicians or men of any stripe can compete with Mr. Nixon's ability to make his position on an issue so perfectly confused. But one thing about the President, he may aid and abet you, he may benignly or malignly neglect you, he may even do worse, but he is far too politically astute to ever forget that you exist. Senator Edward Kennedy, on the other hand, last year conducted two full days of hearings on "Worker Alienation." Research has shown that women are nearly twice as likely as men to express discontent with their jobs. Yet neither the Senator nor his staff remembered to call one single woman to testify at those hearings. And in a putatively more radical vein, three scholars from Cambridge and Canada recently edited a 500-page Random House reader on *Worker's Control*, consisting of more than 40 articles on current work life and how to improve it, again without a single article *by* or about a woman.

Of course these gentlemen could argue that, after all, the issue under discussion is not gender but work. The reasons people become dissatisfied with their jobs—the routine, the lack of autonomy, the low status and pay—have nothing to do with their sex. But if these men say this, then they haven't considered why it is that women just happen to be concentrated in the lowest level jobs. And they haven't stopped saying it or tried to perceive what the women at the Westinghouse workshop knew, what all women know, that try as you will it is impossible to separate life into neat, discrete pieces that don't affect each other, that the areas of family and employment are inseparably related, and that for millions of women they are in conflict.

III

To work or not to work, that is not the question. "The most important fact" to remember, in the words of the HEW reports on *Work in America*, is "that almost all women are working unless they are disabled. Some work in the market for pay; others work in the home; and many do both."

More and more do both. In 1900 about 20 per cent of women were in the paid workforce; today the figure is 50 per cent. In 1900 most job-holding women were young and single (while older, married women then generally confined their labor to the home—working in the fields, doing piecework or other kinds of inhouse jobs in addition to child care and housework). The large increase in women workers since World War II resulted mainly from the influx of older, married women to the labor force. The *new* change is due to the sharp rise in the number of working mothers with young children, including currently a third of the mothers with children under six.

There is now every sign that these percentages will grow. The main reason, it would be nice to say, is the impact of the Women's Movement in sparking our sisters to embark on promising careers. Envision all of us going off in the morning to fight disease in the hospitals, defend justice in the courts, wheel and deal with Henry Ford II on the executive floor, in other words, doing all the things that men in the most prestigious, high paying, and "satisfying" occupations have largely kept as their own preserve.

And it is true that in the upper middle class more women are doing just that—invading the so-called male professions. Unhappily it is equally true that, for all the publicity when it happens, the invasion force is abysmally small. In 1970 women received 8.5 per cent of all M.D.'s awarded, 5.6 per cent of the law degrees, and 3.9 per cent of the Master's degrees in business. Hardly a take-over. Still, low as these percentages were, in each case they represented a large increase over the previous year, hopefully indicating a trend that will continue and accelerate.

Meantime in the so-called female professions a very different situation took place. In 1971 women received 74 per cent of the B.A.'s in education, 83 per cent of the library science degrees and 98 per cent of the nursing degrees. If you want to guess the future career of a woman college graduate, your best bet is still teaching—42 per cent of all professional women are teachers; more than one-third of all female students major in education. The reason for the overwhelming popularity of this choice is very important to understand. As Juanita Kreps notes in her book *Sex in the Marketplace* (Johns Hopkins, 1971):

Are there monetary rewards in certain careers that more than offset the low pay? Is elementary school teaching appealing to women because they like the work itself, or because it is viewed as an extension of their feminine roles, or because it can be timed to enable women to perform their regular household duties? . . . It is not merely that their nonmarket work influences their decision as to whether to enter the labor force; the demands of home and family also influence *which* market jobs women are willing to take. Moreover the period of heaviest domestic responsibility occurs fairly early in a woman's work life, when she is likely to be forced to make some quite long-range decisions: whether to acquire further job training or additional formal education; how many children she will have; whether to continue working, at least part-time, during the child-bearing period. *In the face of demands on her time the young wife is likely to find that the scheduling of her job is the most important single consideration* [my italics].

The scheduling of her job! Thus, although a man is able to enjoy the emotional benefits of a rich family life while at the same time pursuing a demanding career to its fullest, a woman who wants a family *and* a career must somehow find a way to juggle the two or else become a kind of superwoman, generally with the help of a stand-in surrogate worker in the home. The originally strong anti-marriage, anti-family position of the Women's Movement was largely based on the realization of this bind: the sacrifice was too great.

The current debate is tempered by a further realization among some feminists that the abandonment of family life may also be too great a sacrifice for many women—in any case, why should it always have to be the woman who must sacrifice? The growing pressures for truly egalitarian marriages or cohabitational arrangements—sharing equally in both the home and work roles—grows out of this feeling. What is still obviously far away, however, is an occupational and economic structure—with shorter and more flexible hours—that would make the model of shared roles possible for more than a relative handful of upper middle class professionals.

The rapid surge in the number of working mothers has *not* been primarily due to the Women's Movement. Inflation, taxes, and the rising cost of living have been far greater factors. The noble view of a job as a road to self-fulfillment and self-expression may indeed seem laughable to many working-class women forced out of their homes to take menial jobs to help ends meet. If she has a high-school education, she most likely will be involved in clerical or secretarial work. If she has less than a high school education, clerical, factory, or service work is most probable. Only farm workers and domestic workers average less income than clerical workers.

Among these persons, work dissatisfaction is profound. It is in these kinds of jobs that the vast majority of women workers are still found. Compounding all the possible problems of boredom and routine that may face anyone involved in such work is the difficulty of coordinating family responsibilities that the upper middle class professional woman also faces. But while the professional woman often has surrogate child care and household help, plus a husband to some extent committed to the notion of equality in marriage, the working-class woman generally has neither. While the professional woman's husband is often pleased at his wife's status, male workers with low income and education register higher dissatisfaction with their own jobs when their wives work. This was the conclusion of Harold Sheppard and Neal Herrick in their book *Where Have All the Robots Gone?* (The Free Press, 1972):

> The phenomenon of two or more earners in the working class family is not the unmixed blessing it is assumed to be. To put the above facts in a different form, only one-fourth of the single-earner Pennsylvania workers have the "blues" but among workers with additional earners in the family, discontent goes up to nearly two-fifths, 38 per cent . . . Perhaps the belief that satisfaction among male workers should increase as family income is improved through the wife's employment is a projection on the part of the people who write about such problems. These people are primarily professional, upper middle class individuals. Perhaps these professional males feel no threat to themselves if their wives work. Indeed they may even feel proud and gain satisfaction if their wives are so engaged. And the wives themselves may work, not so much for the purpose of adding needed income to the family budget, but more for 'self-fulfillment'. . . .
>
> The working class context may be sharply different from the professional class situation, and the professional class individuals who write about worker discontent may . . . be making some wrong assumptions . . . It may be that these working class men don't feel that they've really succeeded if *all by themselves* they can't provide their families with the necessary income to pay for the level of living to which they aspire.

Here, of course, the emphasis is on the job discontent of the man, not the woman. But the attitudes of a husband are far from unimportant. Among married, professional women, study after study has shown that the supportiveness and encouragement of their husbands has been a crucial factor in their ability to succeed. Among working-class women, the impact of the husband's position toward their working is hardly less crucial. With less commitment generally found in working-class families to the idea of women's liberation, his influence is bound to be even more pronounced. His dissatisfaction with her working adds to her dissatisfaction—his tension to hers. Even if she finds she enjoys her job, even if it turns out to be a relief to have a break from the kitchen and kids, the very hassle of all that surrounds the job—rising early to get the house clean, the kids off to the sitter or school, then rushing home after work to pick them up and start dinner—may outweigh the satisfaction she derives. What to do?

IV

The acute work discontent of so many women needs to be seen in all these terms—personal, social, economic. The meaning of a job to a woman changes as we go from class to class, primarily because of the differences in opportunities available (with motherhood being far more satisfying than many jobs), but also because of the differences in all the factors surrounding work from class to class—the availability of child care and household help, the attitude of the husband and other family members toward her working—all combine to make a woman glad or sorry to be gainfully employed.

One obvious answer to the discontent that appears to be growing is to make it possible for mothers *forced* to take jobs, including welfare mothers, to return to the home. If a woman—or a man—freely chooses to confine her labor to home and child care—and many do—it should be economically possible. In the 1950's we glorified domesticity for women; in the '70's it is equally senseless to glorify the labor market. Whether 'tis nobler for a woman to dish out the ham-and-eggs-over-easy to her family at home or to a stranger at Schraffts—that is hardly the issue women are struggling over. In either instance the content of the work is the same. In one instance the pay is low; in the other, non-existent. To make home and child care possible for those women who want to devote themselves to it full-time, many people are now suggesting we find a way to pay for that work, through government subsidies, tax deductions, or other imaginative measures.

Overall, however, the trend of two-earner families and working women does appear certain to continue and grow. So it is imperative to make sure that current efforts to open better job opportunities and to equalize pay for women do not fade away with the next economic slump, as many are predicting. The notion of eminent domain for the male breadwinner must finally be put to rest.

To make sure it happens, there is also a need to organize women in the low-paying occupations into unions responsive to their needs. Although only 12 per cent of women workers are currently unionized, there has recently been a flood of organizing among women working in the large banks and insurance offices as well as throughout government employment. And it is the unions with large female memberships (teachers, service employees, and state, county, and municipal employees) that are now growing the fastest.

Indeed, slowly and unsurely something may be happening to the conservative labor movement—as well as the rest of the nation—regarding its attitudes toward women. Externally, unions as well as coorporations may now be sued under Title VII of the Civil Rights Act for discriminating against women, and several already have been. Internally, many women union members appear to be going through their consciousness-raising period at conferences and discussion groups where women talk about the discrimination they face on the job and the double burdens they must carry as workers and as women. They are raising issues like child care and maternity (also paternity) with increased force.

Many unions now have women's caucuses. State federations of labor and county labor councils are for the first time starting to adopt resolutions that concern the rights of women. In the San Francisco Bay area a growing group of women from over 70 unions have formed the first voluntary group of trade union women specifically organized to "fight discrimination of women on the job, in unions, and in society." The organization is called Union WAGE (Women's Alliance to Gain Equality), and several groups modeled on it have begun to sprout in other areas of the country.

It was the women of Union WAGE who almost singlehandedly made possible the first statewide women's conference of the California AFL-CIO. Indeed, it took a bitter floor fight at last year's state convention before the women were allowed to conduct it; the male trade union leaders, while willing to make a few concessions to women, obviously didn't want to see women seeking their rightful share of power within the male-dominated unions.

The conference, held in May, 1973, was attended by nearly 400 women from unions all over the state—an historic event. They discussed such topics as working women and the law, how to negotiate women's issues, how to organize the unemployed, how to move into leadership positions within the labor movement. Repeatedly, however, the subject of child care came to the fore. At one point a woman from the Newspaper Guild, a clerk, I believe, rose to voice her irritation about this.

"But what we've said is something else," answered a young woman with a long black braid flowing down her back. "We want women to become more active, to fight for more power. But right now women don't come to union meetings and there are concrete reasons why they don't. Most of the women I work with have to rush home and do all the work on their second jobs as housewives. If we want women to fight for the larger issues, we have to make it possible."

"Yes," said an older woman, a teacher, a mother, a wife, a trade unionist, a person, a veteran juggler of roles. "Yes to child-care centers. The time must come when we can say, 'Listen buddy, tonight it's your turn to start the dinner and take care of the house and the baby. The first battle begins at home."

There are union battles, government battles, business battles, education battles to win if women are ever to gain job equality, but for millions the first battle still begins at home. If the matter of workload is now an issue for negotiation on the job, then it should be no less an issue at home where every working mother moonlights. If job rotation and restructuring are seen as answers to the endlessness and banality of so many work tasks, then the analysis applies with equal force in the nursery and kitchen. If classifying jobs by sex is no longer deemed lawful in business and government, then how can it be fitting at home if both persons also work in the labor market? If wages are still the *sine qua non* of participation in the labor market (and people with the lowest incomes have the lowest satisfaction), then the effect of not assigning an economic value to housework and child care must also be clear. If humanizing the workplace is really a vital issue on the social agenda today, then it is time to recognize that the home is also a place of work.

One usually thinks of professional socialization as preparation for such learned or high-status professions as scientific research, teaching, medicine, or law. In fact there is professional socialization in many service occupations, such as social work and law enforcement. In this selection we look at how "civilians" become police officers through both formal schooling in the police academy and the informal influences of the members of the force and fellow recruits.

What Richard Harris says about the esprit de corps among the recruits he studied has implications for many other socialization experiences, especially in such formal, highly bureaucratic organizations as the military, civil and foreign services, and large corporations.

As you read Harris's article, ask yourself why he places such heavy emphasis on the professional image and why it includes such aspects as physical well-being, moral behavior, and proper deportment. Also ask yourself why becoming a policeman involves resocialization.

Professionalization

RICHARD N. HARRIS

THE PHENOMENOLOGICAL APPROACH

The precise meaning of the term "profession" has long been the subject of debate among students of occupations. On the one hand, the term has been applied to a select group of occupations such as law, medicine, and theology. Taking these occupations as models, students have abstracted qualities that can serve as criteria to determine whether or not an occupation is a profession. On the other hand, so many occupational groups claim the status of profession that the term is virtually meaningless— except to the occupational members themselves. Morticians, realtors, nurses, engineering technicians, journalists, librarians, druggists, and chiropractors are some of the occupations that have entered or are trying to enter the professional ranks. With such a state of affairs, some students have argued that the definition of profession is limited, since it implies that each criterion must be satisfied if an occupation is to qualify. Howard Becker evades the definitional problem by suggesting that if a group succeeds in getting itself called a profession, then for all practical purposes it is a profession.[1]

Everett C. Hughes, however, offers a different framework entirely. He believes that a description of characteristics of a profession to which aspiring occupations may be compared in their own effort to become "professional" should be a secondary focus in occupational research. Such studies neglect the phenomenological facet of professionalism: that is, how do the occupational members themselves define a profession or professional? In the phenomenological orientation, the objective standards, which in essence define what a profession is, become meaningless apart from what the term means to the occupational members. Hughes advises researchers to refrain from continually asking the secondary question: Is this occupation a profession? The circumstances and steps that members of an occupation take to attain the status of profession are more fundamental issues for investigation than is guessing at traits that make up an "objective" definition of profession. The term "profession" is *primarily* subjective, connoting value and prestige to the occupational members and to those outside the occupation.[2]

This is not to say that Hughes was not concerned about the characteristics of so-called professions, since he pointed out some characteristics of his own.[3] A professionally striving group claims that its work is a matter of broad public concern which involves privilege to information on matters of life and death, and honor and dishonor. Since the client is not in a position to judge the quality of the service he receives, the group contends that only a colleague group has the right to make a judgment about whether or not a mistake was made by a member of the colleague group. In an attempt to maintain the guise of competence by keeping internal disagreements unobservable to those not in the colleague group, the group establishes a licensing system that is sanctioned by the state. The licensing system allows the group to make its own standards of admission and to discipline colleagues as it sees fit. Nevertheless, the objective state of affairs is not a paramount question. How the members define the situation and attempt to convince others of their rightful place in the hierarchy is.

While researchers admit that the process of professionalization is an impor-

---

[1] Howard S. Becker, "The Nature of a Profession," *Education for the Professions*, 61st Yearbook of the Society for the Study of Education, Part 2 (Chicago: University of Chicago Press, 1962), p. 33.
[2] Everett C. Hughes, "Professions," *Professions in America*, edited by Kenneth S. Lynn and *Daedalus* (Boston: Beacon Press, 1965), pp. 242–260; and *Men and Their Work* (Chicago: Free Press, 1958), pp. 44–45.
[3] Everett C. Hughes, *Men and Their Work*, pp. 94–95, 116–117, and 140–143.

tant facet of study, in actual practice research in the subjective tradition remains sparse compared to research in the objective tradition. Students of occupations casually dismiss the Hughesian approach and seem to place more confidence in the objective perspective. Certainly this appears to be the case in the literature regarding the police: profession and professionalism are used if they described objective criteria. Scholars and police officials alike explain in what ways policemen are, or are not, professionals or are, or are not, craftsmen. Police officers claim that they are professional; scholars conclude that police are more like craftsmen. To elaborate this point, I refer to two recent studies on the police that specifically deal with police professionalism.

Jerome Skolnick lists two main traditions in the sociological literature regarding professions.[4] One stems from Durkheim's conception of a profession that is based on an enforceable code of ethics. In addition to having high status and a monopoly over certain activities, professions are distinctive in that they infuse their work organization "with moral values, plus the use of sanctions to insure that these moral values are upheld." The second tradition stems from Weber's emphasis on technical efficiency and smoothness. Skolnick notes that police reformers speak of professionalism according to Weber's model of managerial efficiency while they neglect Durkheim's concern about a moral code of ethics. The reason for this, he explains, lies in two conflicting principles of police work: maintaining order and subscribing to the rule of due process of law. Because police efficiency is based on their clearance rates, police officers perceive themselves as controllers of misconduct through the invoking of punitive sanctions, rather than as legal actors within a democratic society. They conceive of themselves as skilled workers who should be free of external authorities, rather than as civil servants who are obliged to comply with the rule of law. The police officer's ideology is that of a craftsman, not of a professional. Although Skolnick is very perceptive in his discussion, just what the difference is between a craftsman and a professional remains unclear. The craftsman demands autonomy, but the professional does, too. The policeman may not comply with the rule of due process of law, but the doctor does not comply with the Hippocratic oath either.

Arthur Niederhoffer goes so far as to list the criteria that define a profession.[5] They are: (1) high standards of admission, (2) a special body of knowledge and theory, (3) a code of ethics, (4) altruism and dedication to a service ideal, (5) a lengthy period of training for candidates, (6) licensing of members, (7) autonomous control, (8) pride of the members in their profession, and (9) publicly recognized status and prestige. If professionalism is perceived as a continuum, the police should be well-along the road to their goal. They

---

[4] Jerome H. Skolnick, *Justice Without Trial* (New York: John Wiley, 1966), pp. 230–245.
[5] Arthur Niederhoffer, *Behind the Shield* (Garden City, N.Y.: Doubleday, 1967), pp. 18–19.

have a code of ethics, professional associations, service ideals, and admission and training standards. Of course, one could argue that police standards are too low to begin with, that the code of ethics is unenforceable, or that the police associations are more like unions than esoteric groups dedicated to improving the quality of their profession. But this begs the question. The point is, what are "high admission standards"? How "autonomous" must an occupation be? Is training by apprenticeship, or is it by classroom study and research? Niederhoffer believes that the New York City police are not professional because the PBA relies on demagoguery as a means of persuasion and is not altruistic.[6] The politics of the New York PBA is well-known, but the AMA has also resorted to distortion, name-calling, and demagoguery when it became the subject for reform. Yet, which occupation is less professional?

My main concern, however, is not whether police work is a profession or not. Instead, I adopt Hughes' phenomenological approach to find out what the police themselves think a professional is and how they go about convincing the public that they are professionals. Topics that I discuss include:

1. how the professional image is defined to in-coming members,

2. the elements of which the professional image was comprised during recruit training,

3. the contribution of the image to a framework for judging others and oneself,

4. the ways in which the image has organizational support or has not,

5. the meaning the image seems to have for the recruits themselves, and

6. how it may have influenced recruit perceptions toward law and justice as they leave for the field.

FIRST STEPS TOWARD PROFESSIONALISM

Education

The same day the recruit took the oath making him a bona fide member of the department, he was given a brief introductory speech while he stood at attention on the drill floor with the other in-coming members. He was at once instructed that he was a professional within a profession and must act accordingly. "You will look like professionals, read like professionals, and study like professionals who are joining other professionals in a profession within the community." It was not until later in the day that the recruit was finally given a hint of what was meant by "professional."

[6] Arthur Niederhoffer, pp. 175, 185–186.

Education was presented as the sine qua non, the indispensable ingredient, of professionalism. That is, the recruit was told that a professional is "recognized by his education"; if RCPD wanted to be professional, its members had to be educated. But while education might have been the key to attaining professional status, high salary seemed to be the real criterion for success. Said one instructor:

You may come up against someone who won't join law enforcement because of the pay. And you'll be able to say, "Whoo, we're professionals. We require a minimum of two years of college and we can start at $15,000." Education is the thing.

During a coffee break, a recruit offered his opinion. If the community wanted professional policemen, it would have to pay for it. ". . . I can tell you why all these guys are here: for the retirement and for the security. You've gotta have the money if you want professionals."

To become acquainted with their educational opportunities, the recruit class spent a day at State College where there was a police science program. The program consisted of a two-year college level degree and covered three required areas. The number following each subject equals its semester hours.

Area 1: Sociology 3, Psychology 3, Physical Science 6, English 6
Area 2: Police Science courses (law, traffic) 36
Area 3: Electives in Social Sciences and the Humanities 10

The state allowed the academy training session to be worth five semester hours, which would be applied to Area 3, in order to encourage the recruit to enter the program. In effect, the liberal arts courses were superseded by police technology courses. By not applying the five credits to Area 2 (which would seem to be the appropriate choice), the department and State College emphasized courses that were mainly technological. Instead of giving priority to courses that were more likely—but certainly no guarantee—to cultivate the use of reason, contemplation, and discourse as instruments for achieving order, "nuts and bolts" courses took precedence. RCPD and the state might have believed that education was necessary for the development of a well-rounded police officer, but unlike the professions that they try to emulate, the quality of their education was essentially vocational.

Esprit de Corps

Even with the vocational orientation in the police science curriculum, the recruit was taught that he was more professional than the members of the classical professions of medicine, law, theology, and education. The police profession became the superprofession, one that overlapped with each of the elite professions but performed its job with more dedication. A tinge of self-righteousness ran throughout a lecture presented by a popular instructor which seemed to set the tone regarding professions for the duration of the session.

I submit, too, gentlemen, that the average attorney is not as dedicated as the average law enforcer. When you get your gun, you are given the power of life and death. Not even the Supreme Court has that power. I submit to you that the legal attorney is guilty of moral prostitution—by that I mean he says one thing and means another. The 1920's showed how an attorney who could circumvent the law was hailed as successful— one who could twist a perhaps inept police testimony.

The leading attorney is not F. Lee Bailey, but Mr. Foreman, who defended Candy and her nephew, who were in an incestuous relationship (but after seeing her picture, you could forgive him that) and who conspired in killing her husband. Yet Foreman got an acquittal. And I quote from Foreman after the trial, "My clients want freedom, not justice." It's rare when a police officer bastardizes the law, while I feel attorneys do, and Foreman succinctly stated their position. The public is very willing to retain the stereotype of the fat, slouchy policeman. We're trying to change that stereotype.

Now let's talk about medicine. Here again we take a profession which used to be dedicated to the citizenry turning to the cash register. One night you may have a grisly accident on Franklin Turnpike that turns your stomach, don't pick up a phone to call a doctor because you won't get one. Your first aid is what saves lives. If you and your first aid weren't there, he'd be in the morgue. The average physician here is making $40,000 clear. A number of med schools have even dropped giving the Oath of Hippocrates. Someone must have had a conscience and realized that it didn't apply to the present medical profession.

. . . We are bound to get some bad apples who smear the badge; what they do smears the badge of everybody across the country. Every profession has its cancers. How many of the clergy betray the cloth by going into sex? How many educators hide behind academia—the homosexuals who warp our children's minds? At least when we get a bad apple, we get rid of him.

The disparagement of the elite professions by the lecturer apparently found willing ears among the recruits, some of whom had their own stories about lawyers and doctors. As in the lecture, the lawyer was never given the benefit of the doubt: he connives to distort the law for his own selfish ends. Tales abounded about the lawyer who got his client off through a legal technicality. As for the doctor, recruits complained how useless it was to try to get a doctor to make a house call. One recruit who had been an ambulance driver recounted an experience of his at a hospital. He had brought a badly injured car accident victim into the emergency room. Because the victim was a "mess," the attendants walked by pretending not to see him. Finally, the driver grabbed a doctor and ordered him to take care of the injured man. "That's the way you have to talk to them," he finished.

Not only was law enforcement projected as the most noble and sincere profession, but the instructors increased recruit enthusiasm and professional distinctiveness by setting up their own department as a paradigm for other police departments.

> If you stay with us, we can be the best—including Metropolis Department; they aren't so good. And with all due respect to those from Megopolis Department, all they have is size and strength; but they can't compare to us because we're professional, and we want to be professional about our job.

Recruits who came from other police departments confirmed the excellence of RCPD. From the first day of the training session, these recruits compared their departments unfavorably with Rurban County's. Several recruits from Megopolis Department referred to it as "the factory." One of them told me that 55 per cent of the force would "love to leave Megopolis Department, but they are either overage or cannot afford the move." Another recruit remarked about a city policeman who gave up a soft job in order to stay on the beat. "He was really dedicated, that's very rare; out here, everyone is dedicated." Still another recruit explained, "We were told not to make any arrests. They kept trying to stop me, but I wouldn't . . . We were told right off not to make any arrests, not to get involved."

Suburban County Police Department, contiguous to Rurban County, fared no better. "They accept false rumors and get rid of you. They back you up all right—with a knife in your back." And, "Jeff even went through Suburban Academy before he came here, but he quit; he saw right away that it was political. You never know where you stand."

In summary, the first steps taken by the staff and visiting lecturers seemed to be the construction of a feeling of specialness—a "we are best" syndrome. The law enforcer was not just equal to the professional with the most status, he was better. Professions were in a hierarchical relationship to one another with law enforcement at the apex. And within the law enforcement profession itself, RCPD was the best. The lateral relationship in which a professional is recognized as an expert in his respective area seems to characterize the "classical" professions because they are secure in their status. On the other hand, the insecure occupations such as law enforcement are too insecure and too competitive to feel comfortable in a lateral relationship, especially when they have not been recognized by those who have "arrived." To be told that the recruit would learn in 12 weeks what the lawyer had to know for his bar examinations reinforced these feelings of inequity. In the following section, the content of the "professional image" as it seemed to be defined to the recruit will be examined.

THE PROFESSIONAL IMAGE

The Physical Image

Once having established an esprit de corps, it remained for the instructors to teach the recruit to be a professional police officer. One way was to look the part. Great stress was placed on the recruit's physical appearance. At first, the emphasis was not apparent.

> We aren't going to inspect you today, but we expect you to always have a neat appearance. Shoes are to be shined . . . Haircuts are preferred to be crew cuts; we aren't strict, but we won't tolerate long sideburns or pompadours.

The recruit soon learned that shined shoes were not enough: they had to be spit-shined on the toe at the very least. Even the recruit's leather equipment (holster, belt, handcuff case, and bullet case) had to be as close to a spit-shine as possible. The result was a patent leather look that seemed to contradict the recruit's image of himself as an officer of the law and as a man of action. Regular haircuts were not enough either. While the staff had said crew cuts were not required, the recruit found that they might just as well have been required.

On the other hand, the staff claimed that the requirements they placed on the recruits' physical appearance were necessary because "with fifty-four recruits, we don't have time to worry about a picayune thing like appearance." Judging from the amount of time the staff spent on inspections during the training session, however, appearance had to be more than a picayune matter. Shoes not only had to be polished, they had to be spit-shined. Haircuts could not only be neat, they had to be cut almost weekly. Uniforms not only had to be tidy, they had to be ironed after each day's use.

Surely the staff had other criteria in mind by which to evaluate a recruit's appearance than what it at first described as a "neat appearance." The stress on the recruit's dress habits was more than an expression of discipline although that, too, was involved. Nor could it be explained away as part of a hazing process characteristic of fraternal or military organizations as an essential part of their rites of passage.[7] For example, a staff member wrote me about this. He thought I might have missed the point of inspections: "The minute harassment was only designed to make the new man, who would be wearing the uniform for the first time, more conscious of his appearance."

---

[7] Sanford Dornbusch, "The Military Academy as an Assimilating Institution," *Social Forces*, 33 (May 1955), pp. 316–321; Arnold Van Gennup, *Rites of Passage* (Chicago: University of Chicago Press, 1960); Frank W. Young, *Initiation Ceremonies* (New York: Bobbs-Merrill, 1965).

On a recognized and intended level he is, of course, correct. But on an unrecognized and unintended level, the attitude that seemed to be translated to the recruit was that a neat physical appearance was professional.

Appearance was not only an end in itself, that is, professional, but it was also a means to convince the public that a new breed of policeman was at its service. Whereas the "old style" cop might have been sloppy, overweight, and cigar smoking—the image associated with police corruption—the image of the new breed would replace the stereotype. As one instructor put it baldly, "Look sharp and impress the public." In spite of the instructors' insistence on a new breed of police officer, a few interesting incidents suggested that at times something resembling the old breed was still desirable.

The tenth day of the session, the staff selected several men from each of our two platoons. The recruits were to shout commands to their respective platoons, and the two who performed to the staff's satisfaction would become platoon sergeants. What stuck me was that the recruit who became my platoon sergeant seemed to earn his position by booming Neanderthal grunts, for I never understood a command he gave. It was as if he were chosen on volume alone. Nevertheless, the "sharp appearance" and the deep voice of authority expressed a realistic need in the field. Said one instructor, "In this job if you don't look the part, forget it. You must project confidence. You are going to be put into an emergency situation sometime in your career, and you have to step in and take charge when everybody else is emotional." Thus, a large and necessary part of the emphasis on appearance seemed to be for its effect on the public.

The second incident occurred right after the completion of the first week of the session. During the night a severe snowstorm put the community into an official state of emergency. Protocol was for a recruit to call the academy 15 minutes before roll call if he would be late or absent during the day. Most recruits, including myself, had called up to find out if classes would be held that day. We were informed by Headquarters that classes were canceled. However, a few recruits had not checked about classes and had staunchly made the trip. For salary adjustments because of the cancellation, the pay for the missed day was to be applied to the day that a recruit would spend at the Communications Center during a weekend. Those recruits who had come to the academy in the aftermath of the storm and found the doors closed were to be paid in full for the day that they would spend at Communications.

The other recruits balked at the rewards granted to those who came to the academy (or at the punishment received for not coming). Their feeling was either that it was impossible to reach the academy and the matter was out of their hands, or that they would have come to the academy if classes had met. Nevertheless, it was interesting that the department rewarded those recruits who did not have the foresight to call headquarters before leaving their homes, while those who did not bulldog their way to the academy were penalized. It became a question of which kind of recruit the department actually wanted: the one who would charge straight ahead impervious to the conditions surrounding him (as the brave but unthinking soldier assaulting a defended hill), or the one who would respond to a situation flexibly and with deliberation (supposedly a characteristic of the new breed). The department seemed to have opted for the "heroic" style.[8]

The Moral Image

The physical image seemed to be closely associated with the moral image, which connotes respectability, convention, piety, virtue, and honor. Physical appearance was used as an indicator of a person's place in the moral structure. A person who shaved each day, kept his hair short, shined his shoes regularly, and wore pressed clothes could be expected to be a respectable, law-abiding, and moral person. Conversely, those persons who grew beards, wore their hair long, and wore unkempt clothes—in short, those who deviated from convention—could be expected to connote something less than the moral.

> Kids want to be like adults in some ways. They want sex, but not the responsibilities that go with it . . . or I'll braid my hair for spite . . . So we want good appearances. Everything is going to look good.

Therefore, the recruit was told he was not allowed to grow sideburns, mustaches, or long hair because he had to "set an example" for the citizenry and because he would then offend fewer people. (I understand that the academy has since become more lax in this respect.)

Of course, there was a screening process that included an evaluation of how the investigators thought the candidate would project the new police image before he was admitted to RCPD. Only one recruit in the class had been given a decidedly unfavorable report during his precandidacy interview. His report read something like this: needed a shave, haircut, hair hanging over his ears and shirt collar [he had a "mod" haircut]; he lacked any kind of military bearing, slouching down in chair during interview; he lacked enthusiasm shown by other candidates. Although his appearance obviously did not disqualify him, and he did have an opportunity to "prove" himself, it is interesting that his hair style and mannerisms during the interview were questionable in the eyes of the interviewers. In contrast, candidates from other law enforcing agencies had the following remark of approval: he has the background that indicates he can adjust to police work well. There was no further elaboration; the fact that the applicant had some previous police experience made him a suitable candidate. The former recruit, however, did not have the image that the department hoped to project to the public; he looked

---

[8] Morris Janowitz, *The Professional Soldier* (New York: The Free Press, 1960), p. 21.

too unconventional for them. Ironically, I thought he was one of the few recruits who believed in and tried to conform to the "new image" beyond surface manifestations.

While this aspect of the moral image may be offensive to some readers, it nevertheless exists and has a bearing on police behavior. No instructor, no staff member, and no recruit ever explicitly stated that a person's physical appearance was a sign of his moral worth. But inferences can be and were made based on comments regarding the unconventionally attired. No instructor made a positive or accepting statement about the unconventionally dressed; only two recruits verbalized their tolerance for such persons. Furthermore, it seemed to be the general consensus that people with long hair or a beard, for example, deserved a different quality of law enforcement than their opposites. Here, then, is another example of a process and relationship that may not have been intended or recognized but did exist and should be recognized.

Integrity, the capacity to be honest with oneself and with others, was the second component of the moral image as it seemed to be presented to the recruit. "Without integrity you cannot be a professional." The recruit seemed to think he had this quality: that was one reason why he entered law enforcement. Consequently, he resented persons in the elite professions who did not always display moral characters, yet apparently had a monopoly of high salaries and prestige. The police officer was only trying to do his job, what the people hired him to do, but all he seemed to find were stumbling blocks in his path. The doctor, lawyer, clergyman, and educator did not seem to fulfill their jobs with as much personal sacrifice and moral discipline as the policeman did, yet the public refused to treat him as a professional. To the recruit, the disparity of rewards seemed unjust. The righteous indignation directed toward the elite professions increased his feeling of moral superiority. This feeling of superiority seemed to serve as a basis for an in-group identity that was continuously set off against the implied moral inferiority of various outgroups. In his envy of the elite professions, he deprecated them and thereby bolstered his own self-image.

The Courteous Image

Professionalism included what a patrolman *did* as well as how he looked.

> Every person who walks in the precinct is entitled at that moment to your undivided attention—whether he is green, a Buddhist, or an atheist. We are going to expose you to the worst kind of treatment, and how you handle it will determine whether you're a professional or just another policeman.

Various reasons were given to the recruit as to why he should behave courteously. One of these reasons was defensive. That is, one should be courteous because the public generalizes from the behavior of one policeman to every policeman in the nation. The department and recruit seemed to resent this necessity for being defensive, since they considered themselves professionals of good moral character. Apparently, anybody could be discourteous to a policeman, but he in turn could not be. "But how you respond to this is what makes the difference between a professional or unprofessional." Hearing this, the recruit responded, "What about our side, don't they care about us?"

Another reason offered to the recruit for acting courteously was that the way a patrolman presented himself could aid him in performing his duties with the least amount of trouble.[9]

> Treat lovers nice. There's no reason to bust their balls. Because they don't forget it. Today we have to use professionalization. Give them time to adjust themselves if you suspect any hanky-panky.

Thus, as one's physical appearance seemed to be identified with professionalism, courtesy was also.

The community itself seemed to support politeness, self-control, and deference as definitions of professionalism. During a sit-in at State University, the police department was commended by community newspapers for its "professional" behavior. Deans, professors, and police officials kept the situation cool and persuaded most of the demonstrators to leave the building. The few students who remained were arrested and escorted out without harshness or bodily harm. The police department was praised for "looking good," they "looked like professionals."

The professional image, then, had three components: appearance, morality, and demeanor. Although these components were defined as ends in themselves, for the most part, the rationale for them seemed to be expediency.

THE PROFESSIONAL IMAGE AND THE CLASSROOM

The Teaching-Learning Situation

Modes of teaching and learning in the classroom offered further insights into the image that the instructors hoped the recruit would inculcate. The classroom situation is particularly important to discuss, since it was there that

---

[9] Erving Goffman, "The Nature of Deference and Demeanor," *Interaction Ritual* (Chicago: Aldine, 1967), pp. 57–95, and *The Presentation of Self in Everyday Life* (Garden City, N.Y.: Doubleday, 1959), pp. 104 and 217, discuss the role of courtesy as a basis for normal face-to-face interaction.

the recruit spent most of his day. They typical classroom situation seemed to be based on the traditional setting in which a teacher talked and students quietly listened at their desks. Even the goals of the classes seemed to parallel those of the traditional style of training—the accumulation of subject matter and the memorization of facts. In addition, the assumption of discipline usually associated with the "old guard" classroom setting was in evidence. Explained one instructor to the class:

> We harass you because we know the requirements you need. . . . We are trying to develop objective people who can think situations through . . . we have to impose our authority on you to get you to know how to respond to situations and rationally deal with a situation.

Discipline was not only a necessary force for the cultivation of rationality and objectivity; it also seemed to be a necessary force for motivating the recruit to learn his lessons. "I'm sorry we have to bear down on you, but we have to watch over you like this in order for this training to have an impact on you."

The instructors might not have been too far off the mark when they assumed the recruit needed an external source of authority. Perhaps the recruit accepted his relatively passive role in the classroom because he placed little worth in "book learning."[10] If the recruit participated in lectures at all, it was usually to ask questions of clarification. When instructors extended their classes into the coffee break time, he became noticeably restless and squirmed noisily in his seat in order to politely indicate that they were going beyond their "allotted" time.

To the recruit it seemed that on-the-job training was more practical than classroom learning: one learns by doing, not by listening. He appeared wary of the scholar who might perform well in the classroom but who would be unable to be depended on in field situations. Lectures that offered practical tools for police work were valued (such as role plays, law, and how to effect a legal arrest), but lectures that seemed unrelated to the necessities of field work were ignored. Indeed, most of the recruits seemed to think that they learned more about police work in one week of field experience than in the previous six weeks of classes, as the following statements indicate.

> You find out that what you learn in the academy isn't so; it's a waste of time.

> I learned more on the precinct in one week than I did here.

> I'm glad I saw how things were really done. If we followed the book, we'd never make any arrests.

[10] Joseph Kadish, "Mental Health Training of the Police," *Mental Hygiene*, 50 (April 1966), pp. 205–211.

To what extent these statements reflected the recruit's true attitudes regarding academy training is debatable. To give an outward sign that the academy did not fit into the needs of the officer in the field seemed acceptable among the recruits; perhaps it was even expected by them. In contrast, when he was alone, a recruit told me, "I know I wouldn't like to go straight on the job without some background." And when I passed out a questionnaire asking the recruits to evaluate their training for field work, 31 of the 52 recruits who filled them out gave positive responses; thus, one should be cautious in forming any generalizations.

If the recruit was biased against classroom training, some of the instructors, though by no means typical, seemed to be also. However, the recruit tended to accept their comments as being more realistic than those of the majority of instructors.

> . . . don't worry about that now. Wait till you get out of the academy. In here, we stick by the book.

> There are tricks of the trade we can't teach you in the academy, but you'll learn them.

These sparse comments seemed to have such an impact on the recruit that he believed that many of his classes were either irrelevant or misrepresentative, for example, Community Relations classes. It appeared that the recruit perceived the academy program as an initial phase of training that he would have to tolerate for a few months.

If he was expected to sit quietly for six or seven hours a day, the recruit seemed to feel that the instructors should, at least, make their lectures entertaining. The need for a gimmick was recognized by one recruit who said, pointing to an instructor:

> Doesn't he look like Jonathan Winters? Look at the way he walks. He's really funny. All he'd have to say was "Hello," "Good-bye" [he accompanied the words with the comedian's mannerisms], and he'd have the whole class listening to what he says. Here he comes; look at the way he walks.

Here, at least, the staff and most of the instructors seemed to agree with the recruit: a gimmick was needed for each class if the recruits were to pay attention to them. There were two general techniques that they used to capture the interest of the recruit. Sexual jokes during the lecture was one technique. Hardly a lecture went by without some off-color joke. A second method used by instructors who accompanied their lectures with slides was to intersperse the slide collection with pictures of nudes. As the nudes flicked across the screen, the recruit's attentiveness, shifting positions, and craning neck contrasted sharply with his earlier sedateness.

In addition to the more general techniques, a few lecturers tried to motivate the class to learn their material in more specific ways. Often it was said that the knowledge in question would protect the recruit from embarrassment, departmental discipline, or lawsuits once he left the academy. For example, in a lecture on arrests, the recruit was admonished with:

> Baby, you better learn this, or your ass will be in the sling! . . . If you don't know the elements of the law, you'll end up looking like a fool or even lose your case.

More notable were the department's formal incentives to encourage the recruit to perform well during academy training. The awards sponsored by police organizations such as the Detectives Association and the Police Brotherhood Association were established specifically to induce "professionalization" among the recruits. An off-duty gun worth $60, required of all departmental members, was presented at graduation to each of the two recruits with the highest overall average in the academy written examinations and to the recruit with the highest firearms average score. The recruit with the second highest firearms average received a $25 savings bond. A $500 scholarship toward tuition for a police science degree was awarded to the recruit selected by the staff for his all-around excellence.

Interestingly, three of the five prizes awarded, in the words of the staff, to "encourage professionalization" were revolvers—especially since the revolver appeared to be an important symbol of the police image for the recruit. During the first day of the session, the recruit was warned, "If you can't shoot a gun, you shouldn't be here." Of all the skills necessary in police work, it was the officer's marksmanship that was periodically evaluated throughout his career. If an officer lost his accuracy, he lost his right to be a policeman. "You must be checked out with firearms once a year, and occasionally we have to drop somebody for this."

Thus it seemed that the intellectual competence image of the policeman was superseded by an action image. While the recruit wore weaponry within two weeks of the session, the training was two-thirds over before he received his wallet-sized card with the Miranda warnings. One instructor remarked, "They give you a gun but not [the Miranda cards]. Well, people like to see a police officer with a gun." Unfortunately, then, the public also identifies the gun with the policeman. In any case, perhaps the department was expressing in another unrecognized way through its training methods the kind of image it really had in mind when it claimed to be developing professional police officers.

Ethic of Masculinity

As in many predominantly male occupations, there were ribald jokes, profanities, and boasts about sexual encounters throughout the academy session. However, it appeared that these displays of masculinity went beyond mere joking, swearing, and boasting. They seemed to show to the recruit that he was, indeed, among men and thereby testified to his own manhood. The phrase "ethic of masculinity" refers to the apparent need of the recruit to confirm his masculine image to others and to himself by exaggerating the characteristics associated with manhood. These characteristics include physical and sexual prowess, courage, profanity, and aggression toward authority.[11]

The man-of-action image, emanating from the ethic of masculinity, seemed to be an important but implicit component of the professional image. The recruit seemed to perceive the police officer as a man of action with the emphasis both on the *man* of action and the man of *action*. A police officer was physically strong, virile, and courageous. Less inclined to depend on persuasion through discourse, he would rely on physical force. Not afraid of dangerous work, his code of loyalty included putting his life "on the line" in order to help a fellow officer. The recruit who did not manifest the man-of-action image was not as highly esteemed by his fellow classmates, and he certainly was not accessible to the inner circles.

In one case in particular, the recruit class expressed disapproval when it thought some fellow recruits were rejecting the image of the policeman as a man of action. It occurred after an announcement that the class was to participate in a murder investigation. This was the first opportunity the class had had to leave the classroom situation for "real" police work. However, the academy staff needed six men to remain behind to help move some furniture. The reaction of the group as the volunteers left ranks was a friendly but critical hissing as if the six men were not making the proper response as police officers.

Sometimes the image of the officer in action had its humorous spots. One example occurred when an alert recruit became suspicious (over a weekend).

> I was parked in my car when I saw a man slink along the side of the drug store and then turn and go around the back. Thinking I was on to something, I got out and went around the other side. The guy was taking a leak!

The second incident occurred during Field Week. The sergeant asked if anybody had a family call during his tour of duty. About ten hands went up, and a voice spoke softly, "I responded to one call; I ran around the back [of the house] and the dog got me."

In contrast, the police academy image, in which a recruit passively sits at his desk while listening to a lecturer and whose spit-shined leatherwork turns him into a "patent leather soldier," ran against the grain of the recruit. To be a "good" recruit implied a docility and childlike conformity that contradicted the man-of-action image. Consequently, the recruit rejected, through subtle

[11] Jackson Toby, "Violence and the Masculine Ideal: Some Qualitative Data," *Annals*, 364 (March 1966), pp. 19–27.

acts of rebellion, the image intentionally or unintentionally defined by the academy. During drill a recruit pushed the man in front of him, who almost collided with the recruit in front of him. One recruit pulled out the back of another recruit's shirt while still another recruit grabbed someone else's memo book and let it drop to the floor. During inspection, ties were pulled off and shirts were pulled out. Instead of running through riot exercises, some recruits danced or walked whenever the instructor's back was turned. Class breaks and lunch hour afforded more time for the men to pull off ties and pull out memo books or blackjacks from otherwise smartly dressed recruits. Once someone placed a blackjack in my empty holster (I was never allowed to carry police weaponry), which I interpreted as a show of disdain for the police academy image.[12] Manliness, then, may also have involved a defiance against leaders and authority; for total conformity meant that one surrendered his freedom to act as an individual.

Physical prowess was esteemed as part of the man-of-action image. On the other hand, mental action seemed not to be defined as action at all, since more prestige was attached to performing well on the pistol range and playing football during coffee breaks than to doing well on written examinations on class lectures. In fact, my willingness and capacity to play football contributed toward my acceptance as a "regular guy." As one recruit remarked to me as we played football during a lunch period, "When you first came, I thought you were a canary-ass brain—you know, those smart guys."

Off-color jokes, profanity, and stories heard or experienced in the military or in police work were typical of many group discussions. The jokes, the use of profanity, and the tales about sexual encounters seemed to confirm the manhood of the recruit. It appeared important for a recruit to confirm his masculinity by contributing some jokes of his own, but lacking these, he should laugh robustly with those recruits who did. In each case, ribald jokes were aggressive toward someone or something, usually an out-group. Many times a police officer was the protagonist, in which case the male made his conquest. Male protagonists who were not policemen turned out to be naive, stupid, or cuckolds.

> You ever hear about the guy who always wanted to be a cop? He could never pass a test, so he bought a uniform and whistle. He's having fun until a broad asks him for directions, but she asks him to get into her car. He gets in, and she strips—she's got a pair of 44's . . . "Go ahead," she says, "touch 'em." "Uh, there's just one thing lady, I ain't a real cop."

Conversations, such as the following, never failed to draw a group of attentive recruits. "Experienced recruits," those who had served in other police

---

[12] These behaviors may be aptly applied to Erving Goffman's concept of role distance in *Encounters* (Indianapolis: Bobbs-Merrill, 1961), pp. 84–152.

departments, shared some of their encounters with females in the past—all in the line of duty. In this example, several recruits were discussing their experiences patrolling areas of parked lovers.

R₁: He [his partner] was a fucking sadist. He'd wait until they were stripped, and then he'd rush up and pull them out of the car. He was really a sadist.

R₂: We'd wait till dark, and then we would go around hoping to catch some couple.

R₃: I know a guy who used to crawl into the ventilating units of the toilets. . . .

The "raw recruits" offered stories heard from their brothers or friends who were police officers or who were themselves abused with their dates. For instance, one recruit claimed that his brother found a parked couple heavily petting. After he comically illustrated how the couple must have tried to cover themselves, he said his brother began questioning them and then chatting with them. After a while, the boy fell asleep, so his brother and the half-naked girl went to the patrol car where he remained with her for most of the night. The listening recruits dreamily sighed to each other as they possibly envisioned themselves in similar circumstances. At the very least, they expressed the enviable position in which this recruit's brother had found himself.

The acting out of the ethic of masculinity may indicate why police officers tend to react personally to an affront on police authority. It would seem that an officer would be less likely to react to disrespect personally if he feels secure with himself. Concomitantly, it would be those officers least secure in their masculine image who are prone to react violently to perceived threats to their masculinity. Thus, while William Westley suggests that violence by police officers emerges when they perceive threats to their authority, he does not appear to go far enough.[13] What people may be doing when they challenge an officer's authority is to challenge his masculinity which he, in part, identifies with authority and respect.

Dirty workers probably place as much esteem on their occupations as do other members of the community. Although some dirty workers see their work as a calling, I suspect that most know that they are doing dirty work. Some may try to romanticize their work, but underneath their bravado may be resentment about their work, and an envy of "clean" workers. Certainly this was true among the police recruits. Consequently, the dirty worker, in his low self-esteem, may embrace the ethic of masculinity, but *not* necessarily because he is insecure about his manhood. Rather he embraces it because, if

[13] William A. Westley, "Violence and the Police," *American Journal of Sociology*, 49 (August 1953), pp. 34–41. See also, Arthur E. Hippler, "The Game of Black and White at Hunters Point," *Trans-Action*, 7 (April 1970), pp. 56–63.

he is nothing else, he is at least a man. Many men can rationalize away their limitations, their subservience, and their lack of prestige, but few can calmly ignore threats or ridicules about their masculinity.

In the case of the recruit, the public may have defined his total identity as "cop," as dirty worker. But the recruit seemed to be saying through his ethic of masculinity that while he was indeed a "cop," it was only a subidentity. First and foremost, he was a man. The recruit and dirty worker exaggeration of masculine characteristics may merely be an affirmation that although they do someone else's dirty work, they are still men.

RECRUIT REACTION

The way in which the staff and lecturers seemed to define professionalism, how they expressed the concept to the recruit, and the kind of image the recruit might have expected the department to formally and informally reward once he was in the field have been outlined. Nevertheless, I have been able to offer relatively little data on the recruit's perspectives toward professionalism outside of his notion of the man of action. This sparse information is probably the result of two factors. First, the lecture on professionalism partly quoted earlier in the chapter seemed to articulate what the recruit was thinking himself. Second, the matter appeared to him to be out of his hands: the potential for police officers to be professional was there, the difference rested with the community. As one recruit said angrily, "How can you be professional when you stop someone and he spits in your face?"

With all the instruction on professionalism, what was really meant by the staff remained vague in the mind of the recruit. To him, professionalism seemed to be something that was described in the cogent speech on professionalism; it implied dedication to one's duty, a conservative and respectful appearance, integrity, courtesy, and self-control. Still, there was no clear presentation of just what a professional was. For example, notice the lack of continuity in one statement.

> We're professional, and we can't do our work in a slip-shod fashion. We have to follow the [Rules and Procedures]. I don't care what it is, use common sense and good judgment, and nobody will burn your ass.

At first professionalism meant performing one's work neatly by following established rules and procedures. This was followed immediately by confidence in common sense as the policeman's most precious tool—but only because the recruit would be able to protect himself from departmental or other external criticisms!

There were a few times, however, when the recruit offered hints at what the term "professionalism" meant to him. Early in the session, I overheard the following stories.

One cop walked into a bank being robbed. He was in plain clothes, so he acted like a scared chicken . . . he backed away, cowering and yelling, "Don't shoot, don't shoot!" One of the two robbers came over and said, "Cool it, take it easy; you won't get hurt." When the robber lifted his arm to hit him, the cop had a gun pointed right between his eyes.

There was one cop in a gun battle. He fired twice, immediately reloaded, then shot four more times. The guy came out saying, "You're out of bullets," and the cop drilled him.

The remark made by one recruit who heard these stories was "They're more professional than we are." Then he added gravely, "You really have to be sharp to get the drop on them." It appeared that to be a professional, an officer had to have the capacity to out-think, outwit, or outmaneuver his opponent.[14]

One of the recruits from Megopolis Police Department offered another perspective on professionalism. A fellow recruit asked him if he thought the police in Rurban County were more professional than those in the city. He replied that he thought there was a better attitude among the men in Rurban County, but that the difference may simply have been because the city force was too large for the individual to count. Then he said, "I don't know; I'll have to find out when I'm brought up on something and see how I'm backed up." For him, professionalism meant support from his superiors in the event that departmental or public charges were placed against him. In his hierarchy of professional values, in-group solidarity seemed to come first.

The image that the recruit desired for himself and for law enforcement seemed to be personified by a visiting lecturer, a member of the Jordanian State Police. The recruit appeared to be very much impressed by the power, prestige, and the assumed competence of the typical Jordanian police officer. His salary was twice that of a school teacher's. He had the power to arrest on mere suspicion, and he could obtain permission to search private property by a phone call to the district attorney. If the officer were knowledgeable in law, he was permitted to prosecute his own case.

Apparently just as impressive to the recruit was the high clearance rate and very low crime rate. The reasons given by the lecturer for this success were strict laws and complete cooperation from the people. In the words of the Jordanian:

There is complete cooperation between police officer and people. If there is a crime and no police officer is around, people will tell all. We solve 95% of cases. We have no robbery and murder. We have low rate of crime because of strict laws, severe sentences, and no mercy. There is no

---

[14] Walter B. Miller, "Lower Class Culture as a Generating Milieu of Gang Delinquency," *Journal of Social Issues*, 14 (1958), pp. 5–19, discusses the focal concern of "smartness" in this sense of conning, outwitting, and duping.

parole system. Hanging is the death sentence . . . Narcotics is ten to fifteen years. ["Beautiful!" cried a recruit.]

Following the class, some recruits compared the American legal system with Jordan's.

R₁: How do you like that in Jordan and with the police state—throw the guy in on suspicion.
R₂: That'll never work in America.
R₃: (regretfully) No, no, it'll never work.

When I asked the latter recruit if he would prefer a police state in America, he answered: "No, not that, but cooperation from the people would be good; imagine, they solve 95 percent of their crime and they don't have much of that!" Living in a society that seemed permissive toward criminals and suspicious toward police officers, the recruits must have thought that the Jordanian police image was ideal.

Thus the general reaction of the recruit class to the whole question of professionalism appeared to be, "Yes, we are professional, but the public doesn't treat us as such," or "if we are not now professional, we could be if the public would get involved in law enforcement and the courts would support our judgment as experts," or "if the public wants professionals, they'll just have to pay more." Therefore, it was useless to debate the issue of police professionalism, since the problem appeared to be basically beyond their control. If there was anything to be done, it was to educate the public that they ought to treat the police as professionals.

LAW AND THE PROFESSIONAL IMAGE

If it is assumed that a person's self-image is closely linked to the organizational structure in which he operates from day to day, then the professional image that seems an integral part of academy training has behavioral and attitudinal outcomes. Since the patrolman is associated with law enforcement, it is necessary to explore the consequences that a recruit's training may have on his conception of the law; this subject is the focus of the remainder of the chapter. The last two major out-groups—lawyers and judges—will be considered in this connection.

Law as Morality

The law seemed to represent two perspectives to the recruit: guidelines that the officer can use to protect himself from charges of malfeasance or incompetence (as discussed in the previous chapter); and principles of morality.

Law, as a set of moral principles that members of a community are obligated to obey, is best discussed in connection with the recruit's image of himself as a morally superior professional. The recruit seemed to think that, since the law was morality per se, it was only just that a violator of the law should be punished according to the seriousness of the offense. Those who guarded, respected, or enforced the law were moral persons. Those who broke or disrespected the law, or who allowed offenders to break the law without the proper degree of punishment, ranged from the less moral to the absolutely immoral. Based on the lessons that he learned in the academy, the recruit appeared to define himself as a moral caretaker of society. Lawyers and judges were often defined as immoral because they made and supported the ground rules of law enforcement that seemed more protective of the rights of the offender than the right of the victim to have the offender properly punished.

It appeared that the basis for this perceived distinction between the recruit and the legal profession in the hierarchy of morality was based on qualitative differences in the law. There are two types of law: substantive law and procedural law. Substantive law defines what behavior may be handled by the legal system. Procedural law is composed of rules that govern how a person who breaks substantive law should be processed through the legal system by police officers and officers of the court.

For the most part, it was the substantive law which the recruit seemed to identify with the morality of the community, as an end in itself. Procedural law was perceived more as a set of prescriptions that interfered with the attainment of justice, that is, the proper punishment of a violation of law. Those who would place procedural law before the primacy of substantive law were seen as immoral, since this reasoning could result in a violator's being only minimally punished if punished at all. Since judges and lawyers operate under the primacy of procedural law (in accordance with the American value of presuming innocence until guilt has been proven), the recruit seemed to perceive them as subverters of law, order, and justice. Nevertheless, judges and lawyers had the last word in the matter, since they controlled the framework of legal activity and established the rules that had to be followed. As a result, the recruit found himself competing with other members of the legal system over the legitimate definition of justice. This did not mean that the recruit (or the patrolman) did not believe in due process of law, for he did. He objected, however, to the "obvious" manipulation of due process for the purpose of restraining the enforcement of substantive law which often allowed an offender to escape punishment.

The recruit's perspectives to both procedural law and substantive law were not without ambivalence. In the previous chapter it was pointed out that the recruit and probably the patrolman would tend to overlook procedural law if they felt threatened. Substantive law was not so simply defined as rules of morality either. At least two recruits thought that the laws prohibiting the use of marijuana should be relaxed, and several others questioned the legality of laws against abortion. Finally, what the recruit and his instructors did not seem to recognize was that police lobbies often opposed attempts at legal reform whether is was substantive or procedural.[15]

To sum up, the recruit seemed to believe that his interpretation of justice, that is, punishment which fits the crime, was one that was more just and humane than a lawyer's or judge's. What could be more just than having a person's violator pay for his misconduct? Several times a recruit complained to me privately or to an instructor during class that the oath he took on entering the academy was "useless," not because he lacked the willingness or capacity to abide by it, but because legal barriers made it inapplicable. According to this view, the problem of law enforcement did not lie so much within the police profession, as it did with lawyers and judges. Indeed, the recruit seemed to believe that lawyers unscrupulously distorted the law while judges encouraged them to do so by providing them the means via their rulings.

Prostitutes of the Law

THE LAWYER. The lawyer seemed to be defined as someone who would deliberately circumvent the law to save a client from a conviction. The client's guilt or innocence would be of no consequence as long as the lawyer received his fee. As Skolnick observed in his study, judges sometimes postponed a case with the implicit understanding that the request was made because of the client's inability to pay at that time.[16]

The lawyer's claim that he was merely conforming to procedural law was belied by some of his tactics in and out of court. For instance, police officers seemed to believe that legislators sometimes constructed the law in ways that would be helpful to their own ends instead of to the community's. As one instructor put it, "The legislators . . . are lawyers, and they are writing the law knowing that they may have to defend a client in court."

Although such a charge is an exaggeration, the behavior of lawyers once in court seemed to offer substantial evidence to the recruit that lawyers subordinated the needs of the community to their own. For example, the recruit seemed to believe that harmony between the police and the community often was disrupted by a lawyer.

We had one time when things were bad in a community, so we brought in all the drunks or people with bottles in their hands. All the people were happy: the problems were decreased significantly. The community was satisfied, and we stuck out our chests. What happend? Some smart

[15] Ed Cray, "Criminal Interrogations and Confessions: The Ethical Imperative," *Wisconsin Law Review* (1968), pp. 173–183.
[16] Jerome H. Skolnick, *Justice Without Trial*, p. 189.

lawyer was crying "unconstitutional," and now everything is as bad as it was.

The lawyer could not claim he was really interested in observing the law by placing procedural law or the "spirit of the law" as primary among the legal values. It seemed that he was concerned about neither procedure nor spirit. Certainly the recruit appeared to think that the lawyer in the following anecdote was not trying to enforce the "spirit of the law" for the good of the client or for the community.

"Person" does nòt just mean the body, but it can mean an individual, a public or private corporation, and now, an unincorporated association. It seems some bright lawyer got a client off by saying that an unincorporated association did not apply to the law as it stood on the books.

In reference to procedural law, it was interesting to notice that according to an assistant district attorney, the complaints of lawyers regarding the rights of their clients had changed as the laws had changed. Instructors claimed that charges of police brutality were declining rapidly because of the new procedural laws. Defense attorneys no longer search for police abuse of their clients; some do not even question whether or not the prescribed warnings were given to the suspect. The first question the attorney seems to ask his client is if he *understood* the warnings. An instructor claimed that the county lost a one-half million dollar arson case because "now the act is. they're stupid."

The sudden change of the defense attorney's charges from police brutality to nonadvisement of legal rights tended to cast doubt on the previous claims of police brutality. Undoubtedly, instances of police brutality occurred, but it might have been that the rates of brutality were inflated by false but strategic charges by lawyers and clients.[17] Judges, including those on the United States Supreme Court, were criticized by instructors and recruits for making rulings that allowed and supported further circumvention of substantive law.

JUDGES AND COURTS OF LAW. If the recruit's feeling of moral superiority relative to judges did not stem directly from his conception of the law as a moral order (which dichotomized people into the moral and the immoral), his fellow recruits and instructors provided him with other convincing arguments for questioning the common sense of judges.

We have what we call the Supreme Court of [District Court]. (Laughter) Now we call them the Supreme Court because they have twelve individual judges, each with his own opinion. (Laughter) The U.S.

---

[17] P. Chevigny, *Police Power* (New York: Pantheon, 1969); and Ed Cray, *The Big Blue Line* (New York: Coward-McCann, 1967) for opposing views.

Supreme Court is no different, except they have more room.

The instructors further attacked the probity of the members of the United States Supreme Court by questioning their qualifications compared to RCPD candidate requirements.

How do you become a Supreme Court Justice today? Well, you go to law school, practice law for three years, and then you go into public office. Then you get appointed Supreme Court Justice—never having rubbed shoulders with a rookie, the D.A.'s, the judges at District Court (although *that* may be okay)—our own Earl Warren.

Since the standards of selection to the United States Supreme Court were presented as being very lax, it came as no surprise when the recruit learned that county, district, state, and national courts deviated from their intended "moral purposes." "Did you ever see that lady blindfolded, holding the scales in District Court? If she ever saw what went on in District Court, she'd throw away the scales."

If the recruit still doubted the moral standing of judges, there was the coup de grace. An instructor informed the recruit class that a couple of years ago the State Supreme Court initiated an investigation of the county's district courts because "it was believed that the District Court was not policing itself." A judge from Megopolis City was consequently appointed to supervise the courts. Thus the recruit seemed to realize that judges, the same ones who were responsible for castigating police officers in court, were so corrupt that their own colleagues from other districts had to supervise them. This knowledge permitted the recruit to place much of the blame for ineffective law enforcement on the courts.

One instructor suggested that the problem of law enforcement could be remedied once the policeman educated the judges. In the case of radar traps, for instance, he claimed that the county was winning 70 percent of its cases because it taught judges how radar worked and that even without radar, police officers were able to make reasonable estimates of speeds.

Indeed, there were times when it seemed that the recruit thought that the intelligence of the judge was insufficient to enable him to absorb fully the testimony that he heard. When discussing a car stealing ring that specialized in Cadillacs, an instructor mentioned the problem of obtaining court support of police efforts. The county had charged a lawyer with the receiving of stolen goods because he had gone to a bar in a slum area and had bought a Cadillac at half its market value. The presiding judge, the recruit was told, acquitted the lawyer, for "how would he know the car was stolen?"

An experience of a recruit from Megopolis Department further illustrated the recruit's sense of frustration in the light of such apparent judicial astigmatism.

I brought a guy in for cock-sucking, and the judge dismissed it because he couldn't believe two men would do that. The judge asked me how long I observed them doing that. Well, it takes only two seconds to see what's going on, but I said ten seconds because he wouldn't have believed me for only two seconds. He dismissed the case because he wouldn't believe they did it at all!

The recruit may have explained away court actions as a consequence of unqualified, naive, and probably some very stupid judges. What he did not seem sensitive to were the different experiences of the police officer and the judge that accounted for their conflicting perspectives.[18] The officer assumes that a man whom he arrests is guilty or he would not have arrested him in the first place; therefore, it is irrational to assume his innocence or to release him. While the judge may see a new face standing in front of him, the officer may have been lenient with the offender in the past. Defining his job as enforcing the law, the officer perceives procedural law as counterproductive. In contrast, the judge defines due process of law as essential to the American legal system: what is a technicality for the policeman is a fundamental principle for the judge. Because of heavy calendars and poor administration, judges are forced to make quick decisions; they rely on dismissals to reduce the chances of injustice to the defendant. None of these issues were presented to the recruit in an enlightened manner. On the other hand, neither the public nor the courts seem to recognize that it is the police officer who must bear the psychological burden for the court's problems.

Much of the apparent animosity of the recruit toward judges seemed to revolve around court decisions that "allowed" violators of the law to escape punishment, set up rigid guidelines for police activity, and freed known criminals on mere technicalities. Perhaps no other Supreme Court decision was more vilified by the recruit and his instructors than the Miranda decision.

Neutralization of Law Enforcement

BENT JUSTICE. The Miranda decision stated that persons in the custody of the police should be informed by a police officer of their right to remain silent and their right to legal counsel even if they could not afford one. The Miranda decision, which applied to the questioning period of police investigations, extended the Escobedo decision of 1964, which held that a defendant in a felony case had the right to counsel once he appeared in court even if he could not afford a lawyer. The instructors seemed to dispel any doubts in the mind of the recruit as to whether the Miranda decision was in the best interests of law, order, or justice.

[18] Jerome H. Skolnick, *Justice Without Trial*, pp. 182–203; James Q. Wilson, *Varieties of Police Behavior* (Cambridge: Harvard University, 1968), pp. 50–52.

Not even the Supreme Court knew what it was doing [in the Escobedo decision]. They said there is a period between investigation and suspicion during which he is entitled to a lawyer. We asked them what they meant, where do you draw the line? Silence. Well, we thought the situation would be okay in a couple of years. They fixed it okay. (Laughter) The Miranda decision, and they shocked the country again. We warn them of their rights. Now we tell them we'll give you a lawyer if you can't afford it. . . . We get them back. But what bothers me is the overall effect on law enforcement.

Apparently, the feeling was that once a client obtained a lawyer whose only concern was to free him, there would be little chance of eliciting any information, much less a confession. The first thing the lawyer would do would be to instruct his client not to say a word and to inform the investigating officers that they were not to question his client. Since, the instructors claim, the only way to solve a crime is to question the suspect, if he either wants a lawyer or he does not understand his rights "you've lost him." The substantial number of cases cleared by confessions could then be expected to decline (in spite of evidence to the contrary).[19] The decline might encourage others to try to break the law.

Even if the Miranda warnings are given to a suspect who agrees to relinquish his rights, the police officer must attend a Huntley hearing. It is a formal judicial hearing that determines whether the suspect waived his rights voluntarily or whether he was apprised of them at all. "Yes, I give up my Constitutional rights; yes, I believe in God; yes, I want to talk; yes, I want to be searched. Then you get a Huntley investigation to see if the waiver is legal."

It appeared to the recruit that lawyers and judges did not want substantive law effectively enforced, since they continued to curtail police discretion. For instance, police officers seemed to believe that wiretapping, judiciously supervised, could be an effective tool of law enforcement. Although they admitted wiretapping infringed on individual rights, they felt that the rights of the community should take precedence in the wake of the apparent power of organized crime. The ruling of the Supreme Court on wiretapping seemed not only unrealistic, but inane: the police must warn those who are supposed to be secretly investigated. "You can tap his phone, but you tell him."

Because of procedural law, many known criminals, including murderers, could not be brought to trial or convicted. The Miranda decision seemed to benefit only the guilty.

As far as I am concerned, the Miranda decision does not help the inno-

[19] Arthur Niederhoffer, *Behind the Shield*, pp. 161–164, cites several findings that the Miranda decision has affected the rates of clearance only minutely, and that confessions clear only 10 percent of the cases anyway.

cent person. It helps the guilty person. No sane person without torture is going to confess a crime he did not commit. And evidence through torture was never admissible long before the Miranda decision.

Thus, the Supreme Court rulings not only seemed to reduce the effectiveness of law enforcement, they seemed unnecessary to the interests of justice. The belief of both recruit and instructor appeared to be that police agents were disproportionately rebuked and controlled compared to other segments of the legal system. A recruit's complaint that police mistakes wind up in a Supreme Court ruling while nothing happens to incompetent judges or lawyers who "twist the facts" raises an interesting point. Kai Erikson observes that the normative boundaries of a society or group (the values that differentiate one group from another) are forever being tested to determine what degree of variation from the norms will be tolerated by the group members.[20] Although the result is often a "rubber band" effect in which the boundaries "bounce back" to the status quo, such is not the case with the police. The police test the limits of their legal boundaries but, since these boundaries do not bounce back to their original state, they find that court actions increasingly *lessen* their areas of activity.

Not only was police discretion seriously hampered, the courts seemed intent on protecting the criminal—even to the extent of granting him immunity from informers and undercover surveillance. The recruit was told about a detective who received a phone call giving the location of the sales of illegal drugs. The next night the detective went to the location and arrested a drug peddler who was selling drugs "right out in the open." The peddler was acquitted, not because the information was false, but because the Supreme Court ruled that a police informer must be one whose reliability has already been tested. The phone caller did not qualify as a police informer.

> They wanted our undercover agents to give the Miranda warnings. (Laughter) No kidding. I asked the judge, "Why? The Miranda decision was for custodial interrogation." The judge said, "Well, I don't read it that way." "What case did you get it from?" "Well, I never read the whole thing." (Laughter) That's what we're up against.

The recruit seemed unable to understand why the criminal merited such protection. It seemed as if one's personal rights included the right to commit a crime without suffering the full consequences.

As if the Supreme Court decisions were not bad enough, local judges seemed to free violators of the law on relatively minor technicalities. It seemed a clear case of finding small technical points in the law to guarantee that the police officer would not win a conviction.

[20] Kai Erikson, *Wayward Puritans* (New York: John Wiley, 1966).

The one thing I like is for a rookie to write out a lot of summonses because he'll have to go to court, and he'll learn. One fellow lost a case because he didn't know the dimensions of a speed sign. He knew what it said, but it was thrown out of court. Don't ask me why.

The recruit seemed to believe that the courts were diametrically opposed to the principles of law, order, and justice. His belief appeared to be reinforced when he learned that judges seemed hesitant to convict a person even when the suspect was clearly guilty.

This is what will bust your balls—the courts. Our Narcotics Squad is doing very well, making good arrests, good evidence, and then they let him plead fourth degree misdemeanor. For what? Because he's a student!

A recruit from Megopolis Department confirmed the apparent court injustice. He had arrested two youths for smoking marijuana. The judge dismissed both defendants, one because he was going to college and the other because he was going into the army. Such permissiveness by the courts toward the criminal, assumed the recruit, could only bring disrespect for the ideals of law and justice. While in the opinion of the recruit and his instructor the courts confused mercy and justice by acquitting defendants, it also appeared that the recruit confused punishment with justice.

Although they were "professionals" responsible for enforcing the moral code of the community, in practice lawyers and judges seemed to leave very little doubt in the mind of the recruit that they were not dedicated to moral values. Hence, they were immoral men. Indeed, what could be more immoral than to leave a victim helpless to have his violator brought to justice?

The————Commission has a very starry-eyed view. "A vehicle can be replaced, a life cannot." And they extended it into the home: the home owner cannot even use deadly physical force! So what happens? A thief robs a house. The owner wakes up and says, "You're under arrest," and he says, "Fuck you," and he's gone. When will it all stop?

Considering himself a professional who was expert in law enforcement, the recruit seemed to think that he should be able to use his own judgment as to what would be the right or wrong procedures. According to the law, an officer may search a person only on the grounds of "probable cause" or if he is in personal danger himself. If an officer searches on suspicion only, his case could be "dismissed" even if the searched person was carrying stolen goods.

As one knowledgeable about the behavior of criminals, the recruit generally felt his judgment should not be subjected to examination by the court. State law insists that a conviction must be founded on the principle of "beyond a reasonable doubt." However, if a jury bases its decision on this principle, it implies that the expertise of the officer is questionable. Indeed, the high standards of "beyond a reasonable doubt" could contribute to a defendant's "beating the rap." If respect for the moral code were to be maintained and if police decisions were not to be questioned, the recruits felt that a more "realistic" principle was needed. What seemed to be the solution was stated by a representative of the state liquor authority who announced to them that many of its convictions were upheld because they were based on a principle that enhanced police competence: "A reasonable man would determine from the facts as a trained observer. . . . ''

JUSTICE BENT BACK. The image of a professional as competent in his field was probably warped when the recruit became aware that court cases were not won necessarily on their merits. His instructors informed him that lawyers "couldn't get through a case if they stuck to the facts." To win a case, lawyers had to advise their clients never to talk with police officers, and once in court, they tried to discredit the officer in the eyes of the jury. The ways in which the lawyer would try to accomplish the latter, the recruit was warned, were to ignore the facts of the case and to attack the officer's demeanor or educational qualifications. The truth did not win cases. One tactic that the lawyer was said to use in order to discredit the officer was to search for misspelled words or errors in the officer's memo book. That was one reason why the recruit was instructed never to overlap notes of two days on one page and to bring only the relevant pages of the memo book to court.

> It can be embarrassing if you are not sure of your facts. The defense attorney may have a piss-poor case, but he makes you look ridiculous to the jury. . . . The moment [the memo book] is introduced into court, you are vulnerable to any mistakes in it.

In addition, the recruit had to use correct grammar and remain courteous if he were ever placed on the witness stand. "Don't murder the English language. You may have a good case, but it doesn't look good when you testify."

One of the new programs of academy training, beginning with our recruit class, was a field trip to county court. The events included a mock Huntley hearing with the staff of the district attorney's office in which some recruits played the parts of witnesses and the suspect. Thirty minutes into the "hearing," the class became bored and impatient with the constant repetition of questions that appeared to be irrelevant. The next day an instructor pointed out the significance of the long mock hearing.

> I just wanted to talk a little about yesterday in court. I know it was tiring, but by God, that's just the way they operate—you feel when are they going to stop those stupid questions. But "sir" them to death.

If judges and juries seemed to rely more on appearances than on the merits of the case, the recruit tended to feel justified to "bend the law" a little to enforce substantive law and justice. The instructor who said, "the judge hates you, the DA hates you, the lawyers hate you—everybody hates you except the defendant," was implying that while the legal staff was concerned about matters other than justice, the defendant knew he was where he belonged. When the legal process seemed to be regulated by immoral persons, it seemed to become the officer's responsibility to compensate for it. As one recruit mentioned to me, "When justice bends you one way, we bend it another."

For example, one way in which the Miranda decision could be countered was to mumble the warnings. If the suspect could not understand the words, that was his misfortune. The important thing was for the officer to be able to swear truthfully in court that he had given the warnings. "You don't need to lie—exaggerate." Notice how one instructor worked in the warning that the suspect is entitled to a lawyer. He had begun by reading all the warnings to the class.

> Basically that's what you're supposed to say. But when you're in the field, try to bullshit them. "Come on, get it off your chest. We'll get an attorney for you. Anybody could have done that—so you made a mistake."

Thus, substantive law and justice seemed to become identified with the morality of the community. Procedural law and justice became rules that hampered law enforcement to the extent that known criminals were allowed to escape the consequences of their actions. As a professional who was competent in his field, as a moral person who was concerned about the rectitude of the community, and as one who had sworn an oath to enforce the law justly, the officer seemed to feel that he had to maintain some respect for the law in some way. Consequently, countertechniques that had the semblance of conforming to procedural law in order to assure enforcement of substantive law seemed to be taught, used, and permitted by members of the police ingroup.

PROFESSIONALISM AS DEFENSIVE

The purpose of this chapter has been to describe and analyze how a police department defined and took steps to achieve a change in the image of police work and the self-image of its members. This was carried out by concentrating on one step of the policeman's career—the time he spends at the police academy—and the consequences of that training. Perhaps the role of professionalism in RCPD (and in other police departments) may be brought into better focus if the simple question is asked: Why does the police academy exist at all?

The answer, aside from the obvious need for training, appears to lie in the department's attempt to convince the public (and itself) that police officers are, indeed, professionals. A police officer today is like the teacher of yesterday. He is called on to engage in a variety of services that touch on intimate facets of people's lives. He must make judgments ranging from administration to public relations, from robbery to first aid, and from law to family disputes. The police officer believes that he is an expert in all these services, but he realizes that his competence as a skilled worker is not recognized by the public. He views himself and his department as being constantly challenged to prove their integrity both in and out of court.

Professionalism seems to connote internal competence and freedom from external regulation. The policeman, considering himself an expert in a wide range of services, seems to believe that nobody but another policeman is able to judge accurately his competence or the quality of his service. As Hughes correctly notes, it is the right to make judgments that is most jealously guarded by professional groups.[21] Consequently, it is assumed "all licensed professionals are competent and ethical until found otherwise by their peers." To be able to be judged by one's peers assures the defendant that "occupational experiences" will be taken into account, and for the profession itself means that its members can discuss any mistakes in secret. The threat of an institutional arbiter such as a civilian review board is seen as antiprofessional and as a demand to discuss police secrets openly. Neither aspect is tolerable since, as the eminent sociologist Georg Simmel points out, secrecy fosters group autonomy.[22]

A publicly recognized professional status seems to be perceived as a panacea for most of the ailments plaguing police work. Courts would question police procedures less frequently, and defense attorneys would be less able to resort to trickery or to disparaging the police officer on the witness stand to win their cases. The press would be less inclined to distort news items against the police, and the status of the law enforcement profession would encourage its selection by high calibre men as a career. The public would be supportive of police actions, and its cooperation would decrease the crime rate as well as make budgetary requests, including salary increases, less problematic.

Since professionalism seemed to be the answer to the problems of police work, the first step was to find out what were the characteristics of a profession so that they could strive to meet these criteria. Characteristics were collected from students of professions. Through the years, progressive departments have tried to conform to these criteria. In RCPD, the establishment of a police academy and a police science degree on the college level were supposed to provide evidence to the public that police work involved specialized

[21] Everett C. Hughes, *Men and Their Work*, pp. 94–95 and 140–142.
[22] Georg Simmel, *The Sociology of Georg Simmel*, edited and translated by Kurt H. Wolff (New York: The Free Press, 1950), pp. 361, 345, 376.

knowledge and training: not just anybody could be a patrolman. Those who were admitted to the police academy had to pass physical and psychological tests, submit to background investigations, swear an oath to a code of ethics, and successfully meet the requirements of the lengthiest police training in the state. On graduating from the academy, the recruit was licensed by the state to engage in specialized activities. Since experience was necessary to acquire competence and knowledge, there was an informal rule that the first five years of field work were still part of the training.

Law enforcement, it was thought, certainly qualified as a profession, since it was an idealistic and service occupation composed of dedicated men. The characteristics that RCPD lacked were (1) complete group autonomy, and (2) publicly recognized status and prestige. Not only were these conditions extraneous to the quality of the department itself, they also happened to be the very problems that caused the effort toward police professionalization in the first place. Thus, according to the police officer, he qualified as a professional. He had only to convince the public of this.

However, there were problems of definition regarding the professional police officer. It was generally agreed that he was one who was competent in his job and deserved the respect of the public, but beyond that, there was less consensus. Professionalism implied abiding by a code of ethics, performing tactfully and efficiently, looking tidy, earning large salaries, and gaining public cooperation. In practice, these characteristics became means as well as ends in themselves. The police officer should enforce the law equally and justly; should perform his job tactfully and efficiently; and should be educated, courteous, and trim to *obtain* complete public cooperation, higher social status, and salaries comparable to doctors and lawyers.

Because of the nebulous image, the instructors were not sure how to train in-coming members to become professional. The haziness of the image was increased by their apparent ambivalence about the worth of a professional police officer even if one could be trained. Notwithstanding their desire to train professionals, the instructors seemed skeptical of the person who did well in the classroom, since he could be ineffective in field situations. Nevertheless, the need to acquire the status of a profession was recognized, and the department simulated the elite professions. Professionals learned in a classroom setting, so a police academy with its certificate of competence replaced the apprenticeship training. Professionals had college degrees, so recruits and patrolmen were encouraged to acquire police science degrees. In spite of these surface attempts, the orientations of the academy and the police science curriculum remained essentially vocational.

The recruit, too, had a funny conception of the professional image. The only anchorage he could fall back on was not what the instructors said, but what they did. The instructors' ambivalence about professionalism was carried over to the recruit. On the one hand, they seemed to want patrolmen who were flexible and independent thinkers, who were tolerant of other people's attitudes and behavior, who relied on dialogue and reason rather than on force to achieve order, and who stressed deliberation. What they taught or reinforced, however, was compliance to authority (which was buttressed by the organizational structure of the department), and intolerance of other people's ways of thinking or acting. The value and theory of due process of law were presented unfavorably or inadequately. Lectures on marijuana were propagandistic and medically questionable: the recruit would not be able to talk intelligently on the subject even if he had wanted to. Role playing was geared to technical proficiency, not to developing interpersonal skills. Consequently, the recruit was very receptive towards instructors who claimed that the real training would occur in the field.

All in all, the image of the patrolman as action-oriented was projected to a significant degree more than the contemplative image. Professionalism was not identified with intellectual or academic training: it consisted of concrete work situations. The neglect of ideological changes may help explain why RCPD and other police departments are having such a difficult time in their "convincing process."

Although, as we have noted, law enforcement may be considered a profession, there still remains a hierarchy of occupations. In survey after survey Americans, when asked to rank them, give Supreme Court justices and surgeons very high occupational ratings. Few of us have direct contact with the chief and associate justices of the high court; however, most of us know a surgeon or two. We know the awe in which surgeons are held and how they command deference in the wider society. As Erving Goffman demonstrates, they demand it of their fellow workers and subordinates as well.

In this selection, sociologist Erving Goffman, author of numerous books on social interaction, uses the concept of role distance to describe and analyze the actual activities of surgeons at work. Goffman suggests that role distance has several functions.

As you read the following essay, consider the other examples of role distance and patterns of deference and what they mean in everyday life.

Surgery as an Activity System

ERVING GOFFMAN

The concept of role distance provides a *sociological* means of dealing with one type of divergence between obligation and actual performance. First, we know that often distance is not introduced on an individual basis but can be predicted on the grounds of the performers' gross age-sex characteristics. Role distance is a part (but, of course, only one part) of *typical* role, and this routinized sociological feature should not escape us merely because role distance is not a part of the normative framework of role. Secondly, that which one is careful to point out one is not, or not merely, necessarily has a directing and intimate influence on one's conduct, especially since the means for expressing this disaffection must be carved out of the standard materials available in the situation.

We arrive, then, at a broadened sociological way of looking at the trappings of a social role. A set of visible qualifications and known certifications, along with a social setting well designed as a showplace, provides the individual with something more than an opportunity to play his role self to the hilt, for this scene is just what he needs to create a clear impression of what he chooses not to lay claim to. The more extensive the trappings of a role, the more opportunity to display role distance. Personal front and social setting provide precisely the field an individual needs to cut a figure in—a figure that romps, sulks, glides, or is indifferent. Later in this paper, some additional social determinants of role distance will be considered.

SURGERY AS AN ACTIVITY SYSTEM

I have suggested some cases where the scene of activity generates for the individual a self which he is apparently loath to accept openly for himself, since his conduct suggests that some disaffiliation exists between himself and his role. But a peek into some odd corners of social life provides no basis, perhaps, for generalizing about social life. As a test, then, of the notion of role distance (and role), let us take a scene in which activity generates a self for the individual that appears to be a most likely one for self-attachment. Let us take, for example, the activity system sustained during a surgical operation. The components consist of verbal and physical acts and the changing state of the organism undergoing the operation. Here, if anywhere in our society, we should find performers flushed with a feeling of the weight and dignity of their action. A Hollywood ideal is involved: the white-coated chief surgeon strides into the operating theater after the patient has been anesthetized and opened by assistants. A place is automatically made for him. He grunts a few abbreviated preliminaries, then deftly, almost silently, gets to work, serious, grim, competently living up to the image he and his team have of him, yet in a context where momentary failure to exhibit competence might permanently jeopardize the relation he is allowed to have to his role. Once the critical phase of the operation is quite over, he steps back and, with a special compound of tiredness, strength, and disdain, rips off his gloves; he thus contaminates himself and abdicates his role, but at a time when his own labors put the others in a position to "close up." While he may be a father, a husband, or a baseball fan at home, he is here one and only one thing, a surgeon, and being a surgeon provides a fully rounded impression of the man. If the role perspective works, then, surely it works here, for in our society the surgeon, if anyone, is allowed and obliged to put himself into his work and get a self out of it.[1]

---

[1] Much the same conceit has already been employed by Temple Burling in *Essays on Human Aspects of Administration,* Bulletin 25 (August, 1953) of the New York State School of Industrial and Labor Relations, Cornell University, pp. 9–10. The fullest published accounts of conduct in the operating room that I know of are to be found in T. Burling, E. Lentz and R. Wilson, *The Give and Take in Hospitals* (New York: Putnam, 1956), Chap. 17, pp. 260–283, and R. Wilson, "Teamwork in the Operating Room," *Human Organization,* 12 (1954), pp. 9–14.

As a contrast, then, to the insubstantial life of horses-for-ride, I want to report briefly on some observations of activity in surgery wards.[2]

If we start with the situation of the lesser medical personnel, the intern and the junior resident, the test will not be fair, for here, apparently, is a situation much like the ones previously mentioned. The tasks these juniors are given to do—such as passing hemostats, holding retractors, cutting small tied-off veins, swabbing the operating area before the operation, and perhaps suturing or closing at the end—are not large enough to support much of a surgical role. Furthermore, the junior person may find that he performs even these lowly tasks inadequately, and that the scrub nurse as well as the chief surgeon tells him so. And when the drama is over and the star performer has dropped his gloves and gown and walked out, the nurses may underline the intern's marginal position by lightly demanding his help in moving the body from the fixed table to the movable one, while automatically granting him a taste of the atmosphere they maintain when real doctors are absent. As for the intern himself, surgery is very likely *not* to be his chosen specialty; the three-month internship is a course requirement and he will shortly see the last of it. The intern may confirm all this ambivalence to his work on occasions away from the surgery floor, when he scathingly describes surgery as a plumber's craft exercised by mechanics who are told what to look for by internists.

The surgical junior, especially the intern, has, then, a humbling position during surgery. Whether as a protection against this condition or not, the medical juniors I observed, like over-age merry-go-round riders, analysands, and carnival pitchmen, were not prepared to embrace their role fully; elaborate displays of role distance occurred.[3] A careful, bemused look on the face is sometimes found, implying, ''This is not the real me.'' Sometimes the individual will allow himself to go ''away,'' dropping off into a brown study that removes him from the continuity of events, increases the likelihood that his next contributory act will not quite fit into the flow of action, and effectively gives the appearance of occupational disaffection; brought back into play, he may be careful to evince little sign of chagrin. He may rest himself by leaning on the patient or by putting a foot on an inverted bucket but in a manner too contrived to allow the others to feel it is a matter of mere resting.

[2] My own material on interaction during surgery, from which all staff practices and verbal responses cited in this paper are drawn, derives from brief observations in the medical building of a mental hospital and the operating rooms of a suburban community hospital. Not deriving from the most formal hospitals, these data load the facts a little in my favor.

I am grateful to Dr. Otis R. Farley, and his staff in the Medical and Surgical Branch of St. Elizabeths Hospital, Washington, D.C., and to John F. Wight, Administrative Director, and Lenore Jones, Head Surgical Nurse, of Herrick Memorial Hospital, Berkeley, California, for full research freedom and great courtesy.

[3] Some of the interns I observed had plans to take a psychiatric residency and, apparently because of this, were doing their stint of surgical internship in the medical building of a mental hospital; they therefore had wider institutional support for their lack of interest in physical techniques.

Interestingly enough, he sometimes takes on the function of the jester, en-dangering his reputation with antics that temporarily place him in a doubtful and special position, yet through this providing the others present with a reminder of less exalted worlds:

> CHIEF SURGEON JONES *(in this case a senior resident):* A small Richardson please.
> SCRUB NURSE: Don't have one.
> DR. JONES: O.K., then give me an Army and Navy.
> SCRUB NURSE: It looks like we don't have one.
> DR. JONES *(lightly joking):* No Army or Navy man here.
> INTERN *(dryly):* No one in the armed forces, but Dr. Jones here is in the Boy Scouts.
>
> SCRUB NURSE: Will there be more than three [sutures] more? We're running out of sutures.
> CHIEF SURGEON: I don't know.
> INTERN: We can finish up with Scotch tape.
> INTERN *(looking for towel clamps around body):* Where in the world . . . ?
> SCRUB NURSE: Underneath the towel.
> *(Intern turns to the nurse and in slow measure makes a full cold bow to her.)*
> SCRUB NURSE *(to intern):* Watch it, you're close to my table! *[A Mayo stand containing instruments whose asepsis she must guard and guarantee.]*
> *(Intern performs a mock gasp and clownishly draws back.)*

As I have suggested, just as we cannot use a child over four riding a merry-go-round as an exhibition of how to embrace an activity role, so also we cannot use the junior medical people on a surgical team. But surely the chief surgeon, at least, will demonstrate the embracing of a role. What we find, of course, is that even this central figure expresses considerable role distance.

Some examples may be cited. One can be found in medical etiquette. This body of custom requires that the surgeon, on leaving the operation, turn and thank his assistant, his anesthetist, and ordinarily his nurses as well. Where a team has worked together for a long time and where the members are of the same age-grade, the surgeon may guy this act, issuing the thanks in what he expects will be taken as an ironical and farcical tone of voice: "Miss Westly, you've done a simply wonderful job here." Similarly, there is a formal rule that in preparing a requested injection the nurse show the shelved vial to the surgeon before its sealed top is cracked off so that he can check its named con-tents and thereby take the responsibility on himself. If the surgeons are very busy at the time, this checking may be requested but not given. At other times, however, the checking may be guyed.

CIRCULATING NURSE: Dr. James, would you check this?

DR. JAMES *(in a loud ministerial voice, reading the label):* Three cubic centimeters of heparin at ten-milligram strength, put up by Invenex and held by Nurse Jackson at a forty-five-degree angle. That is right, Nurse Jackson.

Instead of employing technical terms at all times, he may tease the nurses by using homey appellations: "Give me the small knife, we'll get in just below the belly button"; and he may call the electric cauterizer by the apt name of "sizzler," ordering the assistant surgeon to "sizzle here, and here." Similarly, when a nurse allows her nonsterile undergown to be exposed a little, a surgeon may say in a pontifical and formal tone, "Nurse Bevan, can I call your attention to the anterior portion of your gown. It is exposing you. I trust you will correct this condition," thereby instituting social control, reference to the nurse's non-nursing attributes, and satire of the profession, all with one stroke. So, too, a nurse, returning to the operating room with a question, "Dr. Williams?" may be answered by a phrase of self-satirization: "In person," or, "This is Dr. Williams." And a well-qualified surgeon, in taking the situated role of assistant surgeon for the duration of a particular operation, may tell the nurses, when they have been informed by the chief surgeon that two electric cauterizers will be employed, "I'm going to get one too, just like the big doctors, that's what I like to hear." A chief surgeon, then, may certainly express role distance. Why he does so, and with what effect, are clearly additional questions, and ought to be considered.

THE FUNCTIONS OF ROLE DISTANCE FOR SURGERY

I have suggested that in surgery, in a room that pridefully keeps out germs and gives equal medical treatment to bodies of different socioeconomic status, there is no pretense at expressional asepsis. Role distance is routinely expressed.

But why should the individual be disinclined to embrace his role self? The situation of the junior medical man suggests that defensive activity is at work. We cannot say, however, that role distance protects the individual's ego, self-esteem, personality, or integrity from the implications of the situation without introducing constructs which have no place in a strictly sustained role perspective. We must find a way, then, of getting the ego back into society.

We can begin to do this by noting that when the individual withdraws from a situated self he does not draw into some psychological world that he creates himself but rather acts in the name of some other socially created identity. The liberty he takes in regard to a situated self is taken because of other, equally social, constraints. A first example of this is provided us when we try to obtain a systematic view of the functions performed by role distance in surgery, for immediately we see a paradoxical fact: one of the concerns that prevents the individual from fully accepting his situated self is his commitment to the situated activity system itself. We see this when we shift our point of view from the individual to the situated system and look at the functions that role distance serves for it. We find that certain maneuvers which act to integrate the system require for their execution individuals who do not fully embrace their situated selves. System-irrelevant roles can thus themselves be exploited for the system as a whole. In other words, one of the claims upon himself that the individual must balance against all others is the claim created by the over-all "needs"[4] of the situated activity system itself, apart from his particular role in it.

An illustration of these contingencies is provided by the chief surgeon. Like those in many other occupational positions, the chief surgeon finds that he has the obligation to direct and manage a particular activity system, in this case a surgical operation. He is obliged to see that the operation is effectively carried through, regardless of what this may sometimes express about himself.

Now for the surgical team to function usefully, each member, as already suggested, must sustain his capacity as a communicator, an individual capable of giving and receiving verbal communications and their substitutes. And, as in other activity systems, each member must be able to execute physical actions requiring some coolness and self-command. Anything that threatens either this verbal or physical poise threatens the participant's capacity to contribute, and hence the activity system itself. Each individual member of the surgical team must be in command of himself, and where he is not able to handle himself, others, especially the chief surgeon, must help him do it.

In order to ensure that the members of his team keep their heads during the operation, the chief surgeon finds himself under pressure to modulate his own demands and his own expectations of what is due him. If he exercises his situated rights openly to criticize incompetent conduct, the surgeon may only further weaken the defaulter's self-command and further endanger the particular operation. In short, the chief surgeon is likely to find himself with the situated role function of anxiety management[5] and may find that he must draw on his own dignity, on what is owed his station, in order to fulfil this function. A kind of bargaining or bribery[6] occurs, whereby the surgeon receives a guarantee of equability from his team in return for being "a nice guy"—someone who does not press his rightful claims too far. Of course, the surgeon may save his dignity and lose the operation, but he is under pressure not to do so.

Given the conflict between correcting a subordinate and helping him main-

[4] In the sense used by Philip Selznick in "Foundations of the Theory of Organization," *American Sociological Review*, 13 (1948), pp. 29–30.
[5] This role function is one which the M.D. anesthetist often performs, or tries to perform, sometimes apparently quite intentionally, as a filler for a position that might otherwise not have enough weight for the person who fills it.
[6] The notion of "role bargain" is usefully developed in W.J. Goode, "A Theory of Role Strain," *American Sociological Review*, 25 (1960), pp. 483–496.

tain his poise, it is understandable that surgeons will employ joking means of negative sanction, so that it is difficult to determine whether the joke is a cover for the sanction, or the sanction a cover for the joke. In either case, some distance from usual surgical decorum is required:

(Intern holds retractor at wrong end of incision and goes "away," being uninterested in the operation.)

CHIEF SURGEON *(in mock English accent)*: You don't have to hold that up there, old chap, perhaps down here. Going to sleep, old boy?

CHIEF SURGEON *(on being accidentally stabbed in the finger by the assistant surgeon, who is using the electric scalpel)*: If I get syphalis [*sic*] I'll know where I got it from, and I'll have witnesses.

If some of these jokes seem weak and unnecessary, we must appreciate that to let a small error of conduct go by without comment has its own dangers, apart from what this laxness might mean for staff training. In the presence of a mistake, staff members can ready themselves for the occurrence of a corrective sanction, and unless something pertinent is said, this readiness may act as an anxiety-producing distraction. The immediate expression of a joking sanction, however labored, grounds this source of tension.

Just as a negative sanction may be toned down to prevent the offender from acting still more disruptively, so also direct commands may be softened into requests even though the surgeon's general occupational status and particular situated role empower him to command. Where he has a right to issue a peremptory order for an instrument, he may instead employ courtesies: "Let's have another Richardson," "Could I have a larger retractor." Instead of flaring up when no suitable ready-made instrument is available, he may choose to express a boyish mechanical ingenuity, constructing on the spot a make-do instrument.[7]

I am suggesting that he who would effectively direct an operation at times may have to employ a touch so light as to embarrass the dark dignities of his

[7] In some face-to-face activity systems a participant may be so close to losing poise that a responsible other may have to modify his whole manner, not merely his commands and negative sanctions, if the unreliable participant is to be kept on his feet, and this modification is likely to be at the expense of formal behavior patterns associated with the superordinate's role. To prevent the full weight of his role from frightening or freezing subordinates, the superordinate may therefore employ informalities. The official who asks an interviewee to join him in a cigarette provides the classic example, known as "putting a subordinate at his ease." The strategy employed by a child analyst provides another illustration:

It is so desirable for the psychoanalyst to remain on the less active side with the child patient that for her to knit is often a good device. The knitting should be on something for the patient so that he will not feel that the busy-work takes away from him. The knitting serves to occupy the therapist who may have an inclination to play with the child or the need to press the child into some significant productions. It also serves to modify the seductiveness of the analytical experience of the small patient, who has the exciting opportunity to have a mother figure all alone five hours a week intently engrossed with him and his ideas and encouraging him to express more. (Helen Arthur, "A Comparison of the Techniques Employed in Psychotherapy and Psychoanalysis of Children," *American Journal of Orthopsychiatry*, 22 [1952], pp. 493–494.)

position. In fact, we can expect that the more that is demanded from a subordinate in the way of delicacy, skill, and pure concentration, the more informal and friendly the superordinate is likely to become. If one person is to participate in a task as if he were an extension of another participant, opening himself up to the rapid and delicate feedback control that an individual ordinarily obtains only of and for himself, then, apparently, he must be favorably disposed to the person in command, for such cooperativeness is much easier to win than to exact.[8]

I would like to note here that the chief surgeon may feel obliged to introduce distractions as well as to dispel them. When the spontaneous engagement of the participants in the task activity itself seems likely to tax them too much, the chief surgeon may distract them, for example, by joking. This is just the reverse of the process previously described. Thus, at a point of high tenseness, when a large renal tumor had been completely exposed and was ready to be pierced by a draining needle, a chief surgeon lightly warned before he pierced: "Now don't get too close." Another instance of this easing process is found in the fact that the others often seem to look to the chief surgeon to mark the end of the critical phase of action and the beginning of a less critical phase, one that can be used for a general letdown in the sustained concentration of attention and effort. In order to set the tone for these functionally useful relaxations, at the end of a phase of action, the surgeon may stretch himself in a gawky, exaggerated, and clownish way and utter a supportive informality such as "okey-dokey" or "th'ar sh' be." Before the critical phase is begun, and after it has been terminated, he may engage others present in talk about last night's party, the recent ball game, or good places to fish.[9] And when the patient is being closed up and the critical work

---

I am told by Charlotte Green Schwartz that some male analysts knit or hook rugs during treatment of adult patients, in part, apparently, to divert enough attention to keep themselves from interrupting too frequently.

[8] This is nicely illustrated in multi-situated activity systems on board ship, where, it has been claimed, the one time when the captain unbends and uses easy language not ordinarily associated with his role is when an engine steersman must be counted on to respond exquisitely to steering directions from the helm.

By the same logic, however, we should be prepared for the fact that at times the task-management obligations of the individual may force him to draw back to the formal position accorded him and exact the full swift measure of his authority, for there are times when a flustered subordinate will be steadied better by a sharp negative sanction than by sympathy.

[9] Under strictest possible procedure, no talking would be tolerated except when technically necessary, since germs can apparently be spread through masks in this way. My own experience was in relatively informal hospitals where irrelevant talk and byplays did occur. Burling and Wilson report a similar experience. Presumably the medical traditions of different regions differ in this regard, as suggested by Eugene de Savitsch, *In Search of Complications* (New York: Simon and Schuster, 1940), pp. 374–375:

In a clinic or operating room almost anywhere in the world all would be silence, soft lights, and sustained tension. In France everybody chatters away as merrily as in a cafe. While a brain tumor, for instance, is removed, the surgeon, his assistants, and the audience—if any—argue over the merits of the present cabinet, disclose the shortcomings of their wives, and exchange advice about stocks and bonds.

is quite over, the chief surgeon may initiate and tolerate joking with nurses, bantering with them about their lack of proficiency or about the operation not being nearly over. If no male nurse is present to lift the patient from the operating table to the trolley, the chief surgeon, if he is still in the operating room, may gallantly brush aside the efforts of one of the nurses and insist on lifting the heaviest part of the patient, the middle, himself, acting now in the capacity of a protective male, not a medical person.

Just as the chief surgeon may mark the point where attentiveness may be usefully relaxed, so he, and sometimes others on the team, will put brackets around the central task activity with the result that the level of concern required for it will not be demanded of the team before matters actually get under way and after they have ended. This is nicely shown not merely in the ritual of tearing off one's gloves and immediately leaving the operating room, by which the chief surgeon tells the team that teacher is no longer checking up on them and they can relax, but also in the way in which the body is handled. During the operation, the body of the patient is the rightful focus of a great deal of respectful sustained consideration, technically based, especially in connection with the maintenance of asepsis, blood levels, and respiration. It is as if the body were a sacred object, regardless of the socioeconomic character of its possessor, but in this case the consideration given is rational as well as ritual. As might be expected, then, before and after the operation proper there can be observed minor acts of desacralization, whereby the patient is reduced to more nearly profane status. At the beginning of the task the surgeon may beat a tattoo on the leg of the anesthetized patient, and at the end he may irreverently pat the patient on the bottom, commenting that he is now better than new. The surgeon is not alone in this activity. While scrubbing the anesthetized patient, the nurse may lift up a foot by the toe and speak to it: "You're not sterile, are you?" In moving the now groggy patient from the operating table to the trolley for the trip to the recovery room, the anesthetist, taking charge of this relatively unskilled physical action, may obtain concerted effort from the other persons helping him by saying: "Ready, aim, fire." Similarly, in moving an anesthetized patient on his side for a thoracotomy, the anesthetist may say: "O.K., kids, are we ready to play flip flop? Ready? O.K."

In addition to maintaining the capacities and poise of other members of the team, the chief surgeon has, of course, an obligation to maintain his own. Moreover, he must be concerned not only with sustaining his own mobilization of personal resources, but also with the anxious attention that the other members of the team might give to this. If they feel he is about to lose his temper, or that he has lost his skill, they themselves can become extremely uneasy and inefficient. Thus, when the surgeon runs into trouble that could cause his teammates a distracting and suppressed concern over how he might react to his trouble, we find him engaging in quite standard strategies of tension management, sometimes concealing his own real concerns to do so. He alludes openly to the incident in such a way as to rob it of its capacity to distract the team.[10] When he drops an instrument, he may respond unseriously to his own action by a word such as "oopsadaisy." If he must give an order to one of his assistants which might leave the others not knowing if he were angry or not, he may deliver it in a false English accent, in adolescent slang, or in some other insulating way. Unable to find the right spot for a lumbar puncture, he may, after three tries, shake his head a little, as if to suggest that he, as a person sensitive to ideal standards, is still sensitive to them and yet in quiet control of himself, in short, that the implied discrediting of him has not made him lose poise.

Since the chief surgeon's own self-control is crucial in the operation, and since a question concerning it could have such a disquieting effect upon the other members of the team, he may feel obliged to demonstrate that he is in possession of himself, not merely at times of crisis and trouble, but even at times when he would otherwise be silent and so be providing no information one way or the other about his state of mind. Thus, when puzzled about what to do, he may ruminate half out loud, ingenuously allowing others present a close glimpse of his thoughts. During quite delicate tasks, he may softly sing incongruous undignified tunes such as "He flies through the air with the greatest of ease." In clamping hemostats, he may let them go from his fingers, flipping them back upon the patient's body in a neat row with the verve and control that parking attendants manifest while parking cars, or merry-go-round managers display in collecting tickets while moving around on the turning platform.

What we have here is a kind of "externalization" of such feelings and thoughts as are likely to give security and confidence to the other members of the team. This externalization, as well as the constant cutting back of any distractive concern that might have arisen for the team in the course of action, also provides a constant stimulus to team members' attentiveness and task engagement, in both ways helping to hold them to the task as usable participants. Some surgeons, in fact, maintain something of a running line of patter during the operation, suggesting that whenever there is teamwork, someone is likely to have the role function of "talking it up."

We see that the chief surgeon is something of a host to persons at his party, as well as the director of his operating team. He is under pressure (however he responds to this pressure) to make sure that those at his table feel good about what is happening so that whatever their capacities they can better exploit them. And to do this morale-maintaining job, at least in America, the surgeon makes use of and draws upon activities not expected of one in his dignified position. When he himself does not perform the clown function, he may encourage someone else, such as the intern or circulating nurse, to take on the job.

[10] For a general analysis of this view of tension, see "Fun in Games" in *Encounters.*

In discussing the special responsibilities of the chief surgeon and his frequent need to draw on informality in order to meet these responsibilities, it was implied that the superordinate present may have some special reasons for exhibiting role distance. A further comment should be added concerning the relation between role distance and social ranking.

It seems characteristic of the formalities of a role that adherence to them must be allowed and confirmed by the others involved in the situation; this is one of the basic things we mean by the notion that something is formal and official. Adherence to formalities seems to guarantee the *status quo* of authority and social distance; under the guidance of this style, one can be assured that the others will not be able to move in on one. Reversing the role point of view, we can see that adherence to the formalities one owes to others can be a relatively protective matter, guaranteeing that one's conduct will have to be accepted by the others, and, often, that it will not be difficult to dissociate one's purely covert personal attachments from one's role projection. Finally, it should be added that in general we assume that it is to the advantage of the subordinate to decrease distance from the superordinate and to the advantage of the latter to sustain or increase it.

From these considerations it should be apparent that the exercise of role distance will take on quite different meanings, depending on the relative rank of the individual who exercises it. Should a subordinate exercise role distance, this is likely to be seen as a sign of his refusal to keep his place (thereby moving toward greater intimacy with the superordinate, which the latter is likely to disapprove), or as rejection of authority,[11] or as evidence of low morale. On the other hand, the manifestation of role distance on the part of the superordinate is likely to express a willingness to relax the *status quo,* and this the subordinate is likely to approve because of its potential profitability for him. In the main, therefore, the expression of role distance is likely to be the prerogative of the superordinate in an interaction. In fact, since informality on the part of the inferior is so suspect, a tacit division of labor may arise, whereby the inferior contributes respect for the *status quo* on behalf of both parties, while the superior contributes a glaze of sociability that all can enjoy. Charm and colorful little informalities are thus usually the prerogatives of those in higher office, leading us mistakenly to assume that an individual's social graces helped bring him to his high position, instead of what is perhaps more likely, that the graces become possible for anyone who attains the office.[12] Hence, it is the surgeon, not the surgical nurse, who injects irony into

[11] For example, I know of a nurse who was transferred from an experimental surgery team, in part because she enacted simulated yawns, meant to be humorous, during the ticklish part of a delicate surgical technique, thereby showing role distance above her station.

[12] An empirical illustration of this is presented in an excellent paper by Rose Coser in which she demonstrates the special joking prerogatives of senior psychiatrists during ward meetings; see her "Laughter Among Colleagues," *Psychiatry,* 23 (1960), pp. 81–95. For further illustrations of role distance on the part of superordinates, see Ralph Turner, "The Navy Disbursing Officer as a Bureaucrat," *American Sociological Review,* 12 (1947), pp. 342–348.

medical etiquette. All of this, it may be added, fits other things we know about relations between unequals. It is the ship's captain who has a right to enter the territory of the ordinary seamen, the "fo'c'sle," not they to enter his. An officer has a right to penetrate the private life of a soldier serving under him, whereas the private does not have a similar right. In this connection, one student has been led to speak of the social distance between two individuals as being of different extent depending from whose place one starts.[13]

But, of course, subordinates can exercise much role distance, and not merely through grumbling. By sacrificing the seriousness of their claim to being treated as full-fledged persons, they can exercise liberties not given to social adults.

We can now see that with the chief surgeon on one side and the intern on the other there appears to be a standard distribution of role-distance rights and role-distance tendencies. The intern may sacrifice his character as a full and serious person, becoming, thereby, a half-child in the system, in return for which he is allowed to offend medical role requirements with impunity. The person with dominating status can also offend with impunity because his position gives others present a special reason for accepting the offense.

I would like to add that although the person who manifests much role distance may, in fact, be alienated from the role, still, the opposite can well be true: in some cases only those who feel secure in their attachment may be able to chance the expression of distance. And, in fact, in spite of interns, it appears that conformity to the prescriptive aspects of role often occurs most thoroughly at the neophyte level, when the individual must prove his competence, sincerity, and awareness of his place, leaving the showing of distance from a role to a time when he is firmly "validated" in that role.

Another pecularity should be mentioned. To express role-irrelevant idiosyncracies of behavior is to expose oneself to the situation, making more of oneself available in it than is required by one's role. The executive's family picture on his desk, telling us that he is not to be considered entirely apart from his loved ones, also tells us, in a way, that they are in this occupation with him, and that they might understand his having to work late or open up his house to politically wise sociability.

The differing bases of role distance displayed by the chief surgeon and by the intern imply a division of labor or role differentiation. The nursing personnel exhibit a similar kind of differentiation among themselves: the division of labor and responsibility between the scrub nurse and the circulating nurse is associated with a difference in manifestation of role distance. The scrub nurse, in addition to her continued task obligation during the operation, may feel obliged to maintain the role function of standard-maintainer,

[13] Donald MacRae, "Class Relationships and Ideology," *The Sociological Review*, n.s., 6 (1958), pp. 263–264.

policing the aseptic character of the order that is maintained, as well as keeping a Management's eye on the skills of the physicians. Any withdrawal of herself into the role of female might, therefore, jeopardize the situated system. The circulating nurse, on the other hand, has no such responsibilities, and, apparently, these sexual considerations can be displaced onto her. Further, not needing to be "in" the operation as must the scrub nurse, she can withdraw into herself, or into a conversation with the anesthetist or the nurses in the adjacent operating room, without jeopardizing matters. To place her in a female capacity does not reduce manpower. It is not surprising, therefore, that the circulating nurse, in addition to the intern, is allowed to be flighty— to act without character.

The division of role-function labor that I have described has a characteristic subtlety that should be mentioned again in conclusion. A person with a specialized task not only performs a service needed by the system but also provides a way of being, a selfhood, with which others in the system can identify, thus allowing them to sustain an image of themselves that would disrupt matters if sustained other than vicariously. The "good guy" informality of the chief surgeon can give his subordinates a feeling that they are not the sort to tolerate strict subordination, that in fact the surgeon must see this and has adjusted himself correspondingly, yet this is, of course, a vicarious rebelliousness carried out principally by the very agency against which one would ordinarily rebel. In the same way, the circulating nurse can establish the principle of female sexuality in which the surgical nurse can see her own reflection, even while the surgeon is calling her by a masculine last-name term of address and receiving a man-sized work contribution from her.

Some final points may now be mentioned concerning the function of role distance, now not merely in surgery but in situated systems in general.

First, by not demanding the full rights of his position, the individual finds that he is not completely committed to a particular standard of achievement; should an unanticipated discrediting of his capacity occur, he will not have committed himself and the others to a hopelessly compromised position. Second, it appears that social situations as such retain some weight and reality in their own right by drawing on role distance—on the margin of reservation the individual has placed between himself and his situated role.

An interesting confirmation of the functional significance of role distance in situated activity systems is to be had by examining situations where roles are played *at*.

There seems to be little difficulty in getting stage actors to portray a character who is inflated with pomposity or bursting with emotion, and directors often have to restrain members of the cast from acting too broadly. The actor is apparently pleased to express before a large audience a lack of reservation which he would probably blush to express off the stage. However, this willingness to embrace a staged role is understandable. Since the actor's performed character is not his real one, he feels no need to safeguard himself by hedging his taken stand. Since the staged drama is not a real one, overinvolvement will simply constitute the following of a script, not a threat to one's capacity to follow it. An acted lack of poise has none of the dysfunctions of real flustering.

More significant, there is the fact that in prisons and mental hospitals, where some inmates may constantly sustain a heroic edifice of withdrawl, uncooperativeness, insolence, and combativeness, the same inmates may be quite ready to engage in theatricals in which they enact excellent portraits of civil, sane, and compliant characters. But this very remarkable turnabout is understandable too. Since the staged circumstances of the portrayed character are not the inmate's real ones, he has no need (in the character's name) to exhibit distance from them, unless, of course, the script calls for it.

Becoming a policeman, a surgeon, a priest, or a nun often involves almost complete resocialization. This means that the recruit, the medical student, the seminarian, or the novice must go through a period of transition from well-learned role sets to new ones which may run counter to much of what has already been internalized. For some, such indoctrination is traumatic. For others, unhappy with routine life, becoming a police officer, a doctor, a minister, a nun—or a professional soldier—gives a new lease on life. Such is the case described by Melford S. Weiss.

As you read "Rebirth in the Airborne," think of other examples of voluntary resocialization to new ways of life. In Part Four we also consider examples of imposed resocialization, as is experienced by those incarcerated in a prison, committed to a mental hospital, or interned in a concentration camp.

Rebirth in the Airborne

MELFORD S. WEISS

When an American paratrooper first learns to jump, he does more than step out of an airplane. He steps into a new way of life. Furthermore, his training even takes note of this major transition in his life in a formal ceremonial manner. This training period—marked by pomp and circumstance, superstition and ritual—is what anthropologists refer to as a *rite of passage.*

Rites of passage are universal features of complex as well as simple societies. They mark critical changes in man's life cycle, such as birth, death, and initiation. The paratrooper training program can best be understood as an initiation, a form of entry into an elite group. The process is interwoven with magical and symbolic ritual practices. In one training unit, for example, each time the trainees enter the airplane, the jumpmaster draws a line on the ground in front of the entrance hatch with the toe of his boot. Each prospective jumper then stomps upon the line before entering the airplane to ensure a safe landing. Whether or not they actually believe in the practice (many do not) is of decidedly less importance than the fact that this ritual serves to bind the group together.

A paratrooper's training ends in a ceremonial climax. At the close of training it is customary in some military units to reenact the jumping procedure in a fashion symbolic of rebirth. Newly-qualified paratroopers are invited to a "prop blast" at the noncommissioned officers' club. There a wooden model of an airplane has been hastily rigged. The new initiates line up in jump formation inside the plane. They jump and land facing the jumpmaster, their instructor. He hands each a loving cup full of "blast juice." This must be quaffed within the count of "1000, 2000, 3000," the time between an actual jump from a plane and the opening of the chute. Failure to drain it to the dregs within the allotted span is called a "malfunction," the term for chute failure. The process must be repeated, perhaps three or four times, till success is achieved. Then the initiate is ritually one with his fellows.

INITIATION RITES

Rites of passage vary in different cultures, but according to Arnold Van Gennep a typical rite has three stages:

—*separation* from the former group or state;
—*transition* to the new;
—and, finally, *incorporation*.

In birth and death rites, for example, separation is emphasized most: "The Lord giveth, the Lord has taken away." In the case of paratrooper training the transitional phase is most important. The paratrooper rite described here is a composite of training programs of many groups from World War II to the present time.

The paratrooper school is inside a compound surrounded by barbed wire and guarded by sentries. In this compound the trainee is fed, trained, and occasionally entertained. He is allowed to go out in the evening but usually does so in the company of other troopers. Fraternization with the non-paratrooper world is not encouraged, but separation from the former civilian environment is only partial.

The transitional phase usually lasts three weeks. During the last week the candidate makes five practice jumps which mark stages in his progress toward final acceptance. Not all the jumps are equally important—the first and fifth are most significant.

Paratrooper training is officially a secular affair. But certain superstitious practices which are interwoven show that, in the broadest sense, it is also a religious rite. From the beginning of the transition period the trainees are subjected to continuous periods of anxiety. Since they are all volunteers with a strong emotional investment in success, these stresses serve to bind them more closely to one another and to the group they seek to enter. So do the "magical" devices they learn to use to relieve anxiety. These include the wearing of charms and fetishes, such as a girl friend's picture above the heart, a pair of sweat socks worn on a previous successful jump, or a replica of the "trooper wings" placed inside a boot.

Use of "sympathetic magic" is fostered by the paratrooper mythology to which the trainee is exposed during this stage. The following examples of paratrooper tales illustrate elements of both *mana* (a spiritual force independent of persons or spirits which explains success, excellence, and potency when these qualities are not otherwise explainable) and *taboo* (a prohibition based upon the assumption that disastrous consequences can be averted if certain acts are not performed):

"He was a jinx and was always present at any accident. I would never jump with him in my line. I once touched him before I was about to jump and pretended to be sick in order to avoid jumping that day. Nobody laughed at me when I told them the real reason."

A master jumper told this story: "When I was a youngster, I felt that should I ever lose my original set of wings I could never jump again. They had a natural magic about them which protected me. When I went home I put them in the bottom drawer of my mother's dresser. I knew they would be safe there!"

Legend maintains that the paratrooper compound is off limits, and one myth relates the unhappy story of the intoxicated soldier from another unit who tried to sneak into the compound and was found next morning with his face severely scratched. The soldier claimed that he was attacked by a small bird and then passed out. But paratroopers claim that the bird was in fact the "screaming eagle," the totemic symbol of the 101st Airborne Division.

During the transition period myth and magic help the trainee to identify with paratroopers in general and share their *esprit de corps*. This becomes a formidable force as airborne units are made up entirely of volunteers. Thus a man becomes a paratrooper by choice and remains one all his military life unless he disobeys a direct order to jump. As in the case of other select military units, paratroopers are bound to one another by pride in a common history and system of training. They consider themselves superior to all other such groups—not only in their military virtues, but in their vices as well. A paratrooper is supposed to be able to outdrink, outbrawl, and outwhore any other member of the armed forces.

THE JUMPOUT DROPOUT

Systems of initiation depend for their success upon how much the candidate wants to belong to the group. Sometimes, in the case of paratrooper training, he may not want to badly enough. A young man may decide he does not care to spend his active life plunging out of airplanes with nothing but the silkworm's art for support. Since all trainees are volunteers, this is technically no disgrace. All he has to do is request reassignment.

But because of the problem of preserving group morale the dropout is usually eliminated with almost indecent haste. Many instructors feel that to let him hang around will spread the "rot," and other failures or jumping accidents may result. When a would-be dropout says he wants out at the end of a training day, he is more than likely to be called to the orderly room during the next morning's formation. By the time the other trainees return from their midday meal he will have left the training area forever, usually to spend a month's KP duty in some non-elite holding company. For example one dropout said:

> I was scared and I knew it. I dared not let the others know, but I did not think I could hide it very long. We were listening to a master jumper telling us about his first jump and my stomach got queasy and I was sick. I told my sergeant I wanted out. I left the very next day.

If a trainee should quit during the training day, particularly with a public fuss, more brusque tactics may be used. One would-be paratrooper reports:

> I was fed up with this bastard. I made a scene and cursed the Army and shouted that you can shove the paratroopers. I yelled, "I quit." My training NCO rapidly approached me, ripped the patch from my shoulder, and cut the laces of my jump boots.

In some primitive societies those who fail the tests of manhood may be killed outright. The ripping of the patch and the cutting of the laces serves the same function symbolically. It signifies the separation of the dropout from his companions and thus binds the group more closely together, as does the knowledge that the failure is headed for KP or some other nonstatus duty.

As noted before, the transitional phase of paratrooper training has substages. These occur mainly after the first and fifth (last) practice jump. After the first there is no ceremony, but there is a change in the relationship between the trainees and the seasoned paratroopers. As soon as the jumping experience has been shared, the trainee begins to be treated with at least a modicum of respect by his instructors. Conversation in the barracks becomes less guarded. Before any mention of "spilling silk" or "flying a streamer" was avoided. Now jokes about jumping accidents and chute failures are freely bandied about.

The fifth jump is marked by a definite ritual. After the first four the trainee rolls his own chute. After the last he hands it to the platoon sergeant, who rolls it for him and places it in the supply truck. Then the NCO shakes his pupil's hand, congratulates him, and in some cases invites him to use his, the sergeant's, given name. This reversal of roles marks acceptance into the group. The same evening this is confirmed at a party at the enlisted men's club, usually off limits to officers. The paratroopers-to-be, including officer candidates, are invited to join in the drinking and usually do.

The whole transitional period in paratrooper training closely parallels initiation rites in both Western and non-Western societies. During this stage the initiate learns the formulas, gestures, and chants of the brotherhood. These include a paratrooper prayer and a paratrooper song. The latter is a gruesome chant in which the paratrooper verbalizes, jokingly, his fear of sudden and gory death. It is sung to the tune of "The Battle Hymn of the Republic":

Is everybody ready? cried the Sergeant, looking up.
Our hero feebly answered yes, as they stood him up.
He leapt right out into the blast, his static line unhooked.
O he ain't gonna jump no more!

There was blood upon the risers, there were brains upon the chute,
His intestines were a dangling from his paratrooper boots;
They picked him up still in his chute and poured him from his boots;
O he ain't gonna jump no more!

Chorus: *Glory gory what a helluva way to die!*
Glory gory what a helluva way to die!
Glory gory what a helluva way to die!
O he ain't gonna jump no more!

WINGS AND A THREE-DAY PASS

After transition comes incorporation in two stages—an official ceremony and the unofficial "prop blast" described earlier. The official ceremony is a colorful affair in the tradition of most military rituals. It marks the end of the rigorous training and is a welcome climax to weeks of agonizing tension. It takes place the day after the final (fifth) practice jump. The men in the training unit line up in alphabetical order; uniforms are smartly pressed, faces agonizingly clean shaven, and hair close cropped. They stand at attention while the post band plays the national anthem, followed by "Ruffles and Flourishes." The division flag flies just beneath Old Glory.

The men bow their heads as the post chaplain reads from the Bible. After a congratulatory speech the training commandant presents each man with his diploma. The division commandant passes through the ranks, reviews the troops, and pins "wings" to each man's chest. The chaplain delivers the closing benediction. The band continues to play military music and the men now assemble by training platoon and proudly march by the reviewing stand. As the soldiers reach the stand, they are saluted by the senior officers, and the new troopers return the salute. The men are then dismissed and given a three-day pass.

Many features of this ceremony have symbolic significance. The new paratrooper is being initiated into a special brotherhood within the military forces of an American, predominantly Christian, society. The chaplain's benediction gives the ceremony "divine sanction" and links it, however tenuously, with the prevailing Christian religion. The "American heritage" is reflected by the American flag and the national anthem. The polished boots, clean shaves, and close haircuts set up the image of the "clean-cut, all-American boy." The rest of the rite is military, with calculated differences. The marching, the salute, the respect for rank, and the three-day pass remind the paratrooper that he is a member of the armed forces. But the jump-school graduation certificate and the "wings" belong only to paratroopers and serve as permanent marks of that status.

The brotherhood of all troopers is symbolized by the formation itself. While the platoon is the standard military unit, on this one day the men line up in alphabetical order. This wipes out platoon distinctions and incorporates all the men in a pan-paratrooper sodality. Being saluted first by their superiors, against military protocol, shows the "troopers" that they now occupy a coveted status in the military.

Although the training NCO's are not required to attend, they are present throughout the ceremony. At the close they rush to congratulate the new members and welcome them into the brotherhood. The new status of the members has now been recognized and sanctioned by military society. With the evening's "prop blast" and its symbolic reenactment of the jumping process, the rite of passage is complete. The initiate is now wholly separated from his past life and "reborn" into a new, select brotherhood and a new way of life.

Suggested Readings

The Rites of Passage by Arnold Van Gennep (London, England: Routledge & Kegan Paul, 1960).

Essays in the Ritual of Social Relations, edited by Max Gluckman (Manchester, England: Manchester University Press, 1962).

Reader in Comparative Religion, 2nd ed., by William A. Lessa and Evon Z. Vogt (New York: Harper & Row, 1965).

Religion in Primitive Society by Edward Norbeck (New York: Harper & Row, 1961).

PART IV
COPING WITH CHANGE

Two popular books published in the late 1970s offered accounts and analyses of the rites of passage that all people must face as they grow up and grow older, at least in American society. *Passages* by Gail Sheehy and *The Seasons of a Man's Life* by Daniel J. Levinson et al. mapped out the courses frequently taken by American women and men as they sought to cope with the changes caused by social, economic, and physiological factors. In both volumes special attention is paid to "mid-life," a term that encompasses that time when youth has ended and the "golden age" is still a distant prospect. It is in that period that courtships and marriages take place and that the romance begins to fade; that most people settle into rather fixed career patterns; that the joys and chores of childrearing seem to consume an inordinate amount of time and then end as the children begin to go their own ways. It is in that period that some ask themselves, "Well, now what do I do for the next forty years?"

In Part Four, which includes an essay by Levinson and his colleagues and another by Sheehy, we explore the ways in which people deal with such realities. When one reads the first four articles, one is struck by the fact that, like it or not, many try to make do. They adjust to the end of romance, to empty nests, to lowered aspirations and expectations, even to "middle-aged spread." Others, however, have difficulty accepting the loss of youth. They seek something fresh, something different. Sometimes they abandon spouses or careers (or both). They return to school for new enlightenment and retraining. Many attempt to stay the hands of time by trying to compete with those much younger than they, by altering their lifestyles, their looks, their outlooks. They may try to sort out the confusions in their lives by joining encounter groups or visiting psychiatric counselors.

Normative changes wrought by social pressures, cultural expectations, or biological processes are not the only changes that occur in societies like that of the United States. Some changes are more blatantly political and, in a way, more personal, for they are imposed on specific individuals in the closed space of institutions rather than the more open realms of home and neighborhood and office. Such is the plight of those who are drafted into the military, committed to mental hospitals, sent to prison, or herded into concentration camps. While none of these is the exclusive concern of those in the middle years, we refer to them here and in the last selection in Part Four because there are interesting and important comparisons to be made between the problems of those who face changes that, although they seem inevitable, do not prevent them from controlling their own destinies (or even deciding, for example, that "life begins at forty") and the problems of those who face the far more wrenching reality of having no choice, of being stripped of their personae and having new ones imposed by others. Such intensive resocialization clearly represents the most extreme manifestation of society over self.

*The following essay provides a context for gaining a bet-
ter understanding of what Gail Sheehy called "the
middle passage" in her book* Passages.

*The essay itself, a cooperative venture of a group of
specialized social scientists, offers a progress report on
their thinking about early, middle, and late male
adulthood. They closely examine six stages of adulthood: leaving the family, getting into the adult world,
settling down, being one's own man, the mid-life transition, and restabilization. Note that the article deals
only with men, which explains why the fourth stage,
along with most of the article, is heavily male-oriented.
However, much of what is discussed applies to adult
women as well. The commentary at the end of the article relates several of the points covered to women.*

*As you read "Stages of Adulthood," think of how
accurately it reflects the changing character of the lives
of people you know, including parents and friends who
are about to enter middle or late adulthood.*

Stages of Adulthood

DANIEL J. LEVINSON, CHARLOTTE M. DARROW, EDWARD B. KLEIN, MARIA H. LEVINSON, AND BRAXTON McKEE

This is not a formal research report, but a statement of thinking and progress,
as of May 1972. We are in the third year of a projected four-year study. We
have obtained interview and TAT material on a sample of 40 men, all of
whom are currently aged 35–45. There are 10 men in each of four occupational groups: blue-and white-collar workers in industry; business executives;
academic biologists; and novelists. Each man was seen 6–10 times for a total
of 10–20 hours over a period of 2–3 months. We had a single follow-up interview with most of the men about two years after the initial interviews. The
focus is on the current status of our efforts to construct a theory of adult male
development over the age span of about 20–45. We hope in further study to
get beyond that, but that's where we are now. In view of the comments that

have been made during the discussions of the previous papers, which have dealt heavily with problems of research design, measurement, and statistical analysis, let me say in advance that I shall not talk about methodology or data.

DEVELOPMENTAL PERIODS IN THE ADULT LIFE COURSE

We have found it convenient to distinguish several gross chronological periods in the adult life course: early adulthood, roughly ages 20–40; middle adulthood, ages 40–60; and late adulthood, age 60 + . We are studying early adulthood and the "mid-life transition"—that is, the several years on either side of 40 that constitute a transitional period between early and middle adulthood.

These are descriptive time units that we use to begin making developmental distinctions within adult life. Something even as simple as this is necessary because of the tremendous neglect of development and socialization in the main adult years, roughly 20–65, in psychology, psychiatry, sociology, and so on. We speak as though development goes on to age 6, or perhaps to age 18; then there is a long plateau in which random things occur; and then at around 60 or 65 "aging" begins.

There is little work in sociology on adult socialization. In psychology there are the concepts and "psychohistorical" approach of Erikson and the extensive work of Jungian depth psychology, which is almost totally ignored by the academic disciplines. Like Jung and Erikson, we assume that there is something we can call adult development, that there is a psychosocial evolution just as in pre-adult life, and that we won't understand adults and the changes they go through in their lives if we don't have a conception of what is intrinsic to adulthood. We can then see how derivatives of childhood operate to facilitate or hinder certain kinds of development.

One of our chief theoretical aims is to formulate a sociopsychological conception of the life course and the various developmental periods, tasks, structures, and processes within it. There are, of course, wide individual and group differences in the concrete life course, as our findings show. At a more conceptual level, however, we are interested in generating and working with hypotheses concerning *relatively universal, genotypic, age-linked, adult developmental periods* within which variations occur. As we conceive of these periods, their origins lie both in the nature of man as a biosocial and biopsychological organism, and in the nature of society as an enduring multigenerational form of collective life. The periods do not represent simply an unfolding of maturational potentials from within; they are thus different from the Freudian or Piagetan stages of childhood development, which are seen largely as an internal unfolding. Nor do they simply represent stages in a career sequence as shaped by an occupational, educational, or familial system. In other words, the periods are not simply a function of adult socializing systems, although these systems play an important part in defining timetables and in shaping one's course through them.

We are trying to develop an embracing sociopsychological conception of male adult developmental periods, within which a variety of biological, psychodynamic, cultural, social-structural, and other timetables operate in only partial synchronization. (It could be an important further step to do similar studies of women and to learn about similarities and differences between the sexes under various social conditions.) The remaining sections of this paper set forth our theoretical conception of these periods from roughly age 20 to 45. Within the framework of this overall theory we shall note some illustrative concepts, findings, and areas of exploration. Again, we emphasize that this is a report of work in progress and by no means a final statement.[1]

LEAVING THE FAMILY (LF)

We conceive of Leaving the Family (LF) as a period of transition between adolescent life, centered in the family of origin, and entry into the adult world. In our sample, LF ordinarily occupies a span of some 3–5 years, starting at age 16–18 and ending at 20–24. It is a transitional period in the sense that the person is half in and half out of the family: he is making an effort to separate himself from the family, to develop a new home base, to reduce his dependence on familial support and authority, and to regard himself as an adult making his way in the adult world.

The separation from the family proceeds along many lines. In its external aspects, it involves changes such as moving out of the familial home, becoming financially less dependent, and getting into new roles and living arrangements in which one is more autonomous and responsible. In its internal aspects, it involves an increase in self-parent differentiation and in psychological distance from the family. Of course, these processes start earlier and continue well beyond the LF period. We say that someone is in this period when there is a roughly equal balance between "being in" the family and "moving out." From the point of view of ego development, the young man is in the stage that Erikson has identified as Identity versus Role Diffusion.

LF ordinarily begins around the end of high school (graduation or dropping out). Those who enter college or the military have a new, institutional life situation that is in many respects intermediate between the family and fully adult life in the community. The institution constitutes a home base providing some degree of structure, control, support, and maintenance. It also

---

[1] In May 1973, as we do the final editing of this manuscript for publication, we wish to note that the theory has been elaborated and modified in certain respects but the general framework continues to hold.

provides spheres of autonomy and privacy in which the young person is largely responsible for himself and can strike out in new paths. He has increasing opportunities to form relationships, as a compeer, with adults of various ages and thus to begin experiencing himself as an adult who is part of that world (rather than an adolescent standing reluctantly at the edge of it).

Those who move directly from high school into the labor force—and this is most often the case within the working-class population—have no institutional matrix to shape the transition into adult life. These young men do, nonetheless, go through the LF transition. They may continue to live at home for several years on a semi-boarder status, "leading their own lives" and yet remaining in some ways subject to parental authority and integrated within the family network. This is a common pattern among ethnic groups with strong communal and extended family bonds. Often the young man works with his father or relatives during this period. If he marries during LF, the couple may live for some time with one spouse's parents or relatives. The initial work history has the same transitional character. For several years (in some cases, permanently) the young man has no genuine occupation. He works at various jobs and acquires a variety of skills. But, lacking seniority, influence, and broader competence, he tends to be given the worst jobs in the worst shifts and to have the least job security. Even though a young man in this position may be economically self-sufficient and living on his own, he is still on the boundary between the family and the fully adult world; and getting across this boundary is his major developmental task.

The LF period ends when the balance shifts—when one has for the most part separated from the family (though further work on separation-connectedness in relation to family continues for many years, if not forever) and has begun to make a place for himself in the adult world.

GETTING INTO THE ADULT WORLD (GIAW)

The period we call Getting into the Adult World (GIAW) begins when the center of gravity of one's life shifts from the family of origin (or an equivalent authoritative-protective social matrix) to a new home base and an effort to form an adult life of one's own. This period ordinarily starts in the early 20's and extends until roughly age 27–29. It is a time of exploration and provisional commitment to adult roles, memberships, responsibilities, and relationships. The young man tries to establish an occupation, or an occupational direction, consistent with his interests, values, and sense of self. He begins to engage in more adult friendships and sexual relationships, and to work on what Erikson has termed the ego stage of Intimacy versus Aloneness.

The overall developmental task of the GIAW period is to explore the available possibilities of the adult world, to arrive at an initial definition of oneself as an adult, and *to fashion an initial life structure* that provides a viable link between the valued self and the wider adult world.

The concept of life structure is of central importance in our thinking. In its external aspects it refers to the individual's overall pattern of roles, memberships, interests, condition, and style of living, long-term goals, and the like—the particular ways in which he is plugged into society. In its internal aspects, life structure includes the personal meanings these have for the individual, as well as the inner identities, core values, fantasies, and psychodynamic qualities that shape and infuse one's engagement in the world and are to some degree fulfilled and changed by it. Traditional behavioristic and sociological approaches tend to emphasize the external aspects and to ignore the internal. Conversely, depth psychological approaches tend to emphasize the internal dynamics without taking sufficiently into account the nature of the sociocultural world and the individual's actual engagement in it. Our approach is to use concepts such as life structure to provide an initial focus on the *boundary between individual and society*; from this base, we can then move outward to a fuller examination of the social world and inward to a fuller examination of the personality.

GIAW is, like all entry periods, a time of exploration and initial choice. It involves, to varying degrees and in varying sequences, the processes of exploratory searching, of making provisional choices, of further exploratory testing through which the rightness of an initial choice is assessed and alternatives are considered, of increasing commitment to certain choices and the construction of a more integrated, stable life structure.

There are wide variations in the course, duration, and outcome of this period. These are a few of the patterned sequences we have found:

a. Perhaps the most frequent pattern we find is that of the man who makes a provisional commitment to an occupation and goes through the initial stages of a career. That is, during the 20's he is establishing a tentative structure, including an occupational choice and the beginnings of commitment to an occupational identity. Then, somewhere in the interval between age 28 and 32, he enters a transitional period in which he works on the questions: Shall I make a deeper commitment to this occupation and build a stable life structure around it? or I still have a chance to change; shall I take it? There is a kind of bet that's being made here, at around age 30. Many of our subjects remain in the occupation initially chosen in their 20's; they get married or reaffirm the existing marriage, and they enter a new period, Settling Down.

b. In some cases, the man at around 30 decides that his initial occupational choice was not the right one—that it is too constraining, or that it is a violation or betrayal of an early dream which now has to be pursued, or that he does not have the talent to succeed in it—and he makes a major shift in occupation and in life structure, sometimes including marriage. In this pattern the man makes a provisional structure in his 20's and then makes a moderate or drastic change at about 30.

c. Still another variant is that of the man who during his 20's lives a rather transient, unsettled life. He then feels a desperate need at around 30 to get more order and stability into his life. It is our tentative hypothesis that if a man does not reach a significant start toward settling down by about age 34, his chances of forming a reasonably satisfying life strucutre, and one that can evolve in his further development, are quite small. A number of movies in the last few years have depicted this particular kind of age 30 crisis. One is *Five Easy Pieces*. Another is *Getting Straight*, which is about an ex-college radical who has been in a transient, wandering stage during his 20's. Around 30 his tentative occupational choice is to become a high school teacher, and he makes an effort which he and the educational establishment collude to destroy.

A concept of great value in the analysis of the GIAW period is the *dream*. Many men, though certainly not all, enter adulthood with a dream or vision of their own future. This dream is usually articulated within an occupational context—for example, becoming a great novelist, winning the Nobel Prize (a common dream of our biologists), contributing in some way to human welfare, and so on. Where such a dream exists, we are exploring its nature and vicissitudes over the life course. Major shifts in life direction at subsequent ages are often occasioned by a reactivation of the sense of betrayal or compromise of the dream. That is, very often in the crises that occur at age 30, 40, or later a major issue is the reactivation of a guiding dream, frequently one that goes back to adolescence or the early 20's, and the concern with its failure. We are also interested in the antecedents and consequences of not having a dream, because the dream can be such a vitalizing force for adult development.

A second, crucial concept is that of the *transitional period*. The time around 28–32 seems to be a transitional period, a link between the termination of GIAW and the onset of the next period. We are trying to be very specific about age-linkages in order to counteract the strong tendency to assume that in adulthood very little is age-linked because development isn't occurring. We pursue tenaciously the possibility that the age-linkages are stronger than has been recognized. The Age 30 Transition, and others like it at different points in the life course, may occasion considerable turmoil, confusion, and struggle with the environment and within oneself; or it may involve a more quiet reassessment and intensification of effort. But it is marked by important changes in life structure and internal commitments, and presages the next stage in development.

SETTLING DOWN

The next period is Settling Down (SD). As noted above, this period ordinarily begins in the early 30's. The individual now makes deeper commitments; invests more of himself in his work, family, and valued interests; and within the framework of this life structure, makes and pursues more long-range plans and goals.

The imagery and meaning of Settling Down are multifaceted. One aspect of this period involves *order*, stability, security, control. The man establishes his niche in society, digs in, builds a nest, and pursues his interests within the defined pattern. This aspect may be stronger or weaker in a given case. A second, contrasting aspect has more the quality of *making it*. This involves planning, striving, moving onward and upward, having an inner timetable that contains major goals and way stations and ages by which they must be reached. The executive has to get into the corporate structure by age 40 or has to be earning at least $50,000 by 40; the assistant professor has to get tenure by 40; and so on.

So these are two aspects of SD. One has more to do with *down, in, order;* the other has more to do with *up, mobility, ambition.* Antithetical to both of these is the disposition to be free, unfettered, not tied to any structure no matter how great its current satisfaction nor how alluring its future promise, always open to new possibilities, ready to soar, wander, quest in all directions as the spirit moves one. We see the surgence of this disposition in the present state of society. This disposition is usually not predominant during the early SD period, but this does not mean it is necessarily absent nor that it may not in time reassert itself. Indeed, it frequently reappears toward the end of SD.

The SD period lasts until the late 30's or early 40's, when various internal and external changes bring on new developments. We shall note just a few major characteristics of this period. In creating an integrated life structure, one can utilize only parts of one's self, and this means that important parts of the self are left out. A myth supported by most theories of pre-adult development is that at the end of adolescence you get yourself together and, as a normal, mature adult, you enter into a relatively stable, integrated life pattern that can continue more or less indefinitely. This is a rather cruel illusion since it leads people in early adulthood to believe that they are, or should be, fully adult and settled, and that there are no major crises or developmental changes ahead. The structure one creates in SD cannot fulfill or reflect all of oneself. Parts of the self are repressed or simply left dormant. At some point the life structure must be enlarged, reformed, or radically restructured in order to express more of the self.

One reason the SD structure must change is that it is based to some degree upon illusions—illusions about the importance and meaning of achieving one's occupational goals, about one's relationships with significant others, about what it is one truly wants in life, and so on. A *de-illusioning* process— by which we mean the reduction or removal of illusions and not a cynical disillusionment—is an important aspect of post-SD development. For example, the man in the early SD period tends to regard himself as highly autonomous. He is making his own way, he is not a child anymore, his parents are not telling him what to do, he is on his own. One of his illusions is that he is, in fact, freed of what we would call tribal influences. In actuality, however, the ambitions and the goal-seeking of the 30's are very much tied in with tribal influences. We seek to a large extent what the institutions and reference groups important to us are helping us define. We may be more free of our parents, but we find or invent others who guide us, protect us, tell us what to do. Toward the end of SD, a new step is taken.

BECOMING ONE'S OWN MAN

The next step is Becoming One's Own Man, BOOM. Calling this the BOOM time has a certain metaphorical rightness. We are now inclined to regard BOOM not as a separate period but as a time of peaking and culmination of the Settling Down period and a connecting link to the Mid-Life Transition.

BOOM tends to occur in the middle to late 30's, typically in our sample around 35–39. It represents the high point of early adulthood and the beginning of what lies beyond. A key element in this period is the man's feeling that, no matter what he has accomplished to date, he is not sufficiently his own man. He feels overly dependent upon and constrained by persons or groups who have authority over him or who, for various reasons, exert great influence upon him. The writer comes to recognize that he is unduly intimidated by his publisher or too vulnerable to the evaluations of certain critics. The man who has successfully risen through the managerial ranks with the support and encouragement of his superiors now finds that they control too much and delegate too little, and he impatiently awaits the time when he will have the authority to make his own decisions and to get the enterprise really going. The untenured faculty member imagines that once he has tenure he will be free of all the restraints and demands he's been acquiescing to since graduate school days. (The illusions die hard!)

The sense of constraint and oppression may occur not only in work but also in marriage and other relationships. We have been greatly impressed by the role of the mentor, and by developmental changes in relationships with mentors and in the capability to be a mentor. The word *mentor* is sometimes used in a primarily external sense—an adviser, teacher, protector—but we use the term in a more complex psychosocial sense. The presence or absence of mentors is, we find, an important component of the life course during the 20's and 30's. The absence of mentors is associated with various kinds of developmental impairments and with problems of individuation in mid-life.

The mentor is ordinarily 8 to 15 years older than the mentee. He is enough older to represent greater wisdom, authority, and paternal qualities, but near enough in age or attitudes to be in some respects a peer or older brother rather than in the image of the wise old man or distant father. He may be a teacher, boss, editor, or experienced co-worker. He takes the younger man under his wing, invites him into a new occupational world, shows him around, imparts his wisdom, cares, sponsors, criticizes, and bestows his blessing. The teaching and the sponsoring have their value, but the blessing is the crucial element.

The younger man, in turn, feels appreciation, admiration, respect, gratitude, love, and identification. The relationship is lovely for a time, then ends in separation arising from a quarrel, or death, or a change in circumstances. Following the separation, the processes of internalization are enhanced, since internalization is increased by loss, and the personality of the mentee is enriched as he makes the valued qualities of the mentor more fully a part of himself. In some respects the main value of the relationship is created after it ends, but only if there was something there when it was happening. This is probably true of psychotherapy as well.

The number of mentor relationships in an individual's life does not vary widely. Few men have more than three or four, and perhaps the modal numbers are none and one. The duration of the intense mentor relationship is also not extremely variable, perhaps 3–4 years as an average and 10–12 years as the upper limit. When this relationship ends, the pair may form a more modest friendship after a cooling-off period. The ending of the mentor relationship may take a rather peaceful form, with gradual loss of involvement. More often, however, and especially during the 30's, termination is brought about by increasing conflict or by forced separation, and brings in its wake intense feelings of bitterness, rancor, grief, abandonment, and rejuvenation in the mentee.

The final giving up of all mentors by those who have had them tends to occur in the middle or late 30's. One does not have mentors after 40. One may have friendships or significant working relationships after this, but the mentor relationship in its more developed form is rare, at least in our sample and in our life experience. It is given up as part of Becoming One's Own Man. The person who was formerly so loved and admired, and who was experienced as giving so much, comes now to be seen as hypercritical, oppressively controlling, seeking to make one over in his own image rather than fostering one's independence and individuality; in short, as a tyrannical and egocentric father rather than a loving, enabling mentor. Among the more dramatic examples of this are Freud's relationships with Breuer and Fliess, and Jung's with Freud.

There are clearly irrational elements in this process, such as the reactivation and reworking of Oedipal conflicts, which have their origins in childhood. To focus solely on these, however, is to restrict our vision and to miss the adult developmental functions of the relationship and its termination. Whatever its Oedipal or early childhood-derived meanings, the relationship with the mentor has crucial adult meanings as well. It enables the young man to relate *as an adult* with another man who regards him as an adult and who welcomes him into the adult world on a relatively (but not completely) mutual and equal basis.

The young man must in time reject this relationship, but this is largely because it has served its purpose. He is ready to take a further step in becoming his own man: to give up being a son in the little boy sense and a young man in the apprentice-disciple-mentee sense, and to move toward assuming more fully the functions of mentor, father, and peer in relation to other adults. This kind of developmental achievement is of the essence of adulthood and needs to be studied. It is probably impossible to become a mentor without first having been a mentee.

Relationships of this kind are probably also of crucial importance in initiating and working on the ego stage of *generativity versus stagnation* and its attendant virtue, *caring* (for adults). Erikson has identified this stage as beginning at around 40 and as involving one's relationship to future generations in general and to the next generation of adults in particular. This goes beyond caring about one's small children, which one ordinarily has to learn in the 20's. The issue now is caring about adults, being generative in relation to adults, taking responsibility in the adult world, and getting over being a boy in the adult world. We are saying that one can't get very far with this before age 40 and that the BOOM time of the late 30's is the beginning of work on it.

During BOOM a man wants desperately to be affirmed by society in the roles that he values most. He is trying for that crucial promotion or other recognition. At about age 40—we would now say within the range of about 39 to 42—most of our subjects fix on some key event in their careers as carrying the ultimate message or their affirmation or devaluation by society. This event may be a promotion or new job—it's of crucial importance whether one gets to be vice-president of a company, or full professor in a department, or foreman or union steward. It may involve a particular form of symbolic success: writing a best seller or a prize-winning novel, being recognized as a scientist or executive or craftsman of the first rank, and so on. This event is given a magical quality. If the outcome is favorable, one imagines, then all is well and the future is assured. If it is unfavorable, the man feels that not only his work but he as a person has been found wanting and without value.

Since the course and outcome of this key event take several (perhaps 3–6) years to unfold, many men at around 40 seem to be living, as one of our subjects put it, in a state of suspended animation. During the course of the waiting, the next period gets under way.

THE MID-LIFE TRANSITION

The next period we call the Mid-Life Transition. A *developmental transition*, as we use the term, is a turning point or boundary region between two periods of greater stability. A transition may go relatively smoothly or may involve considerable turmoil. The Mid-Life Transition occurs whether the individual succeeds or fails in his search for affirmation by society. At 38 he thinks that if he gains the deserved success, he'll be all set. The answer is, he will not. He is going to have a transition whether he is affirmed or not; it is only the form that varies.

The central issue is not whether he succeeds or fails in achieving his goals. The issue, rather, is what to do with the *experience of disparity* between what he has gained in an inner sense from living within a particular structure and what he wants for himself. The sense of disparity between "what I've reached at this point" and "what it is I really want" instigates a soul-searching for "what it is I really want."

To put it differently, it is not a matter of how many rewards one has obtained; it is a matter of the *goodness of fit between the life structure and the self*. A man may do extremely well in achieving his goals and yet find his success hollow or bittersweet. If, after failing in an important respect, he comes primarily to castigate himself for not being able to "make it," then he is having a rough time but he is not having a mid-life crisis. He just regrets failure. He is having a crisis to the extent that he questions his life structure and feels the stirrings of powerful forces within himself that lead him to modify or drastically to change the structure.

In making the choices out of which the Settling Down structure was built, he drew upon and lived out certain aspects of himself: fantasies, values, identities, conflicts, internal "object relationships," character traits, and the like. At the same time, other essential aspects of the self were consciously rejected, repressed, or left dormant. These excluded components of the self—"other voices in other rooms," in Capote's vivid image—now seek expression and clamor to be heard.

We shall note briefly some of the major issues within the Mid-Life Transition: (a) The sense of *bodily decline* and the more vivid recognition of one's *mortality*. This brings the necessity to confront one's mortality and to deal in a new way with wounds to one's omnipotence fantasies, to overcome illusions and self-deceptions which relate to one's sense of omnipotence. It also brings greater freedom in experiencing and thinking about one's own and others' deaths, and greater compassion in responding to another's distress about decline, deformity, death, loss and bereavement. (b) The sense of *aging*, which means to be old rather than young. The Jungian concepts of puer and senex as archetypes that play a significant part in the mid-life individuation process are important here. (c) The polarity of *masculine and feminine*. Ordinarily in man's Settling Down structure masculinity is predominant; the emergence and integration of the more feminine aspects of the self are more possible at mid-life. During the mid-life period there is often a flowering of fantasies about various kinds of women, especially the maternal (nurturing and/or destructive) figures and the younger, erotic figures. These fantasies do not represent simply a belated adolescence, a final surge of lasciviousness, or self-indulgence or dependence (though they may have these qualities in part). The changing relationships to women may also involve the beginnings of a developmental effort. The aim of this effort is to free oneself more completely from the hold of the boy-mother relationship and to utilize one's internal relationships with the erotic transformative feminine as a means of healing old psychic wounds and of learning to love formerly devalued aspects of the self. It is the changing relation to the self that is the crucial issue at mid-life.

RESTABILIZATION AND THE BEGINNING OF MIDDLE ADULTHOOD

For most men the Mid-Life Transition reaches its peak sometime in the early 40's, and in the middle 40's there is a period of Restabilization. There seems to be a 3–4-year period at around age 45 in which the Mid-Life Transition comes to an end and a new life structure begins to take shape and to provide a basis for living in middle adulthood.

We are not presenting this as the last developmental change or the one in which everything will be resolved. For many men little is resolved, and the chickens come home to roost later. But it is a time both of possibility for developmental advance and of great threat to the self. Men such as Freud, Jung, Eugene O'Neill, Frank Lloyd Wright, Goya, and Gandhi went through a profound crisis at around 40 and made tremendous creative gains through it. There are also men like Dylan Thomas, F. Scott Fitzgerald, and Sinclair Lewis, who could not manage this crisis and who destroyed themselves in it. Many men who don't have a crisis at 40 become terribly weighted down and lose the vitality that one needs to continue developing through adulthood. Arthur Miller's play *The Price* tells something of the crisis of a man at 50: the sense of stagnation he has because of what he didn't do earlier, especially at 40 when he considered changing his life structure and didn't; he is now sinking in it.

We regard the Restabilization, then, as an initial outcome of the Mid-Life Transition. We are examining various forms of Restabilization and considering their implications for an understanding of the possibilities and problems of middle adulthood.

COMMENTARY

ZUBIN: After such a literary and poetic description of life stages, a hard-bitten differential psychologist like me shouldn't really say anything. However, I have to give a testimonial, I believe he's been reading my autobiography. It is so true! Yet I have enough egocentricity to wonder whether all people are like me—aren't there any individual differences left? I mean, are there not some differences, even within his own group, which could be documented? As Levinson was talking, I began to ask myself, What other classification of stages of man would I have adopted in trying to make sense out of these data? Of course, one can go back to Ethics of the Fathers who had about thirteen stages of man, Shakespeare who had several, Freud who had at least three, and Erik Erikson, Jean Piaget, etc. Mightn't you take a crack at showing what other options are open and what similarities and differences you would have got if you had tried different frameworks?

STIERLIN: Levinson has beautifully shown the complexity of a badly neglected life phase. I would like to add a few comments from my own research, which is a study of underachievers who were high risks for schizophrenia and other serious psychopathology. We conducted family therapy from three months to two years. We followed up the *S*s' parents, becoming increasingly interested in how these parents tried to solve their life crises, and how their life crises affected the separation of their children from the home. For example, we found that parents can get so bogged down with resolving aspects of their middle-age-specific tasks or crises that children are experienced as nuisances and are expelled, or at least insidiously neglected. Many of these children in our sample ran away in a casual, drifting manner (in contrast to other runaways who gave more evidence of inner turmoil [Stierlin, in press]). But other children appeared "delegated" to fulfill aspects of the parents' unresolved life crises. The word *delegate* very nicely conveys two aspects. It conveys, first, "to send out," and, second, to bestow with a mission. Thus, the delegate, while sent out, is also held back, as he remains beholden to the sender. His mission can be to experiment on behalf of the parent. For example, a father who is constantly preoccupied with breaking away from his job or breaking away from a stifling marriage, now encourages his son to experiment with things he is afraid to do himself but is completely preoccupied with. The boy will have a sort of scout function. He runs away, but he comes back and feeds the parent the needed information or enacts some aspect of his (the father's) developmental task. At the other extreme, there are parents who try to solve various aspects of the middle-aged crises you have outlined, holding onto the adolescent in an extremely tight manner. I call these the binding parents. Binding parents maintain on various levels a symbiotically clinging, sucking type of relationship, as salvation for their life crises. They hold on for dear life to what the adolescent offers them. This accounts for a very different kind of separation from the home—a dynamic dilemma which I have outlined in its various ramifications (Stierlin, 1972; Stierlin, Levi, & Savard, 1971; Stierlin & Ravenscroft, 1972).

JESSICA SCHAIRER: As you spoke, I could see that many of the people around me felt that your paper struck very close to home. While not affecting me in the same way, something in what you said is relevant to my situation, which I would like you to think about. Epstein (1970), in a paper on the participation of women in the professions, found that the lack of a mentor is what holds so many women back in professional development. Your whole paper seems to show, almost categorically, that it should be theoretically impossible for a woman to have a mentor in a professional field. This is a sociological problem which people here should think of as professionals and as life historians—even though your paper, like so many others, specifically addresses itself only to men.

LEVINSON: I endorse that. Having more women in senior positions in professional life in the university would have a number of functions. It would give female students female mentor figures. It would give male students female mentor figures, which might help them. I'm greatly indebted to the female mentors that I was lucky enough to have. And it would help to overcome that whole polarization of masculine and feminine with which we struggle so.

SCHAIRER: Was I correct in thinking that your paper says that theoretically it should be impossible because of the psychodynamics of the mentor relationship?

LEVINSON: Well, a man can be a genuine mentor to younger women. I must say that I have worked fairly hard at that myself, and I'm sure Harry Murray could tell stories of his functioning as a mentor. But it's a challenge because the older man who is in that position with, say female graduate students or students in professional school has to be careful that his conscious or unconscious sexism doesn't lead him to make the female student into a little girl, rather than welcoming her into the peer relationship.

Selected References

Brim, O. G., & Wheeler, S. *Socialization after childhood*. New York: Wiley, 1966.

Buhler, C. The curve of life as studied in biographies. *Journal of Applied Psychology*, 1955, 19, 405–409.

Cain, L. Life course and social structure. In R. E. L. Faris (Ed.), *Handbook of modern sociology*. Chicago: Rand-McNally, 1964.

Campbell, J. (Ed.) *The portable Jung*. New York: Viking, 1971.

Epstein, C. F. Encountering the male establishment: Sex-status limits on women's careers in the professions. *American Journal of Sociology*, 1970, 75, 965–982.

Erikson, E. H. Identity and the life cycle. *Psychological Issues*, 1959, 1 (1).

_____. *Gandhi's truth*. New York: Norton, 1969.

Jaques, E. Death and the mid-life crisis. *International Journal of Psycho-Analysis*, 1965, 46, 502–514.

Jung, C. G. *Memories, dreams, reflections*. New York: Pantheon, 1963.

Neugarten, B. L. (Ed.) *Middle age and aging: A reader in social psychology*. Chicago: University of Chicago Press, 1968.

Stierlin, H. Family dynamics and separation patterns of potential schizophrenics. In Y. Alanen (Ed.), *Proceedings of fourth international symposium on psychotherapy of schizophrenia*. Amsterdam: Excerpta Medica, 1972. Pp. 169–179.

———. A family perspective on adolescent runaways. *Archives of General Psychiatry,* in press.

———, Levi L. D., & Savard, R. J. Parental perceptions of separating children. *Family Process,* 1971, 10, 411–427.

Stierlin, H., & Ravenscroft, K., Jr. Varieties of adolescent "separation conflicts." *British Journal of Medical Psychology,* 1972, 45, 299–313.

NOTE: There are excellent biographies and autobiographies of persons such as Sigmund Freud, Eugene O'Neill, Bertrand Russell, Henry James, James Joyce, and F. Scott Fitzgerald. There are also novels and plays about men in the mid-life transition, often written by men during or just following their own mid-life transitions—for example, *The Iceman Cometh* (O'Neill), *Who's Afraid of Virginia Woolf?* (Albee), *The Tempest* (Shakespeare), *The Man Who Cried I Am* (Williams), *Chimera* (Barth), and *Herzog* (Bellow). Works of this kind are of great value, both in forming a theory of adult development and in testing and extending our present theory.

In "Setting Off on the Midlife Passage," writer Gail Sheehy offers a more personal, less analytic view of what Daniel Levinson and his colleagues discussed in the preceding selection. Sheehy, who focuses on both men and women, stresses the fears and anxieties of those who sense that time is beginning to run out, that they are no longer young, and that the dreams of earlier days are rapidly fading. Yet, like Levinson, Sheehy ends on a hopeful note by presenting the possibility of change and renewal in the middle years.

As you read this selection from Gail Sheehy's book Passages, *try to remember the preceding stages and the various roles men and women must learn to play as they move down the road of life.*

Setting Off on the Midlife Passage

GAIL SHEEHY

The middle of the thirties is literally, the midpoint of life. The halfway mark. No gong rings, of course. But twinges begin. Deep down a change begins to register in those gut-level perceptions of safety and danger, time and no time, aliveness and stagnation, self and others. It starts with a vague feeling . . .

I have reached some sort of meridian in my life. I had better take a survey, reexamine where I have been, and reevaluate how I am going to spend my resources from now on. Why am I doing all this? What do I really believe in?

Underneath this vague feeling is the fact, as yet unacknowledged, that there is a down side to life, a back of the mountain, and that *I have only so much time before the dark to find my own truth.*

As such thoughts gather thunder, the continuity of the life cycle is interrupted. They usher in a decade that can be called, in the deepest sense, the Deadline Decade. Somewhere between 35 and 45 if we let ourselves, most of us will have a full-out authenticity crisis.

We see the dark at the end of the tunnel first. The apprehension is often sudden and sharp. We don't know what to do with it or even what "it" is; no young person really believes his end will come. The first time that idea breaks through, no matter how sound the state of our health and how substantial our position, most of us become intensely preoccupied with signs of aging and premature doom.

Does this make sense? Not rationally, no. If our apprehensions were logical, then the fear should mount as we grow older and come closer to dying. Usually, it doesn't. As people restabilize on the other side of the midlife passage, the specter of death moves farther back in their minds. They talk about it a lot and compare protective strategies, but by then "it" is real, not a private, unmentionable gargoyle.

This chapter will explore some of the predictable inner changes most of us can expect to feel in the Deadline Decade as we move through it: seeing the dark first, disassembling ourselves, then glimpsing the light, and gathering our parts into a renewal. The remainder of the book will describe men and women actually groping toward authenticity, each in his or her own pattern, trying to find his or her own truth. Or running away from it, or blocking it until something explodes.

This is not to suggest that people who suffer the most severe crisis always come through with the most inspired rebirth. But people who allow themselves to be stopped, seized by the real issues, shaken into a reexamination— these are the people who find their validity and thrive.

SEEING THE DARK AT THE END OF THE TUNNEL

The sudden change in the proportion of safety and danger we feel in our lives is seldom anticipated, which is why people often feel depressed at the start of this passage. When we were buoyed by the optimism of the early years, we could easily steer clear of the dark side by sailing from one channel of vigorous activity to another. Our juices were running full. Ordinarily, our potency was building in every sphere—stronger bodies, better sex, bigger accomplishments, more friends, higher salaries—and oh, how we loved to exhibit our powers! It seemed they could do nothing but increase. They defended us well against the inadmissible truth that no one has forever.

Ask anyone over 35, when did you first begin to feel old? Was it when you looked at yourself in the buff and realized that everything was half an inch lower?

"Hold your stomach in, Mom."

"It's in."

Most of us notice first the cracks in our physical shells and see them in distortion, as if in a funny-house mirror. A comedian gave as ridiculous an answer as any. "I knew I was middle-aged when I woke up one morning to find a twenty-three-inch hair growing out of my ear."

What we turn away from in the mirror, we can't escape seeing in our friends, our children, our parents. These are the "others" who register the fact that "you" are soon going to be different.

You go to a reunion. Your classmates now have titles. You listen to the accounts of their achievements and you can hear they are impressive, but you are not impressed. What you are obsessed with is the pink glacier pushing back the class president's hairline. You hear about Harry; he dropped like a fly while dancing the bump.

In the locker room you, a woman recently past 35, find yourself staring at the women well into their forties, at the purple bull's-eyes in their thighs where it looks as though a BB gun went off under the skin. You wonder if they still undress in front of their husbands.

Your mood swings up and down by sheer caprice. Madcap optimism in the morning, in the doldrums by lunch. You make a joke to yourself about acting like "some nutty menopausal woman." But you don't believe it, of course. You are a woman still menstruating regularly, and women of 38 are at the sexual *peak*. Or you are a man, and after all, Charlie Chaplin was making babies at 81.

It is a paradox that as we reach our prime, we also see there is a place where it finishes.

CHANGE IN TIME SENSE

Going into this crisis decade, every one of us can expect a distortion in our sense of time. We have stumbled onto that apostrophe in time between the end of growing up and the beginning of growing old. Like the apprehensions associated with death, this disruption in time sense is most unsettling at the start of the passage. The jolt as felt by men and career women sounds something like this:

"Time is running out. Time must be beaten. Can I accomplish all that I'd hoped before it's too late?"

To women who have been at home, time is suddenly seen as long:

"Look at all the time ahead! After the children are gone, what will I do with it?"

Social psychologist Bernice Neugarten in an interview confirmed this broad difference in change of time sense for the two sexes. Career position is significantly involved in the personality changes for men, and health is more of an age marker for them than for women.[1] Women are much more likely to see a realm of unimagined opportunities opening up in the middle years. An initial sense of danger and timidity may give way to invigoration. For most of them there are still so many firsts ahead.

The change in time sense forces each of us to a major task of midlife. All our notions of the future need to be rebalanced around the idea of time left to live.

CHANGE IN SENSE OF ALIVENESS VERSUS STAGNATION

Before we are able to do this rebalancing, the time problem will have most of us feeling stalled. Our distorted perspective foreshortens the future so falsely we are likely to create our own inertia, saying, "It's too late to start something new." Boredom is what it *feels* like, but as author Barbara Fried explains so nicely, we have boredom mixed up with time diffusion.[2] They are different. Routine boredom can be cured by seeking out simple novelties of experience. Time diffusion is a deeper malaise that stems from our sudden, drastic lack of trust in the future and an unwillingness to believe there is anything to look forward to.

Trust is the foundation of hope formed in earliest childhood. Now we are back to "go," reckoning all over again the balance we can expect between our needs and when, or if, they will be met. Except that now there is no caregiver. *We* are our hope. And we can't very well trust in our own resources for enlivening the future until we find out who we want to be on the other side of the meridian. That's the circle. It's not vicious; it's the runaround that leads to revitalization. We have to go all around it, stagnate in it, before we are spurred to break out and make use of the time left. "Yes, I can change. It's not too late to start what I put aside!"

It is a paradox that as we come out of the crisis, although we have less actual time left, the depression and ennui lift. The future is again seen in truer perspective because we infuse it then with the faith of our redefined purpose.

CHANGE IN SENSE OF SELF AND OTHERS

About now, your son beats you at tennis for the first time. Or he asks if he and his girl friend can take their sleeping bags out in the backyard. You stew all night, wondering how do they *do* it? The next morning you ask a few oblique questions. But by his expression, it is clear that your son knows your interest is less parental than lascivious.

Your daughter wants to go shopping. You stare in the store windows and see yourself in the same clothes. Inside the store your daughter looks shocked when you try on a supersexy dress. "Oh Mom, that's disgusting."

It is a paradox that teenage children are totally intolerant of midlife parents for having much the same romantic fantasies they have.

You look to your parents for comfort and find they have weakened. Their eyes aren't so good. They would rather you drive. When a parent contracts a terminal illness, who is next? You, the 40-year-old, are abruptly flung to the front of the generational train, followed only by your own children.

With your own role as child to your parents intact, you still felt secure.

With the death of your father or mother, you are exposed. "Today there are a tremendous number of people who experience death for the first time with a parent's passing when they themselves are 35 to 40," as Margaret Mead observes. "This is altogether new in the world." The death of the remaining parent has been documented as one of the most constant crisis points in the individual's evolving image of self.

Your curiosity at looking into the funny-house mirror mounts to morbidity. You never read the obituaries before; now you note age and disease. For the first time in what might have been a spectacularly healthy life, you become a minor-league hypochondriac.

People in the middle years will often say, "All my friends are dying of cancer." *All* their friends aren't, but if even one or two are, it comes as a shock. We hear so much about our increased longevity, how is it so many people become seriously ill in their late forties? Because infant mortality has been sharply reduced in recent years, more people who would have died at birth survive infancy but are not as physically strong as our grandparents had to be to survive. Consequently, as indicated by government analysis of life-span statistics, there is an ever-increasing population of middle-aged people and hence a larger pool susceptible to death in the middle years.[3]

Had any such sudden tragedy struck a friend or relation when you were 25, your sympathetic reaction would have been of a safely distant kind. The pestilence would have been theirs, a life accident. Now it is a red alert to make more of your own life before it is too late. And that is all to the good.

It is a paradox that as death becomes personalized, a life force becomes energized. In the very jaws of this danger is opportunity, the chance for no less than a second christening.

DE-ILLUSIONING THE DREAM

The changes in perception are most vividly reflected in the way the dream is now seen. Whatever your occupation, you cannot help but face up to the gap between your vision of yourself in the twenties and the actuality of your arrival at 40. If you are a 40-year-old mother, your purpose will soon slip from your arms. If you are a chief executive officer, the business psychologists who proclaim "no man over 45 should be in a line position" will soon be talking about *you*. Saying that you should be put out to pasture in a staff job. Saying that all they want are young hustlers whose whole focus is the bottom line. Never mind these philosophical middle-agers who want to make a social contribution.

The affirmation you have or have not accrued by 40 will tell you in what league you can expect to play out your life. No matter what your position you will wonder, "Is this all there is?"

The same disillusionment seizes everybody, steam fitter or top brass, and that is crucial to remember if you are to save yourself from wallowing in self-pity. Studs Terkel collected the stories of Americans in over a hundred occupations for his extraordinary book *Working*, and the one common denominator he found was concern with age. "Perhaps it is this spectre that most haunts working men and women: the planned obsolescence of people that is of a piece with the planned obsolescence of the things they make."[4]

You must give up believing that all the riches of life will come from reaching the goals of your idealized self. If your ideal self is evidently not going to be attainable and you refuse to adjust down, you will go the route of chronic depression. On the other hand, if you recognize that you will never be president of the big-city bank, you can get on with becoming branch manager in your favorite community and maybe find your greatest pleasure in becoming a Little League coach or starting a choir.

If your ideal self *has* been achieved, what happens after the dream comes true? If you don't replace it with a new dream, there may be no zeal left for the future, although there may be plenty to fear. On the other hand, you are freed by your success to take old passions off the shelf, to open that funny little restaurant you always had a yen to cook for, to throw yourself into song writing or helping minorities or landscape gardening for your friends. I know people in midlife who have turned to all these things. They are far more ebullient people than their counterparts who stay with the old, achieved dream and find themselves in their fifties literally squeezing it for lifeblood.

It is a paradox that while medical science has increased our longevity, business psychology seeks to shrink our work span.

GROPING TOWARD AUTHENTICITY

As our distorted glimpses of the dark side grow into convictions and the dream disappoints our magical hopes, *any* role we have chosen seems too narrow, *any* life structure too confining. *Any* husband or wife, mother, father, child, mentor, or divinity to whom we have given faith can be felt as part of the clasped circle hemming us in.

The loss of youth, the faltering of physical powers we have always taken for granted, the fading purpose of stereotyped roles by which we have thus far identified ourselves, the spiritual dilemma of having no absolute answers—any or all of these shocks can throw us into crisis. But in all of us, before this decade is out, the crisis makes sweeping changes in personality possible. And some degree of personality change is probably inevitable.[5]

These changes may permit a woman to assert herself, a man to allow his emotions, and any one of us to let our narrow occupational and economic definitions fall away. When that happens, we are ready to look for a sense of purpose truly our own. The very act of striking out on that path can pave the way to a new, freestanding intimacy between us and the ones we love.

But first, letting the dark side open up will release a cast of demons. Every loose end not resolved in previous passages will resurface to haunt us. Even chips off the archaic totem pole of childhood will come to the surface. Buried parts of ourselves will demand incorporation or at least that we make the effort of seeing and discarding them.

These demons may lead us into private hells of depression, sexual promiscuity, power chasing, hypochondria, self-destructive acts (alcoholism, drug taking, car accidents, suicide), and violent swings of mood. All are well documented as rising during the middle years. The midlife crisis has also been used by psychiatrists as an explanation for why so many highly creative and industrious people burn out by their mid-thirties. Even more dramatic is the evidence that they can die from it.[6]

If we do admit the dark side, what are we likely to see?

We are selfish.
We are greedy.
We are competitive.
We are fearful.
We are dependent.
We are jealous.
We are possessive.
We have a destructive side.

Who's afraid of growing up? Who isn't? For if and when we do begin the process of reexamining all that we think and feel and stand for, in the effort to forge an identity that is authentically ours and ours alone, we run into our own resistance. There is a moment—an immense and precarious moment—of stark terror. And in that moment most of us want to retreat as fast as possible because to go forward means facing a truth we have suspected all along:

We stand alone.

We are the only ones with our own set of thoughts and bundle of feelings. Another person can *taste* them, through shared experience of conversation, but no other person can ever really *digest* them. Not wives or husbands, although they may be able to finish our sentences; not mentors or bosses, although they may be of goodwill in working out their own ambitions through us; not even our parents.

From the childhood identifications with our parents we carry along the most primitive layer of imaginary protection: the protection of that dictator-guardian I have called the inner custodian. It is this internalized protection that gives us a sense of insulation, and even into the middle years, shields us from coming face to face with our own absolute separateness. We look to our mates, to our children, to money or success, hoping they will extend the protection of the caregivers from our childhood. The illusory power of the inner custodian has made us believe that if we don't stick our necks out, if we don't test our full potential, we are somehow insulated from danger, failure, getting sick, dying. But it is an illusion.

Trying to keep that illusion alive by maintaining what psychiatrists call an "incomplete identification" only soothes us against the *idea* of separation. It does nothing actually to protect us from being separate.[7]

We push and strain against all of these truths. Retreat and tremble. Chase after the sweet birds of our youth. Stop. Stagnate. And finally we come to know the unthinkable: The dark side is within us. So powerful becomes the sense of internal collapse that many of us are no longer willing to prevent it.

People whose biographies I have taken can say at 44 or 45, "I really went through hell for a few years, and I'm just coming out of it," but their capacity to describe what "it" felt like is often limited. People right in the middle of midlife passage may be so panicky that the only descriptions they can summon are of "living in a state of suspended animation" or "I sometimes wonder in the morning if life is worth getting up for." To be any more introspective seems dangerous.

A 43-year-old designer was able to articulate the feelings that bring on the emotional vertigo of this period. "What I've discovered over the last year is how much of what is inadmissible to myself I have suppressed. Feelings that I've always refused to admit are surfacing in a way *I am no longer willing to prevent*. I'm willing to accept the responsibility for what *I really feel*. I don't have to pretend those feelings don't exist in order to accommodate a model of what I should be."

By his own admissions, this man is engaging the midlife crisis. "I'm really shocked now at the range and the quality of those feelings—feelings of fear, of envy, of greed, of competition. All these so-called bad feelings are really rising where I can see them and feel them. I'm amazed at the incredible energy we all spend suppressing them and not admitting pain."

The consensus of current research is that the transition into middle life is as critical as adolescence and in some ways more harrowing. Can it possibly be worth it to ride with this chaos and see it all? Is it worth it to become real?

I'm rather partial to the answer given in a children's book, *The Velveteen Rabbit*. One day the young rabbit asks the Skin Horse, who has been around the nursery quite some time, what is real? And does it hurt?

"Sometimes," said the Skin Horse, for he was always truthful. "When you are REAL you don't mind being hurt."

"Does it happen all at once, like being wound up," he asked, "or bit by bit?"

"It doesn't happen all at once," said the Skin Horse. "You become. It takes a long time. That's why it doesn't often happen to people who break easily, or have sharp edges, or who have to be carefully kept. Generally, by the time you are REAL, most of your hair has been loved off, and your eyes drop out and you get loose in the joints and very shabby. But these things don't matter at all, because once you are REAL you can't be ugly, except to people who don't understand.''[8]

FROM DISASSEMBLING TO RENEWAL

While the dilemma of this decade is the search for authenticity, the work is to move through a disassembling to a renewal. What is disassembling is that narrow self we have thus far put together in a form tailored to please the culture and other people.

It is the form we hurried through our twenties to find, the identity we developed in order to stabilize ourselves, and around which we built the life system of the early thirties: the ambitious executive, the supermom who always copes, the fearless politician, the wife who asks permission. We could not afford then to act on our own *internal* authority. The unspoken promise was, if we did a good job and stayed within that straight and narrow form, we would be liked and rewarded and live forever.

The shock of this turning point is to discover that the promise was an illusion. That narrow, innocent self is indeed dying, must die, in order to make room for the fully expanded self who will take in all our parts, the selfish, scared, and cruel along with the expansive and tender—the ''bad'' along with the ''good.'' No matter how shattering is this collision with our suppressed and destructive impulses, the capacity for renewal within each human spirit is nothing short of amazing.

It is not *either* disassembling *or* renewal. It is both. By allowing this dis-integration, by taking in our suppressed and even our unwanted parts, each of us prepares at the gut level for the reintegration of an identity that is truly our own. We are free to seek the truth about ourselves more vigorously and thus to see the world in truer perspective.

Along the way to that freedom, we must do some grieving for the old ''dying self'' and take up a conscious stance with regard to our own inevitable mortality.[9] It is this mature insight that will protect us from slavishly following what the culture wants us to do and from squandering our time in seeking the approval of others by conforming to their rules. Moreover, when we act on this knowledge, we can be less defensive toward others.

''Take back your silly rules!'' we can shout at last. ''No one can dictate what is right for me. I have glimpsed the worst, and now I can afford to know whatever there is to know. I am my own and only protection. For the fact is, this is my one and only journey through life.''

Through the process of disassembling, then, we provide for the grandest expansion. By the end of this period we can include inside our boundaries all that we are and have experienced—and *re*value it. That is renewal.

RIDING OUT THE DOWN SIDE

One solution is to go into the darkness and explore it. Stick in the mire for a while. Take a sabbatical and become a midlife delinquent, or pit oneself against nature on a backwoods canoe trip. It is one way to know our own depths and possibly to be reinvigorated by that knowledge toward making the most of our lives.

Others appear to wing it past this midstation without pause. Their solution is to continue denying the down side. To play more tennis and run more laps, give bigger parties, seek better hair transplants and higher face lifts, find younger partners to take to bed. That is not to suggest that jogging isn't worthwhile or that younger partners can't help to revitalize a stagnant sex life, but people who rely on only these outlets may be losing in the bargain even more than a critical chance for personal development. To disallow the momentous changes underneath forces a skimming of all experience. The eventual price is superficiality.

Still others block this passage in a razzle-dazzle of compulsive activity. Whiz-kid businessmen or hyperactive hostesses or politicians, for example, seem to have no time for a midlife crisis. They are too busy starting a new business that year or giving dinner parties or running for higher office. They consume themselves with externals for the very reason that they fear dipping into what might be the poverty of meaning inside.

The catch is, inner issues pushed down in one period tend to swing up in the next one with an added wallop. To face a midlife crisis for the first time at fifty is horrifying (although people can get through it). Or development may simply be halted for the person who continues to wear blinders. He becomes more narrow in view, self-indulgent, and finally juiceless and bitter.

"If a man goes through a relatively bland period when midlife transition is going on," Levinson asserts, "it will limit his growth. Many men who don't have a crisis at 40 become weighted and lose the vitality they need to continue developing in the rest of the adult stages."[10]

The only way, finally, to make fear of the down side go away is to allow it entry. The sooner we allow the truths of this period to fill our container, the sooner they can be integrated with our youthful optimism and reground us with true strength.

The most important words in midlife are—Let Go. Let it happen to you. Let it happen to your partner. Let the feelings. Let the changes.

You can't take everything with you when you leave on the midlife journey. You are moving away. Away from institutional claims and other people's agenda. Away from external valuations and accreditations, in search of an inner validation. You are moving out of roles and into the self. If I could give everyone a gift for the send-off on this journey, it would be a tent. A tent for tentativeness. The gift of portable roots.

To reach the clearing beyond, we must stay with the weightless journey through uncertainty. Whatever counterfeit safety we hold from overinvestments in people and institutions must be given up. The inner custodian must be unseated from the controls. No foreign power can direct our journey from now on. It is for each of us to find a course that is valid by our own reckoning. And for each of us there is the opportunity to emerge reborn, *authentically* unique, with an enlarged capacity to love ourselves and embrace others.

Notes

Most helpful to me in synthesizing the many aspects of the midlife period were personal interviews with research scientists Bernice L. Neugarten at the University of Chicago, Roger Gould at the University of California at Los Angeles, Daniel Levinson at Yale University, Marylou Lionells and Carola Mann at the William Alanson White Institute in New York, and writer Barbara Fried. A primary written source is Jung, the first important analytic thinker to conceptualize personality changes in the second half of life (and the only one who distinguishes between the age at their onset in men and women). References to the work of Elliott Jaques (an American psychoanalyst now practicing in London) throughout this and the next chapter are from his paper "Death and the Mid-Life Crisis." Jaques's analysis of creative genius and interpretation of midlife processes has become a classic in the field. Also useful are some of the findings in Kenneth Soddy's book, *Men in Middle Life*.

1. From an interview with Bernice Neugarten. Amplified in "The Awareness of Middle Age," *Middle Age and Aging* (1968), pp. 93–98.
2. Fried (1967).
3. Source is U.S. Public Health Service, table on Expectation of Life in America (based on 1968 data).
4. Quote from Terkel, *Working* (1972), p. xviii.
5. Jung, Jaques, and Levinson make the strongest case for the inevitability of personality change.
6. A 1973 report by the Dept. of Health, Education, and Welfare on "Work in America" indicates that some executives would suffer fatal consequences rather than face a reduced image of themselves: "A general feeling of obsolescence appears to overtake middle managers when they reach their late thirties. Their careers appear to have reached a plateau, and they realize that life from here on will be a long and inevitable decline. There is a marked increase in the death rate between the ages of 35 to 40 for employed men, apparently as a result of this 'midlife crisis'. . . ."

7. Psychiatrist Roger Gould was particularly helpful in formulating the ideas about subjective changes in self and object representations during the midlife period. Psychoanalyst Judd Marmor also describes midlife crisis as a developmental stage, the central theme of which is a separation loss involving the giving up of fantasy hopes of youth and a confrontation with personal mortality. In a paper read before the annual meeting of the American Orthopsychiatric Association in March 1967, Marmor cited four modes of coping with midlife crisis: denial by escape in frantic activity; denial by overcompensation (as in sexual escapades); decompensation, including anxiety, depression, and diffuse rage; or integration at a higher level with less narcissistic self-involvement.

8. Quote from *The Velveteen Rabbit* by Margery Williams, Doubleday (1958).

9. Jaques (1965) discusses the ''grief work'' of midlife and the return to the infantile depressive position. This mourning for our lost illusions and innocence is what gives the crisis of midlife its depressive quality.

10. From an interview with Dr. Levinson.

Humor has its place in any serious discussion of social affairs and personal life. Hence we include Gerald Nachman's brief essay, which satirizes the tendency of some writers to exaggerate the significance for everyone of various rites of passage, including the "mid-life crisis." Beneath the satire is an interesting view of what W. I. Thomas once called "the definition of the situation," the idea that if we define situations as real, they may become real in their consequences. Thus Nachman's piece brings to mind sociologist Robert K. Merton's notion of the "self-fulfilling prophecy," the prediction that is made to come true.

As you read Gerald Nachman's essay, relax and have a good laugh.

The Menopause that Refreshes

GERALD NACHMAN

I seem to be the last boy in town to get my Midlife Crisis. After listening in awe to wild tales of this chic new male malaise, I've looked forward to having one of my own, like all the other guys. I don't plan to be left behind again, as I was in the Sexual Revolution and the Cultural Boom.

When I hit 35, I said: "Well, kid, this could be your big year," but I was early. At 37, still nothing very upsetting had happened, unless a kidney stone counts as a Midlife Crisis. This year, turning 39 and frantic, I tried to coax my Midlife Crisis along by calling a psychiatrist to see what was wrong.

"Many men are late bloomers," he said, "but I must level with you—some fellas never suffer a Midlife Crisis. It's rare now, thank God, but it does occur. Last month, an Iowa man experienced delayed adolescence at 93, so don't ever say die."

I replied that if I didn't catch at least a mild identity crisis pretty soon I would consider my entire middle years a waste of time. Last October, feeling a twinge of *angst*, I almost quit my job and got a hair transplant, but it went away. (This is known as a "hysterical Midlife Crisis," but it doesn't keep you from having the real thing.)

LOOSE ENDS

Worried—for fear my Midlife Crisis is that I won't have one—I consulted a friend who, at 46, is just wrapping up the loose ends of his own private turmoil and was shocked to hear I'd yet to start mine. "You're nearly 40, which leaves you less than a year to mess up your life," he warned. "Better get a move on."

Men who pass from their 30s to 40s in utter tranquillity, he adds, later feel cheated out of one of life's greatest miseries. At 70, they're full of regrets, with nothing left to look forward to but a Latelife Crisis (sometimes labeled "death"). He told me not to be fooled by peace of mind. "If you ask me," he said, "you're not looking hard enough for disappointment and dissatisfaction."

I asked how he'd enjoyed his own voyage from Throbbing Thirties to Forsaken Forties, and he smiled, "I wouldn't have missed it for the world. Every man should go through a stage of chaos and collapse. It builds character. A Midlife Crisis is a lot like the Army, only the food is better."

He claims too many males plunge into their 40s unprepared and flounder about happily when they could be having a truly hellish period. "These men overlook the many opportunities for despair right in their own backyards. They're hung up on contentment; they have a maturity complex. When overwhelmed by unhappiness, they quickly come to their senses. If beset by problems, they have a tendency to solve them."

BLOCKED PASSAGES

My mid-40s friend sighed, "Gee, if only I'd had somebody to take *me* aside when I was 39 and show me the ropes. You younger chaps don't appreciate the grief that's out there, just waiting to be wallowed in. You're much too busy adjusting to reality."

Introspection, he insists, is the key to a successful, fulfilling and indeed ripsnorting Midlife Crisis, or "the pre-senility crazies" as the boys down at the barbershop call it. "With proper exercise and diet, a healthy man entering middlescence can expect a good year of trapped desires and thwarted dreams."

I wondered what I might do to trigger an all-out MC, and he suggested taking matters into my own hands by asking a few close friends and family in to celebrate my rite of passage into midmanhood. "You want to let as many people in on your woe as possible. Half the fun of a Midlife Crisis is depressing others."

(He advises notifying your wife at least ten days ahead of time so she can get her own life in disorder. Then, if anybody calls for you, she can just say, "Fred's out having his Midlife Crisis but he said he'd be back in a year or so and not to wait supper for him.")

Some men, he explained, have a Midlife Crisis block that prevents them from having facelifts or second marriages. They must be gently initiated into middle age by experienced pals and older brothers, who can introduce them to a plastic surgeon or slip them the phone numbers of some eager, bored housewives. "Many men are naturally nervous about their very first encounter with bags under the eyes and intimations of mortality, but later they go around bragging what a dismal Midlife Crisis they had."

When I called my shrink back and said it looked hopeless for me, menopausewise, he told me, "Don't fret—social science has come to the rescue once more. Have you ever heard of Midlife Crisis camp?"

Inspired by tennis ranches and marriage retreats, Old Camp Torment is for men incapable of devising their own midlife traumas, he explained. You sign up for a week of intensive anguish, located on 227 acres of choice desolation reminiscent of the usual barren atmosphere of Midlife Crises—drab hotel rooms, murky bars, obscure cafés, empty parks. The camp guarantees to produce a maximum sense of worthlessness and tortured self-doubt in a minimum amount of time.

A PLACE IN THE SHADE

I told him that midlife camp sounded ideal, so he described a typical day's activities on the grounds overlooking Lake Failure, N.Y.:

"Every second of your day is rigidly planned," he said. "You begin with drifting-apart exercises and selfishness training, then spend an hour pulling up stakes and kicking over traces, followed by a little ego deflation and self-flagellation—your Daily Doldrums. That's the morning session.

"At noon," he went on, "you break for lunch with some tootsie at a noisy French bistro, holding hands and grim discussions about relationships. The afternoon consists of experiencing decreased sexual desire, growing old in a youth-oriented society and confronting the inevitability of death. At 5 o'clock, everybody shuffles into a singles bar for unhappy hour, followed by a sordid and meaningless one-night stand . . ."

"I feel life's futility already," I said. "I think I'm finally able to stop making the best of things."

"That's the first sign of real growth," he smiled.

Just as parenting is something for which few people are properly socialized, so too is unemployment. This is especially true for middle-aged, middle-class professionals, who cannot imagine losing their jobs and find it difficult to cope if they do.

In the following article, Douglas Powell and Paul Driscoll describe what happened to one group of scientists and engineers who were laid off during a recent economic recession. The authors detail the reactions and adjustments of people who are ill-prepared to deal with unemployment and its attendant loss of money and status.

As you read the essay, note the periodic shifts in mood and behavior. Ask yourself how different the experiences of those described might be from those of poor inner-city dwellers who have rarely known steady employment.

Middle-class Professionals Face Unemployment

DOUGLAS H. POWELL AND PAUL F. DRISCOLL

"I knew it was coming. . . . For over a year I hadn't been sleeping very well because I could see business falling off and knew they didn't need me. When I was finally laid off I stopped worrying . . . for a while, anyway." Many unemployed professionals share the feelings of this purchasing agent when faced with the prospect of joblessness. The actual layoff comes as a relief from the anxiety and tension of anticipation and they do not begin to look for a job immediately. One man went to Europe for a month's vacation and others expressed guarded optimism: "I don't feel unemployed," and "No question in my mind I'll be employed in a few months."

We began to understand the feelings and attitudes of these unemployed professionals while meeting with groups of out-of-work scientists, engineers and technical people at an experimental Professional Service Center in Massachusetts. While we knew of several studies dealing with the reactions of

---

How the Study of Middle-class Unemployed Men Was Made

Our initial impressions of how middle-class men feel and act during a period of lengthy unemployment came in the course of 30 discussions with groups of about 25 unemployed scientists and engineers at an experimental Professional Service Center in Massachusetts. The intent of the meetings was the development of job-seeking skills and remotivation, but our preliminary observations encouraged us to look more carefully. We interviewed an additional 50 men picked randomly from among those coming to the job center. The men in our sample had these characteristics:

	MEAN	RANGE
AGE	41 years	25–53
EDUCATION	16 years	14–20
LENGTH OF UNEMPLOYMENT	9.5 months	2–18 months

Our open-ended interviews with these unemployed men were not viewed as a test of the theoretical scheme. They were intended to provide data which would illuminate our initial impressions as well as to suggest new directons for inquiry. We treated the interview data inductively, tabulating reports of changing patterns of job-seeking behavior, feelings and attitudes, and relationships with others when they occurred. The result is the clinical description in this article—supported by the evidence of our interview material—of the four stages which unemployed middle-class people seem to go through if they are not able to find a job within a short time. The stages are progressive and appear to have characteristic emotional and behavioral patterns related to how long the individuals have been out of work. Among our sample of unemployed scientists and engineers, each man reported going through at least two of the stages, and most of them had been through three or four. At the time of the interviews five men were in Stage I, nine of the men were classified in Stage II, ten in Stage III and 26 in Stage IV.

---

lower-class and minority workers to unemployment, we had little information about the feelings and behavior of middle-class men facing lengthy periods of unemployment. From our research and discussions with these middle-class professionals we constructed a four stage description of their difficulties and responses to a situation which threatens to become increasingly widespread.

STAGE I: PERIOD OF RELAXATION AND RELIEF

Most of the men in our survey reacted to the initial period of unemployment with a sense of relief. Like the purchasing agent, they had seen their companies failing to find new business, contracts terminating and their friends laid off. The period following layoff became one of relaxation and relief. Sometimes they are bitter toward their employer, but most men understand why they are laid off. The intellectual awareness of the reasons for their unemployment tends to dampen anger or bitterness—or even depression—they may feel when first fired.

During this time, the unemployed scientists and engineers don't like to think much about being out of work. There is a sense of being "between jobs;" they feel confident and hopeful of finding a job as soon as they are "ready" to go back to work. Although most of the men make at least one clearcut effort to look for work at this stage, they do so on a casual basis: "I feel I know people and can get into places." They call a friend or agency or respond to an ad.

The newly unemployed seize gladly upon any excuse not to look for work. "I stopped looking because I figured no work was coming for the holidays," explained a quality control engineer; one physicist said, "I wanted to have companies get over their summer doldrums before I looked." They spend time very much as they would on a vacation at home—being with the family, sleeping late, reading or tinkering in the workshop. Sometimes they travel, but they all tend to find some release to recuperate and prepare for intensive job-seeking.

Relationships with others do not change much during this period of relief and relaxation. Family relationships remain normal. Neither husband nor wife openly airs their mutual concerns at this time and family equilibrium is maintained.

Newly unemployed men talk openly about their situation to co-workers and friends in other divisions of their companies (contacts who know their situation as a matter of course). But they do not initiate contacts with friends who wouldn't know about their situation unless told.

STAGE II: PERIOD OF CONCERTED EFFORT

After a period of approximately 25 days, the individual begins to feel rested, often somewhat bored and edgy. Now he starts to make a systematic and usually well-organized attempt to find work. This is a period of concerted effort. The individual relies on job-finding strategies which have been successful in the past, including calling friends, sending resumes to blind ads and going back to the university placement center. He tries to follow the advice of job counselors who say, "You have a full-time job. Your full-time job is to find a full-time job!" More time is spent actually looking for work or thinking about it than in other activity.

This is a time of optimism and planning. Among the scientists and engineers we talked with these descriptions were common:

"I do my homework. When I have an interview I study everything concerning the company that I can get my hands on."

"I went door-to-door, private agencies, resume send-outs."

"I'd literally memorize the want ads."

"I'm pushing, trying to hit all bases."

During this stage a logical, consistent approach is followed:

"I laid out my plan of action, contacted all friends, agencies and ads."

"I get up every morning at 7, get the paper, check to see what I have to do for the day."

"I keep a notebook of contacts. Keep close tabs on where I've been, where I have to go."

If an unemployed man finds himself blocked in one area—for example, the local want ads—he looks elsewhere. He shows flexibility. He contacts other sources of potential jobs such as employment agencies and the Division of Employment Security. He is willing to make "cold calls."

Though the average amount of time devoted to these activities was about three months, individual variation was substantial. There was evidence that this period could be very short indeed—a matter of days for some—and rather lengthy for others. The length of time an unemployed person was able to sustain his confidence seemed to depend on several factors. The men we interviewed who were able to maintain themselves three months or longer mentioned these reasons:

> Just didn't think about failure; financial security from pension or savings; received reinforcement from job market and support from family and friends.

Critical to the maintenance of a concerted effort is the capacity to avoid becoming overly depressed or anxious in the face of rejection letters from potential employers—or worse, no response at all. The unemployed person must bounce back quickly to remain active. He tries not to think about how tough it is to find jobs or why he failed in his last attempt. Any encouragement from the market place helps immensely: a note indicating that an application is being processed, a call from a friend saying a company had called for a reference or a letter asking for more information results in renewed optimism.

Having savings or other money to tide the family over while the individual is out of work is vitally important to maintaining a sustained effort. Those with greater financial resources continue to look for work in a positive, organized manner much longer than those who do not.

This appears to be a time of maximum support and encouragement from family and friends. To the extent he receives support, the unemployed scientist and engineer's capacity to maintain a concerted effort is enhanced.

Overall, family relations during this period are good. The wife helps in the job search by taking care of the secretarial chores often necessary to finding a job and giving moral support and encouragement. Often she becomes as emotionally involved as her husband is about his getting a particular job—if he fails she becomes very upset too. Her ability to maintain her resiliency and optimism directly influences her husband's continuing efforts.

So, too, do friends provide maximum support. As one engineer said, "I opened up a bit. I don't plead, just tell them the facts. My company has been hit by the layoffs. If you know of anybody looking for a good guy, I'm available." Most men we talked with reported a cordial response from friends and neighbors whom they told about their problem. Friends took resumes, made phone calls, gave advice, volunteered to talk to people they know who might be able to help. It appears that friends are motivated to help because the unemployed person is actively looking for a job.

But this is not a time when the unemployed individual likes being in the presence of other unemployed people. Usually he avoids them. "I'm not like *them*," one engineer said, "They are out of a job. I am waiting for an offer from Corning Glass." When he met other unemployed men, he would often greet them with the enthusiasm he would normally show a leper—afraid that whatever they have might be catching.

Men who have a prior history of being laid off seem to adjust better to unemployment than those who have never been out of work. They spent less time in the stage of relaxation, were more open in telling others about their unemployment, and were more appropriate in their job-seeking strategies. Furthermore, these men had saved a greater proportion of their salary while they were working, and when it was possible for the wives to work this reversal of roles was handled smoothly.

STAGE III: PERIOD OF VACILLATION AND DOUBT

At this point the individual usually has been unemployed longer than he has been out of work before, or it becomes clear to him that the usual ways of finding a job are inadequate. His mood is characterized by vacillation in many areas. Job-seeking behavior is sporadic, a less than half-time process with alternating periods of intense activity and lying fallow. Doubt begins to undermine the process of decision making. He becomes intensely moody. Relationships with family and friends deteriorate.

With repeatedly unsuccessful encounters with the job market, the controlled optimism which produced earlier efforts starts to erode. The unemployed man begins doubting his judgment, second-guessing himself and becoming more self-critical. Fears and doubts—earlier suppressed by working hard, looking for work and trying not to think about the last unsuccessful attempt—trouble the unemployed scientist and engineer much more than before. Anxiety surrounding these feelings intensifies.

Preparation and organization, the unifying strategies of previous efforts, are gradually discarded. Much of the individual's job-searching strategy is aimed at reducing anxiety. One way was to "do" something. One chemical engineer said, "I was sitting around, getting edgier and edgier. . . . So I just went down to the Northwest Industrial Park and went from door to door." Another reported almost the same behavior. He looked at the parking lot first and dropped in on only those companies where the lot was filled with cars.

Identity problems become a serious issue as the scientist or engineer tries to decide which aspects of his occupational experience and skill he should feature in order to find a job. The men have a tendency to lose a sense of who they are vocationally, allowing the market to define their abilities. Some men write four resumes which describe four different people. They are ripe to be taken in by unscrupulous job placement agencies who seem to promise jobs at enormous cost but are not in fact helpful. But most men don't complain. They are ready to grab at anything promising relief for their anxiety.

This was the time many men said they began to think seriously about making a significant change in their careers. A number actually began to pursue a specific alternative, the most common being taking the civil service exam, and going back to college for a teaching certificate. But unemployed scientists and engineers at higher levels of technical proficiency appear to be resistant to changing fields, while those who have climbed the management ladder seem more willing to shift careers. A project manager for a large defense contractor with an M.S. in physics justified his attempts to switch fields with the comment, "Managing people is the same regardless of the business product." His administrative experience offered him a number of options which he pursued early in his unemployment.

During this third stage many men develop an increasing sense of being past their prime. The majority of unemployed scientists and engineers over 35 said in one way or another, "They're looking for a younger man," to explain why they could not find a job. There is some truth in the statement—younger men are cheaper. But it also appears to be true that unemployed men in this period of vacillation and doubt have a premature sense of not being the men they once were.

Part of the problem is that engineering and technology fields condition men to feel obsolete quickly when they are out of work. Procedures and techniques change so rapidly that it is difficult for a man to begin working at the same level of responsibility if he has been unemployed and not in close contact with his field for a year or more.

Particularly hard hit are men in the aerospace industry who have had marginal formal education, but have grown through on-the-job training into positions usually requiring a degree in engineering. So long as they remain within a company they have no problems. Their coworkers know what they can do. But when the layoffs come these men with lots of experience but no degree find it more difficult than degree holders to get a job. For some non-degree holders this means returning to technician status again. Sometimes it is not the financial regression that hurts but the loss of the hard-earned professional status.

Extreme moodiness characterizes men in this stage. A young unemployed personnel manager put his feelings this way:

It's like being on a roller coaster of mental attitude, a yo-yo of mental attitude. Sometimes I feel depressed—I mean *really* depressed, and wonder if I'll ever snap out of it. After a while I begin to feel really agitated . . . you know, filled with energy. Then I'm really hyper! I spend a lot of energy, though I don't seem to get much done. I race through want ads but don't get much (from them) . . . then I go to the unemployment (sic) office for help . . . I only have pieces of conversation there, cutting short any help they might be, acting as if I have to go somewhere important in a hurry. I know what I'm doing is not helping. . . . Yet, it feels better when you're on the move.

Frustration builds and keeping cool is increasingly difficult. Several men reported they lost jobs they were qualified for because they couldn't restrain themselves from badgering the potential employer for a decision.

Violent Rage

During this period most unemployed men feel extremely angry. They censure the government for breaking up the aerospace industry and are furious at the universities for training men for jobs that no longer exist. They feel a violent rage that sometimes turns back on them in the form of a deep depression. Unable to find a suitable external object to direct their anger against, some men internalize these intense feelings of fury and accumulated frustration. The despair and sense of panic they feel is at its greatest point and during this period men who commit suicide are likely to decide to do it.

Relations with others are severely impaired and the strain weighs heavily on marital relations. The men described two common family problems. Some felt they were a burden on their family, "I'm moody, beginning to pick on my wife for small things;" others said their wives annoyed them a great deal, "Her worrying bothers me" or "She's questioning me and I don't like it." Seeing her husband fail to obtain a job and then apparently fall into periods of no activity at all, a wife badgers her husband to try harder or begins to doubt his ability and transmits these concerns to him. Already doubting himself and wondering if he will ever find a job, the husband often responds acrimoniously to well-intended queries about how things are going, and what should be done if he doesn't soon find a job. Problems at home are further exacerbated in those cases where the unemployed man is not actively looking for a job, yet expects his wife to continue to do all the household work. In homes where the roles are strictly defined, the difficulties were most severe. These problems are intensified when the wife actively considers going back to work.

Relations with friends sometimes change in this phase. About one man in four said they felt their friends began to avoid them when their concerted efforts to find work were not productive. A substantial minority reported their friends offered money or other support. Reactions to these offers ranged from tearful appreciation to hostile rejection because of the implication that a man out of a job needs charity.

After an average of six weeks of sporadic activity (it varies between three and nine weeks), there is a definite winding down of job hunting. Describing themselves toward the end of this stage, the scientists and engineers in our sample commented: "I'm not looking for a job as much any more." "I've stopped using certain approaches like sending out resumes. They don't pay off." "It's sporadic. I push a little harder only when an opportunity comes up." These statements reflect a gradual constriction of continuing efforts to find work, and movement toward the stage of malaise and cynicism.

STAGE IV: PERIOD OF MALAISE AND CYNICISM

Now looking for a job becomes an infrequent endeavor. Job-seeking strategies are often oriented toward protecting self-esteem. Moods stabilize as do relationships with others. As opposed to the transition from Stage II to Stage III which is marked by a great deal of anxiety and depression, the transition from Stage III to Stage IV appears to be a smoother one.

The individual goes longer and longer between positive attempts to secure a job, substantial efforts to change his job strategy, or active consideration of retraining. We found that one of the clearest indications that the individual has given up completely is where he has not had personal contact with a potential employer, job counselor, agency or college placement group in a 60-day period.

When the unemployed scientist or engineer looks for a job he often does so in a manner designed to cushion himself against the pain which could come from a possible refusal rather than adopting a more aggressive strategy and opening himself to disappointment if he is turned down. He protects his self-esteem by responding mostly to blind ads which ask for applicants to send their resumes, but don't require a personal contact. In this impersonal exchange, no response is the worst thing that can happen. There isn't much of an investment in getting the job—and not much chance of getting it either. Scientists and engineers responding to a blind ad typically face odds of 100 to 1 or worse against their being considered.

The men look for perfect matches as a way of guarding against getting turned down. Many unemployed scientists and engineers won't seek a position unless the job description fits their experience and training exactly. A systems engineer in our sample with sub-specialties in radar communication and automatic test equipment looked for openings that required his primary, secondary and tertiary skills. It appears that the longer a man remains in this fourth period, the more rigidly he holds to this highly differentiated view of himself. By holding on to this narrow vocational self-image he, in effect, avoids looking for a job.

The reasons men give for not looking for work are interesting: "I've lost all my drive and don't care." "What's the use of looking? I'll just get turned down." "I'm sick of being humiliated by people who act like they're doing you a favor just talking to you." Unemployed men in our sample described themselves as apathetic and listless in most aspects of their lives. One unemployed mechanical engineer described his behavior to us this way: "Not only have I lost my drive (looking for a job), but I'm not doing much of anything. I'm just staying around the house." Sentiments like this were expressed by two-thirds of the scientists and engineers.

In this stage most unemployed scientists and engineers start to lose the sense they are in control of their own vocational lives or futures. Luck seems more important in getting a job than anything he can do. As one scientist said, "No matter what I do it just doesn't make any difference. It's just a throw of the dice, whether I'll get the job or not." The feeling of powerlessness and pessimism are also characteristic of men in this stage. "Why go in for an interview," a physicist said, "I'll never get past the secretary anyway."

There is an enormous amount of cynicism in the ranks of the out-of-work scientists and engineers during this fourth stage. Programs designed to retrain out-of-work professionals are often greeted with superficial sarcasm about their real purpose being to keep bureaucrats busy and the minds of the unemployed off their troubles. At a deeper level there is frequently the conviction that nothing can really help.

This cynicism seemed to be a way of avoiding a very painful confrontation with the necessity of making a major change in life style in order to be able to return to work. This was illustrated by a conversation with an engineer who had been out of work for 15 months. He had not pursued any job opening in the last nine months. He recounted his several initial efforts to find work which turned up nothing. Noting he had several education courses in college, a job counselor suggested he might retrain in that field and plan to teach math or science. His initial response was, "Who's going to pay for the education I am going to have to get to retrain?" When it was determined he could capitalize on some veteran's benefits which would support much of the cost, he said, "Hell, there's no money in education anyway!" The job counselor responded that there were many jobs in education which paid as well as most jobs paid in his field. His final response was, "Well, even if I get a job in education I'll never get one of those high-paying jobs because everything is all political anyway."

The psychological mood of unemployed scientists and engineers becomes typically more quiet and stable than in the previous period. Most individuals don't feel as upset and anxious as they did earlier. The desperate feelings that are so intense in Stage III are tempered by helplessness and quiescence.

In this fourth period of unemployment, relations between husband and wife become markedly better. The wife stops asking her husband why he isn't actively looking for work anymore. Roles begin to be shifted or shared more equally. Mindful of financial realities the unemployed man faces the need for his wife to find work if she can. As many scientists and engineers marry close to their own educational background, their spouses are able to find work rather easily.

Relationships with others are more limited, largely restricted to a few very close friends and relatives. This constriction in interpersonal relationships cannot be explained solely on the basis of limited funds for entertainment or that the husband has lost contact with colleagues at work. In fact, most unemployed individuals report that they and their wives turned down a number of social invitations. Though the reasons vary, a major factor is that the family altered their life style to accommodate the husband's unemployment. It was easier for them to stay at home than to be with acquaintances whose way of life is now very different from theirs. Here the cycle comes to a close and the future depends upon the vagaries of the job market and the willingness of the professional to consider a change in career fields.

Several intriguing questions arise about the fate of the unemployed professionals in Stage IV and beyond. We would like to know more about how they find their way back to work and what the effect of lengthy unemployment has been on their careers.

In our sample some of the men were remotivated by special training programs. Others were sought out by previous employers or colleagues. Individuals who were more future oriented in their job-seeking strategy found these efforts paid off many months later. Men who made a number of contacts with potential employers who did not have openings at the time, or with whom the application process was lengthy, often were surprised later on by a job offer when they had nearly abandoned hope. One scientist in Stage IV was finally called back to his old company because when he was making a concerted effort to find work he had reinitiated contact with them, expressed his continued interest when a position opened up and attempted to keep them aware of his availability even though he was sure nothing would materialize immediately. An engineer finally received a civil service appointment even though it had been several months since he had contact with the potential employer. The individual realized at the time he initiated this contact that it might not pay off but went ahead anyway.

Interestingly, both of these men said they would not have made contacts of this type in Stage IV. Their limited job-seeking activity was mainly present oriented. This sentiment was shared by many men in Stage IV with whom we talked.

We think these ideas about progressive stages of unemployment, each with unique behavioral and emotional characteristics, are likely to apply to any unemployed middle-class group. But to what extent these observations differentiate the upper-middle-class engineer from a working-class laborer is not clear. Much behavior characteristic of unemployed scientists and professional groups in Stage IV—malaise, cynicism, a sense of powerlessness—has been described as typical of the poor and minority group workers as well as of workers in other countries. Our suspicion, therefore, is that these characteristics are human reactions to unemployment and the frustrations associated with it, and are not restricted to a specific group of individuals.

The success of programs designed to help unemployed groups such as scientists and engineers as well as men in other occupations might be enhanced by an understanding that these men have very different needs depending upon which stage of unemployment they are in. These needs and related patterns of behavior make them responsive to specific kinds of help and indifferent or hostile to others. For example, a man in Stage II doesn't need counseling, he needs job openings to pursue; a man in Stage III may require a good deal of counseling before he is ready to look for a position; and giving a man in Stage IV a list of job openings is not likely to be very helpful. Often they will require a good deal of outside help aimed at restoring self-confidence and changing job-seeking strategies before they will take a job interview.

The image of competent and energetic men reduced to listless discouragement highlights the personal tragedy and the loss of valuable resources when there is substantial unemployment. It presses us to seek more thorough and intensive methods of remotivation and more dignified avenues of return to the world of work. Perhaps more significantly, the situation of these middle-class unemployed further dramatizes the plight of the larger number of unemployed non-skilled workers whose fate is to deal with unemployment often during their lifetime.

There are many situations in which individuals are expected to cope with changes. The most common are those relating to phases in the life cycle. Transitions from childhood to adulthood, from being single to being married, from being a student to joining the work force, from employment to retirement are all examples of "normal" passages in societies such as our own. Such changes involve resocialization, the learning and taking of new roles.

There are other situations in which people, individually or collectively, voluntarily or sometimes involuntarily, are resocialized—even "remade." Basic training turns civilians into soldiers, law school prepares students to become attorneys, seminaries change laypersons into members of the clergy. Other examples are the indoctrination of new inmates into prison life, new patients into the world of a mental hospital, prisoners of war and other internees into oppressive, alien settings. The most intensive resocialization takes place in controlled, authoritarian environments in which one is removed from everyday life.

In the following pages sociologists Peter I. Rose and Myron Glazer and historian Penina M. Glazer discuss such intensive resocialization, citing four case studies. Included are personal descriptions of basic training, entry into a mental hospital, an experimental study of a prison, and a devastating look at the ultimate total institution, the concentration camp.

As you read "In Controlled Environments," keep in mind the similarities and differences between the concepts of socialization and resocialization. Also note the clear connection between the altering of a person's lifeways and changes in personality and character.

In Controlled Environments: Four Cases of Intensive Resocialization

PETER I. ROSE, MYRON GLAZER, AND PENINA MIGDAL GLAZER

What happens to people who go through a resocialization process designed to give them new self-concepts, values, and norms? Resocialization . . . usually occurs in special contexts, often in special places. Some sociologists, such as

Erving Goffman, call them *total institutions;* we prefer to call them *controlled environments* because the term *institution* generally has a different meaning in sociology.

Controlled environments are established for a variety of purposes. Some exist to help or force people who are considered deviant to come back into society. Prisons and mental hospitals are examples. Others are designed to prepare people for new and different roles in specialized subcultures, such as military or monastery life. Whatever the purpose, so elaborate are the requirements and so all-encompassing are the activities that controlled environments often represent miniature social systems. They have their own hierarchies of authority, codes of conduct, and patterns of socialization. When successful in attaining their goals, they are able to block out most other aspects of life for the recruits, nuns, or inmates.

In this section we examine the resocialization that takes place within several of these environments, exploring both similarities and differences among them. There are important differences, for example, between the places a person enters voluntarily in order to be "remade" and the places he or she enters involuntarily. The range of voluntary entrants is wide: from the young drifter who decides to let the army turn him into a fighting man, to the devout Catholic adolescent who chooses the rigors of a career in the clergy, to the mentally disturbed person who seeks psychiatric help by entering a mental hospital.

The degree of voluntarism affects the entire resocialization process. For example, it is easier to resocialize people into becoming armed fighters if that is what they want to be than if they have to be forced into the role. Thus, the armed forces voluntary enlistment program may have an easier time producing trained troops than the draft. Similarly, it is far easier to help persons with emotional problems who are seeking assistance than it is to cure reluctant, confused, or belligerent people who have been committed by others.

In some instances, of course, voluntarism does not exist at all. The most extreme controlled environments, such as prisoner-of-war camps or concentration camps, make no pretense of remaking people in a more positive image. Rather, in the interests of political or military authorities, inmates are simply controlled or are actually destroyed as we see later in this chapter.

SHARED CHARACTERISTICS OF CONTROLLED ENVIRONMENTS

Although controlled environments are established for different purposes (and different inmate groups), they do tend to share certain characteristics. Erving Goffman, who studied these environments, noted four common traits.[1] First, all aspects of life are conducted in the same place and are under the control of

[1] Erving Goffman, *Asylums* (New York: Doubleday Anchor, 1961).

the same authority. Most people interact in a variety of settings. They assume many roles. No matter how successful their socialization to these roles is, there is always competition from the demands of the others. "Sorry I can't stay and listen to music. I have to get to work," or, "Hello, Pat. I'll be late getting home from school because I'm staying for practice."

All of us depend on getting time out from the demands of a particular setting. "Thank God, it's Friday," exclaim workers, teachers, and students alike. What they really mean is, "I want to get away from work. I'd like to do some other things, interact with different people."

In a controlled environment, whether it is a merchant ship or a monastery, the inmates eat, work, and sleep in the same place with the same authorities regulating their lives. Usually a large number of people are managed by a small staff, and the interaction among role-players in different positions is carefully regulated.

A second characteristic of controlled environments is that all aspects of daily life are conducted in the company of others who are in the same circumstances. Army recruits, novices in a convent, and prisoners generally enjoy little privacy. They spend most of their days with others in similar circumstances. Contact with the outside world is regulated and occurs under conditions specified by the establishment's authorities.

A third characteristic is that all activities are scheduled by the authorities without consulting the participants. Very often a formal routine prescribes such details of life as when to get up and go to bed, what to wear, when and what to eat, the work to do, and the leisure activities offered.

Finally, the activities in a controlled environment are all designed to meet the same goal: to fulfill the purpose of the organization. Physical training, harassment by authorities, strict enforcement of rules and regulations, and limitations on contact with the outside world are all used by military authorities, for example, to transform civilians into fighting men. Similarly, all activities in a monastery are centered around prayer and communion with God, while prison activities are designed to keep antisocial people in order, if not to change their antisocial attitudes.

In the remainder of this essay we examine in detail the intense resocialization process in four environments—the army, the mental hospital, the prison, and the concentration camp. These establishments do not share every element of a controlled environment to the same degree. Some allow inmates to have passes, while others do not, for example. What distinguishes these settings from other places, however, is, as Goffman points out, "that each exhibits to an intense degree many items in this family of attributes."[2] That is, each sufficiently resembles the ideal type to be classified as a controlled environment.

[2] Ibid., p. 5.

BOOT CAMP

The armed forces prepare men (and some women) to endure hardship, obey orders, have group solidarity, and acquire the skills and attitudes necessary for war. To do this, military authorities demand that recruits leave behind their families, possessions, ideas—indeed, their whole civilian selves—and forge new identities as military personnel. How this occurs is well described by Steven Warner, a young man who had been given a conscientious objector designation by his local draft board but nevertheless was drafted by the marine corps. Warner, like the other recruits, found that many of his previous beliefs were challenged as the corps attempted to turn him from a citizen who hated war into a soldier who would obey on command. Warner was quickly labeled a deviant by his superiors and singled out for special harassment. The experience had a deep impact on him.

> Our Greyhound drove onto Parris Island at ten that night. A few seconds after we stopped, a staff sergeant wearing the Smokey Bear hat all drill instructors wear came on the bus and said: "You're on Parris Island. There are two ways to leave here: on a bus like this in eight or nine weeks or in a box. . . . If you have any cigarettes, put them out. If you have any gum, swallow it. . . . You have ten seconds to get into that building. . . . Move!"
>
> A staff sergeant began . . . telling us how we were to behave from that moment on. . . .
>
> Recruits must stand at attention at all times. Recruits will not eyeball. Recruits will double-time everywhere. Recruits will do nothing without permission: they will not speak or swat bugs or wipe off sweat or faint without permission. Recruits will call everyone, except other recruits, "Sir." Recruits will never use the word "you" because "you" is a female sheep and there are no ewes on Parris Island. Recruits will never use the word "I" because "I" is what a recruit sees with, not what he calls himself.[3]

An initial part of the resocialization process began with *depersonalization*. The young men were no longer called by their names. Their possessions were taken away, and a hundred rules or new norms were thrown at them. Merging with the group was stressed, rather than individual identity. Recruits were no longer treated as individuals, but had to speak, look, and act like every other

[3] Steven Warner, "A Conscientious Objector at Parris Island," *Atlantic,* June 1972, p. 46. Copyright © 1972 by The Atlantic Monthly Company, Boston, Mass., reprinted by permission, and by permission of Paul R. Reynolds, Inc., 12 East 41st Street, New York, N.Y., 10017.

recruit—or else. Uniforms and haircuts were important components of that transformation. To accomplish the depersonalization, the men had to do some *unlearning*. It no longer mattered whether a recruit had been a high school baseball star, a talented carpenter, a big man on campus, or his parents' pride and joy. Former roles and identities simply did not count. The sooner they were forgotten, the better the recruit would get along.

The resocialization process included another crucial component made clear by Warner's first exposure to the marines. The drill instructor (DI) immediately became the recruits' most important *significant other*. The welcoming speech not only set out a whole series of new norms but also established that the DI controlled rewards and punishments. If the recruit did not live up to his role obligations, he would be observed and quickly reprimanded. The DI's opinion and reactions were what counted now. He and his fellow DIs were in control.

This was made abundantly clear when the men were ordered to pick up their gear and follow their DI after the initial speech. Those recruits who couldn't keep the double time pace were cajoled, cursed, and ultimately punished. The message was clear. Tough days were ahead. The DIs had the difficult task of turning soft-bellied individual civilians into a disciplined fighting unit. It may not have been a task they relished, but it was necessary, and they did it in a relentless manner.

The DIs' definition of their own roles seemed abundantly clear and reflected their sensitivity to the process of resocialization. The recruits brought with them a vast baggage of previous roles and cultural definitions. It was the assumption of the armed forces that all of these had to be broken down and discarded if the recruits were to become military men capable of responding to orders, working as a group, and living together. New norms had to be repeated continually and appropriate behavior demanded. No exceptions could be made. The DIs' role demanded that they be constantly alert for infractions of the rules and be ready to "chew out" or "ream" offenders. The DIs' vigilance and consistency in playing their roles were important defenses against letting the recruits slide into former civilian patterns of behavior.

Each DI's vigilance also served to remind his men that he represented the authority of the entire military chain of command. His legitimacy stemmed from his position in the military hierarchy, and he had clearcut obligations to his superiors to bear down hard. The DI, as well as the men, was judged by the unit's efficiency in performing its tasks.

Warner's training continued. Physical exercise was peppered with constant harassment and emphasis on the cunning and toughness of North Vietnamese soldiers. Although Warner came to training camp with no fear of or ill will toward the "enemy" in Southeast Asia, exposure to the training sessions instilled such fear in him. The controlled environment was having its effect. Other things were also happening. A sense of group solidarity was beginning to take hold. The men reached out to help each other in time of trouble and provided comfort. As in actual combat situations, the recruits came to act out the belief that they could depend on their buddies. Primary group relations were clearly developing under the supervision of the authorities.

Since the first days of boot camp, we had been warned about the PRT (Physical Readiness Test) we would take during the last week. This would be our initiation into the Marine Corps. . . .

We climbed some ropes in full gear, carried one another over our shoulders for a while, crawled a lot. . . . Then came the last hurdle: a three-mile run in full gear—steel helmet, boots, pack, rifle.

Everyone was grim. Our commanding officer, also in full gear, ran in front of the company. Gordon [the DI] was in front of our platoon. . . . We ran silently for a while. The only sounds were heavy breathing and boots hitting the ground. Then Gordon started us on our chants: "Here we go-o! HERE WE GO-O! Long Road! LONG ROAD! Hard Road! HARD ROAD! Won't Stop! WON'T STOP! Gimme More! GIMME MORE! Marine Corps! MARINE CORPS!"

Two or three recruits were having a hard time. They had run the distance many times before, but now they gasped for air and stumbled trying to keep up. Other recruits took turns, carrying their rifles, their packs, and even their helmets. If the stragglers continued to fade, they were held up by the arms, even carried. . . . The point was, the platoon kept on running, and no one was left behind. We had learned our lesson.

When it was over, everybody was grins and back-slapping. Gordon, sweating more than I had ever seen before, came into the barracks and gave us a small smile and said: "MARINES . . . take a shower." It was the first time he had ever called us that.[4]

This episode includes some telling points about the process of resocialization. The men's new status required far more than putting aside previous statuses. It required them to forge a new identity, a new set of role definitions to go along with their new status as marines. A positive identity was developing. This identity included the belief that the recruit could overcome difficult physical challenges, that he must and could make sure that the others made it as well, that this successful outcome came under the leadership of competent authorities. The reward was a shared satisfaction that the unit had succeeded and that each member could take personal pride in the achievement. Thus, while former statuses had been suppressed in the process of resocialization, the new one—marine—once achieved, made all the sacrifices easier to bear.

[4] Ibid., p. 51.

In this effort, the peer group had played a central part. Feelings of "We're doing it together" or "We can make it, if we stick together" reflect a sense of interdependence that reinforces the value of the authorities that the unit is more important than the individual. In essence, resocialization of each participant is attained more effectively if the peer group comes to support the values of the authorities.

How do the characteristics of a controlled environment that we described earlier apply to the military basic training situation? All aspects of the recruit's life are conducted at one particular place—the military base—and under the control of one authority—the DI. All aspects of the recruit's life are conducted in the company of other recruits who are in the same circumstances and playing the same role. All activities of the day are scheduled by the authorities without the consent of the recruits. No one asks them what time they care to get up, what they would like to wear or eat during the day, or which tasks they prefer to perform. Finally, the activities were designed to fulfill the main purpose of the military—to prepare men to fight in wars. This means socializing men to do tasks and respond to authority even when their lives are at stake. Behavior that had been perfectly acceptable in civilian life was now defined as deviant and subject to punishment. Even a conscientious objector like Steven Warner found his previous beliefs undermined. His last statement is particularly revealing, for he writes that, if his own son ever has to be in the armed forces, he hopes the boy will serve in the marines.[5]

Warner's experiences in marine basic training show us several other characteristics of controlled environments. For one thing, depersonalization is a central component of resocialization. It forces the recruit to leave behind former positions and the roles and identities associated with them. Warner's experience also shows that unlearning former role behavior is a painful procedure that people are likely to resist. Significant others are crucial in the unlearning process. They are more likely to have their expectations met when these are set out clearly and consistently and when resources are available to reward conformity and punish deviance. An individual is more willing to play new roles if these roles are shown to have some relation to past definitions of the self. Thus, recruits may vehemently dislike obeying orders, but they are more likely to do so if they can be convinced that this shows they "can take it," "are growing up," or are now fit to be called "marine." In essence, resocialization occurs more easily if conformity to the roles of the new position is shown as competence rather than subservience. Finally, resocialization proceeds more smoothly if the individual finds new groups with which to identify within the controlled environment. This occurred in Warner's marine basic training. As we see next, it can also occur in mental hospitals.

[5] Ibid., p. 52.

THE MENTAL HOSPITAL

The patient in a mental hospital, like the military recruit, must learn a new set of behaviors and attitudes for interactions with a variety of new persons. Like boot camp, the mental hospital has a goal: to take people who have been defined—by their physicians, their families, or themselves—as emotionally disturbed and transform them, if they are capable of responding to therapy, into functioning members of the larger society.

The mental patient spends virtually all his or her time in the hospital, is cut off from playing former roles, and is usually deprived of regular clothing and possessions. The patient experiences the depersonalization process in many subtle and obvious ways. Yet the experience in a mental hospital is much more individualized than that in basic training. Patients do not enter or leave as a group. Though similar behavior is demanded of the patients, each patient must adjust on his or her own to the new setting, and each must progress individually to a healthier condition in order to be released.

Sociologist Lewis Killian described his experience as an actual patient in a small mental hospital in New England. He was suffering from severe depression, and his psychiatrist had recommended hospitalization.

> I remember my admission to the hospital only in fragments. I kissed my wife goodbye and heard the appalling words, "No visitors for 72 hours," and then I was alone among strangers. I didn't care: I wanted to be alone. . . . But immediately the [staff] began to break through my shell. "Have you eaten supper, Lewis?" "We all use first names here—patients and staff; I'm Helen, I'm a nurse". . . .
>
> We inventoried everything I had brought into the hospital. I was required to give my keys to the nurse for safe keeping because the small knife on my key chain constituted a "sharp" in the lingo of the ward, and all sharps had to be kept behind the nurses' station. I was reminded by this that I really was suspect—I did not just imagine that I was in a somewhat abnormal state. I could accept this, though, for I wasn't sure that I might not harm myself. After I went to bed that night it reassured rather than disturbed me to realize that an attendant looked in on me every hour throughout the night. . . .
>
> The power vested in the staff was so evident that one of my first reactions to the ward was, "This is like a prison!" When I found that a staff member had to accompany me on the short walk down the corridor to the lavatory; when I saw patients with "hospital privileges" asking the charge nurse for a pass to go to the gift shop; when I realized that I was

forbidden to go out the doors of the ward without permission, I was reminded of the pervasive system of control which I had observed in a maximum security military prison while training there as a reserve officer. For me as for our prisoners "being out of place" was an offense against the norms of the total institution.[6]

Despite the apparent differences between Killian's first hours in the mental hospital and the marines' initial exposure to basic training, there are important similarities. In both instances the authorities have a clear-cut goal and a method that they believe is effective in resocializing people in accordance with the goal. They are confident that, in the context of a highly structured and even authoritarian environment, they can reshape individuals' behavior and conceptions of themselves. At first, individuals go along, because they are made acutely aware of the imbalance of power. But this is not sufficient. Ultimately, in order to create well-motivated fighting men or cured patients, the authorities must convince those in their charge that the establishment's goals and methods are appropriate:

> My conception of the power of the staff changed as I reacted to their behavior. I came to feel that it was . . . essentially supportive rather than threatening. A patient saw his therapist only two or three times a week, and then for an hour at a time. On the other hand, at least one member of the nursing staff was on the floor at all times, and usually there were three present. . . .
>
> This almost constant observation and intervention made it very difficult for a patient to withdraw and nurse his troubles in private—something I was certainly inclined to do when I entered the community. . . . I soon reached the conclusion that it was easier to keep active and involved with other people than it was to justify going into a shell. This change of behavior pattern was, of course, just what I needed to break the cycle of my depression, and it came about without anyone's explicitly prescribing it for me.[7]

Lewis Killian's ability to understand himself increased as he became an active participant in the hospital community. He grew to feel close to both staff and patients. For a short but crucial period, the hospital became his home. Patients shared their problems and helped each other find new strength. Killian thrived in an environment where people could freely discuss what was troubling them. There was no need to fool themselves or each other. In effect, the authorities fostered the development of primary group relations. It was important for the therapeutic method that close bonds develop among people

[6] Lewis M. Killian and Sanford Bloomberg, "Rebirth in a Therapeutic Community: A Case Study," *Psychiatry* 38 (1975): 43–45.
[7] Ibid., pp. 48–49.

of diverse ages, backgrounds, and interests who could support each other in the rehabilitation process. Perhaps Killian's last sentence best captures his feeling. When friends say they are sorry to hear he was in the hospital, he replies: "Thank you—but it was one of the most wonderful experiences of my life."[8]

Killian's experience shows that secondary deviance—being defined by others as emotionally ill—can have positive consequences. It was only in the company of others who were similarly defined that he was able to come to terms with his illness. The hospital staff provided the social structure in which his "rebirth" would take place.

Other mental patients have encountered very different experiences, however. Not all mental hospitals are so clearly directed toward healing as the one described by Killian. Patients may not know of such a place, or they may not be able to afford one. Also some patients are too difficult to control in such a setting. These people are most likely to be placed in facilities that emphasize management, control, and caretaking. Here the depersonalization and powerlessness are not as likely to produce beneficial results for the patient as they did for Killian in his setting.

In a project directed by D. L. Rosenhan, a number of graduate students and professionals studied mental hospitals by pretending to be patients.[9] The researchers were interested in finding out how easily they could be diagnosed as mentally ill and admitted to a mental hospital, and how easily they could obtain their discharge. All understood that once they entered the hospital they would be released only when they convinced the staff that they were sane. This turned out to be no simple task.

Each went to the admitting office of a mental hospital and claimed to be hearing unfamiliar voices. All were admitted to their chosen hospitals. No researcher was recognized as a pretender by the staff. At all times they were treated as real patients. Other patients, however, frequently noticed that the researchers did not seem ill. They asked if they were journalists or professors.

Rosenhan's description of what the researchers experienced tells us a great deal about the resocialization process in a mental hospital. As you read it, compare this resocialization experience with Steven Warner's account of boot camp.

> Consider the structure of the typical psychiatric hospital. Staff and patients are strictly segregated. Staff have their own living space, including their dining facilities, bathroom, and assembly places. The glassed quarters that contain the professional staff, which the pseudopatients came to call "the cage," sit out on every dayroom. The staff emerge

[8] Ibid., p. 52.
[9] D. L. Rosenhan, "On Being Sane in Insane Places," *Science* 179 (1973): 250–58.

primarily for caretaking purposes—to give medication, to conduct a therapy or group meeting, to instruct or reprimand a patient. Otherwise, staff keep to themselves. . . .

. . . It has long been known that the amount of time a person spends with you can be an index of your significance to him. If he initiates and maintains eye contact, there is reason to believe that he is considering your requests and needs. If he pauses to chat or actually stops and talks, there is added reason to infer that he is [treating you as an individual]. In four hospitals, the pseudopatient approached the staff member with a request which took the following form: "Pardon me, Mr. [or Dr. or Mrs.] X, could you tell me when I will be eligible for grounds privileges?" (or ". . . when I will be presented at the staff meeting?" or ". . . when I am likely to be discharged?"). . . . Care was taken never to approach a particular member of the staff more than once a day, lest the staff member become suspicious or irritated. . . .

. . . By far, their most common response consisted of either a brief response to the question, offered while they were "on the move" and with head averted, or no response at all.[10]

This kind of response reduces the patient to childlike status. The question is not worthy of an answer. The doctor's answer is almost like a pat on the head. Rosenhan concludes:

No data can convey the overwhelming sense of powerlessness which invades the individual as he is continually exposed to the *depersonalization* of the psychiatric hospital. . . .

Powerlessness was evident everywhere. The patient is deprived of many of his legal rights. . . . His freedom of movement is restricted. . . . Personal privacy is minimal. Patient quarters and possessions can be entered and examined by any staff member, for whatever reason. . . . The water closets may have no doors. . . .

On the ward, attendants delivered verbal and occasionally serious physical abuse to patients in the presence of other observing patients. . . . Abusive behavior, on the other hand [ended quickly] when other staff members were known to be coming.[11]

Rosenhan's critique echoes those made by other researchers,[12] civil libertarians, and public officials. Most mental hospitals seem far more capable of giving custodial care than of providing therapy. Their patients most often are resocialized to play a passive and apathetic role rather than an active one in an effort to change troublesome patterns of feelings and behavior. Depersonalization and powerlessness make patients easier to handle. Authority

[10] Ibid., pp. 254–55.
[11] Ibid., p. 256.
[12] For a recent statement, see Martha R. Fowlkes, "Business as Usual—At the State Mental Hospital," *Psychiatry* 38 (1975): 55–64.

figures often do not use these techniques to achieve therapeutic goals as they did in the hospital described by Killian.

THE PRISON

Prisons, unlike mental hospitals, have long been a favorite subject of movie makers. Striped uniforms, marching men, the tough, good-guy warden have all been part of the scenario. Yet these films give the audience only a glimpse of prison life. They cannot fully detail the years of boredom, the meaningless work, the fear of violence, the deprivation of heterosexual activity, and the humiliation of forced homosexual participation that often characterize a prison sentence.

In the 1950s Gresham Sykes wrote a detailed account of a maximum security prison in New Jersey.[13] Several years later Willard Gaylin did a study of a group of conscientious objectors who were serving time in a minimum security federal prison.[14] The settings differed, and the men were in prison for entirely different reasons, yet the experiences were alike in many ways.

In both studies, the prisoners learned that prison means loss of self-expression. Prisoners are allowed little sense of individuality. Closely cropped hair and prison uniforms strip inmates of the personal distinctions that help tell them who they are. They are thoroughly searched upon arrest and are deprived of any privacy. Prisoners who attempt to gain rights or organize others to do so may be singled out for swift and often cruel punishment.

For centuries prisons have been places of incarceration and punishment. Only in modern times has the idea of rehabilitation of society's deviants become a central task. However, programs designed to accomplish the preparation of prisoners for life on the "outside" have had limited success. As evidence of the failure of rehabilitation, critics point to the high proportion of ex-convicts who return to their former activities and end up back in prison. Of the 228,032 adults arrested for federal crimes during 1970–72, 25 percent had one previous conviction, 9 percent two, 5 percent three, and 8 percent four or more. . . .

Other critics say it is not the idea of rehabilitation that is at fault but the inadequate training of prison personnel and insufficient funding to support effective programs. Moreover, some suggest, most prison authorities still see their jobs as keeping inmates securely behind bars and maintaining order.

Is it necessary for prisoners to be treated so differently from the rest of us in our everyday lives? Prisons have been established by the larger society to control and isolate men and women convicted of breaking some law. Does the attempt to control prisoners require guards to play their role in a certain way?

[13] Gresham M. Sykes, *The Society of Captives* (Princeton, N.J.: Princeton University Press, 1958).
[14] Willard Gaylin, *In the Service of Their Country: War Resisters in Prison* (New York: Viking Press, 1970).

As husbands, fathers, or friends, these same men may be kind and gentle. Yet most guards seem to believe that such traits are a weakness in the prison community and therefore a threat to the order they are hired to maintain.

An Experiment in Intensive Resocialization

To understand more about how guards and prisoners learn to play their roles, a group of social scientists set up a mock prison in the basement of a building at Stanford University as an experiment.[15] Into this prison they sent ten "prisoners" and eleven "guards." All the men were actually ordinary college students who had answered an ad offering them the chance to make fifteen dollars a day by participating in .an experiment. The interaction between prisoners and guards was carefully recorded by hidden recorders and video tape.

The people chosen to play the role of prisoner agreed to remain in the jail for two weeks, and each was arrested and booked by the local Stanford police, who cooperated in the experiment. Prisoners wore special smocks for uniforms and nylon stocking caps to imitate short haircuts. Guards were dressed in uniforms and sunglasses (to avoid eye contact), and carried billy clubs, whistles, and handcuffs. They were told that they were responsible for maintaining law and order. They were informed that the situation was dangerous.

Prisoners were not allowed to write letters, smoke cigarettes, or go to the bathroom without first obtaining permission. Roll-call was held during each of three guard shifts, and prisoners were often awakened for special counts. Prisoners had to remain silent during rest periods, meals, and outdoor activities, and after lights-out. They were required to address each other by ID numbers only and to address guards as "Mr. Correctional Officer." . . .

The experiment revealed that normal college students placed in a prison setting quickly assumed behavior that actual prisoners and guards display. When interviewed by the researchers, guards said how angry they became with prisoners who resisted their control. The guards enjoyed feeling the power they held over the prisoners and resented any attempt by the prisoners to stand up to them. One guard, for example, told how he listened to a conversation a prisoner had with a visitor. The guard interrupted whenever he disagreed with anything the prisoner said. The guard reported that he relished the feeling of superiority. Yet this same guard described himself as a pacifist and was deeply surprised by his own actions.

Most of the guards were sorry when the experiment ended. They did not like giving up the money they were making by participating in the experiment. But, even more important, they had really enjoyed their sense of power.

[15] Philip G. Zimbardo, W. Curtis Banks, Craig Haney, and David Jaffe, "A Pirandellian Prison," *New York Times Magazine,* April 8, 1973, p. 38.

Prisoners, on the other hand, were glad when it was all over. In their cells they had talked almost constantly about the prison—the food, their treatment, how they could escape. Prison had been a real and deeply troubling experience for them. Very quickly they learned to play passive roles, accommodating themselves to unjust rules, finding it easier not to assert themselves or stick up for their rights. The experiment revealed that the prison affected the volunteers the way it does actual prisoners. They were afraid, hated their guards, and tried to rebel. They seemed to forget that they were to be there for only two weeks. Finally, they adjusted to their environment, became passive, and began to toe the line.

The guards, too, responded much the way real guards do to hostile, threatening prisoners. Some were kinder than others, but no guards ever stopped their colleagues from treating prisoners cruelly.

In fact, the study concluded, even normal, healthy, educated young men can be transformed or resocialized under the pressures of the prison environment. It did not seem to matter that the situation was an artificial one. Nor did it matter that the subjects had individual personalities at the outset. Once put into their prison roles, they responded very similarly to others in those roles. Philip Zimbardo, the chief researcher, concluded that

> the mere act of assigning labels to people and putting them into a situation where those labels acquire validity and meaning is sufficient to elicit pathological behavior. . . . The prison situation, as presently arranged, is guaranteed to generate severe enough pathological reactions in both guards and prisoners as to debase their humanity, lower their feelings of self-worth and make it difficult for them to be part of a society outside their prison.[16]

Zimbardo's conclusion, based on a carefully conducted experimental study of a small group of students, is supported by numerous official reports published over the years. A recent effort focused on the Attica prison uprising in which forty-three prisoners and hostages were killed by New York State police on September 9, 1971.[17] The report of the New York State Commission on Attica strongly criticized this nation's entire prison system. Massive establishments like Attica, with 2,200 prisoners, are unlikely to provide an environment in which prisoners can be treated humanely, it contended. (We might say the same of large-scale mental hospitals.)

The New York commission found that confinement and security were far more important to Attica authorities than rehabilitation. Shortages of staff and funds prevented the prison from offering education or job taining programs for prisoners. Rarely were guards and other officials trained to com-

---

[16] Philip G. Zimbardo, "Pathology of Imprisonment," *Society*, April 1972, p. 6.
[17] *Attica: The Official Report of the New York State Commission on Attica* (New York: Bantam Books, 1972).

municate with prisoners in a meaningful way. Personnel did not think it was part of their job to understand the inmates. Facilities were so crowded that it was even difficult to maintain personal cleanliness and health. Most prisoners could shower only once a week, change their clothes only once a week, and rarely replace worn-out clothing.

It was impossible for prisoners to distinguish between incompetence and harassment. They became less and less willing to cooperate with authorities and less and less convinced that the resocialization process was beneficial to them. Inmates defined the bureaucracy as the enemy. One inmate, for example, received much-needed undershorts and pajamas from his family; unfortunately, the underwear was blue, which was prohibited. He raged, "How can you tell a grown man that he is violating security by wearing a blue pair of shorts? . . . They actually think that we believe that? You know why that rule was made? For harassment and for harassment only."[18]

Under the severe limitations of inadequate clothing, minimal food, lack of spending money, and endless regulations, many prisoners adapted by "hustling." Unlike the therapeutic community, in prison primary groups were not organized by the authorities to help reshape or train their charges. Rather prisoners themselves created these groups to get around the authorities. For example, the Attica commission reported that, to get clean laundry, prisoners "bought a laundry man" (someone working in the laundry) for a carton of cigarettes a month. Many deals were made to meet sexual needs. Because of the lack of women and the denial of visits by wives and sweethearts, many formerly heterosexual men in prisons turn to homosexuality. Small prostitution and pimping groups emerged in Attica, the report found. Similar groups developed for production and distribution of "moonshine," drugs, and medicines.

Throughout the history of prisons, inmates have gone on hunger strikes, invented codes to communicate with and help one another, made implements out of the most primitive materials, and organized internal social systems to get around the rules. An elaborate system of theft and bribes in prisons and other controlled environments helps make life a bit more bearable for the inmates. In his book *Asylums,* sociologist Erving Goffman referred to this phenomenon as "make-do's"—a response that he claims characterizes people in all highly controlled environments.[19] This seems especially true where little effort is made to reshape people to a positive identity, and where the environment is geared toward isolation and control.

THE CONCENTRATION CAMP

Many modern societies have had internment camps, occasionally or as a constant feature. An internment camp in many ways resembles a prison, except

[18] Ibid., p. 46.
[19] Goffman, *Asylums,* p. 207.

that its purpose is neither punishment nor rehabilitation. It is designed to hold people who have been removed from the general society in times of unrest or war because they are considered a threat to the social or political order. For example, at the outset of World War II, as hostile feelings against the Japanese rose, Americans adopted an official policy of holding all Japanese-Americans in internment camps.[20]

These people—most of whom were living in California—had committed no crimes. Many had been born in this country and had always been loyal to it. One Japanese-American battalion that was later formed distinguished itself for bravery in European combat, suffering the highest casualty rate of any battalion and boasting the lowest desertion rate in military history—zero. Yet Japanese-Americans had their property confiscated and were denied all civil liberties and rights, without charges, trial, or conviction. Official histories tend to ignore or underplay this episode, because it is now recognized as cruel, unnecessary, and nakedly racist—no Germans or Italians were interned even though their ancestral nations were also declared enemies of the United States in that war, and some German-Americans had formed organizations to promote sympathy for Nazism before the war.[21]

These American internment camps have been compared to the Nazi concentration camps of the 1930s and early 1940s. Yet there is an essential difference: the Nazi camps were engaged in a program of genocide (annihilation of a whole people considered racially or morally degenerate). In both kinds of camps, there was no training of recruits for army service as in the boot camp, no treatment of illness as in the mental hospital, no rehabilitation of prisoners or even simply holding inmates captive until they had served their sentences as in the prison. But the Nazi concentration camps had one extremely significant additional feature: they were established to work the inmates to death or to kill them outright if they became unfit to labor for the German war machine. Those who were not sent immediately to the gas chambers soon saw how worthless their lives were in the eyes of their captors. They learned the techniques of adaptation quickly or not at all. Bare survival was the only reward of the lucky few.

The inmates of the concentration camps included political activists and intellectuals who had resisted the Nazis, prisoners from invaded countries such as Poland and Russia, and Jews from many lands—including Germany, its allies, and occupied countries. Thus, although Italy under Mussolini fought on the side of Hitler's armies, Italian Jews were rounded up by their own countrymen and shipped to German concentration camps far across Europe.

Among these Italians was Primo Levi, a young man who fled to the mountains when the arrest of Italian Jews began but was captured by the Italian

---

[20] See Alexander H. Leighton, *The Governing of Men* (Princeton, N.J.: Princeton University Press, 1945).
[21] Audrie Girdner and Anne Loftis, *The Great Betrayal: The Evacuation of Japanese Americans during World War Two* (New York: Macmillan, 1969).

militia. His story illustrates how resocialization occurs in the most extreme form of controlled environment.

A dozen SS men stood around, legs akimbo, with an indifferent air. At a certain moment they moved among us, and in a subdued tone of voice, with faces of stone, began to interrogate us rapidly, one by one, in bad Italian. They did not interrogate everybody, only a few: "How old? Healthy or ill?" And on the basis of the reply they pointed in two different directions. . . .

In less than ten minutes all the fit men had been collected together in a group. What happened to the others, to the women, to the children, to the old men, we could establish neither then nor later: the night swallowed them up, purely and simply. Today, however, we know that in that rapid and summary choice each one of us had been judged capable or not of working usefully for the Reich; we know that of our convoy no more than ninety-six men and twenty-nine women entered the respective camps of Monowitz-Buna and Birkenau, and that of all the others, more than five hundred in number, not one was living two days later. . . .[22]

The initiation rite continued. Heads were shaved, the people were thrown in boiling showers, then immediately forced to run, naked and barefoot, in the icy snow. Finally they were given uniforms to put on.

There is nowhere to look in a mirror, but our appearance stands in front of us, reflected in a hundred livid faces, in a hundred miserable and sordid puppets. . . .

Then for the first time we became aware that our language lacks words to express this offense, the demolition of a man. In a moment, with almost prophetic intuition, the reality was revealed to us; we had reached the bottom. It is not possible to sink lower than this; no human condition is more miserable than this nor could it conceivably be so. Nothing belongs to us anymore; they have taken away our clothes, our shoes, even our hair; if we speak, they will not listen to us, and if they listen, they will not understand. They will even take away our name; and if we want to keep it, we will have to find in ourselves the strength to do so, to manage somehow so that behind the name something of us, as we still were, still remains. . . .

Driven by thirst, I eyed a fine icicle outside the window, within hand's reach. I opened the window and broke off the icicle but at once a large, heavy guard prowling outside brutally snatched it away from me. "Warum?" I asked him in my poor German. "Hier ist kein warum" (there is no why here), he replied, pushing me inside with a shove.

[22] From *Survival in Auschwitz* by Primo Levi, translated by Stuart Woolf. Copyright © 1959 by The Orion Press, Inc. All rights reserved. Reprinted by permission of Grossman Publishers, a division of The Viking Press, Inc.

The explanation is repugnant but simple: in this place everything is forbidden, not for hidden reasons, but because the camp has been created for that purpose. . . .

And we have learnt other things, more or less quickly, according to our intelligence: to reply *"Jawohl,"* never to ask questions, always to pretend to understand. We have learnt the value of food; now we also diligently scrape the bottom of the bowl after the ration and we hold it under our chins when we eat bread so as not to lose the crumbs. We, too, know that it is not the same thing to be given a ladleful of soup from the top or the bottom of the vat, and we are already able to judge, according to the capacity of the various vats, what is the most suitable place to try and reach in the queue when we line up.

We have learnt that everything is useful: the wire to tie up our shoes, the rags to wrap around our feet, waste paper to (illegally) pad out our jackets against the cold. We have learnt, on the other hand, that everything can be stolen, in fact is automatically stolen as soon as attention is relaxed; to avoid this, we had to learn the art of sleeping with our head on a bundle made up of our jacket and containing all our belongings, from the bowl to the shoes.

. . . The prohibitions are innumerable: to approach nearer to the barbed wire than two yards; to sleep with one's jacket; or without one's pants, or with one's cap on one's head; to use certain washrooms or latrines. . . .

We Italians had decided to meet every Sunday evening in a corner of the Lager, but we stopped it at once, because it was too sad to count our numbers and find fewer each time, and to see each other ever more deformed and more squalid. And it was so tiring to walk those few steps and then, meeting each other, to remember and to think. It was better not to think.[23]

We have stated that socialization is the process of learning the ways of society and that resocialization is the process of relearning codes of conduct and patterns of behavior appropriate to new circumstances. Often, intensive resocialization in controlled environments has some supposedly positive goal for those undergoing the process. This is true of boot camp, where citizens are trained to be soldiers, and mental hospitals, where people are presumably helped to adjust to or overcome their psychological difficulties. Even prison officials sometimes claim that they are rehabilitating people found guilty of violating its rules. But the goal of the concentration camp had no positive value for the inmates. Those who were not physically destroyed were mentally broken. Hitler succeeded in annihilating millions of those confined, and nearly succeeded in eradicating European Jewry.

Controlled environments are found in every modern society. They are inevitably problematic. Governments seem to have found no other way to reso-

[23] Ibid., pp. 21–34.

cialize people intensively. No military establishment in the world would consent to have recruits simply take a few classes and read some books about soldiering, and then consider them "combat-ready." Similarly, societies almost always demand that people defined as mentally disturbed or dangerous to themselves and others be isolated in highly controlled environments.

These places invariably violate the inmates' individual liberties and rights. They succeed more often in controlling people than in rehabilitating them. And when people are confined strictly for political reasons, as in internment or concentration camps, the most reprehensible features of controlled environments predominate. Societies in which large numbers of citizens are subjected to or threatened by this kind of punishment for political activities are defined as totalitarian. In more democratic systems, there is a continual tension between those who seek to solve social problems by the use of controlled environments and those who fight to preserve the civil liberties of inmates—mental patients, the elderly in nursing homes, prisoners, and military recruits. Some contend that intensive resocialization in controlled environments tends to worsen existing problems rather than solve them.

SUMMARY

[Various individuals] experience resocialization, the process of learning new roles, or adapting known roles to new needs, and unlearning previous values, norms, and roles. Some forms of resocialization occur in controlled environments designed to promote rapid, drastic changes in a person's behavior. Prisons, mental institutions, military training camps, convents and monasteries, concentration camps, and prisoner-of-war camps are examples of controlled environments.

Despite many differences in their details of administration, the voluntariness of entry, and the establishment's goals, they share certain basic features of institutions engaged in extreme resocialization. In each, the identity (or definition of self) of inmates is assaulted by techniques of depersonalization and denial of autonomy. The individual is deprived of most personal possessions and most distinguishing features of appearance. He or she can perform few tasks or functions without first obtaining permission, and punishments for infractions of rules are chosen and administered by the authorities. These techniques are planned to replace the inmate's old identity with a new one that is submissive to the demands and goals of the environment.

PART V
THE LATER YEARS

"WE GROW TOO SOON OLD AND TOO LATE SMART." SO GOES AN OLD Pennsylvania Dutch expression. And, it seems, there is more than a kernel of truth in the statement.

As we grow older time seems to fly by with ever-increasing rapidity. Before we know it we are listed among those who have entered Shakespeare's last stages of life. Sometimes the comeuppance occurs abruptly: one day we are happily employed; the next day we are given the proverbial gold watch and ushered out into the ranks of the retired. Sixty-five is usually the watershed year, but it sometimes occurs earlier. Whenever it happens, it is difficult because, in a youth-centered culture like ours, people are seldom prepared for the loneliness, loss of status, and downward mobility that often occur in "the later years." This period may last a long time. Medical advances have prolonged life, although social norms have hardly kept pace. There is a cultural lag which, until recently, few have recognized and even fewer have dealt with effectively.

Of course, not all people in this society grow old in misery, isolation, or poverty. A steadily increasing number are finding that the "golden years" can be rewarding and productive and are establishing their own niches and communities and even their own political organizations (such as the Grey Panthers). They are making demands on those who can bring about changes in policies relating to the elderly, and they are making contributions to a wide range of activities.

In order to deal more effectively with senior citizens, many behavioral scientists and professionals in the human services are studying the social aspects of aging: the ramifications of retirement, family adjustment, housing problems, and the ways in which individuals deal with loss. In addition to the growing concern with aging, professionals and lay people alike are paying increasing attention to death and dying as sociological phenomena.

The selections in Part Five include discussions of growing old both in dignity and in misery, personal accounts of three who work with families of the dying, a presentation of practical aspects of bereavement, and a penetrating discussion of the ultimate exercise in the life-long process of socialization, learning to die.

*America is not only characterized as the land of the free
and the home of the brave; it is also the country of
youth. Yet, each year census figures suggest that more
and more citizens fall into older age brackets and that
the whole demographic picture is changing. Only recently have we begun to face this fact of social life.*

*As we turn our attention to the problems of older
people, a number of questions arise about the health
and welfare of our "senior citizens." In this* Newsweek
*article, reporter Kenneth Woodward provides a brief
overview.*

*As you read the following article, think of the special
problems of being old in a youth-centered society and
the attendant matter of loss of status.*

Growing Old Happy

KENNETH WOODWARD

Growing old in the country of the young has always been a fearsome
prospect—and with the aging of the whole population it is one that more and
more Americans can look forward to. But it may not turn out to be so bad. In
reality, the lives of millions of older Americans suggest that growing old is
nowhere near as fearful—or unfulfilling—as it is thought to be.

Most interesting, in fact, is what old people are not. Contrary to popular
belief, only 5 percent of the 23 million Americans over 65 are confined to nursing homes and institutions, and only 10 per cent more, experts say, ought to
be. Most senior citizens do not move to Florida—or anywhere else for that
matter: only 5 percent of the population pulls up stakes after retirement.
Over half of America's elderly live with their spouses in independent
households, usually in communities where they have roots; one-fourth live
alone and only 15 per cent live with their children.

And most old people aren't poor and neglected: the percentage of older
Americans living below the poverty line has dropped from 25 percent in 1969
to 16 percent in 1974. At latest tally, older citizens reported a median family
income of $4,800, compared with $12,400 for those between 18 and 64, but
those figures do not include interest from savings, supplementary support
from children or income derived from bootleg jobs. "The old characterization

of the elderly as impoverished, debilitated and depressed is badly wrong,'' claims Dr. George Maddox, director of the Duke University Center for the Study of Aging and Human Development in Durham, N. C. ''That description fails to describe 85 per cent of older Americans.''

FEAR OF DYING—AND LIVING

In reality, the aging process is a series of progressive stages, beginning with one that can be genuine fulfillment. With proper planning, the first ten years of retirement can result in a most gratifying mental, physical and social life. ''The watershed age is 75, when illness, disability or financial conditions begin to take their toll,'' says sociologist Robert Atschley, a specialist on aging at Miami University in Oxford, Ohio. Yet even the later years can offer a peace of mind in preparation for death, which the elderly often accept more willingly than their relatives. ''Older people want to talk about death, but when they do, their 40-year-old children change the conversation,'' says psychologist Gisela Labouvie-Vief of Wayne State University in Detroit. ''More older people are coping with death, but what is significant for them still remains a taboo for large segments of society.''

There are still many serious problems for older Americans. According to a Harris poll prepared in 1974 for the National Council on the Aging, what bothers the aged most, after fear of crime, is poor health, not having enough money to live on and loneliness. The elderly are afraid of dying and at the same time, afraid of outliving their capacity to cope with sickness. The worst nightmare is that of a long-term illness which wipes out their financial resources and leaves them hanging—indefinitely—between life and death.

Medicare and Medicaid have substantially eased the financial burdens of health care for the elderly, ensuring that they can withstand even serious illness without losing everything. Similarly, Congressional action to link social-security payments to the cost of living has gone far to ease money worries for the majority of old people who rely on the system as their main source of income.

For many Americans, however, retirement itself—whether by force or choice—can be the most traumatic experience of growing old. The shock of suddenly having nothing to do, the feeling of being put on a shelf, can bring on profound physical and emotional crises, especially among people who derive their self-esteem from work. When Max Joseph was forced to retire last year at the age of 64, the hard-driving production chief for a New England garment firm immediately sought other employment. But wherever he applied, he was told that he was overqualified—and too old—for the job. ''I felt beaten by life,'' the tall, white-haired Bostonian recalls. ''I was ready for a psychiatrist. I am too intelligent to get up in the morning and wonder what I am going to do." Last fall, Max signed on as a volunteer in the state consumer-protection office. "This volunteer business is a beautiful thing," he says, "but I'm still resentful at giving my ability for nothing."

Unlike older, more traditional societies, the U. S. has yet to institutionalize a role for its elderly, so each retiree must create his own life-style. For the few who can afford it, there are communities like Leisure World, an expensive cluster of Spanish-style dwellings in Laguna Hills, Calif., where life is so safe, ordered and busy that younger widows sometimes lie about their age (minimum requirement:52) when applying for a condominium. Among other diversions, residents can swim in four heated pools, play golf on a 27-hole course, ride horses, take up almost any craft or organize any sort of club. By day, the women sew, play bridge and give each other parties. By 10 o'clock each night, there are no empty parking spaces outside the five community club houses. About the only activity Leisure World doesn't offer is work. "If you play golf or pool five times a week for a couple of months, it becomes a pain in the neck," says one restless retiree.

Most older Americans, however, do not move to distant retirement communities. They either haven't got the money or are pinned to homes they cannot manage to sell. Others do not want to leave their neighborhoods and lose the friendships they have developed there. Although the elderly often say they like to live among young people they in fact prefer to associate with friends their own age.

STAYING YOUNG

High concentrations of the aged urban poor, however, can turn into squalid—and dangerous—geriatric ghettos. In New York City, for example, apartment rentals are so high (37 per cent above the national average) that fully one-third of the over-60 population lives in the city's 26 poorest neighborhoods, where the risk of mugging, rape and murder is a constant worry. In Miami Beach, Fla., where a majority of the 90,000 residents are over-65 pensioners, some of the elderly have become a public nuisance. Though actual crime runs mainly to jaywalking and shoplifting, police find that they must maintain lists of senile residents who stray from home, unable to remember who they are or where they live. "We are the only social agency open around the clock and on weekends," says police chief Rocky Pomerance.

The most successful retirees, according to some experts, are teachers who have become accustomed to long summer vacations and blue-collar couples who look forward to retirement as a release from dull and taxing jobs. Thanks to their combined pensions, retired postman Stanley Goldberg, 69, and his wife Eda, a former secretary, can afford a six-room apartment in Chicago plus annual vacations to Europe, Israel or the West Coast. At home, they keep busy with hobbies. "We can't see the difference between now and when we were younger," bubbles Eda.

The main goals of healthy older people and those dedicated to helping them are to stay active and feel good about themselves. At Chicago's Chelsea House, a middle-income retirement hotel where only eight of the 325 residents are married, romance flavors social activities. "You pick it up very quickly," says Nancy Gilmore, director of social programing. "Jack and Dorothy are a couple now. Then there's Julia and Frank, and Abe and Dorothy. If we can't find Florence, we just look for Bill."

The need for companionship and the ability to function sexually, experts say, continue into ripe old age. "Even if and when actual intercourse is impaired by infirmity," explains gerontologist Alex Comfort, author of "The Joy of Sex" and "A Good Age," "other sexual needs persist, including closeness, sensuality and being valued as a man or as a woman."

As older Americans are making their real needs felt, business, government and private organizations are adjusting their goals to serve the aged. Pilot programs under the aegis of the Federal Older Americans Act now have 2,000 elderly people performing work as homemakers and teacher aides, and taking care of children. The Illinois Department on Aging has pumped $450,000 into a program to establish craft centers, health care programs and businesses, run by as well as for the aging.

"MEALS ON WHEELS"

One of the most impressive community-service programs is the Older American Resources and Services program (OARS) at the Duke University Center. Aside from providing legal, medical and at-home nursing care, OARS arranges for "chore workers" who cook and do odd jobs in the house, "meals on wheels" to provide shut-ins with home-delivered meals, and a volunteer corps of drivers who take the disabled on trips. "We try to come up with a service package to allow each person to stay in the community," says director Dan G. Blazer. In Massachusetts, officials of the Department of Elder Affairs are experimenting with a variety of alternative-living arrangements. Instead of purely social Golden Age Centers, they have established eight day-care centers and are experimenting with boarding houses and communes, where small groups of residents can care for each other, and an "adoption center" through which old people can live with young families.

Gradually, a country that has long been obsessed by youth is beginning to discover the needs and joys of the last quarter of life. But America still has a lot more to learn about providing for its elder citizens. In the next few years, the sheer numbers who are graying will force the nation to face up to that problem. But the good news is that it can be done, and done well—as the old folks themselves can proudly attest.

Common portraits of homes for aged persons are bleak and depressing—and for good reason. Many nursing homes are inadequately staffed, poorly regulated, and medically inferior places where patients suffer isolation and alienation. But not all are such human wastelands.

Consider the following description of several Jewish institutions visited by Judith Wax. She found that many residents learned to feel that "It's like your own home here."

As you read this essay, think about the differences that make these places home-like in contrast to more typical nursing homes. Think, especially, of the meaning of community and, again, of the process of resocialization.

"It's Like Your Own Home Here"

JUDITH WAX

Evanston, Ill. "To be exact and to be truthful to the fact, my nerves are a little out of commission," she sighs, putting down the silverware she'd been dispensing. She's wearing white tights, like a little girl going to a party—but the black oxfords are orthopedic, and she is 83.

"So you'll sit and I'll set," says a fork-arranger in green house-slippers. There are 12 places at the big dining room table. Still another white-haired woman grasps the table's edge as she lays napkins in the fork lady's wake.

Soon 11 women—their average age is 82—have seated themselves beneath a reproduction of Chagall's painting "The Praying Jew." On a blackboard hung nearby, a wavering hand has written, "Sarah, remember you should take yr. medcine." As one man straggles in last, the green-slippered woman calls, "Over here, Abe boy."

"You'll try this soup, your nerves will commission themselves," white tights is advised. "Also, your appetite."

"At my age, what is appetite? A spasm!" Nevertheless, her appetite turns out to be impressive. But Bessie, 86, only looks at her food. She just arrived today, and the large brown eyes are watchful, wary. "I'm a greenhorn again," she sighs softly. "A greenie!"

The one named Rose is 85. She baked the poppyseed cake she'll cut only after the visiting rabbi has admired its speckled wholeness. "Sure, I use only butter. On the coldest day, I still would get it from the store."

Later, some diners clear plates, others load the dishwasher. Two women linger on in hot debate over teaspoon etiquette; finally they phone Marshall Field's silver department for a ruling to settle the matter. "We fight every day," one assures me. "It's absolutely wonderful." Newcomer Bessie looks doubtful.

The dozen diners are geriatric communalists, among the first in America. Most have been at the Weinfeld Group Living Residence—an experiment in "congregate housing" for the elderly—since it opened nearly four years ago in a renovated townhouse complex here in Evanston, one block from the northern boundary of Chicago. Before Weinfeld, they had lived alone or with relatives, in nursing homes or even in psychiatric hospitals. Like the 1.1 million older Americans the Urban Institute estimates could manage living outside institutions if they had an alternative, the Weinfeld 12 couldn't quite make it on their own in public or private housing. Now, pooling what strengths age permits, they give each other emotional and physical sustenance in an environment that feels and smells more or less the way home once did.

Like similar innovations in Philadelphia and Bethesda, Md., Weinfeld depends on funding and strong backup social services from an outside agency. Adapted from programs studied in England and Sweden, Weinfeld is one of many projects supported by the Council for Jewish Elderly, an offshoot of the Jewish Federation of Metropolitan Chicago. The aim is to encourage each resident's independence by maintaining community and family ties while providing only as much help—counseling, homemaking, health care—as is needed, no more, no less. That demands careful staffing: a cook and "careworker" on-site daily, a part-time activities therapist, a domestic who comes twice a week, a nurse who comes when she is needed and a nutritionist who visits to plan menus and special diets. "Our baby sitter," a college student, sleeps in each night: council social workers are on call, and a psychiatrist helps screen candidates for the traits that will make them compatible members of the Weinfeld group.

It costs $500 a month to live at Weinfeld, and few of the residents can swing the full amount, even with Social Security benefits and some family supplements. Jewish Federation philanthropy makes up the difference.

"Weinfeld costs half what would be spent by the taxpayers if these same people were institutionalized," says Ronald Weismehl, the council's executive director. "But when government is unable to meet needs, sectarian agencies have to do it as innovators."

The U-shaped complex of townhouses, located on a quiet, middle-class street and convenient to shopping, cultural and religious centers, makes an ideal setting for the experiment. After its purchase in 1971, the one-story complex was remodeled into one big home; dividing walls were torn down so that residents can stroll to each other's living rooms and the communal dining and recreation rooms at the center. You can't be a recluse at Weinfeld, but privacy is easy; each of the six units, shared by two residents, has two bedrooms, a bathroom, a spacious living room and a door to the outside that may be used at will. Nobody needs to ask permission to be part of the world. Most prized: the small private kitchens, for snacks, treats and breakfast at any hour one chooses.

Colors and fabrics are different in each unit, and though the basics are provided, residents are encouraged to add on—plants, photographs, old treasures and new handicrafts. Hung over the entrance to one woman's bedroom, a cherished stole keeps perpetual vigil; long retired from active duty, it is a permanent decor.

"I'm 84," Anna Cleaver says, "and with my blood pressure—today I *feel* it." She spent a decade in nursing and old-age homes before Weinfeld ("I thought I'd be stuck in those places till I died!") She and her vivacious suitemate, Ethel Honnet, have just finished the breakfast they made in their own kitchen, and tidied their rooms—dusting gingerly around the homemade figurines that Anna creates and Ethel explains to visitors. Anna is off to a new job, baby-sitting ("the beauty part—it's in the neighborhood"). Ethel has a job to do, too: She consults with the others to compile her master list of supplies they need for their kitchens. Though shopping is done in bulk by the council, residents "fill in" from nearby stores.

Later, the council's blue minibus with "SHALOM" painted on it will take a few Weinfelders on an architectural tour. But Rose Brauer will stay home. She's sewing children's clothes to be sent to Israel in the "Ship-a-Box" programs for which some Weinfelders do handicrafts.

One woman is packing, a little nervously, for a visit to her out-of-state children. Another feels ill and is napping; later, her suitemate brings an offering—the prize she's won that day at a charity luncheon. People do as bones and energy allow.

At the end of the day, after evening dishes are cleared, some settle with newspapers, others compare highlights—and shortcomings—of afternoon excursions. "Played out," one heads for bed, but not before evaluating the day just ending. "A good one," she proclaims. "Everybody was busy and buzzy." It wasn't all that good for the anxious new arrival, Bessie Bassuk. She's spent the last six years living with a daughter; both carefully considered and then agreed on the move to Weinfeld. But on her second day here, the frail white-haired woman—twice widowed—has a sternness that suggests fear on the still lovely face.

"Unless you're senile—maybe I'd be better off that way—you mind change. I'm sad, sure; not because its not nice here but it's a new life." Still, it's clear she has the instinct for sociability the consulting psychiatrist looks for in deciding who's a good Weinfeld candidate. When Rimma Kwartwski, the Russian émigré cook, says she gets complaints about her cooking, Bessie forgets her own distress and gives counsel. "They're probably just depressed, Rimma. When my daughter didn't like my soup, I knew it was already another problem."

Cook Rimma, still learning English, is a 42-year old mother figure for some. After all, she provides familiar tasting food twice a day. "They got 11 mothers here, and I *their* mother. I work this place with a full heart, some people think I the social worker. Old people getting depressed, the past is coming on their minds." She dispenses counsel in Yiddish, as she dispenses aromatic offerings from either of the two kosher kitchens, meat and dairy.

Rimma's "full heart"—not to mention the residents'—was battered recently by the deaths of three of the four male Weinfelders. (Men generally wait longer than women to relinquish independence and request housing help; they therefore tend to be frail when they arrive at Weinfeld.)

One of the recent deaths ("Oscar was everybody's darling") hit everyone particularly hard. Oscar had owned an apparel store for women, a background the psychiatrist thought would help him cope when outnumbered by them at Weinfeld. It did. For some he was father, for others, surrogate husband or indulged brother—even rumored suitor of one woman. ("A little hand-holding," she says, glowing. "A little kissing.")

The remaining Weinfeld male, Abe Mendelsohn, is leaving the residence now, going to live with his only daughter and her husband in a Las Vegas mobile-home community. "My doctor says the winter here won't be good for my foot," he says. But the staff at Weinfeld is concerned. One social worker says, "When the last two men died, Abe must have started worrying he'd be next. Of course he has a right to leave, but we think he'd be better off here. And what will 11 *baleboostehs* do with no one to spoil?"

Mendelsohn—the women tend to call him "Abelah"—protests that "to me it's immaterial there's all these women around; you just got to learn their ways and means. It's like your own home here; the food is good, it's sociable— what can you expect? These women are satisfied. They cook a little, play bingo, go shopping. But for a man, if he belonged to organizations, it's hard. If I want to help, to take off the dishes from the table, they say, 'That's for ladies.' Can I fight with them? One man who died, I miss very much. We went to the park every day. He was very well readed—American history. The other man, him I miss too." The dark eyes got a little moist. "But especially I miss the one who was well readed."

"One of the men used to sit next to me at the table," says 80-year-old Gert Ginsburg. "I kept his things from spilling. It was our habit—like I was a mother again. We look after each other. If one leaves the table we want to know why. And we all run out of bed in the night if, God forbid, someone gets sick. You do get attached, even if you don't want to."

Dr. Sanford Finkel is the council's consulting psychiatrist. "It's a family unit, so intense emotion becomes involved, which is nurturing. But these people have already sustained losses—that's why they're at Weinfeld—and death in the group means having to deal with loss again when you've already been weakened by it." Still, Finkel agrees, emotion is feeling, and feeling proves you're alive.

Wearing the coveted Table Setter badge the nutritionist awarded her, tiny Sylvia Abelson arranges luncheon plates around the big table. The only resident who has never married, she has severe hearing and visual problems and at 69 is Weinfeld's youngest—"They call me the baby." An ardent luncheon-goer, she returned from one at a nearby temple with a bag of treats for the newcomer, who has been named Bessie New York—she has lived in Manhattan—to distinguish her from Bessie Karbelnig, now called Bessie Senior. "I couldn't sleep last night," says Bessie New York at lunch. "I don't think I can eat much today either." The others manage to touch her often, encourage her to talk about husbands and achieving children. She maintains her "let's be frank" directness. "My first husband? A lawyer sure, but not a Clarence Darrow." When she leaves the table at meal's end, she's still struggling for composure. But this time she smiles a little when she calls herself "the greenie."

Bessie Senior, 84, who describes her memory as "a little viggle-vaggle," says that Weinfeld is wonderful. "But I would like a little business of my own." There are a few sarcastic mumbles about her relentlessly cheery declarations—"Ladies should *always* smile!"—and her requests for goodbye kisses as others leave the table. ("What does Bessie think, we're still sailing to America?")Still, she's protected. Prodded by the sailing-to-America woman to take off her sweater in the warm dining room, Bessie does, happily. "You got something there," she beams. "The right advice in the right moment." And grasping furniture to keep her balance, Bessie Senior goes off to check on Bessie New York—in whom she has taken a proprietary interest.

I wanted to find out—tactfully—if those who had grown-up children would rather have lived with them than at Weinfeld. Theirs, after all, is a generation that remembers when it was the expected golden-years arrangement. Still, I didn't want to ask one Weinfelder ("I'm on the last ship") outright if she would have preferred it. "Do you think it's generally better," I stammer, "to—um—live with —um—one's children?"

"I don't know," she says, giving me the Myron Cohen eyelid drop. "*One* never got a chance to find out."

For many, Weinfeld is as close to domestic scenes past as you can get without the original cast. Not that the original cast has necessarily disappeared. "We want to alleviate families of the anxiety they feel about their parents," says a council executive, "but not of their responsibility to continue relating to them." Middle-aged children (often confronting life crises of their own just when a parent is finding that he can no longer get along by himself) feel comfortable visiting here. It's pleasant, homey, there's no sense of having deposited Granny on the ice floe. Great-grandchildren can run in and out, examine the contents of the refrigerator and choose from a dozen eager cheek-and-botton pinchers. Weinfelders are touchers. They're kissers, too—they'll plant one on your hand or cheek after a conversation because, "You talk so nice on a person!"

Volunteers are part of the Weinfeld ecology. One, retired engineer-inventor Justin Wetzler, is the all-purpose visiting handyman. "I came out of Hitler's Germany, " says Wetzler, 69, "and I saw so much misery there that helping is my way to relieve people's unhappiness." "Wetzler's better than a husband," says one admirer. "He can fix anything and you don't get kvetching."

Volunteer Shirley Rothstein gathers up Weinfelders for frequent outings: to see the movie "Hester Street," to visit a museum of Jewish artifacts. "On birthdays, I take them out to lunch and say, 'Order anything you want.' One once chose a ham sandwich, a scandal. They love to give, too—a little door prize when we go to the recreation center, a dollar to charity."

"I was raised in a children's home," says the zesty Mrs. Rothstein, who is 54, "so I guess this is the family I never had."

Harry Borisy arrives on Tuesdays. He first came to visit a friend who has since died; now he comes to read Yiddish stories and discuss them with the group. The morning's tale is about an old widower's search for a new bride on the Coney Island boardwalk. "His appetite was good," Borisy reads, "but the legs . . . the legs wouldn't go too fast." His listeners laugh and nudge each other at the best ironic bits.

Later, a literary exchange:"Roth, Malamud, those guys don't know the *shtetl*." "Roth writes ashamed and I get aggravated." Abe Mendelsohn is hard on I. B. Singer. "He's too open. I know what a woman is undressed; Singer don't have to tell me. Peretz lets us know there's more to a human being and Aleichem says you gotta laugh at the world. Listen, we all know what a woman is."

Cyd Noble, like Borisy, comes once a week. She's the middle-aged daughter of whom anyone could be proud—trim figure, jaunty scarf that matches her blouse. She reads and leads discussions, too. Her sessions are in English and about historical and world events, mostly with a Jewish angle. Her visits are particularly cherished by a tall and handsomely immaculate gray-haired woman (the sign on her bedroom door proclaims: "This is Trudy

Lefkovitz's room"). Though there's no hint of it in her graceful movements, Trudy is functionally blind. Her Germanic preciseness is sometimes misunderstood by the others, but she's the acknowledged resident intellectual. Failing sight forced Trudy to stop reading, the favorite activity of a lifetime. Now she's devoted to "talking books" for the blind and is an ardent, alert participant in this discussion group.

Noble reads them an article on anti-Semitism in Mexico City. But the group is shaken by something closer to home, a local columnist's report of an anti-Semitic campaign planned by the Chicago Nazi Party. "What is the Government doing?" one asks. "Look how we're talking Mexico and this happens here."

"Anywhere it can happen," Trudy says. "Since I left Germany, I always knew that." "They voted against us at the United Nations," someone else says, "and still Jews run to Mexico like it was Miami."

The discussion gets more impassioned; philosophies and theories heat up the roast-chicken-scented air. Though most ignore it, sweet-faced Bessie Senior waves a fist. "We should give 'em a klop!" says the militant in white stockings and a flowered apron. Sylvia wants to know when Cyd will review "Golda's book, since once we saw her personally, even, downtown." And everyone wants to hear the next installment of "90 Minutes at Entebbe."

Andrea Glassner is 24; her title is resident careworker. She's at Weinfeld five days a week, alerts outside staff to "positive or negative interaction, illness, a stove that breaks down."

Andrea worries about the balance between too much and too little help. "Sometimes I catch myself doing more than I should. I say. 'Look, they're old, why shouldn't I bring a cup of tea?' That's what I was doing for one woman who wasn't well, but she got to the point she'd see me sitting down and then ask for it. Today, another lady looked at me and said, 'Coffee, please!' I said, 'What am I, a waitress?'

"Yesterday, I was helping load the dishwasher—they all help clear the table—and Trudy corrected the way I was doing it. I took the hint . . . it's *their* kitchen.

"I try to handle problems of depression right away," says Andrea, "but I flag the social worker for help if the problem isn't getting better. Holiday time is the toughest. They remember old cooking, big families."

"Andrea," comes a voice from the next room, "you could help a little, maybe, with a bath?"

"Sure thing," she calls out. Then she adds: "They manage pretty well. These are super people, in a super place."

"We don't know exactly how to evaluate Weinfeld's effectiveness," says Dan Silverstein, program operations director for the council. "Are we improving the 'quality of life', and if so—by whose definition? Does this program help them live longer and is that our ultimate goal? Do we still foster too much dependency? And what is too much?''

Despite such questions, the council is optimistic enough at this point in the Weinfeld experiment to be planning the next group residence. The new one will probably house 24, though staff size will stay nearly the same to stabilize cost. "We do know some things we want to do better next time," Silverstein says. "We'd like a live-in couple who would function as staff as well as be part of the family. We know we need more continuity of family ties and that we have to keep building up outside contacts, too, because there's a tendency among the elderly to retreat."

There's a waiting list for Weinfeld, but it isn't everybody's glass of tea. Not everyone goes gently into group living. "Many older people don't want to share with a stranger or live in a strange house," says Marie Thompson, housing expert at the International Center for Social Gerontology. "But as they become more needy—for help or company—they're more open to sharing arrangements. People from rural environments seem to come to it more naturally than city people."

Thompson, like others committed to concerns of the elderly, sees group housing as a vital part of the national trend to provide older Americans with a variety of responses to their needs. "The need for all types of congregate housing is acknowledged," says Mrs. Thompson. "The trouble is getting bureaucratic backing for new concepts." A recent H.E.W. grant is underwriting a feasibility study of cooperative living for the elderly. But legislation meant to fund congregate projects is often hobbled by its own restrictive language.

But the council is hardly discouraged, "Whatever the problems," says Silverstein, "we're sure now that interdependence works. That every person should feel useful, have connections and responsibilities. We believe older people have a potential for growth . . . not just for growing older."

"Sometimes, when you're old, you feel you're just waiting to die," says Weinfeld's Mrs. Ginsburg. "But we know that the way we live here is the best way for us that there is!"

Mary Ellen Lavery is a lot taller than most of the Weinfelders; a few put their heads on her chest when they reach up to hug her in greeting. She's administrator of health care for the Council for Jewish Elderly's many programs, and every Friday afternoon she meets with the assembled Weinfeld residents to talk about what's on their minds. It's a free-floating forum, but important, so that even the women setting the Sabbath dinner table—the retired rabbi will arrive before dinner to say the blessing and exchange stories over steaming matzoh balls—tuck errant slip straps under their housedresses and gather in the recreation room to meet with Mrs. Lavery. A few have fresh hairdos; there is evidence of newly applied nail gloss. All the women will put on best dresses for the Sabbath meal.

Some notes from the Weinfeld meeting held several days before Yom Kippur, the holy Day of Atonement:

Lavery is presented with a list of things to do: draperies need cleaning, there's a folding chair shortage. . . .

Bessie New York arrives a little late, wary still, her features slightly woeful. Trudy tells administrator Lavery that Bessie needs a bedroom chair. A short history of Weinfeld bedroom-chair problems and logistics. Trudy persists—Bessie New York *needs* one, despite the newcomer's reticent "I'll tide myself over." (Later, though she can see only vague outlines, Trudy is spotted carrying a chair into Bessie's room. "Trudy says some people call her Hitler," says Bessie, "but she's so kind!")

Bessie Senior chides Lavery. "You wonder why I'm laughing; you stopped Important Matters and settled on chairs."

This weeks's important matter has been a pre-Yom Kippur debate. Andrea, the young careworker is scheduled for duty on that holiest of days in the Jewish religion. Rose Brauer, the expert baker, doesn't think a Jewish girl should work that day, even at Weinfeld. Yesterday, passions ran so high about the issue, Sylvia says she expected the riot police.

ROSE: Jewish girls shouldn't work Yom Kippur. And that's that.

SARAH: I don't mind it. (The other women take "let Andrea herself decide" positions.)

ROSE: Abe agrees with me.

ABE: Let there be peace in the family. Once there was a great sage who was on his way to the temple on Yom Kippur when he heard a baby cry. It was the Holy of Holies; everybody was looking for him at shul. But the great sage was taking care of the baby. And if Andrea wants to help *us*, so what's the matter?

ROSE: She still shouldn't come. Why didn't they get a gentile to take care of that baby?

TRUDY: In Israel the farmers have to take care of the animals, even holidays.

ROSE: Let the rabbi decide later.

LAVERY: I think Abe is just as wise. But we'll work this out earlier before the next holiday. I guess the majority wants Andrea to work, Rose.

ROSE: O.K., settled. But the last time somebody worked Yom Kippur, I got so nervous my glasses broke.

Everyone airs what they call their shticks. The group decided to take up Sarah's son's offer ("He's in the business") of fabric for their dining-room chair seats. They'll do the work. They decide on a wedding gift for their nighttime "baby sitter," and skirt around somebody's treatment for a disease no one's ready to call by name.

And, gradually, everyone draws out the new resident. Bessie New York, shyly at first, begins to talk out feelings about her life—old regrets, new fears. "If I praise my product," she says of her children, "I better be extra careful."

They all laugh when she confesses she spent "years in the bathroom" while one daughter practiced the violin. Bessie has misgivings now about the time she spent away from her husband—at his insistence—living in another city with this child to be near the best violin teacher. "I'm the fool of music," she says, "and 'fool' of baloney." Between exchanged rue, and laughter, the essential Bessie is emerging.

The rabbi, Morris Guttstein, arrives and is introduced to her. "I think you must be a very smart woman," he says expansively, "smart because you lived in New York." She looks him over. "Eight million people can't all be smart," she says. "And if they were so smart, Rabbi, would a city be in that kind of financial trouble?"

The 86-year-old "greenhorn" is clearly going to make it in group living. They're admiring her wit. . . she'll be somebody at Weinfeld and she's begun to feel comfortable, maybe even optimistic. Next day, you can tell all that just by looking at her cane. Bessie New York has tied a pink chiffon bow on it.

Although it may be easier to grow old in America today than it was a decade or two ago, there is still the matter of downward mobility, the loss of status that often accompanies the retirement of workers. This is the subject of sociologist Thomas Tissue's careful study of 256 aged public-assistance recipients.

Tissue reviews the relevant literature and then describes his own research. Interestingly, he reports that the aged poor from middle-class backgrounds faithfully adhere to belief in the equity and propriety of the larger social system even though they have suffered because of its rules.

As you read "Downward Mobility in Old Age," ask yourself why the aged poor from middle-class origins still support traditional American ideals and values despite their own problems.

Downward Mobility in Old Age

THOMAS TISSUE

In a recently translated paper, Simmel (1965:139) remarked that poverty "is the common end of the most diverse destinies, an ocean into which lives from the most diverse social strata flow together." Nowhere does the image ring so true as in the case of the aged poor. It seems clear by now that poverty in old age is not restricted to the lifelong poor, the profligate, nor the shortsighted. Public assistance programs currently include a considerable number of aged recipients with middle-class biographies. Many just outlived their economic endurance and resources. It is a simple arithmetic fact that the longer one lives past retirement, the greater one's chances for impoverishment (Sheppard, 1965). Others have lost their savings to unanticipated illness, the death of a spouse, or the ravages of an inflationary economy. In any event the aged poor as a welfare category embraces a broad variety of antecedent histories and life styles, many of them at sharp variance from the popular image of the public assistance recipient. As Solomon (1967:214) wryly observes, "This may be somewhat surprising to those who still believe that thrift and industry are guarantors of financial independence in one's old age, while impecuniousness is a sign of a misspent early life."

It is my intent to examine some of the personal correlates and consequences of downward mobility in old age. More specifically, how do aged public assistance recipients of middle-class origin differ from those drawn from working-class backgrounds? What differences exist in regard to details of biography, current life style, and maintenance of morale?

Two basically antithetical models may be brought to bear upon the matter of morale or accommodation to poverty in old age. The first may be traced to Durkheim (1951:246–254), whose category of anomic suicide is based essentially upon an individual's inability to tolerate rapid change in social position and the attendant normative collapse. Subsequent studies have emphasized the relationship between mobility and diminished bonds of social integration, e.g., mobility and mental illness (Hollingshead and Redlich, 1958), job mobility and anomia (Aiken and Ferman, 1966), mobility-induced strains on primary and secondary group structure (Janowitz and Curtis, 1957), constriction of interpersonal alternatives associated with mobility (Blau, 1956), and even with the system-wide implications of a society's endorsement of a high mobility ethic (Tumin, 1957). Also of interest is the Wilensky and Edwards (1959:228) finding that "work life skidders" (manual workers who have experienced clear-cut losses in occupational status over time) are more rigidly conservative than non-skidders and retain an exaggerated and incongruous middle-class value structure; "Like a man falling from a skyscraper, our skidder reaches not in the direction of his fall, but back up the structure."

Compatible with the studies cited above is the Lenski (1954) concept of "status crystallization." Based on the assumption that every actor occupies a multiplicity of statuses at any given time, Lenski anticipates special difficulty for those persons with incongruous, poorly crystallized status patterns. As Kolack (1968:366) later put it, " . . . he is likely to be denied rewards and to be subjected to social rebuffs more often than other persons." Subsequent studies have demonstrated some association between status inconsistency and right wing extremism (Rush, 1967), reduced social contact (Lenski, 1956), low job satisfaction, and non-participation in professional organizations (Kolack, 1968).

On the basis of the evidence cited above, one is led to predict considerable difficulty for aged public assistance recipients who might be called "post-work-life skidders." The drop from middle class to public assistance status may be expected to elicit the alienation and isolation which accompanies abrupt downward mobility, as well as creating the value imbalance mentioned by Wilensky and Edwards (1959). Furthermore, one can assume that middle-class life styles and comparatively high education will combine with poverty in old age to produce poorly crystallized status configurations. In any event, one must envision poverty in old age as a more solitary, painful and disorienting experience for the declassé aged than for the lifelong poor or working class older person.

Diametrically opposed is the contention that middle-class life styles are productive of skills and personal resources singularly adaptive to the problems of aging, regardless of income. Peck and Berkowitz (1964:33) maintain that, "Adjustment to the aging process comes most easily, it would appear, to upper status people, but not primarily because they are economically advantaged. Lower-class people suffer genuine economic and social deprivations which handicap them as they grow old. At the same time, their ill-developed personalities also interfere with good adjustment at least as early as middle age. The social class differences in adaptability and adjustment, thus, are not only a matter of financial resources but also of inner psychological resources." A variety of other sources may be introduced in support of the thesis of middle-class resilience and adaptability, to include capacity for cooperative action (Riesman and Glazer, 1950), effective self direction (Kohn and Schooler, 1969), and self confidence in confronting one's immediate environment (Knupfer, 1947). More to the point, a recent study of the aged indicates that retired men of higher socioeconomic origin are able to maintain high levels of life satisfaction despite major discontinuities in life style, whereas the most severe satisfaction losses associated with life discontinuities were found within the lower socioeconomic group (Bultena, 1969).

Middle-class life styles also provide specific recreational skills and experience which seem well suited to the aged role. Excluded from major productive roles, such as employment and child rearing, the aged are progressively forced into a sedentary, leisure oriented, and relatively unstructured role. Middle-class life styles offer a considerably richer variety of material with which to augment such a role. Middle-class adults have greater experience with voluntary organizations (Komarovsky, 1946; Wright and Hyman, 1958; Dotson, 1951; Scott, 1957), more hobbies (Reissman, 1954), more diversified cultural involvement (Clarke, 1956), more community participation (Reissman, 1954), and more interest in politics and voting (Hastings, 1956; Connolly and Field, 1944).

On balance, then, the principal question relates to the ability of middle-class persons to maintain and exploit class-related advantages when confronted with poverty in old age. Can such initial advantages soften the impact of late life poverty or, as Clark and Anderson (1967:102) have put it, " . . . is sliding down to the bottom of the economic scale in old age worse than having never been able to rise above it?"

METHODOLOGY

The sample consists of 256 Old Age Assistance recipients in Sacramento County. Ranging in age from 65 years to 88 years, all were recently approved for cash payments at the time they were interviewed. Starting with a complete roster of cases approved in July-October, 1969, study staff excluded from the sample only those cases in which the respondent a) lived in an institutional setting or b) was unable to participate in an extended interview because of language difficulty, hearing loss, or extremely poor health. The sample thus consists of 256 English-speaking, non-institutionalized, old welfare recipients who were healthy enough to undergo a two hour interview.

Their class of origin was determined by use of the Hollingshead (1958) two-item Index of Social Position. For men and single women, the ratings were based on the respondent's own education and occupation. For married women, the husband's occupation was substituted. Because of the relative scarcity of cases, the usual five interval class scale was compressed to two categories. The original Levels I, II and III are grouped into the Middle Class category, while Levels IV and V constitute the Working Class. By dichotomizing the sample along these lines, we obtain almost equal numbers of cases in each category, as well as retaining basic educational and occupational distinctions between groups.

Middle Class respondents worked primarily as skilled laborers, small entrepreneurs, and lesser administrators and executives. They include nearly all the high school and college graduates in the sample. The Working Class is evenly divided among unskilled and semi-skilled laborers, whose education seldom exceeded junior high school. The sample contained 112 men and 144 women. Women made up 61 percent of the Middle Class cases and 51 percent of the Working Class cases.

BIOGRAPHY

The designation of cases as Middle Class or Working Class is helpful only if these labels correspond to demonstrable differences in former life style and personal history. The data indicate that such differences do exist, even back to childhood. Those we have called Middle Class on the basis of education and occupation were more likely to have been raised in conventional circumstances as children. As shown in Table 1, they were more often raised by their natural parents and less frequently shifted from one living arrangement to another. Their own parents or caretakers were of higher socioeconomic status as well. The family's standard of living was more often described as "wealthy" or "better than most families," and the family's breadwinner had considerably more formal education than did his counterpart in the Working Class respondent's family.

As adults, the Middle Class less frequently held regular employment than did the Working Class. Although statistically significant (at .02 by X^2), the disparity is entirely an artifact of differential employment rates for women; 62 percent of Working Class women were employed regularly as adults whereas only 46 percent of the Middle Class women had worked steadily.

Past use of free public services in the community was most characteristic of Working Class backgrounds. Although the actual magnitude of difference is small, the direction is consistent. Working Class respondents were the highest consumers of free medical service at county hospitals, free job placement through the State Department of Employment, and emergency employment with WPA or CCC during the depression years. They were also more likely to have received general relief from the county when younger.

The classes do not differ appreciably in regard to details of marriage and family. Both had remarkably similar numbers of marriages and virtually identical numbers of children.

CURRENT LIFE STYLE

The most striking aspect of the current Middle Class life style is its comparative solitude. Middle Class respondents simply do not see as many other people per month as do those with Working Class histories. As measured by

TABLE 1. *Childhood*

	MIDDLE CLASS	WORKING CLASS
a. Principal Living Arrangement as Child**		
With Both Natural Parents	82%	69%
	(127)	(129)
b. Number of Living Arrangements as Child*		
Raised in One Home	69%	64%
Raised in Two Homes	23	17
Raised in Three or More Homes	8	19
	100%	100%
	(127)	(128)
c. Family's Standard of Living**		
"Wealthy" or "Better Than Most"	21%	9%
"About the Same as Most"	62	64
"Poorer Than Most" or "Very Poor"	17	27
	100%	100%
	(127)	(128)
d. Breadwinner's Education (if known)***		
Less than 4th Grade	27%	44%
5th–8th Grade	42	42
More than 8th Grade	31	14
	100%	100%
	(102)	(104)

*SIGNIFICANT AT .05 BY X^2.
**SIGNIFICANT AT .02 BY X^2.
***SIGNIFICANT AT .01 BY X^2.

the Cumming and Henry (1961) index of Life Space (based on monthly contacts with friends, neighbors, relatives, trades-people, and others in the household), the current social sphere of the Middle Class is significantly smaller than that of the Working Class.

TABLE 2. *Use of Public Services*

	MIDDLE CLASS	WORKING CLASS
a. Ever Used County Hospital	44%	54%
	(127)	(129)
b. Ever Used Dept. of Employment	38%	47%
	(125)	(129)
c. Ever Worked for WPA or CCC*	17%	29%
	(127)	(129)
d. Ever Received General Relief	14%	20%
	(126)	(129)

*SIGNIFICANT AT .05 BY X^2.

Similarly, the Middle Class has sustained the greatest comparative loss in social contact over time. When asked to compare current activity in five major roles (churchgoer, relative, friend, organization member, and consumer) to that which they enjoyed when 45 years old, more than half of the Middle Class respondents acknowledged loss in at least four of the five roles. Also a Cumming and Henry measure, this index of Perceived Life Space yields results offering considerable support to the contention that downward mobility is indeed associated with a significant constriction in the previous level of social interaction.

Although both groups were virtually identical in regard to number of marriages contracted and children produced, the Working Class more frequently maintains an intact, functional family unit. The Working Class aged are more likely to live with the latest spouse, and to do so in a home that he or she owns. Despite the fact that Middle Class parents are more likely to have children living in the state, it is the Working Class parent who most often sees at least one of his children every day.

It was suggested earlier that Middle Class life styles typically include forms of recreation and leisure roles which might profitably be extended into later life. An examination of current recreational activities indicates a consistent (though not statistically significant) association between Middle Class origin and participation in a variety of sedentary leisure pursuits. Middle Class aged are more likely to read newspapers, to do more reading in general, to attend movies and the theatre, to participate in hobbies, and even to watch television. In the latter regard, 57 percent of the Middle Class respondents admitted to three or more hours of television per day.

The unifying element in all of these activities, however, is their capacity for solitary enjoyment. One needn't have friends or relatives about in order to read, go to the movies, sew or make knick-knacks for the house (the most common hobbies), or to watch television. It is worth noting that there were no class related differences in respect to recreation which involves other people. Class origins are not, for example, related to belonging to a group of close friends who see one another frequently, nor to getting together with others to play cards or other table games.

TABLE 3. *Life Space and Perceived Life Space*

	MIDDLE CLASS	WORKING CLASS
a. Life Space**		
Low (0–49 contacts)	47%	32%
High (50 plus contacts)	53	68
	100%	100%
	(127)	(129)
b. Perceived Life Space**		
Severe Loss (in at least 4 of 5 roles)	55%	40%
Moderate to No Loss (in 3 or fewer roles)	45	60
	100%	100%
	(127)	(129)

··SIGNIFICANT AT .02 BY X^2.

TABLE 4. *Family*

	MIDDLE CLASS	WORKING CLASS
a. Currently Lives With Spouse*	23%	36%
	(127)	(129)
b. Lives in Own Home*	17%	28%
	(127)	(129)
c. Children Living in California*		
(For those with living children)		
Has None	11%	26%
Has One	28	30
Has Two	29	20
Has Three or More	32	24
	100%	100%
	(104)	(105)
d. Sees at Least One Child Daily	26%	38%
(For those with living children)	(103)	(105)

·SIGNIFICANT AT .05 BY X^2.

CURRENT SATISFACTION

The data do not indicate class related differences with regard to the Srole (1956) measure of anomia. Middle-Class respondents are no more likely to manifest this dimension of generalized alienation and systemic distrust than are the Working-Class aged. Middle-Class respondents are, however, significantly less happy about their current situation in general, and specific elements of it in particular.

Responses to general questions about current happiness and satisfaction with present life style show that Middle-Class origins are significantly related to feeling "not too happy" and "unhappy" as well as to a general dissatisfaction with one's circumstances as a whole. These differences persist with controls on age, sex, perceived health, and presence of spouse.

Retirement more frequently constitutes an unpleasant experience for the Middle Class. All persons who had worked during the past were asked to compare their actual retirement experience to what they had anticipated at the time they stopped working, to identify the most satisfying element of their current age, and to identify what they missed most about their usual jobs. A single point was awarded for each "positive response," i.e., finding retirement as anticipated or better than anticipated, identifying free-time and absence of responsibility as the best element of one's current age, and missing nothing about one's past job. As shown in Table 6, a zero or perfectly negative score was more common to Middle- than Working-Class retirees. In other words, feeling that a) retirement was working out worse than anticipated, b) that freedom from responsibility and additional free time were not the major benefits of old age, and c) missing at least some part of one's previous job, was a response pattern more common to those with higher socioeconomic origins.

Response to one's current housing is also conditioned by class of origin. The feeling that one's current housing is inferior to that occupied when younger is

TABLE 5. *Happiness and Satisfaction*

	MIDDLE CLASS	WORKING CLASS
a. Current Happiness*		
"Not too happy," "Unhappy"	29%	17%
	(125)	(129)
b. Satisfaction With Current Life**		
"Dissatisfied"	17%	8%
	(127)	(129)

*SIGNIFICANT AT .05 BY X^2.

**SIGNIFICANT AT .02 BY X^2.

more common to Middle-Class backgrounds. Conversely, the belief that one's own standard of living is currently superior to that of one's friends is more common to the Working Class.

Parenthetically, the data lend substantial support to the Wilensky and Edwards (1959) conclusions regarding retention of middle-class values among the downwardly mobile. Despite their currently precarious status, the Middle-Class aged still cling to an ethic of hard work for its own sake and a belief that one's fate is the result of personal diligence rather than chance or fate. They more frequently rejected statements to the effect that the only reason for working is to earn a living, and that one should never work without being paid for it. They were correspondingly stern about the basis for a person's success in life—significantly fewer Middle-Class responses dealt with "the breaks" than did Working-Class answers.

TABLE 6. *Retirement, Housing, and Standard of Living*

	MIDDLE CLASS	WORKING CLASS
a. Response to Retirement*		
Most Negative (0 pts.)	21%	12%
	(117)	(121)
b. Housing Comparison*		
Current House Worse Than Those		
Occupied When Younger	35%	22%
	(127)	(129)
c. Standard of Living Comparison		
Better Than That of Peers	25%	35%
	(126)	(129)

*SIGNIFICANT AT .05 BY X^2.

SUMMARY AND DISCUSSION

In general, the data offer tentative support for the hypothesis which predicts special difficulty for the downwardly mobile aged. As compared to their counterparts with Working-Class backgrounds, the ex-Middle-Class, aged poor have sustained greater loss in social interaction over time, maintain lower levels of current interaction, and more frequently described themselves as unhappy and dissatisfied with their current lives. They are less likely to live with a spouse or to see their children on a daily basis (despite the fact that they are more likely to have children living in the state). They are most likely to resent retirement, to denigrate their current housing, and paradoxically, to adhere to elements of a classically puritanical ethic of hard work and personal responsibility.

Particularly interesting is the fact that class of origin has no association with anomia, as measured by the Srole scale. As Messer (1968) suggests, anomia and morale may indeed constitute two conceptually independent dimensions of adjustment. Thus, the downwardly mobile aged can be more unhappy and dissatisfied with the objective circumstances of their lives, without embracing a world-view characterized by alienation, despair, or hopelessness. They have fallen on hard times and are quite aware of it, but they have not lost faith in the essential propriety and equity of the larger order of things. On the contrary, like the Wilensky and Edwards (1959) "older work life skidders," they respond to status loss by exaggerated allegiance to the values of the system in which they have failed. Thus, the anomia and despair component of mobility theory is not borne out by the present study. As shown by their response to retirement, the dilemma faced by the downwardly mobile aged does not consist of disenchantment with the system, but with being forced to view its operation as spectators rather than participants.

TABLE 7. *Work Ethic*

	MIDDLE CLASS	WORKING CLASS
a. "The only reason for working is to get enough money to live on."***		
Agree	55%	78%
	(127)	(129)
b. "A person shouldn't work overtime or on weekends unless he is paid for it."*		
Agree	67%	78%
	(127)	(129)
c. Success in Life Due to "Hard work" or "Breaks"**		
The "Breaks"	9%	23%
	(127)	(129)

*SIGNIFICANT AT .05 BY X^2.
**SIGNIFICANT AT .02 BY X^2.
***SIGNIFICANT AT .001 BY X^2.

The persistence of middle-class leisure activities into old age and poverty does not seem productive of the individual benefits usually anticipated. Although the ex-Middle-Class respondents did retain leisure interests and activities consistent with their backgrounds, these activities did not produce increased rates of social contact, satisfaction, or happiness. Television, newspapers, books, hobbies, etc., may serve to pass the time; but they do not appear to provide a sufficient buffer against the combined shock of retirement, downward mobility, and poverty.

However, the tentative nature of these findings must be noted. It is apparent that the inter-class differences are typically small. Although quite consistent in direction, the percentage comparisons most often result in modest net differences. Also important is the fact that the data are adequate to establish various associations between class of origin and life style-satisfaction, but are not of the sort which permit tracing the sequence of events which underlie the associations. For example, we can demonstrate that Middle-Class public assistance recipients are more isolated and less likely to be involved in a functional family unit. However, we cannot determine the degree to which these factors may operate differently within the two classes to influence the initial need for, and eventual receipt of public assistance. The data are not adequate to separate the causes of downward mobility from its putative effects.

Within the constraints mentioned, the data do serve at least two important functions, nonetheless. As mentioned before, they offer an additional, somewhat different test and partial confirmation of the downward mobility thesis outlined earlier. More importantly, the study focuses attention upon the dynamic aspect of class and mobility among the aged. All too often in the past, considerations of socioeconomic status among the aged have been manifested in repetitive comparisons of the life-long poor to the life-long affluent. Subsequent studies must attempt to deal with the question of what happens as the affluent start to skid.

References

Aiken, M., and L. Ferman
    1966   "Job mobility and the social integration of displaced workers." Social Problems 14(Summer): 48–56.
Blau, P.
    1956   "Social mobility and interpersonal relations." American Sociological Review 21(June): 290–295.
Bultena, G.L.
    1969   "Life continuity and morale in old age." The Gerontologist 9(Winter): 251–253.
Clark, M., and B.G. Anderson
    1967   Culture and Aging: An Anthropological Study of Older Americans. Springfield: Charles C Thomas.
Clarke, A.C.
    1956   "The use of leisure and its relation to levels of occupational prestige." American Sociological Review 21(June): 301–307.
Connelly, G.M., and H.M. Field
    1944   "The non-voter—who he is, what he thinks." Public Opinion Quarterly 8(Summer): 175–187.

Cumming, E. and W. Henry
1961   Growing Old: The Process of Disengagement. New York: Basic Books.

Dotson, F.
1951   "Patterns of voluntary association among urban working class families." American Sociological Review 16(October): 687–693.

Durkheim, E.
1951   Suicide. Glencoe, Illinois: The Free Press.

Hastings, P.K.
1956   "The voter and the non-voter." American Journal of Sociology 62(November): 302–307.

Hollingshead, A.B., and F.C. Redlich
1958   Social Class and Mental Illness. New York: John Wiley & Sons.

Janowitz, M., and R. Curtis
1957   "Sociological consequences of occupational mobility in a United States metropolitan community." Working Paper One, Fourth Working Conference on Social Stratification and Social Mobility: International Sociological Association (December).

Knupfer, G.
1947   "Portrait of the underdog." Public Opinion Quarterly 2(Spring): 104–110.

Kohn, M.L., and C. Schooler
1969   "Class, occupation, and orientation." American Sociological Review 34(October) 659–677.

Kolack, S.
1968   "A study of status inconsistency among social work professionals." Social Problems 15(Winter): 365–376.

Komarovsky, M.
1946   "The voluntary association of urban dwellers." American Sociological Review 11(December): 686–698.

Lenski, G.
1954   "Status crystallization—a nonvertical dimension of social status." American Sociological Review 19(August): 405–413.
1956   "Social participation and status crystallization." American Sociological Review 21(August): 458–464.

Messer, M.
1968   "Race differences in selected attitudinal dimensions of the elderly." The Gerontologist 8(Winter): 245–249.

Peck, R.F., and H. Berkowitz
1964   "Personality and adjustment in middle age." P. 43 in Bernice L. Neugarten (ed.), Personality in Middle and Late Life. New York: Atherton Press.

Riesman, D., and N. Glazer
1950   "Criteria for political apathy." P. 534 in Alvin Gouldner, Studies in Leadership. New York: Harper & Bros.

Reisman, L.
1954   "Class, leisure and social participation." American Sociological Review 19(February): 76–84.

Rush, G.B.
    1967   "Status inconsistency and right wing extremism." American Sociological
            Review 32(February): 86–92.
Scott, J.C., Jr.
    1957   "Membership and participation in voluntary organizations." American
            Sociological Review 22(June): 315–326.
Sheppard, H.L.
    1965   "The poverty of aging." Pp. 85–101 in Ben B. Seligman (ed.), Poverty as
            a Public Issue. New York: The Free Press.
Simmel, G. (Tr. C. Jacobson)
    1965   "The poor." Social Problems 13(Fall): 118–140.
Solomon, B.
    1967   "Social functioning of economically dependent aged." The Geron-
            tologist 7(September): 213–217.
Srole, L.
    1956   "Social integration and certain corollaries: an exploratory study."
            American Sociological Review 21(December): 709–716.
Tumin, M.
    1957   "Some unapplauded consequences of social mobility in a mass society."
            Social Forces 36(October): 32–37.
Wilensky, H.L., and H. Edwards
    1959   "The skidder: ideological adjustments of downward mobile workers."
            American Sociological Review 24(April): 215–231.
Wright, C.R., and H. Hyman
    1958   "Voluntary association memberships of American adults: evidence from
            national sample surveys. American Sociological Review 23(June):
            284–294.

*Studs Terkel, a radio and print journalist, is also a good
listener. In preparing his books* Division Street, Hard
Times, *and* Working, *he listened to and recorded the
thoughts of hundreds of people about their lives and
their jobs. For* Working *he interviewed factory workers,
farmers, professionals, managers, and some people who
are engaged in rather specialized occupations, such as
Carmelita Lester, a practical nurse who cares for a
ninety-three-year-old helpless patient; Herbert Bach, a
"memorial counselor"; and Elmer Ruiz, a gravedigger.
Their roles as practitioners in the business of death and
dying are described in their own words and in Terkel's.*

*As you meet the people Terkel interviewed, think
about the methods they each employed to cope with
their seemingly gruesome chores. Why do they all appear to assume the mantle of professionalism?*

Last Rites: Three Practitioners

STUDS TERKEL

CARMELITA LESTER

*She arrived from the West Indies in 1962. She has been a practical nurse
for the past five years. "You study everything about humanity, the human body, all the way through. How to give the patient cares, how to
make comfortable . . . Most of the time I work seven days."*

*We're in a private room at a nursing home for the elderly. "Most of
them are upper, above middle class. I only work for private patients.
Some may have a stroke, some are maybe confused. Some patients have
nothing wrong with them, but relatives just bring them and leave them
here."*

*As she knits, she glances tenderly at the old, old woman lying in the
bed. "My baby here has cerebral thrombosis. She is ninety-three years
old."**

I get in this morning about eight-thirty. I shake her, make sure that she was
okay. I took her tray, wipe her face, and give her cereal and a cup of orange

---

* Four years before, I visited "her baby" when she was eighty-nine years old. It was a gracefully
appointed apartment; she was most hospitable. Bright-eyed, alert, witty, she recounted her experiences during the Great Depression.

juice and an egg. She's unable to chew hard foods. You have to give her liquids through a syringe. She's supposed to get two thousand cc per day. If not, it would get dry and she would get a small rash and things like those.

The first thing in the morning, after breakfast, I sponge her and I give her a back rub. And I keep her clean. She's supposed to be turned every two hours. If we don't turn her every two hours, she will have sores. Even though she's asleep, she's got to be turned.

I give her lunch. The trays come up at twelve thirty. I feed her just the same as what I feed her in the morning. In the evening I go to the kitchen and pick up her tray at four o'clock and I do the same thing again. About five thirty I leave here and go home. She stays here from five thirty until eleven at night as floor care, until the night nurse comes.

You have to be very, very used to her to detect it that she's having an attack. I go notify that she's having a convulsion, so the nurse come and give her two grains of sodium amytal in her hips. When she gets the needle it will bring down her blood pressure. Because she has these convulsions, her breathing stops, trying to choke. If there's nobody around, she would stifle.

Some days she's awake. Some days she just sleeps. When she's awake she's very alert. Some people believe she isn't, but she knows what's going on. You will hear her voice say something very simple. Other than that, she doesn't say a word. Not since she had that last heavy stroke last year. Before that, she would converse. Now she doesn't converse any more. Oh, she knows what's going on. She's aware. She knows people by the voices. If a man comes in this room, once she hears that voice, I just cannot undress her. (Laughs.)

She knows when I'm not here. If I'm away too long, she gets worried, sick. But she got used to it that I have to go out sometimes. She knows I'll be back, so she's more relaxed now. Oh, sometimes I sit here and get drowsy. I think of the past and the future. Sometime I think when I was a little girl in Cuba and the things I used to do.

If I'm not doing nothing after I get through with her, it's a drag day. I laugh and I keep myself busy doing something. I may make pillows. I sell 'em. Sometimes I'll be writing up my bills. That's my only time I have, here. If I don't feel like doing that, well, I'll make sure she's okay, I'll go down into the street and take a walk.

The work don't leave my mind. I have been so long with her that it became part of me. In my mind it's always working: "How's she getting along?" I worry what happened to her between those hours before the night nurse report. If I go off on a trip, I'll be talking about her. I'll say, "I wonder what happened to my baby." My girl friend will say, "Which baby are you talking about?" I'll say, "My patient." (Laughs.) I went to Las Vegas. I spent a week there. Every night I called. Because if she has these convulsions . . .

My baby, is not everyone can take of her through this illness. Anybody will be sittin' here and she will begin to talk and you don't know it. So you have to be a person that can detect this thing coming along. I called every night to find out how she was doin'. My bill was seventy-eight dollars. (Laughs.) If she's sick, I have to fly back. She stays on my mind, but I don't know why. (Laughs.)

She works through a nurses' registry. "You go where they send you. Maybe you get a little baby." She had worked at a general hospital before. "I used to float around. I worked with geriatric, I worked with pediatric, I worked with teen-agers, I worked with them all. Medical-surgical. I've been with her two years. As long as she's still going." *(Laughs.)*

In America, people doesn't keep their old people at home. At a certain age they put them away in America. In my country, the old people stay in the home until they die. But here, not like that. It's surprising to me. They put them away. The first thing they think of is a nursing home. Some of these people don't need a nursing home. If they have their own bedroom at home, look at television or listen to the radio or they have themselves busy knitting . . . We all, us foreigners, think about it.

Right now there's a lady here, nothing wrong with her, but they put her away. They don't come to see her. The only time they see her is when she say "I can't breathe." She wants some attention. And that way she's just aging. When I come here, she was a beautiful woman. She was looking very nice. Now she is going down. If they would come and take her out sometimes . . .

We had one lady here about two years ago, she has two sons. She fell and had a broken hip. They called the eldest son. He said, "Why call on me? Call the little one. She gave all the money to that little one." That was bad. I was right there.

All these people here are not helpless. But just the family get rid of them. There is a lady here, her children took her for a ride one day and push her out of the car. Let her walk and wander. She couldn't find her way home. They come and brought her here. And they try to take away all that she has. They're tryin' to make her sign papers and things like those. There's nothing wrong with her. She can dress herself, comb her hair, take a walk . . . They sign her in here, made the lawyers sign her in. They're just in for the money. She will tell you, "There's nothin' wrong with me."

Things that go on here. I've seen many of these patients, they need help, but they don't have enough help. Sometimes they eat and sometimes they don't. Sometimes there's eight hours' wait. Those that can have private nurse, fine. Those that can't suffer. And this is a high-class place. Where *poor* old people . . . (She shakes her head.)

"The reason I got so interested in this kind of work, I got sick. One evening my strength just went. My legs and everything couldn't hold. For one year I couldn't walk. I had twelve doctors. They couldn't find out what was wrong. I have doctors from all over the United States come to

*see. Even a professor from Germany. A doctor from South Carolina
came, he put it in a book. My main doctor told, 'You have to live with
your condition 'cause there's nothing we can do.' I said to him, 'Before I
live this way, I'd rather die.' 'Cause I couldn't feed myself, I couldn't do
nothin'. This life is not for me.*

"*They took me home. I started prayin' and prayin' to God and things
like those and this. Oral Roberts, I wrote to him several letters. Wrote
from my heart. Still I was crippled. Couldn't put a glass of water to my
mouth. The strength had been taken away. I prayed hard.*

"*One night I was in bed and deeply down in my sleep, I heard elec-
tricity. Like when you take an electric wire and touch it. It shot through
both my legs. Ooohhh, it shocked so hard that I woke up. When I woke
up, I felt it three times. The next morning I could raise this leg up. I was
surprised.*

"*The next night I felt the same thing. The third night I felt the same
thing. So I got up and went to the bathroom, I went back to the doctor
and he said, 'That's surprising.' Ooohhh, I can't believe it. There is a
miracle. This is very shocking.*"

What do you think cured you?

"*God.*"

Did Oral Roberts help?

"*Yes.*"

How?

"*By prayin' sincere from his heart.*

"*I was a nurse before, but I wasn't devoted. I saw how they treated
people when I was there. Oh, it was pitiful. I couldn't stand it. And
from that, I have tender feelings. That changed me. That's when I decided to devote myself.*"

I feel sorry for everybody who cannot help themselves. For that reason I
never rest. As soon as I'm off one case I am on another. I have to sometimes
say, "Don't call me for a week." I am so tired. Sometimes I have to leave the
house and hide away. They keep me busy, busy, busy all the time. People
that I take care of years ago are callin' back and askin' for me.

Plenty of nurses don't care. If they get the money, forget it. They talk like
that all the time. They say to me, "You still here?" I say, "Yes." "Oh, you
still worry about that old woman." I say, "That's why she pays me, to worry
about her." Most of the nurses have feelings.

If I had power in this country, first thing I'd do in nursing homes, I would
hire someone that pretended to be sick. 'Cause that's the only way you know
what's goin' on. I would have government nursing homes. Free care for

everybody. Those hospitals that charge too much money and you don't have insurance and they don't accept you, I would change that—overnight.

Things so bad for old people today—if I could afford to buy a few buildings, I would have that to fall on. You got to be independent. So you don't have to run there and there and there in your old age. They don't have enough income. I don't want to be like that.

An elderly person is a return back to babyhood. It give you a feeling how when you were a teen-ager, you're adult, you thing you're strong and gay, and you return back to babyhood. The person doesn't know what's happening. But you take care of the person, you can see the difference. It makes you sad, because if you live long enough, you figure you will be the same.

POSTSCRIPT: *A few months after this conversation, her "baby" died.*

HERBERT BACH

We are called memorial counselors. We use telephone solicitation. We use direct mail. We put ads in papers. In any kind of field you look in the haystack for needles.

We call ourselves the Interment Industry. The funeral industry is a little bit different. You conduct a funeral, it takes one or two or three days, and that's the end of that. But we're responsible for fifty, a hundred, two hundred years. People will come in and say, "Where is my great-grandfather?" If you don't have a record of that, we're in trouble.

We're in a creative field. We get into engineering, into landscaping, into purchasing for flowers. We get into contracting and road building. We cover areas from working with a bereaved family to dropping a sewer thirty feet into the ground so it will properly drain. Oh yes, there have been significant changes in cemetery management.

In the old days the cemetery was strictly a burial ground. When somebody died, they would dispose of the remains. They left it to each family to put in some sort of tombstone. Today the cemetery is a community institution. It should be a thing of beauty, a thing of dignity.

In the old days the cemetery served a simple pupose. Today we think of it in terms of ecology. Green acres in the center of residential and commercial areas, newly built. We have 160 acres here. Around us are industrial parks. Still, we have this green . . . The cemetery field has become professionalized.

In the old days each little church, each little synagogue, would buy a piece of land, and the sexton would keep the records of who and what was buried where. There was no landscape design, there were no roads, there was no draining. Our landscaper does the annual World Flower Show. One of our architects had done the Seagram Building. We use forward-thinking people who make the cemetery serve the whole community.

The olden days, the maintenance of the cemetery was left to the individual family. One family would pay and the others didn't. You would have weeds in one area and someplace else cared for. Today, in a modern cemetery, you have trust funds. Whenever a family purchases, a part of that money is put into a trust. This trust in inviolate. In this state it's held by a third party, a bank. You know that cemetery is gonna be cared for.

We have eliminated tombstones and monuments. We use level bronze memorials. You get away from this thing of a marble orchard—and the depression of cold, cold stone. What you see are shrubs and flowers and trees. The beauty represents something for the entire community.

We are only fifteen years old and our trustee has close to a million dollars to help pay for the maintenance. When the park is complete, the trust will run between twelve and fourteen million dollars. Only the interest can be used. So we put in works of art.

I am not a grief psychologist. (Laughs.) I think death is a personal thing. We feel we have to do something to help people overcome their grief. At every interment service we erect a chapel tent. We have an outdoor chapel. We call it the Chapel in the Woods. We hold annual memorial services. So the family knows—even if they don't come to the service—their loved ones are being remembered. We have a lowering device—the casket is put on that—covered with green. So people don't see the bare hole in the ground, which is very traumatic.*

Funerals are more restrained today. In the past people got very, very emotional. Today there is a dignity to the service. They don't have to get emotional. They don't have to do the kind of thing they did in the past to show everybody how much they loved the one that went away. The one big thing at the time of death is the guilt complex. We always felt we haven't done enough for the person who passed away. So we try to overcome this at the time of death.

One of the big things people say at the time of death is: "Oh, I loved him so much. I want him to get the very best." I want to get the finest of this and the finest of that. They are subjected to emotional overspending. At the funeral chapel they'll buy the casket they can't afford. At the cemetery they'll buy the interment space they can't afford. We try to avoid that. We say it should be planned, like you plan life insurance. You wouldn't drive a car without automobile insurance. You wouldn't move into a house without fire insurance. Why not memorial insurance?

---

* Joe Matthews, a clergyman, recalls his aged father's funeral: "I sat alone with my father the day before his burial. The cosmetics shocked me. It wasn't my father as I had known him. I wanted to see his wrinkles again. I helped put those wrinkles there. My brothers and sisters helped put those wrinkles there. My mother helped put those wrinkles there. Those wrinkles were part of me. They weren't there that day. It was as if they had taken away *my* life. It was as if I were ashamed of my father as he was. No. The mortician was friendly, though bewildered. He brought me the soap, sponge, and basin of warm water I asked for. I took the make-up off of papa. I never got him to look ninety-two again. But he didn't look fifty any more when I was finished."

They can budget it over a period of time. If people don't budget, they have to pay cash, right? If you don't pay for a refrigerator, they can repossess it. If somebody passes away and you make an interment, you can't very well repossess the body. (Laughs.) So, they have to pay cash here in advance. It's a matter of budgeting.

ELMER RUIZ

Not anybody can be a gravedigger. You can dig a hole any way they come. A gravedigger, you have to make a neat job. I had a fella once, he wanted to see a grave. He was a fella that digged sewers. He was impressed when he seen me diggin' this grave—how square and how perfect it was. A human body is goin' into this grave. That's why you need skill when you're gonna dig a grave.

He has dug graves for eight years, as the assistant to the foreman. "I been living on the grounds for almost twelve years." During the first four years "I used to cut grass and other things. I never had a dream to have this kind of job. I used to drive a trailer from Texas to Chicago." He is married and has five children, ranging in age from two to sixteen. It is a bitter cold Sunday morning.

The gravedigger today, they have to be somebody to operate a machine. You just use a shovel to push the dirt loose. Otherwise you don't use 'em. We're tryin' a new machine, a ground hog. This machine is supposed to go through heavy frost. It do very good job so far. When the weather is mild, like fifteen degrees above zero, you can do it very easy.

But when the weather is below zero, believe me, you just really workin' hard. I have to use a mask. Your skin hurts so much when it's cold—like you put a hot flame near your face. I'm talkin' about two, three hours standin' outside. You have to wear a mask, otherwise you can't stand it at all.

Last year we had a frost up to thirty-five inches deep, from the ground down. That was difficult to have a funeral. The frost and cement, it's almost the same thing. I believe cement would break easier than frost. Cement is real solid, but when you hit 'em they just crack. The frost, you just hit 'em and they won't give up that easy. Last year we had to use an air hammer when we had thirty-five inches frost.

The most graves I dig is about six, seven a day. This is in the summer. In the winter it's a little difficult. In the winter you have four funerals, that's a pretty busy day.

I been workin' kinda hard with this snow. We use charcoal heaters, it's the same charcoal you use to make barbeque ribs or hot dogs. I go and mark where the grave is gonna be tomorrow and put a layer of charcoal the same size of a box. And this fifteen inches of frost will be completely melt by tomorrow morning. I start early, about seven o'clock in the morning, and I have the park cleaned before the funeral. We have two funerals for tomorrow, eleven and one o'clock. That's my life.

In the old days it was supposed to be four men. Two on each end with a rope, keep lowerin' little by little. I imagine that was kinda hard, because I imagine some fellas must weight two hundred pounds, and I can feel that weight. We had a burial about five years ago, a fella that weighed four hundred pounds. He didn't fit on the lowerin' device. We had a big machine tractor that we coulda used, but that woulda looked kinda bad, because lowerin' a casket with a tractor is like lowerin' anything. You have to respect . . . We did it by hand. There were about a half a dozen men.

The grave will be covered in less than two minutes, complete. We just open the hoppers with the right amount of earth. We just press it and then we lay out a layer of black earth. Then we put the sod that belongs there. After a couple of weeks you wouldn't know it's a grave there. It's complete flat. Very rarely you see a grave that is sunk.

To dig a grave would take from an hour and a half to an hour and forty-five minutes. Only two fellas do it. The operator of the ground hog or back hoe and the other fella with the trailer, where we put the earth.

When the boss is gone I have to take care of everything myself. That includes givin' orders to the fellas and layin' graves and so on. They make it hard for me when the fellas won't show. Like this new fella we have. He's just great but he's not very dependable. He miss alot. This fella, he's about twenty-four years old. I'm the only one that really knows how to operate that machine.

I usually tell 'em I'm a caretaker. I don't think the name sound as bad. I have to look at the park, so after the day's over that everything's closed, that nobody do damage to the park. Some occasions some people come and steal and loot and do bad things in the park, destroy some things. I believe it would be some young fellas. A man with responsibility, he wouldn't do things like that. Finally we had to put up some gates and close 'em at sundown. Before, we didn't , no. We have a fence of roses. Always in cars you can come after sundown.

When you tell people you work in a cemetery, do they change the subject?

Some, they want to know. Especially Spanish people who come from Mexico. They ask me if it is true that when we bury somebody we dig 'em out in four, five years and replace 'em with another one. I tell 'em no. When these people is buried, he's buried here for life.

It's like a trade. It's the same as a mechanic or a doctor. You have to present your job correct, it's like an operation. If you don't know where to make the cut, you're not gonna have a success. The same thing here. You have to have a little skill. I'm not talkin' about college or anything like that. Myself, I didn't have no grade school, but you have to know what you're doin.' You have some fellas been up for many years and still don't know whether they're comin' or goin'. I feel proud when everything became smooth and when Mr. Bach congratulate us. Four years ago, when the foreman had a heart attack, I took over. That was a real tough year for myself. I had to dig the graves and I had to show the fellas what to do.

A gravedigger is a very important person. You must have hear about the strike we had in New York about two years ago. There were twenty thousand bodies layin' and nobody could bury 'em. The cost of funerals they raised and they didn't want to raise the price of the workers. The way they're livin', everything wanna go up, and I don't know what's gonna happen.

Can you imagine if I wouldn't show up tomorrow morning and this other fella—he usually comes late—and sometimes he don't show. We have a funeral for eleven o'clock. Imagine what happens? The funeral arrive and where you gonna bury it?

We put water, the aspirins, in case somebody passes out. They have those capsules that you break and put up by their nose—smelling salts. And we put heaters for inside the tents so the place be a little warm.

There are some funerals, they really affect you. Some young kid. We buried lots of young. You have emotions, you turn in, believe me, you turn. I had a burial about two years ago of teen-agers, a young boy and a young girl. This was a real sad funeral because there was nobody but young teen-agers. I'm so used to going to funerals every day—of course, it bothers me—but I don't feel as bad as when I bury a young child. You really turn.

I usually will wear myself some black sunglasses. I never go to a funeral without sunglasses. It's a good idea because your eyes is the first thing that shows when you have a big emotion. Always these black sunglasses.

This grief that I see every day, I'm really used to somebody's crying every day. But there is some that are real bad, when you just have to take it. Some people just don't want to give up. You have to understand that when somebody pass away, there's nothing you can do and you have to take it. If you don't want to take it, you're just gonna make your life worse, become sick. People seems to take it more easier these days. They miss the person, but not as much.

There's some funerals that people, they show they're not sad. This is different kinds of people. I believe they are happy to see this person—not in a way of singing—because this person is out of his sufferin' in this world. This person is gone and at rest for the rest of his life. I have this question lots of times: "How can I take it?" They ask if I'm calm when I bury people. If you stop and think, a funeral is one of the natural things in the world.

I enjoy it very much, especially in summer. I don't think any job inside a factory or an office is so nice. You have the air all day and it's just beautiful. The smell of the grass when it's cut, it's just fantastic. Winter goes so fast sometimes you just don't feel it.

When I finish my work here, I just don't remember my work. I like music so much that I have lots more time listenin' to music or playin'. That's where I spend my time. I don't drink, I don't smoke. I play Spanish bass and guitar. I play accordian. I would like to be a musician. I was born and raised in Texas and I never had a good school. I learned music myself from here and there. After I close the gate I play. I don't think it would be nice to play music when the funeral's goin' by. But after everything . . .

I believe we are not a rich people, but I think we're livin' fair. We're not sufferin'. Like I know lotsa people are havin' a rough time to live on this world because of crises of the world. My wife, sometimes she's tired of stayin' in here. I try to take her out as much as possible. Not to parties or clubs, but to go to stores and sometimes to go to drive-ins and so on.

She's used to funerals, too. I go to eat at noon and she asks me, "How many funerals you got today? How many you buried today?" "Oh, we buried two." "How many more you got?" "Another." Some other people, you go to your office, they say, "How many letters you write today?" Mine says, "How many funerals you had today?" (Laughs.)

My children are used to everything. They start playin' ball right against the house. They're not authorized to go across the road because it's the burial in there. Whenever a funeral gonna be across from the house, the kids are not permitted to play. One thing a kid love, like every kid, is dogs. In a way, a dog in here would be the best thing to take care of the place, especially a German Shepherd. But they don't want dogs in here. It's not nice to see a dog around a funeral. Or cats or things like that. So they don't have no pet, no.

I believe I'm gonna have to stay here probably until I die. It's not gonna be too bad for me because I been livin' twelve years already in the cemetery. I'm still gonna be livin' in the cemetery. (Laughs.) So that's gonna be all right with me whenever I go. I think I may be buried here, it look like.

Doctors, clergymen, funeral directors, gravediggers—
these and others are, at one time or another, practi-
tioners involved in the "business" of dying. They often
receive specialized schooling or on-the-job training to
deal with death, dying, and bereavement. But what of
the dying themselves? How do they prepare for the in-
evitable?

In recent years preparation for death has become of
considerable interest to sociologists, anthropologists
and psychologists. In the following article, Thomas
Powers discusses death preparation and expresses some
views on this ultimate socialization experience.

As you read "Learning to Die," consider the im-
portance of understanding the meaning of life and
death in our society and the social and religious sources
of these learned and shared beliefs.

Learning to Die

THOMAS POWERS

On November 8, 1970, Barbara B., a woman in her middle sixties, was admitted to New York Hospital with an unexplained intestinal blockage.
Because it was a Sunday and her own doctor was unavailable, the doctor of a
friend took over. He had never met Mrs. B. and knew nothing of her medical
history. When he asked what was wrong she described her symptoms during
the preceding few days but volunteered nothing else. Dr. C. began making
arrangements for an exploratory operation in the next day or two if the situation did not correct itself.

A friend had accompanied Mrs. B. to the hospital. Later that day her
daughter and son-in-law came up to see her. Mrs. B. was in considerable pain
so there was not much conversation. When they did talk, it was about matters
of little consequence. Not knowing exactly what Mrs. B.'s condition was they
all hoped that an operation would not be necessary, but they did not speculate as to what might have caused the blockage. Each of the four had a pretty
good idea of the cause: none of them mentioned it that first day.

On Monday Dr. C. contacted Mrs. B.'s regular doctor and was told she had
had a cancerous breast removed in the summer of 1968, that malignant skin
nodules had reappeared in the summer of 1970, and that laboratory tests

showed spreading cancer. It was obvious to Dr. C. that Mrs. B.'s cancer had reached her abdomen and that she did not have long to live. When he spoke to Mrs. B.'s family, however, he was somewhat more tentative. He said he was not sure (which was true; he was not *absolutely certain*) what was causing the blockage, that the blockage might disappear, that he advised waiting for a few days to see how things developed. He admitted, in response to direct questions, that Mrs. B. was suffering from a serious case of cancer and that serious in her case probably meant fatal. He muted only the probable (but not yet *certain*) fact that Mrs. B. had already begun to die.

During the following few days Mrs. B. was in continual discomfort but nevertheless remained the same person her family had always known: witty, unsentimental, interested in gossip, a passionate reader, a stern critic of everything about President Nixon except the good looks of his daughters, in all things a woman determined to be strong. When friends or family came to visit she talked about politics, life on Tenth Street, what she was reading, and so on. Everyone asked how she was feeling. She always answered, "Oh, all right," with a look of disgust. Once or twice she said she hoped she would not need an operation. A kind of unspoken agreement was in effect: cancer was not to be mentioned. The reasons for the agreement varied. Mrs. B. felt it was weak to discuss bodily ills, and wanted to spare her daughter. Her daughter wanted to spare her mother. Mrs. B. and her family all knew her cancer had reappeared, but discussion of the possible operation was based on the unstated assumption that the cancer and the intestinal blockage were two entirely separate conditions. In other words, everyone knew the end was coming, but resisted the notion that it was coming *now*.

When the blockage persisted into the middle of the next week, however, it became increasingly difficult to ignore the seriousness of Mrs. B.'s condition. Mrs. B. has nothing but contempt for people who complained and was inclined to think that any mention of her own condition was a kind of complaining. In spite of this, she began to refer to it elliptically.

One evening, as her son-in-law was just leaving, she abruptly mentioned a Kingsley Amis novel she had once read in which a character visits a hospitalized friend who is dying with cancer (Mrs. B. winced at the word) of the stomach. In the novel, the dying friend makes little pretense of interest in the conversation; he is simply trying to hold on until his next pain shot.

"I'm beginning to feel that way myself," Mrs. B. said with a bitter smile, apologizing for her failure to keep up her end of the conversation and ashamed of herself for bringing it up. "When something really hurts, all you live for is that pain shot."

A couple of days later Mrs. B.'s son-in-law arrived just as Mrs. B.'s roommate was coming out of anesthesia following an operation to determine if she had breast cancer. The son-in-law asked what the verdict had been. "She had two tumors but neither was malignant." Mrs. B. said "Some people have all the luck."

Mrs. B. refrained from talking about her feelings directly on all but one or two occasions. Once she told her daughter, "I've got so little to look forward to," but then regained her composure. "Sometimes I can't help feeling blue," she explained. There were other slips, but generally she refused to talk about what she was going through, or to let anyone else talk about it. Neither she nor anyone else had yet admitted fully what was now the one great fact in her life: she was dying.

Dying is not a subject to which doctors have traditionally paid much attention. Their first purpose is to preserve life, and once life can no longer be decently extended they tend to lose interest. Until fairly recently, the medical profession reacted to death as if the subject were adequately covered by the children's old skip-rope song:

> *Doctor, doctor, will I die?*
> *Yes, my child, and so will I.*

Since death was inevitable, discussion was restricted to secondary matters, centering on three main questions. The first was how to determine when the patient was really dead. Before the twentieth century, people were occasionally buried while still alive, and wills sometimes included a stipulation that the deceased remain above ground until his body actually began to smell. The second question, still much discussed, was whether or not to tell the patient he was dying. The third question, of more interest to doctors of divinity than of medicine, concerned the individual after the process of dying was complete: specifically, did the soul survive, and if so, in what form? All three questions are still open to dispute, and the first has attracted considerable scientific attention since the advent of organ transplants. Laws that require embalming before burial preclude the possibility of being buried alive, but there is still plenty of contention about identifying the precise moment at which a patient becomes sufficiently dead to justify the removal of vital organs.

The question of dying itself has been ignored. In 1912 a Boston doctor, Roswell Park, suggested that nothing was known about the subject and coined a word for its study—thanatology. No one remembered the word or undertook the study. With the exception of books on death as a religious event, almost nothing was published on the subject. The few books that were often had a cultist flavor, like *Death: Its Causes and Phenomena,* also published in 1912, which included a chapter on "Photographing and Weighing the Soul." Medical scientists acted as if Woodrow Wilson had adequately described death and dying in his last words before slipping into unconsciousness: "I am a broken machine. I am ready to go." Scientists were interested in the machine during, not after, its breakdown. They described dying exclusively in terms of the specific diseases or conditions which accompanied it, almost as if dying would not occur if there were no disease.

Since the second world war the subject has begun to receive some attention. In 1956, the American Psychological Association held a major symposium on death at its annual convention. In 1965, Dr. Elisabeth Kübler-Ross began a prolonged study of dying patients at the University of Chicago's Billings Hospital. Other organizations, institutes, and centers, usually with a highly specialized focus, have been established in Cleveland, Boston, Durham, North Carolina, and elsewhere. In 1967, a number of doctors in New York created the Foundation of Thanatology (the coincidental use of Dr. Park's word was not discovered until later) to encourage the study of death and dying from a broad perspective. They chose the word thanatology to make it easier to raise funds, figuring that philanthropists, like others, would find the word death so disturbing they would prefer to have nothing to do with it. La Rochefoucauld, the seventeenth-century French writer, said "One can no more look steadily at death than at the sun." The Foundation of Thanatology has found that the attention span of those they approach for funds is generally just long enough to say no. Independent researchers have experienced similar difficulties and disappointments, including outright hostility on the part of doctors, nurses, and hospital administrators. Nevertheless, some important work has been done, and dying as a biological and psychological event is beginning to be understood.

The biological aspects of death have received the most attention. In most, but not all, cases an autopsy will reveal exactly how an individual died, by which doctors now usually mean what caused his brain to cease functioning. Since respirators and other machines can keep the heart beating and other organs functioning virtually indefinitely, doctors have begun to accept "brain death" as adequate confirmation that the patient is actually "dead." The brain is considered to be dead when an electroencephalogram (EEG) is flat, which means that it detects no electromagnetic activity within the brain. It is a useful definition, compromised to some degree by the fact that patients have, if only rarely, recovered completely following two or even three days with an absolutely flat EEG. Brain death is generally (but not always) caused by a lack of oxygen, which is generally (but not always) caused by failure of the heart or lungs. The number of exact ways in which a human can die are, however, vast. Medical scientists are successful in describing how the body breaks down, not quite so successful in explaining why it breaks down; they admit that in a significant number of cases death occurs for no apparent medical reason whatever.

Dying as a psychological event, as an experience, is even more elusive. The principal obstacle to its study has been the fear of death on the part of patients, relatives, doctors, nurses, and the dispensers of funds for research. Since no one can say convincingly what death is, it is not easy to say why people fear it. In general, the fear of death has been broken down into the specific fears of pain, loneliness, abandonment, mutilation, and, somewhat more difficult to define, fear of the loss of self. This is not just another way of saying fear of death, but a kind of disassociation of the self as a conscious entity (the sense of *me*-ness one feels) from the self as a particular individual, with his particular history in the everyday world. That individual is one's closest associate and one fears his loss.

The fear of death also has a primitive, nonrational dimension, like fear of the dark and fear of the unknown. Conscious effort can bring such fear under control but cannot suppress it entirely. One doctor in New York uses complaints about the food in hospitals as a rule of thumb for gauging the fear of death: the more passionate and unreasonable the complaint, he has found, the greater the fear of dying. Everyone apparently experiences the fear of death in some degree, but reacts to it in his own way. People tend to die as they have lived, as suggested in the saying, "Death is terrible to Cicero, desirable to Cato and indifferent to Socrates."

The experience of death is obviously related to its immediate cause. Heart disease and stroke are the conditions most likely to grant the widespread wish for death to occur in sleep. Heart patients who have been saved by modern techniques report they felt only a sudden pain in the beginning of mingled alarm and surprise. In earlier times, those sensations would have been death (as they presumably still are for those not saved). Patients who have suffered severe heart attacks often regain consciousness in some hospital's intensive-care unit with the words, "I'm dying, I'm dying," suggesting that awareness of death can be almost, but not quite, instantaneous. Nurses then find themselves in the awkward position of having to explain that the patient is not dying, without making clear the fact he still might at any moment. Diseases which do not attack vital centers directly and massively, and especially the forms of breakdown associated with old age, allow considerable warning before death actually arrives.

When an individual begins to die, much of what he suffers is the result of the fear of death on his own part and on the part of those around him. He reminds people that they, too, are going to die, which they naturally are not eager to consider. As a result, the first problem faced by the dying individual is to discover the truth about his condition.

In some rare instances doctors make a practice of telling patients the truth immediately, but in most cases the patient has to find out by himself. In their book, *Awareness of Dying*, Barney G. Glaser and Anselm L. Strauss describe a struggle for the truth which is sometimes Byzantine in its complexity, with patients trying to pick up clues while doctors, nurses, and relatives join in a conspiracy to conceal the patient's actual condition. The reason for withholding the truth, doctors say, is that the patient would find it too upsetting, that he needs hope in order to keep on fighting for life, that one can never be absolutely certain of a diagnosis, that patients really do not want to know.

A number of studies have shown, however, that 80 per cent (more or less, depending on the study) of doctors oppose telling dying patients the truth, while 80 per cent of their patients want to be told. Doctors apparently shy from the subject because death represents a defeat and because, like everybody else, they find death upsetting to talk about. The psychological stratagems of medical students confronting death for the first time are notorious. The atmosphere of autopsy rooms is one of macabre humor, a degree or two short of hysteria. Doctors generally end by suppressing awareness of death so thoroughly some researchers speculate that that is why they are drawn to medicine in the first place.

Even while doctors and nurses do everything in their power to withhold the truth, resorting with a smile or outright lies, they customarily believe that the majority of their patients know the truth anyway. Relatives of the dying have the same mixture of feelings, trying to suppress the truth and yet assuming that eventually the patient will realize what is happening. Husbands and wives, each knowing the truth, often tell a third party that *they* know, but not to let the *other* know because he (or she) "couldn't stand it." The pretense naturally grows harder to sustain as the dying patient approaches a final decline. Nevertheless, the pretense is often maintained by sheer will until the end, even when all parties know the truth, and know the others know it too.

In rare instances patients refuse to recognize the truth, ignoring the most obvious clues (such as the visit of a relative who lives thousands of miles away) and insisting up until the end that they will be better in no time. For such patients almost any explanation will suffice. One woman dying of cancer, for example, believed (or pretended to believe) that she was only the victim of a slightly new strain of flu. Dr. Kübler-Ross describes a woman Christian Scientist who insisted until the end that faith in God was sufficient physic for an open cancer which was clearly killing her. As the woman declined she put on ever more garish makeup, until finally she was painting her white and withered cheeks a deep red, suppressing the distinctive smell of cancer with perfume and using false eyelashes and deep green eye shadow to insist she was still alive and even attractive. In most cases, however, patients eventually sense they are not getting better and either ask their doctors directly (by no means always getting an honest answer) or set verbal traps for nurses, relatives, and other patients, checking their responses for every discrepancy. One woman fatally ill with a rare disease discovered her condition when she casually ran across an article in *Newsweek* which described every symptom in exact detail. Nurses believe that "way deep down" patients sense when they are dying, and there is some evidence this is true. Patients who know they are dying will often tell a nurse, "I'm going to die tonight," and then do so. Occasionally, however, patients feel they are going to die when, in fact, they are going to live. Persuading such a patient he's going to recover can be a frustrating experience, particularly when he has watched doctors and nurses deliberately deceive other patients who really were dying.

When patients finally do realize they are dying, a pattern of behavior often follows which was first described in detail by Dr. Kübler-Ross. Based on interviews with hundreds of dying patients over the past five years, she divides the reaction to knowledge of impending death into five distinctive stages.

The first stage is one of denial, even when a patient has suspected the worst and fought to determine the truth. All his life he has casually accepted the fact that "we all have to go." He is stunned to realize that now *he* has to go. After the discovery, patients often retreat into a self-imposed isolation, remaining silent with friends or relatives or even refusing to see them, while they get used to the fact that no mistake has been made, that they are *now* in the process of dying. Dr. Kübler-Ross believes that the dying never completely lose hope that a cure for their disease will be discovered at the last minute or that an outright miracle will occur ("the Scripture says that nothing is impossible with God"). This hope remains a deep-seated thing, and for practical purposes, such as writing wills and settling their affairs, the dying generally accept the fact they are dying once they have been told, directly or indirectly, that it is truly so.

The second stage is one of anger, especially when the dying individual is young. The anger can be released in any direction: at the doctors for doing nothing, at relatives who are going to live, at other patients for not being quite so ill, at nurses for being young and healthy, at God for being unjust. In 1603, when Queen Elizabeth was told by her physician, Sir Robert Cecil, that she was seriously ill and must go to bed, she flared back, "*Must*! Is *must* a word to be addressed to princes? Little man, little man! Thy father, were he alive, durst not have used that word." Her mood quickly shifted to gloomy self-pity. "Thou art so presumptuous," she said, "because thou knowest that I shall die."

Eventually the anger subsides and the dying patient enters a curious stage in which he tries to bargain for his life. He begins to talk about all the things he has failed to do but will undertake if he recovers. He laments the fact he spent so much time earning a living and so little with his family, promising to alter his priorities if he gets home again. The most explicit bargains, generally proposed to God, are usually kept a secret. They are often legally precise, offering regular church attendance and sincere belief in return for a few more years. The bargains tend to be selfless, for the dying person knows he is about to lose himself altogether. Bargains can be offered for almost anything, for the chance to attend a son's wedding or to see another spring, but they all have one element in common: they are *never* kept. If the dying person actually does live until spring he immediately proposes another bargain.

Religious individuals often insist they submit themselves happily to God's pleasure ("Thy will be done") but are prepared to propose a reasonable compromise. St. Anselm, the Archbishop of Canterbury, dying in 1109, told fellow clerics gathered about his deathbed, "I shall gladly obey His call. Yet I should also feel grateful if He would grant me a little longer time with you, and if I could be permitted to solve a question—the origin of the soul." God did not accept the offer, and St. Anselm shortly died, but if He had, Dr. Kübler-Ross suggests that St. Anselm would quickly have proposed another bargain.

The fourth stage is one of altogether reasonable depression, part of the process doctors refer to as "anticipatory grief." In effect, the dying patient is grieving for himself before the fact of death, since he is about to lose everything he loves. It is this grieving which is probably most feared by doctors and relatives. It is painful to witness a death, and doubly painful when the dying person reacts in a fearful or hysterical manner. This is exceedingly rare, and yet doctors and relatives, perhaps unsure what their own reactions would be, fear the possibility so greatly that they put off discussion of death as long as possible and sometimes, as mentioned above, deny the truth until the end. In every other circumstance of life, no matter how bleak, some consolation can be genuinely offered; with those who are dying, there is nothing to say. Dr. Kübler-Ross has found, however, that the grieving patient will often come out of his depression and face the prospect of death more calmly for having been through it.

The final stage, not always reached, is one of acceptance.

When Mrs. B. woke up one afternoon following a nap, she saw her daughter standing by her bed with tears streaming down her cheeks. "Now, we're not going to have any tears," Mrs. B. said.

Nevertheless, she, too, had recognized the seriousness of her condition. During the first week she was in the hospital she made a point of telling her daily visitors they really didn't have to come so often. Now she admitted to looking forward to every visit. "It's nice to wake up and find somebody there," she confessed. Her last roommate had remained only a day before moving into a single room, so Mrs. B. was entirely alone between visits. The roommate, a woman in her forties who had also had a cancerous breast removed, had been shifted by her husband when he learned of Mrs. B.'s medical history. He said he wanted to protect the feelings of his wife, but she was acutely embarrassed by the move and came to see Mrs. B. every day. When the woman left the hospital she stopped by to say goodbye and suggested that she and Mrs. B. meet in New York for lunch someday. "Or," she said, "we have a place near you in the country. Maybe we can get together next spring." Mrs. B. said that would be fine and then added, "Good luck."

By the second week it was obvious Mrs. B.'s intestinal blockage was not going to clear by itself. Her doctors told her family the cancer had reached her liver and had probably affected her entire abdominal area. The sole remaining question was how long it would take Mrs. B. to die and whether or not she would be able to go home again in the time remaining. The only way she could leave the hospital, the doctors said, would be to undergo an operation in order to remove whatever was obstructing her intestine. They warned that she was in a weakened condition and might die during the operation, or that cancer might have affected so much of her intestine nothing could be done. The alternatives were also presented to Mrs. B., although in less detail and more tentatively. Both she and her family decided it would be better to go ahead.

Mrs. B.'s eldest daughter, living in California, already had made plans to come East for Thanksgiving, knowing it would probably be her last chance to see her mother. When she was told about the operation she asked over the phone, "Shall I wait until next week or should I come now?"

"I think you'd better come now," her brother-in-law said. She arranged for someone to take care of her three children and made a plane reservation for the day after the operation. Mrs. B.'s two brothers were also called, but they decided to wait until after the operation before coming to New York. "If I came now it would scare her to death," said the brother who lived in Washington.

The operation was scheduled for the morning of Thursday, November 19. Her family remained by the phone throughout the day. At 6 P.M. the surgeon finally called and said Mrs. B.'s intestine was blocked by cancer every two or three inches. There was nothing he could do. He was asked how long Mrs. B. might live. "Perhaps a week," he said.

Later that evening Mrs. B.'s family visited her briefly after she came up from the recovery room. She was pale and drawn and barely able to speak. The operation had obviously been an ordeal. "Never again," she whispered. "Never again."

The next day Mrs. B.'s eldest daughter flew to New York and went to see her mother, already beginning to regain her strength after the operation. Before the family went to see her on Saturday they tried to decide what to say if she should ask about her condition. The hard thing was finding out what Mr. B. already had been told by her doctors. Until they reached Dr. C., they decided, they would tell Mrs. B. everyone was worried but didn't yet know the full results of the operation. They feared she would press them, and they knew that if she asked directly whether or not the cancer had been cut out, the only possible answers would be the truth or an outright lie. They did not want to lie, knowing how much Mrs. B. would hate being lied to, but they dreaded equally talking about the true situation. They could not have explained why.

As things turned out they need not have worried. Mrs. B. had cross-examined her doctors on a number of occasions since Thursday night, when she had found the strength to say, "It was my cancer, wasn't it?" Dr. C. later explained that Mrs. B. kept after him until she had the truth. His practice was to answer all questions truthfully, leaving it up to the patient to decide which questions to ask. Some patients asked nothing. Others stopped as soon as Dr. C. indicated their condition was serious. Mrs. B. had been unusual, he said, in questioning him precisely about her condition.

On Sunday Mrs. B. began to weaken again. When her son-in-law arrived about 11 A.M., she shooed the nurse out of the room. "I want to be alone with my son-in-law," she said. As soon as the door was closed she said, "I'm dying. There's no use kidding ourselves."

She told her son-in-law where all her papers were and what was in her will, asking him to make sure his mother got the red leather box which Mrs. B. had bought for her in Czechoslovakia the previous summer, and then had liked so much she kept it. "I've been feeling guilty about that," she said.

She also asked her son-in-law to get the lawyer on the phone so she could give him "a pep talk." When she reached him she said, "Now listen, you take care of the kids and try and keep the government from getting it all." She gave her best to his wife and said goodbye.

Finally Mrs. B. asked her son-in-law to make sure her eyes went to the eye bank and that her body was given to "science." (Mrs. B.'s surgeon told her son-in-law he wanted to do an autopsy, but that cancer had destroyed her body's usefulness as far as "science" was concerned. Mrs. B.'s second choice had been cremation without any service, and that wish was carried out.)

After Mrs. B. had straightened out her affairs to her own satisfaction, she relaxed and began to chat and even joke about her situation. A few minutes later she suddenly weakened and seemed to doze off. After awhile she started awake, staring intently at the ceiling. "Is there anything up there, right over my bed?" she asked her son-in-law. He said there was not. A look of resigned disgust came over Mrs. B.'s face. "I'm afraid I'm going to have hallucinations," she said.

During the following days her decline was obvious to herself and her family. She spent more time dozing, was coherent for shorter periods which came farther apart. During one such moment she told her daughter, "I hadn't believed it would happen so fast."

In most American hospitals the experience of death is clouded by drugs. When drugs are necessary to relieve pain there is no alternative, but heavy sedatives, tranquilizers, and pain-killing drugs are also used for purposes of "patient management." In the final stages of dying the greatest fear of patients is abandonment, with good reason. When possible, hospitals will try to send patients home to die. Doctors often cut back their visits, overworked nurses save most of their attention for "those who can be helped," and even families of the dying frequently begin to detach themselves. The belief that life must go on can be carried to brutal limits, with relatives and even husbands or wives acting as if the dying individual were already dead. When dying patients pester the nursing staff for attention, they are often simply trying to alleviate their loneliness; if the pestering becomes irksome there is a tendency to respond with drugs.

The abandonment which dying patients fear can be as much emotional as literal. Nurses say they do not become hardened to death and often dream about the death of their patients. As a result they attempt to distance themselves from the dying by thinking of them as no longer quite there, referring to the care of unconscious patients, for example, as "watering the vegetables." The terrible moment which demands that life-sustaining equipment be turned off is emotionally masked by the phrase, "pulling the plug."

The impulse to abandon the dying can become overwhelming. It is policy in most hospitals to move dying patients into single rooms as death approaches. Doctors, nurses, and even relatives tend to find good reasons to stay out of the dying patient's room. The pretense is that no one wants to "disturb" the dying person while he is "resting," but nurses say they have seen too many clusters of relatives outside hospital rooms at the moment of death to consider it a coincidence.

As death approaches, the world of the dying gradually shrinks. They talk less of their disease and more about their exact symptoms, how they feel, what they plan to do tomorrow, or this afternoon, or in the next hour. Hope generally remains until the final moments, but its focus tends to shift. The Rev. Robert Reeves, Jr., the chaplain of Columbia-Presbyterian Hospital in New York, tells of one middle-aged man who hoped to get back to his business up until five weeks before his death. During the first week after that he talked about getting home for Thanksgiving. During the second week he hoped to be able to get out of bed again. In the third week he hoped to regain the ability to swallow food. At the beginning of his final week of life he hoped for a good night's sleep. A day later he hoped his pain medicine would work. The day before he died he hoped he would die in his sleep. He was denied evey hope except the last, and yet each had eased his way toward death.

When the layman speaks of death he is referring to *somatic* death, or the death of the entire organism. The traditional signs of somatic death are *rigor mortis* (the stiffening of certain muscles), *algor mortis* (the cooling of the body) and *liver mortis* (the purplish-red discoloration of the skin caused by the settling of the blood). Somatic death includes the death of all bodily tissues, but an individual is commonly said to be "dead" long before all his tissues have died. The death of the "person," then, is only one stage in what an increasing number of doctors tend to think of as a distinct physiological process.

One doctor likens the process of death to menopause, which has long been known to include profound biological changes in women going far beyond the simple cessation of ovulation. The fact of putrefaction can also be cited as evidence that dying is a coherent biological event, and not simply the exact condition which precipitates death (heart failure, say, or kidney shutdown). When the body dies, organisms escape the gastrointestinal tract and begin the process of general decomposition by which the body is returned to Biblical ashes and dust. Built into the body, in other words, is the biological mechanism of its own dissolution, a fact which hardly can be dismissed as a coincidence. In arguing for an expanded notion of death, doctors also mention the characteristic return of the dying to infancy. Gradually they sleep longer each day, until they wake for only minutes at a time. Emotionally, the dying become increasingly dependent. Waking in the night they may cry if they discover they are alone, or sink back to sleep if someone is there.

Given a choice, the vast majority of people would prefer to die in their sleep. The next best, they say, would be a "peaceful" death, a consummation largely under the control of doctors. "Dear gentlemen," said the eighteenth-century English doctor, Sir Samuel Garth, to his physicians whispering together at the foot of his bed, "let me die a natural death." The ability of doctors to extend the process of dying, if not life, is incomparably greater now. Medical "heroics" can keep the heart beating, the lungs breathing, the kidneys functioning, the brain flickering long after death would normally have arrived. The deterioration of the body from disease, and especially from cancer, proceeds further than it would without medical intervention. The result is that patients often lose consciousness long before they die because doctors, or relatives, refuse to give up when the body does. One nurse with years of experience in an intensive-care unit says she finds it increasingly difficult to tell when a patient has died, since machines sustain his vital signs.

Once the process of dying has begun, death can arrive at any time. Some patients die quickly; some linger for months with conditions that ought to have been quickly fatal. Doctors are still exceedingly cautious about predicting when someone will die, since they are so often surprised. Thomas Lupton, a sixteenth-century English writer, made the following attempt to list sure signs of imminent death:

> If the forehead of the sick wax red, and his brows fall down, and his nose wax sharp and cold, and his left eye becomes little, and the corner of his eye runs, if he turn to the wall, if his ears be cold, or if he may suffer no brightness, and if his womb fall, if he pulls straws or the clothes of his bed, or if he picks often his nostrils with his fingers, and if he wake much, these are almost certain tokens of death.

Signs which modern nurses look for are dilated nostrils, sagging of the tongue to one side of the mouth, and a tendency for the thumbs to tuck in toward the palms of the dying patient's hands. Just as dying people frequently sense the imminence of their own death and predict it accurately, nurses develop a sense which tells them (but not always correctly) when a patient is going to die.

In the early stages of dying, the patient remains essentially himself, afflicted only by the knowledge of impending death and the effect of that knowledge on himself and those around him. In the final stages, consciousness in the dying sometimes undergoes qualitative changes. This experience is the least well understood of all, since the nearer a patient approaches to death, the less he can describe what he feels. The crisis for the dying patient characteristically arrives when he stops "fighting" to live. Doctors cannot say just how patients "fight," but they are unanimous in saying that patients do so, and that "fighting" can make all the difference in situations which can go either way. A man fighting to stay alive apparently duplicates the experience of a man fighting to stay awake, i.e., alternating flashes of lucidity and delirium. Patients often signal the approach of death by simply saying. "I can't fight any longer." The period that follows is unlike any other experienced in life.

Until the twentieth century, this final period was often called "the dying hour," although it can last considerably longer than an hour. Physicians described it as being a peaceful period in which the dying person, accepting the lost struggle and the inevitable end, is relaxed and ready to depart. The patient may gradually distance himself from life, actually turning away from close friends and relatives, literally turning to the wall (as suggested by Lupton) as he prepares himself to die. Accepting the fact of their own death, the dying frequently turn their attention to those who will live, who are sometimes aggrieved by the readiness of the dying to leave them behind. At the end it is often the dying who comfort the living. Even so self-centered a figure as Louis XIV said to those around his deathbed, "Why weep ye? Did you think I should live forever?" After a pause he reflected with equanimity, "I thought dying had been harder."

Dying patients who remain fully conscious, or nearly so, say they are tired, feel a growing calm, are ready to go, are perhaps even happy. When Stephen Crane died of tuberculosis in England in 1900, only twenty-nine years old, he tried to describe the sensation to a friend: "Robert—when you come to the hedge—that we must all go over. It isn't so bad. You feel sleepy—and you don't care. Just a little dreamy anxiety—which world you're really in—that's all."

Dr. Austin Kutscher, one of the creators of the Foundation of Thanatology, has been studying death and related questions since the death of his wife in 1966. He emphasizes that in some ways the living tyrannize over the dying, studying the experience of the latter for the sake of those who remain. An example is the effort of medical scientists to narrow the definition of death in order to allow the organs of the dying to be used for transplants. The decision to accept brain death as death itself may be valid, Kutscher says, but it can hardly be argued that the definition was framed for the benefit of the dying. As a result of this natural bias on the part of the living, the study of death and dying has tended to ignore the nature of the event, and of its experience.

"Isn't there something rather magical about life that defies measurement by a piece of apparatus?" Dr. Kutscher says. "We are begging the issue by trying to define death when we can't even define life."

The scientific study of dying is relatively recent, but there exists a vast literature, amounting to case studies, of the approach of death. The final moments of great men have always been minutely recorded, these accounts ranging from those in the *Lives of the Saints*, which tend to a dull predictability, to the moment-by-moment narratives of death as experienced by generals, poets, and kings. Again and again the last words of the dying concede their readiness to depart; an unfeigned peace seems to ease the final flickering out. History and modern research agree that, for unknown reasons, the dying do not find it hard to die.

The very last moments are, of course, the least accessible. Some doctors have found evidence that the experience of patients still conscious has an element of the mystical. The doctors are quick to say that they are not talking about God and religion and parapsychological cultism; also they admit that such experiences might be the result of anoxia, or oxygen starvation in the brain. Nevertheless, they say, there is reason to believe the dying can experience a sense of surrender which borders on ecstasy. In a secular age, as practitioners of a science which tends toward mechanism, doctors reluctantly speak of "soul" or "spirit." But, in the safety of anonymity, they return again and again to the puzzle of what it is that dies when the body ceases to function. One doctor, attempting to describe the mystery he had sensed in dying patients, quoted the dying words attributed to the ancient philosopher Plotinus: "I am making my last effort to return that which is divine in me to that which is divine in the universe."

During her final five days of life, Mrs. B. was rarely conscious. The hospital left the second bed in her room empty. Her doctors and family decided not to attempt extreme efforts which could only prolong her dying, but Mrs. B. continued to receive intravenous feeding and was regularly turned by the nurses as a precaution against pneumonia.

On two occasions Mrs. B. started violently awake and insisted, "Something is terribly wrong." She did not know her daughters and believed her doctors were conspiring against her. She was given heavy sedation, and her daughters felt that, in effect, she had already died. Nevertheless, on a few last occasions she regained consciousness and knew her family, if only briefly. Two days before she died, as her surgeon was examining her, she suddenly asked, "Why don't I die?"

"Because you're tough," the surgeon said.

"I don't want to be tough that way," Mrs. B. said.

Because one test of a patient's grip on life is the ability to respond, the doctors and nurses would call her name loudly from time to time to ask if she wanted anything. "Mrs. B.?" one of the nurses nearly shouted one night. "Mrs. B.?"

"I'm gone," said Mrs. B. in a faint whisper.

"No, you're still with us," the nurse said.

Mrs. B. grew steadily weaker. Her kidneys began to fail. She began to breathe rapidly and heavily, then stopped altogether, and after a moment began again. A nurse called this "Cheyne-Stokes breathing" and said it was probably a sign that the end was approaching. Some of the nurses thought Mrs. B. was completely unconscious; others felt she had only lost the ability to respond. Not knowing who was right, her family spoke as if she could hear and understand everything said in the room.

When Mrs. B.'s youngest daughter arrived about 11 A.M. the morning of Thanksgiving Day, November 26, she found her mother breathing slowly and regularly. Her body was completely relaxed over onto one side. It was a bright sunlit day. Mrs. B.'s daughter sat down by the large bank of windows overlooking Manhattan to the south and tried to read, but found herself thinking of her mother. After a while she looked up and saw that her mother had stopped breathing. So long expected, death had arrived unnoticed. For eighteen days Mrs. B.'s daughter had restrained her tears. Now, finally, when her mother was no longer there to comfort or be comforted, she began to cry.

There is life after death. By this we do not mean ex-
istence in another world, but rather life for those who
survive. As they go on with their lives, they must deal
with the void created by the departure of a loved one.

In this concluding essay of Part Five, Austin Kutscher
confronts the social and psychological management of
loss and grief. He sees it as being like an illness that
seriously affects a patient but from which, in most
cases, he or she eventually recovers.

Kutscher's article begins with a lengthy case history
and ends with some practical advice from bereaved in-
dividuals who willingly responded to a survey of the
problems they had recently faced in the dying of a loved
one, in grief, and in mourning.

As you read this essay, note that most of the bereaved
argue that life must go on and that the important thing
is to help the living cope with their loss by providing
comfort and support. At the end of a life, as at the
beginning, others are significant for maintaining the
social order.

Bereavement

AUSTIN H. KUTSCHER

Certain conclusions are evident to one who explores in retrospect the management and resolution of "practical problems" confronting the bereaved: 1)
there is a need for thorough investigation of the subject of recovery from
bereavement; 2) ways must be found to communicate to the bereaved available information and advice that may be helpful; 3) bereavement should be
treated as an illness which may result in serious, even fatal, physical ailments
or complications; 4) an essential factor in recovery is the bereaved's acceptance
and at times understanding of his grief; 5) the bereaved's efforts at recovery
must be channeled into constructive efforts which will sustain him through
the depths of his grief; and finally, 6) those who would minister to and care
for the bereaved must be familiar with the numerous practical problems
which add an enormous burden to his grief.

The discussion which follows gives emphasis to the practical problems confronting the bereaved. That the bereaved needs help in meeting the practical

problems of bereavement is not simply a theoretical concept but a stern reality. Such key issues as what the bereaved can and should do, what others (doctors, family, ministers, and friends should do in his behalf, and for how long a period of time such help should be provided must be dealt with.

The term "practicalities" refers to those concrete immediacies of day-to-day living which must be acted upon by the bereaved himself or by someone acting in his behalf. The knowledge and skills of different disciplines must be utilized in order to assist the bereaved family to regain the pleasures and gratifications of daily living. Although philosophic, psychologic, and religious determinants affect the course of action it is important to remember that the action taken represents the need to *do* in order to relieve urgent and formidable pressures and burdens. Not only is there a tremendous gap between the bereaved's need to meet everyday problems and the quality of information and advice offered by concerned individuals, but unfortunately there is, as a rule, less than adequate recognition by the "helping professions" of the importance of dealing with such practicalities. Even when the need for advice may be recognized, there is lack of knowledge as to how such words of advice are to be delivered, how advice can be effectively utilized, and how the bereaved can find and avail himself of the specialists to advise him. By way of illustration, one individual's experience is cited below:

> After the long-anticipated death of his wife from cancer, the bereaved called upon a psychiatrist, a lifelong acquaintance, for advice and suggestions as to how to proceed through the days that lay ahead. None of the questions he had in mind were unusual for someone in this situation. The questions dealt with the first moves to be taken and steps which might hasten recovery. They were concerned with such practicalities as: What should one do for the first days following the funeral? What should be done for and with the children? Should one stay about the house, or visit others, or leave home for several days? Should one accept condolence calls or simply avoid all contact with commiserators? Even cursory examination of each aspect of the life to be continued had already uncovered a multitude of such questions that required answers.
>
> The psychiatrist replied, "What made you call *me*? *Why* did you call me?" As it developed, this response to what might well have been an SOS was an indication of the paucity of well-defined information available to the bereaved from any source.
>
> Yet the psychiatrist did listen, and finally suggested that the bereaved and his sons visit with him at his suburban home that next weekend. The Sunday visit, the culmination of the first weekend of bereavement, was concluded with the accomplishment of at least the start of several important phases of the work of mourning. Words, verbalization of feelings,

and advice all contributed to charting an initial course of action. Nothing actually looked brighter but beginnings had, in fact, been made, certain excesses had been abandoned, and initial perspectives had been achieved. The process of acceptance had been initiated and the past had made the first uncertain steps of retreat into memory.

The failure of anyone to provide the bereaved with comfort, information, or understanding increases feelings of isolation and despair and leads to inappropriate or detrimental responses. Such failures can create a sequence of inopportune or harmful events, just as the heeding of effective advice can create a beneficial sequence.

Dealing with practical tasks readily stirs feelings of guilt, loneliness, regret, abandonment, and despair in the bereaved. These feelings in turn, confront the bereaved with additional problems.

In grief, thoughts of what has taken place persistently reappear and reverberate. Feelings of guilt and loneliness stir up doubts and insecurities. What had one done wrong? Should the patient have been told the truth or should denial and false encouragement have been continued until the end? Should an autopsy have been permitted? If it had been performed, had it served any real purpose? Despite the suffering occasioned by ruminating on these and other matters, the practicalities of daily living must be faced. Advice is required on such basic matters as to how to take care of the children, where to live, and how to continue one's daily life. The more positive areas having to do with regaining the pleasures of living and the question of remarriage begin to emerge much later for consideration and are frequently dealt with more effectively as the result of discussions with informed friends, physicians, clergy, and family members.

It is one matter to consider how to bring comfort to the bereaved: it is another matter to consider just how well the individual can or will function in the emotional and physical turmoil of the bereavement state. Some feel that the tendency for the bereaved to drift in an unstructured and directionless manner must be dealt with forcefully. When and to what extent should the bereaved be encouraged to resume responsibilities, and how much time should the bereaved be encouraged to spend with dependent members of the family (children)? For how long should friends and relatives continue to give assistance? There are many factors, determined by individual circumstance, which materially influence such long-term goals as returning to full working capacity, resuming normal social and familial structures, and re-entry into that most satisfying social unit of all, marriage. The bereaved can be guided toward sources of advice concerned with financial arrangements, homemaker services, companionship activities, return to social living, and the myriad of other elements of daily life. Failure to do something specific and practical can have far-reaching ramifications.

The approach must be two-fold: 1) it must take into account the subjective experience of the bereaved (understood from both individual and collective accounts); and 2) the evaluation by the counselor of the beginning and later needs of the bereaved. Infallible guidelines cannot be formulated and applied to all bereaved, since each individual enters the bereavement state with complicating practical factors, including differences in religious, ethnic, social, and economic background as well as, where children are involved, their number, age, and sex. Timing may also be critical for those needing help. It should also be borne in mind that, for many bereaved, the problems of loss and grief do not begin at the time of death but during the period of anticipatory grief. There are also profound practical differences between the widow and widower state. By anticipating the bereaved's anxieties, fears, and fantasies, and recognizing the problems of daily practical decision-making, obligations, and household necessities, the physician can develop a far better perspective and approach to his helping role.

BEREAVEMENT AS AN ILLNESS

Although it is recognized that the illness and death of a patient may precipitate emotional or physical disturbances in persons who have loved and cared for him, there is little acceptance of the concept that bereavement states *per se* may be considered an illness. The bereaved may be regarded as a patient with a definite complex of symptoms, often subclinical, which may become exacerbated, severe, and even fatal. Despite this, the bereaved's illness, in general, is left untreated. His state is usually diagnosed from the medical and psychological points of view as a normal response to the circumstances of his situation—until overt signs and symptoms reach pathologic proportions.

The bereaved, as a patient, requires treatment, especially in the early stages, to prevent a more serious progression. Unfortunately, our culture tends to ignore the fact that the problems of loss and grief do not begin at the moment of the loved one's death and that there is anticipatory grief which follows notification of the patient's unfavorable prognosis. Anticipatory grief also ushers in a multitude of practical problems, difficulties which cannot be deferred or ignored and which also affect events subsequent to the death of the patient.

In other areas of medicine, when an illness is regarded as being potentially serious, strenuous efforts are made to achieve early intervention and preventive treatment. In the management of bereavement, it is primarily the responsibility of the physician (perhaps the bereaved's own or that of the dying patient) to assume the initiative for the well-being of the "new" or secondary patient. Although the bereaved individual may appear to be progressing "normally," there is little reason for complacency in the physician's responses to the psychological and practical aspects of the bereaved patient's management. There always remain innumerable personal supportive measures which may positively influence the course of convalescence and the long-term physical and emotional prognosis.

Medical educators, too, must recognize that bereavement can be studied as an illness replete with multiple etiologies, diagnostic criteria, and practical features, as well as with a prognosis.

Still another problem exists which has its roots in the failure of communication among professionals. The primary physician is far too willing to ignore the entire matter or to deal with emotional complications in the context of an illness—bereavement. Until recently there has been a generalized apathy among professionals regarding the treatment and management of the bereaved. Compounding this state of affairs has been failure of communication between the primary physician and the specialist, as well as between the physician and paramedical personnel. The insensitive and perfunctory platitude, "Time will heal all," has often substituted for empathic intervention. Perhaps the members of the health professions are shielding themselves from their own fears and insecurities since, in the words of La Rochefoucauld, "One cannot look directly at either the sun or death."

What is often lacking is the intense depth of feeling for the bereaved which can be summoned by few persons regardless of training, who have not themselves passed through an intimate emotional experience associated with death. A quotation from a letter written by an eminent professional colleague speaks for itself:

> One of the reasons I am so tardy in responding has been the death of my mother. Yes, grief and I have come to know one another in a very firsthand way. Mother had been making a good recovery from serious surgery—and then, a clot developed and that was it. All of the small inconsiderations—the phone call not made, the word said and the word not said, the thoughtfulness I might have shown and didn't, all of it came to me—too late. I have often heard the bereaved speak of guilt for which it was too late to atone in the way one might wish to; now I, too, have experienced it.

The practitioner, when he has gained understanding of the problems of the bereaved, can give the bereaved deeper insight concerning his problems and provide assistance in meeting the day-to-day problems. Those involved in the mourning process include the entire family, friends, as well as the physician who has just lost the battle with death. To be of real assistance, it is important that the physician make himself available to discuss the practical aspects of bereavement with the family. This availability may, in turn, be an important step toward resolving feelings of loss by the physician, so that he *can* provide comfort, reassurance, and medical care.

Few teaching or training programs exist which prepare the physician to manage the vicissitudes of grief in medical practice. Recognition of the stages of bereavement, including anticipatory grief, is important not only for the physician but also for the nurse, social worker, and chaplain. As part of his assigned duties, the staff physician should be permitted the opportunity to visit and counsel the bereaved-to-be as he awaits the termination of his vigil. How the physician should be paid for the time he spends in the management of anticipatory grief or the grief of bereavement requires mention since it, too, is very clearly a practical problem.

There is no justification for the abandonment of the bereaved immediately following the death of a loved one in a hospital. Everyone, including interns, nurses, nurses' aides, becomes submerged in routine hospital activities, apparently quite oblivious to the needs of the bereaved, at a time when innumerable problems present themselves. Abandonment should be recognized for what it is: for the professional and paramedical personnel it is a retreat from their own unresolved conflicts concerning death.

Important practical patterns to be followed by the bereaved have been established by etiquette and religion. It is ironic that certain aspects of assisting the bereaved should be well appreciated by an authority on the subject of etiquette, Emily Post, and so poorly appreciated by those who have numerous opportunities to utilize the information:

> At no time are we so indifferent to the social world and all its code as when we stand baffled and alone at the brink of unfathomable darkness into which our loved one has gone. The last resource to which we would look for comfort at such a time is the seeming artificiality of etiquette. Yet it is in the hours of deepest sorrow that etiquette performs its most real service. All set rules of social procedure have for their object the smoothing of personal contacts, and in nothing is smoothness so necessary as in observing the solemn rites accorded to our dead.

The effect which the condolence call may have on the bereaved is not fully appreciated. The religious aspects of the funeral have been dealt with at great length in many writings and yet the positive practical value of these proceedings has only in recent years been duly appreciated by the health professions.

Recovery from bereavement is achieved, in part, through the management of practical day-to-day problems. In this process, we must accept the assumption that the bereaved requires "room to move around in," with as many alternatives as possible offered at the level of practical problem-solving. It is critically important to listen during this period to requests for help in regard to seemingly minor difficulties and decisions. They may represent a plea for help at a far more complex level—including a call for psychiatric assistance. If unresolved, severe emotional or physical problems may develop.

The ultimate goal is the reconstitution of the individual into someone who, having dealt successfully with grief and its attendant practical problems, has much to live for and much to contribute to his family and society. With proper support, he can emerge sustained by the knowledge that he has been able to survive his darkest hours and is able now to reengage himself in constructive living.

Four concepts which illustrate some of the practical problems confronting the bereaved are described in the following case history: 1) the numerous intellectual and psychological burdens which become practical problems as they create the milieu for emotional and physical illness; 2) the procedural details, such as funeral rites, legal routines (for example, dealing with lawyers, reading the will, opening of the vault, filing for social security, etc.) which are required by law and custom, and which may also impose unreasonable and cumulative physical burdens; 3) the additional physical strain of coping with the minutiae of daily living (for example, marketing, cooking, housekeeping, and of continuing to perform a job); and finally, 4) the compounded problems inherent in a failure to find positive solutions for many of the issues confronting the bereaved.

A 43-year-old university professor, after his wife's death from cancer, continued to face many of the uncertainties that had complicated his life during the months of her protracted and painful illness. Although he was able to function as the head of a household of three young sons, aged 17, 15, and 11, and to satisfy the minimum demands of his professional obligations, he suffered from weight loss, lassitude, fatigue, irritability, anorexia, restlessness, insomnia, physical and emotional exhaustion, and depression. Many practical problems had begun at the time of the original diagnosis and unfavorable prognosis of his wife's illness.

Initially, and again subsequently when she required hospitalization, he had encountered an emotional conflict within himself over whether or not to tell his wife the truth about her illness. His first instinct was to spare her. On the other hand, he realized that the truth might be unavoidable since she, having more medical knowledge than the average lay person, might recognize the significance of her symptoms and physical deterioration. Also to be considered was the fact that a sharing of their mutual thoughts and concerns at this time might afford both greater emotional strength. Yet at what point should he tell her, where, and in whose presence? Should he wait until her questions showed that the truth would be better than her doubts and uncertainties as she realized that she was dying? Should their physician or clergyman assume the responsibility for the decision?

Without seeking advice, he decided to withhold the truth. Their relationship had been such that words did not seem to be necessary; yet he did want to tell her of his present grief and previous happiness with her, and to share with her future plans for their children. Because he could not find the words and because he was convinced that such a course was not destructive, he did not tell her. Consequently, he was never certain of how much she did or did not know about her condition.

He was also confronted with the question of whether or not to tell the children the facts concerning their mother's illness, and if so, how—alone or together; whether to reveal the true prognosis to them or to maintain a wide margin of hope until the truth could no longer be concealed; whether to permit them to continue their visits as her condition deteriorated.

Could support and advice be obtained from his friends, relatives and associates, who included psychiatrists, physicians, clergy, writers? Could they provide answers to his immediate day-to-day problems? Could someone give the children the emotional support and physical presence that he realized he was withdrawing as he spent more time at his wife's bedside in the hospital?

Although those to whom he did turn for advice had few answers, they were able at times to provide temporary relief from the extraordinary and ever-present strains of the situation. He had no desire to keep up his usual social contacts but realized that the children were able to benefit from association with family and friends who tried to fill the gaps in their lives. Just finding a way to decline invitations and to respond to inquiries about himself and the family was a source of great distress.

However, he knew that more help, help of a different sort and on a permanent basis, had to be provided for the children. Some semblance of a stable home life had to be established for them. Hence, the home would have to be maintained, and a housekeeper would have to be hired. Should he advertise in the newspapers, or be in touch with community service agencies, such as Homemaker Service or Cancer Care?

Toward the end, controversial problems had to be considered concerning the administration of drugs for pain control or as psychopharmacologic agents. As body functions failed, the continuation of intravenous infusions became increasingly traumatic, and venous cut-down appeared barbarous.

When death did come in the unhospitable environment of the hospital, it was only early evening—but not a professional colleague was in sight. The heartrending task of informing the children remained for still later that night, following a visit to the undertaker. Other family members, friends, and associates then had to be notified. In each instance there were questions of how, when, and where. Strong feelings surrounding the problem of autopsy permission were avoided because the husband had reached a decision on this issue earlier. The obituary, too, had been an earlier subject for thought; he wrote it alone and readily, but no less painfully.

While most questions concerning the funeral were explicitly answered by established religious rituals, certain procedures were open to the personal preferences of the bereaved. How should a casket be chosen? In what clothes should the deceased be buried? Should keepsakes be buried? Should the casket be kept open or closed? How should the cemetery plot be chosen? Or the gravestone? Where should the family and friends go after the funeral? To what degree should the children participate in all the arrangements and rites?

Soon after her death, the bereaved husband expressed to his wife's physicians his appreciation for the care and support they had given. He knew that every available means had been used to sustain his wife's health while this was still possible. He also knew that no pain or suffering had gone unrelieved because of his own unconcern. He soon began to realize that he had neglected himself during his wife's illness; and many problems concerning his own physical and emotional well-being were becoming apparent.

Were his symptoms psychogenic or of purely physical origin? Were they what everyone called "normal?" Should he seek physical attention or psychiatric assistance, or both? Should he consider his state as "normal grief"? How would he recognize an abnormal grief pattern? What were the stages and timetable of grief and mourning? How had anticipatory grief modified his overall grief experience? How could he best counteract his despair and loneliness? Would frequent visits to his wife's grave be harmful? Should he and his family spend the mourning period away from home, with others, or alone?

Longer-range plans had to be made. Should he accept a new job offer and move to another city? What would be the advantages and disadvantages of such a move for the children? If they remained in their present house, many trivial but nevertheless emotionally stressful decisions had to be made. Should he rearrange the furniture, change the furnishings, remove disturbing mementos? Who should be given his wife's clothes, her jewelry? Should he place photos of her about the house? Should he discard keepsakes that were now painful to look at or store them until a later time when the family might better be able to live with them and perhaps enjoy them again? What kind of remembering would be of a healthy sort—deliberate recall or a simple openness to whatever memories revived from day to day? What days of commemoration should be observed—birthdays, anniversaries, nostalgic occasions? Should he participate in religious ceremonies and rites on those days?

How much should the children be included in decision-making? Would it be best for them to continue their normal patterns or should they establish new ones in order to avoid certain memories? How could the routine of their daily living be continued with no mother to see them off to school in the morning or to greet them as they returned home with tales of their daily successes and disappointments?

Legal and financial matters had to be attended to: immediate financial distress; funeral costs; service as executor of the will; the opening of the bank vault and taking inventory of its contents with a tax examiner; the problems of the joint bank account and reorganization of bank accounts; rewriting of his own will to provide guardians and care for his children in the event of his own death; etc. These adjustments imposed heavy burdens on him both physically and emotionally; they also deprived him of time and energy that he preferred to spend with and for his children.

Re-engagement in any activity had to be assessed. Relationships with friends, old and recent, had to be re-evaluated. Should a widower continue to socialize with the friends he had shared as a married man? Responsibilities toward in-laws remained, but what would happen in this regard if he were to remarry at some later date?

A hopelessly desolate, seemingly unending period followed, bereft of any reason to go on, except for the children. Then the agonizing beginning aimed at regaining the pleasures of living developed. Finally, the implications of remarriage presented problems of still greater complexity. The first difficulties involved profound feelings of guilt over having thought of meeting and loving another woman. Would this mean that the memory of his love for his wife need be diminished? If so, should he try to stand independently and allow a series of paid housekeepers to help raise his children? Should he try to assuage his loneliness in a manner that did not involve remarriage?

His own self-knowledge made him realize that his faithfulness to his wife could be only in terms of remaining worthy of her; of fulfilling his responsibility to their children; and by sharing with another wife the faith and trust in love he had experienced with her. But how was he to make such a new beginning? Should he tell his children and relatives of his intentions? Would he meet someone through friends, associates, or social organizations? How would his children react? He thought their response would be favorable, but he couldn't be absolutely sure.

Would a new marriage restore the pleasures of life for himself and his children? Could two families (presuming that he married a widow with children) learn to live together and share with each other their memories, their material possessions, and even their parents? Could two households be reorganized so that everyone's treasured keepsakes could be retained and shared to recreate a home filled with love and happiness for all?

How could new relationships be fostered in his current frame of mind with the physical debilitation born of his grief? All the energy he could summon was being utilized in his job and in maintaining his home. He could not anticipate ever being able to make the effort to initiate new social relationships. Indeed, emotionally and physically he felt too ill to have any desires beyond those of remaining alive to care for his children.

Tranquilizers offered a modicum of relief. He was eventually able to seek out and derive spiritual comfort in diverse ways. He urgently sought a philosophy of life on which to base a pattern of living. As his physical symptoms subsided, his emotional responses became more stable, and he was able slowly to reintroduce into his life the pleasurable activities. Months later he remarried; and since then his normal health has been restored; a new mode of living, a mixture of old and new, has been achieved. The patient has attributed a major part of his recovery to his own recognition of grief as an illness.

CONCLUSION

The problems described in this case history are but a small fraction of those ordinarily encountered. Although some are unique to this given case, the majority replicate those faced by nearly every bereaved person. In retrospect, each aspect of daily living assumes forbidding proportions and ramifications. The conclusions become self-evident: bereavement is an illness and as such, even under the circumstances of so-called normal grief, should be considered in the context of any necessary preventive or therapeutic measures.

Research is needed to fill the void as to how, when, by whom, and through what means these measures should be provided. In virtually all health problem areas, particularly those wherein crises are encountered, research programs are organized to collect information and data to permit the purposeful design and administration of medication or care in order to effect healing. So too, in confronting bereavement as an illness, specific programs must be established for research into and treatment of this crisis.

It is hard to rechannel a life back into creative activity. Dr. George Crile, Jr., eminent surgeon of the Cleveland Clinic, has expressed the essence of the problem in his book, *More Than Booty*, written as a memorial to his wife (who had succumbed to cancer):

> We are gathered together in memory of Jane Crile. If you seek her memorial, look about you—in the hearts of her family, in the faces of her children, in her writings and in her home. Life has been given and life has been taken away. Life and death are one, even as the river and the sea are one. Death is only a horizon and a horizon is but the limit of our sight.

His further message that pleasures can be restored, that a life can be renewed, is very difficult to transmit to the bereaved. Yet all who advise them should be aware that the bereaved's agony in accepting this counsel is but a small price to pay for taking the first step.

It is now more than a year since Jane died. For the first few weeks there was numbness and obsession with sorrow. Some of it may have been because of insecurity. Through the years I had become so dependent on Jane that it did not seem I could find a way to live without her. But gradually I found I was competent to do or arrange for many of the things Jane had always done for me. Interest in my work returned. I began again to find pleasure in people.

As is often the case with those who have been deeply in love and the husband or wife dies, I married again. A new life began, filled with new interests and with a continuation of the old.

I still live in the same house. Many of the same birds, the wood ducks and the swan, are still in our backyard. Many of the relics that Jane and I collected in our travels are about our house. But there are no ghosts. Memories that for a time were inexpressibly sad have once again become a source of deep pleasure and satisfaction.

Since we know nothing of death except that it comes to all, it is not reasonable to be sad for the person who has died. The sorrow that once I felt for myself, in my loss, now has been transformed to a rich memory of a woman I loved and the ways we traveled through the world together.

MANAGEMENT OF THE FAMILY

Opinions of the Bereaved

In order to provide physicians with suggestions regarding preferred approaches to the management of the bereaved family as offered by the *bereaved*, the editors present here the results of [a] survey . . . of attitudes of the bereaved toward problems inherent in the dying process, grief, and mourning.

The survey, to which 125 bereaved responded, also dealt with: 1) signs and symptoms of bereavement; 2) guilt and bereavement; 3) what the bereaved should be told by the physician; 4) what the bereaved should be encouraged to do; and 5) advice concerning remarriage. Cited below are the responses of the bereaved.

Signs and Symptoms of Bereavement

Regarding the appearance of grief prior to the death of the patient, 48 per cent of the bereaved predict the appearance of symptoms such as loss of appetite and/or weight, sleeplessness, feelings of despair, and feelings of help-lessness in the bereaved-to-be always or frequently.

Approximately 90 per cent of the bereaved anticipate that dreams of the deceased will occur at least sometimes; 39 per cent reported that such dreams will occur always or frequently. Illusions of the deceased occur at least some-times, according to 51 per cent of the bereaved, although 22 per cent believe these illusions never occur.

Over half of the bereaved believe that angry thoughts and feelings toward the deceased never occur; guilt feelings are predicted to occur always or fre-quently by only 19 per cent; feelings of infidelity are predicted to occur rarely or never by 67 per cent.

That the bereaved will at least sometimes have subjective symptoms similar to the deceased is the opinion of only one-third of the group of widows and widowers.

Symptoms in the bereaved such as diminished sexual desire, impotence, and greater inclination toward masturbation are reported relatively rarely by the bereaved respondents. For example, only 32 per cent anticipate impo-tence at least sometimes; diminished sexual desire is reported by 58 per cent to occur at least sometimes—but 38 per cent assume that it rarely or never oc-curs; one-third predict an inclination to masturbation will never occur.

Guilt and Bereavement

Guilt is always or frequently less likely when there has been free expression of feelings between the dying person and the "bereaved-to-be," according to 69 per cent of the bereaved. Approximately 60 per cent expect that the bereaved will rarely or never experience guilt under the circumstances of beginning to function on his or her own, accepting the inevitability of the death, and then beginning to take up old or new interests once more. When more specific questions are asked concerning putting away pictures of the deceased, having renewed interest in members of the opposite sex, and deciding to remarry, over half of the bereaved group expects there will rarely or never be such guilt feelings. They do not, however, anticipate early experiences of pleasure in the bereavement state—only 19 per cent expect it within a few weeks after the de-ceased passed away.

What the Bereaved Should Be Told by the Physician

It is always or frequently important to advise the bereaved how often death is faced with serenity by the dying, 41 per cent of the bereaved respondents believe, and 78 per cent feel that such advice is at least sometimes important. One-third of the group feels that bereaved individuals should always be made aware of the patient's right to die, although 12 per cent believe this should never be the case. More than 58 per cent of the bereaved believe that the practitioner should always advise the bereaved in detail that everything was done.

More than half of the bereaved group feel that physicians should encourage the bereaved to think that he will experience less fear of future tragedies following the current loss. Approximately three-fourths tend to feel that emphasis should be placed at least sometimes on the bereaved's being fortunate to have a child by the departed spouse, if that is the case.

What the Bereaved Should Be Encouraged to Do

On the subject of seeking care and advice, 72 per cent of the bereaved feel that regular visits to the physician during the first year should be encouraged at least sometimes; there is strong agreement that the bereaved should not be hospitalized for an elective procedure soon after or during the course of bereavement. More than two-thirds suggest that the bereaved seek advice at least soon after the funeral; however, only 29 per cent suggest that such advice should, at the least, be considerable, and more than half prefer that it be minimal. The group of bereaved suggests turning to the clergyman (27 per cent), the lawyer (25 per cent), and the physician (21 per cent). When the bereaved is religiously inclined, 79 per cent of the widows and widowers suggest that at least sometimes he should be urged to attend religious services on the day(s) which have special significance with regard to the deceased. More than 74 per cent agree that psychiatric advice would be of benefit at least sometimes, and 65 per cent feel that this would also be true of vocational guidance at this time.

Over 88 per cent of the bereaved feel that expression rather than repression of feelings, and crying, should be encouraged at least sometimes. Almost half feel that repression of distressing memories should rarely or never be encouraged. They favor encouraging the bereaved to speak about the recent bereavement: 87 per cent agree that the bereaved should be encouraged to talk to old friends at least sometimes; 92 per cent encourage talking with someone who has had a similar experience at least sometimes; nearly all encourage the bereaved to talk to someone about feelings related specifically to the deceased.

Over half of the widows and widowers favor keeping the deceased's wedding ring permanently. As to various other personal belongings of the deceased, there seems to be general agreement: keep some, give some to family or friends, give some to charity. Promises made by the bereaved to the deceased during life should be followed if practical and reasonable, but hardly any bereaved indicated that such promises should be followed if not practical. The bereaved should always or frequently be encouraged to relinquish excessive attachments to the deceased, according to 72 per cent of the bereaved respondents.

It was commonly felt that at least sometimes the person in grief should obtain a pet, seek a companion (if elderly), travel, go shopping, change jobs if he had long wanted to do so, move to a new living location, or seek vocational guidance. They are also predominantly in favor both of continuing old hobbies and beginning new ones at this time. About half would encourage the bereaved to resume work within a week, and three-quarters within two weeks. Some 14 per cent would encourage a return to work only when the bereaved feels up to it. More that 78 per cent indicate that at least sometimes this might be a time to encourage the bereaved to change jobs, if this had been his longtime desire. More than 90 per cent see working as frequently or always being good for the bereaved—of those, nearly two-thirds emphasized "always." Many (37 per cent) suggest that the bereaved always or frequently make major decisions as early as possible.

Advice Concerning Remarriage

An impressive majority of the widows and widowers—92 per cent—indicated that the bereaved should always be encouraged to remarry if age permits; 78 per cent regard remarriage as the major problem of the young bereaved spouse. That those who have loved deeply and satisfyingly tend to remarry more quickly is the opinion of 59 per cent of the bereaved. However, 63 per cent feel that it is not desirable to encourage the bereaved to make the decision whether or not to remarry before a particular person is considered, and 80 per cent also feel that it is not desirable to inform relatives and in-laws of a decision to remarry before a particular person is considered.

Differences Between Advice Received from the Bereaved and from Physicians

There appears to be general agreement between the group of widows and widowers and the physicians, who were also surveyed, concerning attitudes toward death and mourning, although some differences can be noted.

It is relevant to consider what factors may have influenced those differences which appear most consistently (namely, opinion regarding the appearance of signs and symptoms of bereavement), since both groups represent, in a sense, "experts" who have had either personal or professional knowledge of the bereaved state. It may be that physicians' impressions are in part a result of the fact that their experience is limited to bereaved persons who have chosen to turn to a physician for help or whose reactions are so intense as to require medical assistance.

On the other hand, the differences may testify to the lack of understanding and the need for education on the part of both groups concerning what occurs during bereavement. Physicians might develop greater sensitivity as to what the bereaved expect, seek, and find acceptable to themselves in this most critical period. The lay public which includes the bereaved and those who are involved with him also should be educated as to what bereavement entails. More open recognition of the difficulties and decisions which present themselves including the necessity of dealing with feelings which are difficult to tolerate at the time because they appear inconsistent with the loss, might help all individuals in their attempts to integrate death, separation, and loss when these occur. It is hoped that the results of this survey will contribute data in this direction.

When a person is born, all his dear ones rejoice. When he dies they all weep. It should not be so. When a person is born, there is as yet no reason for rejoicing over him, because one knows not what kind of a person he will be by reason of his conduct, whether righteous or wicked, good or evil. When he dies there is cause for rejoicing if he departs with a good name and departs this life in peace.

Talmud

ACKNOWLEDGMENTS (continued from page iv)

Joseph Bensman and Bernard Rosenberg: From *Mass, Class, and Bureaucracy: An Introduction to Sociology*. Copyright © 1976 by Praeger Publishers, Inc. Reprinted by permission of Holt, Rinehart and Winston.

Peter L. Berger and Brigitte Berger: Chapter 3 from *Sociology: A Biographical Approach*, © 1972 by Peter and Brigitte Berger; by permission of Basic Books, Inc., Publishers, New York, and Penguin Books Ltd.

Paul Bohannan: Extracts from "The Six Stations of Divorce," in *Divorce and After*, edited by Paul Bohannan. Copyright © 1968, 1970 by Paul Bohannan. Reprinted by permission of Doubleday & Company, Inc.

Thomas J. Cottle: "Encounter in Color," reprinted by permission from *Psychology Today* Magazine. Copyright © 1967 Ziff-Davis Publishing Company.

Norman Denzin: "Children and Their Caretakers" is published by permission of Transaction, Inc. from *Transaction*, Vol. 8, #9–10, Copyright © 1971 by Transaction, Inc.

Richard Flacks: Excerpt from *Youth and Social Change*, published by Rand McNally College Publishing Company, 1971, is reprinted by permission of the author.

Barbara Garson: Extracts from *All the Livelong Day*, Copyright © 1972, 1973, 1974, 1975 by Barbara Garson. Reprinted by permission of Doubleday & Company, Inc. and Barbara Garson c/o International Creative Management.

Dair L. Gillespie: "Who Has the Power? The Marital Struggle" is reprinted by permission from *Journal of Marriage and the Family*, August 1971. Copyright 1971 by the National Council on Family Relations.

Erving Goffman: From *Encounters*, copyright © 1961 by The Bobbs-Merrill Company, Inc. Reprinted by permission.

Richard N. Harris: Excerpt from *The Police Academy: An Inside View*, copyright © 1973 by Richard N. Harris. Reprinted by permission of John Wiley & Sons, Inc.

Florence Howe: "Sexual Stereotypes Start Early," *Saturday Review*, October 16, 1971. © *Saturday Review*, 1971. All rights reserved. Reprinted by permission.

Louise Kapp Howe: "Women in the Workplace" first appeared in *The Humanist*, September/October 1973, and is reprinted by permission.

Robert L. Kahn: "Stress: From 9 to 5," reprinted by permission from *Psychology Today* Magazine. Copyright © 1969 Ziff-Davis Publishing Company.

Austin H. Kutscher: From *Loss and Grief: Psychological Management in Medical Practice*, B. Schoenberg, A. C. Carr, D. Peretz and A. H. Kutscher, editors. New York: Columbia University Press, 1970, pp.280–297, by permission of the author and the publisher.

Daniel J. Levinson et al.: "The Psychosocial Development of Men in Early Adulthood and the Mid-Life Transition," from *Life History Research in Psychopathology, III*, edited by Ricks et al. © Copyright 1974 by the University of Minnesota, Minneapolis. Reprinted by permission.

Gerald Nachman: "The Menopause that Refreshes," from *Newsweek*, April 18, 1977. Copyright 1977 by Newsweek, Inc. All rights reserved. Reprinted by permission.

Douglas H. Powell and Paul F. Driscoll: "Middle-class Professionals Face Unemployment," published by permission of Transaction, Inc. from *Society*, Vol. 10, Number 2. Copyright © 1973 by Transaction, Inc.

Thomas Powers: "Learning to Die," Copyright © by Thomas Powers 1971. Used by permission.

Peter I. Rose, Myron Glazer, and Penina Migdal Glazer: From *Sociology: Inquiring Into Society*. Copyright © 1977 by Peter I. Rose, Myron Glazer, and Penina Migdal Glazer. By permission of Harper & Row, Publishers, Inc.

Alice S. Rossi: "Transition to Parenthood" is reprinted by permission from *Journal of Marriage and the Family*, February 1968. Copyright 1968 by the National Council on Family Relations.

Gail Sheehy: From *Passages*. Copyright © 1974, 1976 by Gail Sheehy. Reprinted by permission of the publisher, E. P. Dutton, and the author.

Robert Paul Smith: Reprinted from *"Where Did You Go?* *"Out."* *"What Did You Do?"* *"Nothing."* with the permission of W. W. Norton & Company, Inc. Copyright © 1957 by Robert Paul Smith.

Rafael Steinberg et al.: "A Cog in the Machinery," from a chapter in *Man and the Organization*, a title in the Human Behavior series, published by Time-Life Books, Inc., Alexandria, Virginia.

Studs Terkel: From *Working: People Talk About What They Do All Day and How They Feel About What They Do*. Copyright © 1972, 1974 by Studs Terkel. Reprinted by permission of Pantheon Books, a Division of Random House, Inc. and Wildwood House Limited.

Thomas Tissue: "Downward Mobility in Old Age" is reprinted by permission of the Society for the Study of Social Problems from *Social Problems*, 18:1 (Summer, 1970).

Judith Wax: "It's Like Your Own Home Here," from *The New York Times Magazine*, November 21, 1976. Copyright © 1976 by Judith Wax. Reprinted by permission of Judith Wax c/o The Sterling Lord Agency.

Melford Weiss: "Rebirth in the Airborne" is published by permission of Transaction, Inc. from *Transaction*, Vol. 4, #6, Copyright © 1967 by Transaction, Inc.

Kenneth L. Woodward: "Growing Old Happy" from *Newsweek*, February 28, 1977. Copyright 1977 by Newsweek, Inc. All rights reserved. Reprinted by permission.